Favorite Recipes

Chinese

Favorite Recipes

Chinese

This is a Parragon Publishing Book
This edition published in 2003

Parragon Publishing
Queen Street House
4 Queen Street
Bath BA1 1HE, UK

ISBN: 1-40540-485-X

Printed in China

Produced by Haldane Mason, London

Notes

This book uses imperial, metric, or US cup measurements. Follow the same units of
measurement throughout; do not mix imperial and metric.
All spoon measurements are level: teaspoons are assumed to be 5 ml and tablespoons
are assumed to be 15 ml unless otherwise stated.
Milk is assumed to be whole, eggs and individual vegetables such as potatoes are
medium, and pepper is freshly ground black pepper.
The preparation times include chilling, marinating and making fresh stock.
The times given for each recipe are an approximate guide only because the
preparation times may differ according to the techniques used by different people and
the cooking times may vary as a result of the type of oven used.
Ovens should be preheated to the specified temperature. If using a fan-assisted oven,
check the manufacturer's instructions for adjusting the time and temperature.
Recipes using raw or very lightly cooked eggs should be avoided by infants, the
elderly, pregnant women, convalescents, and anyone suffering from an illness.

Contents

Introduction   10

Soups

Appetizers

Salads & Pickles

Poultry

Meat

Meat (continued)

Fish & Seafood

Vegetables

Vegetables (continued)

Tofu

Rice

Noodles

Noodles (continued)

Desserts

Introduction

The abundance of Chinese restaurants testifies to the fact that Chinese cuisine is hugely popular in the West. This book will show you how to recreate authentic Chinese dishes in your own home. Along with the more famous Cantonese and Szechuan specialties, there are also less familiar but equally delicious recipes from other regions for you to try.

There can be few places in the world nowadays that are unfamiliar with Chinese cuisine. It first became known in the West with the arrival of Chinese workers in the United States during the Gold rush years and today there are Chinese restaurants from

San Francisco to Helsinki and from Sydney to Edinburgh. Home-cooked Chinese food is a more recent phenomenon—at least, in the Western kitchen—but, once the ingredients and the wok became easily available and people realized how quick and easy it is to prepare, it soon became popular.

Besides being quite delicious, which is undoubtedly its most attractive characteristic, Chinese food is both healthy and economic. Carbohydrates, such as rice, which release energy slowly and are recommended by nutritionists as an important part of a healthy diet, are served at every meal. Vegetables, too, play a starring role and they are cooked in ways, such as stir-frying and steaming, which preserve most

Introduction

of their vitamins and minerals. With a few exceptions, high-cholesterol, high-fat ingredients, such as cream and other dairy products, and red meat, are either absent altogether or served sparingly.

To a considerable extent, the distinctive flavors of Chinese food resulted from the need to be economical. Bulky but bland foods, such as noodles, were served in relatively large amounts to satisfy the appetite. Expensive ingredients such as meat and fish could be used in only small quantities, so they had to

be prepared in ways that made the most of them—combined with herbs, spices, and other flavorings. As a result, Chinese cuisine probably has the largest repertoire of any in the world. Fuel was scarce, so "fast food" was a necessity, resulting in the art of stir-frying, in which ingredients are tossed in a round-based, cast iron wok over high heat to cook in a short time. This preserves their flavor, colour, texture, and nutrients. Steaming, also a favourite Chinese cooking technique, similarly results in flavorsome, attractive and nutritious dishes. Bamboo baskets are stacked one above another over a single heat source, thus saving fuel.

A desire for balance and harmony has permeated all aspects of Chinese life since the days of Confucius and this applies to food as well as everything else. Spicy dishes are complemented by sweet-and-sour ones, dry-cooked dishes are balanced with those bathed in sauce, meat is matched with seafood. Dishes are chosen to complement each other in texture, flavor, and colour and it is not considered correct to serve more than one dish with the same main ingredient or to cook them using the same technique. Consciously or unconsciously, Chinese cooks, from the housewife to the professional chef, all work to this ancient Taoist principle of Yin and Yang, in which balance and contrast are the key. Mealtimes, too, are a time of harmony, when the family—often three generations—gather and share a selection of different dishes, as well as their daily news.

Regional Cooking

China is a huge country and the terrain and climate vary dramatically from one region to another. The crops grown and the livestock raised are equally diverse, giving rise to distinctive regional culinary traditions.

The North

Beijing has been the capital of China for about 1,000 years and, as befits such an important city, its culinary tradition is venerable. The Emperor's chief chef was a highly respected figure whose responsibilities included maintaining the health of the Imperial family through a careful balance of herbs, spices, and other ingredients, not simply creating appetizing dishes. Each newly appointed chef considered it a matter of honor to outdo his predecessors and there was also much rivalry with visiting chefs, who accompanied dignitaries from other provinces when they came to Beijing. As a result, Beijing cuisine, which still tends to be called Peking in culinary circles, is varied and elegant. It has also been influenced by the Moslem culinary traditions of Central Asia through a number of Tartar invasions. Sesame seeds and the oil and paste made from them, which now feature in the cooking of all regions of China, were originally introduced by the Tartars. The popularity of lamb, rather than pork, unique to the Northern provinces, is probably also a result of Moslem influences. Outside the city, the cooking is simpler and lacks the light-handed touch that is characteristic of Beijing. Sauces and dips tend to be strongly flavored and leeks, onions, and garlic are popular vegetables. Mongolian or chrysanthemum fire pot dishes—a kind of stock-based fondue—are a specialty.

Wheat, rather than rice, is the staple ingredient in Northern Chinese cuisine and it is used to make noodles, dumplings, pancakes, and steamed buns. The climate can be quite harsh, but produce in this region includes bok choy, onions, grapes, and peaches. Freshwater fish, especially carp, are popular in the area around the Huang Ho River and shrimp and other seafood are abundant in the coastal regions. Drying, smoking, and pickling are typical preserving techniques.

The South

The first Chinese emigrants came from Kwangtung in the nineteenth century, so this is probably the best-known style of Chinese cuisine in the West. The capital of the province, Canton, was the first major trading port in the country and so was open to many foreign influences. However,

Regional Cooking

probably the most important influence, from the culinary point of view, was internal. In 1644 the Ming dynasty was overthrown and the Imperial Household, together with its retinue of chefs, fled to Canton from Beijing. This has resulted in a style of cooking that is renowned for its variety, sophistication, and excellence.

Steaming is a characteristic technique in Southern China and small fish, little pockets of meat or patties, and, above all, dumplings are often cooked this way. Dim sum, which literally means "to please the heart" are a Cantonese specialty. These small, steamed, filled dumplings are as popular in the West as they are in China, but there, they are never served as an appetizer. Rather, they are eaten as snacks at teahouses in the morning or afternoon. In fact, an alternative way of saying "going to a dim sum restaurant" is "going out for morning tea."

Char siu roasting is another Cantonese technique. No kind of roasting is common in Chinese homes, which often do not have ovens, but this method is popular in restaurants. Meat is seasoned and marinated well and then roasted at very high temperatures for a short time. This results in the marinade becoming encrusted on the meat in a crisp outer layer, while the inside remains succulent and juicy. Only very tender cuts of meat, particularly pork, can be prepared in this way.

Agricultural produce in this semi-tropical region is abundant and varied. Vegetables are often simply stir-fried and served plain or just with oyster sauce. They may also be combined with meat or fish. Spinach, bok choy, and dried mushrooms feature widely. Fresh fruit, frequently served on its own as a dessert, may also be combined with meat or fish in sweet-and-sour dishes. Fish and seafood, particularly abalone, crab, lobster, shrimp, and scallops, are plentiful. They are usually stir-fried or steamed, often flavored with ginger, and cooking meat with fish is typically Cantonese. Generally, food is not highly spiced, as the Cantonese prefer to enjoy the natural flavors of the ingredients. Light soy sauce is a popular flavoring and other typical sauces include hoisin, oyster, black bean, and plum.

The East

The delta of the Yangtse River makes this one of the most fertile regions in China. The abundant produce includes broccoli, scallions, sweet potatoes, bok choy, soybeans, tea, wheat, rice, maize, and nuts and the region is well known for its superb vegetarian dishes, noodles, and

Regional Cooking

dumplings. Freshwater fish are found in the many streams and lakes, especially in Kiangsu, which also has a long tradition of deep-sea fishing.

The provinces that comprise this region each have a particular style of cooking, but all are characterized by their richness. The vast cosmopolitan city of Shanghai has assimilated many influences from both other parts of China and abroad. Its cuisine is unusual in that it features dairy products and uses lavish quantities of shortening. Shanghai dishes are typically rich, sweet, and beautifully presented. The school of cooking in the surrounding area is known as Kiangche, the name being an amalgamation of the two provinces of Kiangsu and Chekiang. Duck, ham, and fish dishes are specialties, often

prepared with piquant spices.

This region produces the best rice wine in the country. It is one of the most prosperous parts of China and has a long gourmet tradition. In Fukien to the south, the cuisine is less sophisticated, relying mainly on fish and a wealth of fresh produce. It is strongly influenced by the neighboring Kwangtung region.

The West

Surrounded by mountains, Szechuan has a mild, humid climate and rich fertile soil. Its cuisine is most noted for its robust, richly colored dishes flavored with hot spices, such as chiles and Szechuan peppercorns. Strongly flavored ingredients, such as garlic, ginger, onions, leeks, and sesame seed paste are typical and hot pickles are a specialty.

Food preservation techniques, for which Western China is famous, include smoking, drying, salting, and pickling. Yunnan, to the South of Szechuan, produces superb cured, smoked raw ham.

Szechuan cooking is traditionally described as having seven kinds of flavors—sweet, salty, sour, bitter, fragrant, sesame, and hot—based respectively on honey or sugar, soy sauce, vinegar, onions or leeks, garlic or ginger, sesame seeds, and, finally, chiles. Methods of cooking are varied, ranging from dry-frying with very little oil and no additional liquid to cooking in a clear, well-flavored broth, which is then reduced to make a thick rich sauce. Deep-fried, paper-wrapped pockets of marinated meat or fish are a Szechuan specialty.

Equipment

It is not essential to buy a vast array of special equipment for Chinese cooking, but some items, especially a good-quality wok, are easier to use than their Western equivalents and will result in more authentic-tasting dishes. Most utensils are inexpensive and easily available from Chinese supermarkets and good kitchenware shops.

Wok

This bowl-shaped "skillet" with sloping sides is designed to ensure that heat spreads quickly and evenly over the surface so that food can be cooked rapidly, which is crucial for stir-frying. Once the ingredients have been added to the wok, they are tossed and stirred constantly for a short time over very high heat. It is possible to stir-fry in a large Western-style skillet, but it is more difficult and the texture of the dish is likely to be less crisp. Woks can also be used for a variety of other cooking techniques, including braising, deep-frying, and steaming.

Traditionally made from cast iron, they are now available in a variety of metals and in a wide range of prices. Carbon steel is a good choice, but stainless steel tends to scorch. Non-stick woks are also manufactured, but the lining cannot really withstand the high temperature required for stir-frying. Handles may be single or double, semicircular or long, or a combination of the two. Wooden handles are safer than metal ones. It is important that a wok is large enough for the ingredients to be stirred and tossed all the time they are cooking and a range of sizes is available. One with a diameter of about 14 inches/35 cm is adequate for most Western families without being so heavy, whatever it is made of, that it is an effort to use. Flat-based woks are now manufactured for use on electric stoves.

New woks, apart from those with a non-stick lining, must be seasoned before they are used. First wash well with hot water and cream cleanser to remove the protective coating of oil. Rinse and dry the wok and then place it over low heat and add about 2 tablespoons of vegetable oil. Rub the oil all over the inner surface of the wok with a thick pad of paper towels, taking care not to burn your fingers. Heat the oil for 10 minutes, then wipe it off with a fresh pad of paper towels, which will become black. Repeat this heating and wiping process until the paper towels remain clean—this can take quite a long time.

Once the wok has been seasoned, it should not be washed with cream cleanser or detergent. Simply wipe it out with paper towels, then wash in hot water and dry thoroughly. If the wok is used only occasionally, it may become rusty. In this case, scour the rust off and season again.

Wok Accessories

Some woks are supplied with lids, but if not, these can be bought separately. They are dome-shaped, usually made of aluminum and are tight-fitting. A lid is necessary when the wok is used for steaming, but a dome-shaped pan lid will work just as satisfactorily.

A metal stand is an essential safety feature when the wok is used for steaming, braising, or deep-frying. It may be an open-sided frame or a perforated metal ring.

A wok scoop is a bowl-shaped spatula with a long handle. Some resemble a perforated spoon and others are made from reinforced wire mesh. The handle may be wood or metal. The scoop makes it easier to toss the ingredients during stir-frying, but a long-handled spoon is an adequate substitute. Chinese cooks also use the scoop for adding ingredients to the wok.

A trivet is used for steaming. It is placed in the base of the wok and supports the dish or plate containing the food above the water level. It may be made of wood or metal. A wok brush of split bamboo is used for cleaning the wok.

Bamboo Steamer

Bamboo baskets with lids are available in a range of sizes and can be stacked one on top of another. They are designed to rest on the sloping sides of the wok above the water level.

Cleaver

This finely balanced tool is seen in every Chinese kitchen and is used for virtually all cutting tasks, from chopping spare ribs and halving duck to slashing fish and deveining shrimp. Cleavers are available in a variety of weights and sizes and although they look unwieldy, they are precision instruments. The blade should be kept razor sharp.

Chopsticks

Long wooden chopsticks may be used for adding ingredients to the wok, fluffing rice, separating noodles, and general stirring. They are not essential, but are useful and add a feeling of authenticity. Because they have a lighter touch than a spoon or fork, they are less likely to break up or squash delicate ingredients. Chopsticks are easy to handle once you have acquired the knack. Place one chopstick in the angle between your thumb and index finger, with the lower part resting on your middle finger. Hold the other chopstick between the thumb and index finger as you would hold a pencil; this is the one you manipulate.

Ingredients

Many ingredients used in Chinese cooking are also typically found in the Western kitchen—eggs, meat, poultry, fish, bell peppers, scallions, carrots cucumbers, and so on. Some, such as bean sprouts and soy sauce, have become familiar. A few, such as wonton skins and chile sauce, may not be so well known.

A comprehensive range of specialist ingredients can be obtained from Chinese foodstores and many can be purchased from good supermarkets.

Bamboo Shoots

Used for their texture rather than their flavor, which is very bland, bamboo shoots are readily available in cans. Fresh young bamboo shoots can sometimes be obtained. To prepare them, remove the tough outer skin and boil them in water for 40–50 minutes. Adding two red bell peppers to the water helps to remove the bitter taste.

Bean Sauce

Also known as bean paste, this savory purée may be black or yellow. It is made from crushed, salted soybeans, flour, and spices and is often used instead of soy sauce when a thicker consistency is required. It is available in cans and jars. Sweet bean sauce is red and is used as a basis for sweet sauces and as an accompaniment to char siu dishes.

Bean Sprouts

This term usually refers to the shoots of the mung bean, although the shoots of many other pulses and grains can also be eaten. They are widely available, fresh and in cans from supermarkets. It is easy to sprout beans at home to provide a fresh supply when needed. They are used to give texture to dishes and can be stored in the refrigerator for two or three days.

Black Beans

Salted fermented soybeans are available in cans and packets. They should be soaked in cold water for 5–10 minutes before use to remove some of their saltiness. They have a distinctive flavor and are always combined with other ingredients, such as meat or fish.

Cellophane Noodles

Also known as transparent noodles or bean threads, these opaque white noodles are sold in bundles that resemble candy floss in appearance. They should be soaked in hot water for 5 minutes before using, when they will become translucent. They

Ingredients

are never eaten on their own and are good combined with soups and soupy dishes because they absorb a lot of liquid, making them very tasty.

Chile Bean Sauce

This fermented soybean sauce flavored with chiles and other spices is available in cans and jars. Some varieties are fiery hot, so use with caution.

Chile Oil

This is a very hot, red-colored oil used for flavoring spicy dishes. It should always be used with caution. Some varieties contain chile flakes. You can make your own by adding a few dried chiles to a small bottle of bland vegetable oil.

Chiles

Many varieties of both red and green fresh chiles are widely available and they range from relatively mild to scorchingly hot. It is often not possible to tell which variety you are buying and some look very similar to each other, but taste quite different. As a general rule, large, round chiles are usually milder than small, pointed ones. The seeds are the hottest part, so if you prefer a milder flavor, remove and discard them before use. Take care when handling chiles, as the juice can burn. Wear protective gloves if you have sensitive skin and avoid touching your face, especially the eyes. Always wash you hands thoroughly afterward. Dried red chiles are also used in Chinese cooking. They are often hotter than fresh chiles and can also burn.

Chinese Five-Spice Powder

This flavoring contains star anise, fennel seeds, cinnamon, cloves, and Szechuan pepper. It has a distinctive taste and a pungent aroma, so it should be used sparingly. It is a popular flavoring for soy-braised dishes and roast meat. It will keep more or less indefinitely in an airtight container. When buying, make sure you look for Chinese five-spice powder because the Indian flavoring is a different mixture.

Napa Cabbage

Also known as Chinese cabbage, the commonest variety of this leafy vegetable resembles a tightly packed, pale green romaine lettuce. Another variety is rounder with curly

yellow leaves. A large proportion of the vegetable consists of the crunchy stems, which add texture to stir-fries and other dishes.

Chinese Pancakes

These are made from flour and water and are available fresh and frozen. Frozen pancakes should be thawed before steaming.

Chinese Pickles

A variety of pickles is available from Chinese foodstores in jars and cans. They include salted cabbage; salted mustard greens; Szechuan hot pickle, made from kohlrabi; and Szechuan preserved vegetable, made from the root of mustard greens. They should be rinsed well before using.

Chinese Rice Vinegar

White rice vinegar, which is distilled from Chinese rice wine, has a stronger flavor than the red variety, which is made from fermented rice. Cider vinegar or white wine vinegar may used as a substitute.

Chinese Rice Wine

Made from glutinous rice, this has a rich, sherry-like flavor and is golden in color. In fact, its alternative name is yellow wine. The best type, called Shaoxing, comes from Chekiang in Western China and is made from sticky rice, millet, ordinary rice, and mineral water. Another famous wine, Chen Gang, comes from nearby Fukien. These are both well-matured and quite expensive. Ordinary quality rice wine, made from sticky rice alone, is adequate for cooking and dry or medium sherry may be used as a substitute. Be careful not to buy Mao Tai, which is also sometimes marketed as a "wine," because this is a spirit distilled from sorghum and is even stronger than pure vodka.

Cilantro

Also known as Chinese parsley, the fresh leaves are widely used in Chinese cooking. Tearing the leaves, rather than chopping them, produces a more subtle flavor. Although it resembles flat-leaf parsley in appearance, cilantro tastes quite different.

Dried Mushrooms

Dried Chinese or shiitake mushrooms are used in many dishes. They are expensive, but as their flavor is very strong, only a few are required. Soak them in hot water for 20–30 minutes before using. The soaking water can be used as stock. Dried mushrooms keep more or less indefinitely in a cool, dry place.

Ingredients

Egg Noodles

These yellow noodles range in size and shape from long, narrow strands, like spaghetti, to broad, flat ribbons, like tagliatelle. They are available both fresh and dried.

Ginger

The fresh root is an essential ingredient in many Chinese dishes. Ground ginger is no substitute, as it will burn during stir-frying and does not impart the same delicate flavor to other dishes. Choose plump sections of root with shiny, unblemished skins. To use, peel with a swivel vegetable peeler or a small sharp knife and thinly slice, finely chop or grate, according to the recipe. Fresh root ginger will keep for several weeks in a cool, dry place.

Hoisin Sauce

Sweet and spicy, this dark brownish red sauce is made from soybeans, sugar, flour, vinegar, garlic, chiles, sesame oil, and salt. It is often combined with soy sauce for flavoring stir-fried dishes and may also be used on its own when cooking seafood, spare ribs, and duck. It is sometimes provided in a small bowl at the table as a dipping sauce.

Lemon Grass

This aromatic herb has a mild citrus flavor. It is available fresh, in jars or powdered. Use only the lower part of the stem, which should either be removed from the dish before serving or very finely chopped, as it is quite woody.

Lily Buds

Tiger lily buds, also called golden needles, are dried flower buds with a rather musty flavor that is something of an acquired taste. They should be soaked in water for 20 minutes before use.

Lotus Leaves

The leaves of the lotus plant are very large and are used to enclose food to be steamed. Although they are not eaten, they impart a subtle flavor to the contents of the pockets. They are sold dried and should be soaked in warm water for 20 minutes before they are used.

Lotus Root

Available dried or canned, lotus root is cooked as part of a mixed vegetable dish. Soak the dried root in cold water overnight before use. Fresh lotus root is not widely available in the West.

Ingredients

Lotus Seeds

These oval seeds, about $1/2$ inch/1 cm long, are available dried or canned. They are used in vegetable dishes and soups.

Oyster Sauce

Made from boiled oysters and soy sauce, this salty, brown sauce should be used moderately. It is widely used in Cantonese cooking. Vegetarians can use soy sauce as a substitute. Oyster sauce will keep in the refrigerator for several months.

Pak Choi or Bok Choy

This is an attractive vegetable with white stems and dark green leaves and can be used raw or cooked.

Plum Sauce

Especially popular in Cantonese cooking, this thick, rich, spicy fruit sauce is available in jars and cans.

Rice Stick Noodles

About 10 inches/25 cm long, these white thread noodles are more popular in Southern than Northern cuisine and go particularly well with fish. They do not require soaking before cooking.

Sesame Oil

Made from toasted sesame seeds, this oil is strongly flavored and aromatic. It is rarely used for frying, but a little is often added to a dish at the end of the cooking time for extra flavor. Be sure to buy a Chinese variety, as Middle Eastern sesame oil is less aromatic and flavorsome.

Sesame Seeds

Widely used in all Chinese cooking, sesame seeds add a nutty flavor, pleasant aroma, and crunchy texture to many dishes.

Soy Sauce

This is the sauce most widely used in Chinese cooking and is made from fermented soybeans, salt, yeast, and sugar. Light soy sauce has a stronger flavor than dark and is mainly used in cooking. Dark soy sauce is sweeter and richer and is frequently used as a condiment. When used in cooking, it imparts a rich color to the food and is integral to the technique known as red-cooking. Japanese soy sauce has a much lighter flavor and is not an adequate substitute.

Spring Roll Skins

These are made from wheat flour or rice flour and water and are wafer-thin. They are available in a variety of sizes. Wheat-flour skins are sold frozen and should be thoroughly thawed before separating and using them. Rice-flour skins must be soaked before use.

Straw Mushrooms

Named because they grow on beds of rice straw, these mushrooms are used for their unusual slippery texture rather than their flavor, which is quite bland. They are widely available in cans, but fresh straw mushrooms cannot be obtained easily in the West.

Szechuan Peppercorns

These reddish brown or pink peppercorns, also known as farchiew, grow wild in Western China. They are very aromatic, but not so hot as either black or white peppercorns. They are often roasted and ground before use.

Tofu

Also known as bean curd, this soybean product is used extensively in Chinese cooking. It has a fairly bland flavor, but readily absorbs the flavors of other ingredients. Firm tofu, ideal for stir-frying, is usually sold in cakes. It should be handled carefully, as it breaks up fairly easily. It can be sliced, diced, or shredded. Silken tofu has a more jelly-like consistency. Tofu is high in protein, making it a very popular vegetarian food. It can be stored, submerged in water and covered, in the refrigerator for several days. Dried tofu is sold in cakes and can be cut into strips or slices before being cooked with other ingredients. Smoked and marinated tofu is also available, but these are less suitable for Chinese cooking.

Water Chestnuts

These roots of an aquatic plant resemble chestnuts in appearance only and peeling them reveals crisp, white, sweet-tasting flesh. They are available fresh and in cans, but the latter have less flavor and texture. Store fresh water chestnuts, submerged in water and covered, in the refrigerator for up to a month, changing the water every two or three days.

Wonton Skins

These are made from flour, egg, and water. You can make your own or buy them ready-made.

Wood Ears

Dried fungi that grow on trees, wood ears and the similar cloud ears are like mushrooms. They are used more for their texture than flavor and provide contrasting color in some dishes. They are available dried and should be soaked in hot water for 20-30 minutes and thoroughly rinsed before use. Discard the soaking water.

Basic Recipes

Chinese Stock

This basic stock is used in Chinese cooking not only as the basis for soup-making, but also whenever liquid is required instead of plain water.

MAKES 10 CUPS

1 lb 10 oz/750 g chicken pieces

1 lb 10 oz/750 g pork spare ribs

15 cups cold water

3–4 pieces fresh gingerroot, crushed

3–4 scallions, each tied into a knot

3–4 tbsp Chinese rice wine or dry sherry

1 Trim off any excess fat from the chicken and spare ribs; chop them into large pieces.

2 Place the chicken and pork in a large pan with the water; add the ginger and scallion knots.

3 Bring to a boil, and skim off the scum. Reduce the heat and simmer uncovered for at least 2-3 hours.

4 Strain the stock, discarding the chicken, pork, ginger, and scallions; add the wine and return to a boil, simmer for 2-3 minutes.

5 Refrigerate the stock when cool; it will keep for up to 4-5 days. Alternatively, it can be frozen in small containers and be defrosted as required.

Fresh Chicken Stock

MAKES 7½ CUPS

2 lb 4 oz/1 kg chicken, skinned

2 celery stalks

1 onion

2 carrots

1 garlic clove

few sprigs of fresh parsley

9 cups water

salt and pepper

1 Put all the ingredients into a large pan.

2 Bring to a boil. Skim away surface scum using a large flat spoon. Reduce the heat to a gentle simmer, partially cover, and cook for 2 hours. Leave to cool.

3 Line a strainer with clean cheesecloth and place over a large pitcher or bowl. Pour the stock through the strainer. The cooked chicken can be used in another recipe. Discard the other solids. Cover the stock and chill.

4 Skim away any fat that forms before using. Store in the refrigerator for 3-4 days, until required, or freeze in small batches.

Fresh Vegetable Stock

This can be kept chilled for up to three days or frozen for up to three months. Salt is not added when cooking the stock: it is better to season it according to the dish in which it its to be used.

MAKES 16¼ CUPS

9 oz/250 g shallots

1 large carrot, diced

1 celery stalk, chopped

½ fennel bulb

1 garlic clove

1 bay leaf

a few fresh parsley and tarragon sprigs

8 cups water

pepper

1 Put all the ingredients in a large pan and bring to a boil.

2 Skim off the surface scum with a flat spoon and reduce to a gentle simmer. Partially cover and cook for 45 minutes. Leave to cool.

3 Line a strainer with clean cheesecloth and put over a large pitcher or bowl. Pour the stock through the strainer. Discard the herbs and vegetables.

4 Cover and store in small quantities in the refrigerator for up to three days.

Fresh Lamb Stock

MAKES 7½ CUPS

about 2 lb 4 oz/1 kg bones from a cooked
   joint or raw chopped lamb bones

2 onions, studded with 6 cloves, or sliced
   or chopped coarsely

2 carrots, sliced

1 leek, sliced

1–2 celery stalks, sliced

1 bouquet garni

about 2 quarts water

1 Chop or break up the bones and place
in a large pan with the other
ingredients.

2 Bring to the boil and remove any
scum from the surface with a
perforated spoon. Cover and simmer
gently for 3-4 hours. Strain the stock and
leave to cool.

3 Remove any fat from the surface and
chill. If stored for more than 24 hours
the stock must be boiled every day, then
cooled quickly and chilled again. The
stock may be frozen for up to 2 months;
place in a large plastic box and seal,
leaving at least 1 inch/2.5 cm of
headspace for expansion.

Fresh Fish Stock

MAKES 7½ CUPS

1 head of a cod or salmon, etc, plus the
   trimmings, skin and bones or just the
   trimmings, skin and bones

1–2 onions, sliced

1 carrot, sliced

1–2 celery stalks, sliced

good squeeze of lemon juice

1 bouquet garni or 2 fresh or dried bay
   leaves

1 Wash the fish head and trimmings
and place in a pan. Cover with water
and bring to a boil.

2 Remove any scum with a perforated
spoon, then add the remaining
ingredients. Cover and simmer for about
30 minutes.

3 Strain and cool. Store in the
refrigerator and use within 2 days.

Cornstarch Paste

Cornstarch paste is made by mixing
1 part cornstarch with about 1½ parts
of cold water. Stir until smooth. The paste
is used to thicken sauces.

Plain Rice

Use long-grain rice or patna rice, or
better still, try fragrant Thai rice

SERVES 4

9 oz/250 g long-grain rice

about 1 cup cold water

pinch of salt

½ tsp oil (optional)

1 Wash and rinse the rice just once.
Place the rice in a pan and add
enough water so that there is no more
than ³/₄ inch/2 cm of water above the
surface of the rice.

2 Bring to a boil, then add salt and oil
(if using), and stir to prevent the rice
sticking to the bottom of the pan.

3 Reduce the heat to very, very low, then
cover and cook for 15-20 minutes.

4 Remove from the heat and let stand,
covered, for 10 minutes or so. Fluff up
the rice with a fork or spoon before
serving.

Fresh Coconut Milk

To make it from fresh grated coconut,
place about 9 oz/250 g grated coconut
in a bowl, then pour over about 2½ cups
of boiling water to just cover and leave to
stand for 1 hour. Strain through
cheesecloth, squeezing hard to extract as
much "thick" milk as possible. If you
require coconut cream, leave to stand
then skim the "cream" from the surface
for use. Dry unsweetened coconut can
also be used in the same quantities.

How To Use This Book

Each recipe contains a wealth of useful information, including a breakdown of nutritional quantities, preparation and cooking times, and level of difficulty. All of this information is explained in detail below.

The nutritional information provided for each recipe is per serving or per portion. Optional ingredients, variations, or serving suggestions have not been included in the calculations.

The number of chef's hats represents the difficulty of each recipe, ranging from easy (1 chef's hat) to difficult (5 chef's hats).

This amount of time represents the preparation of ingredients, including cooling, chilling, and soaking times.

This represents the cooking time.

The ingredients for each recipe are listed in the order that they are used.

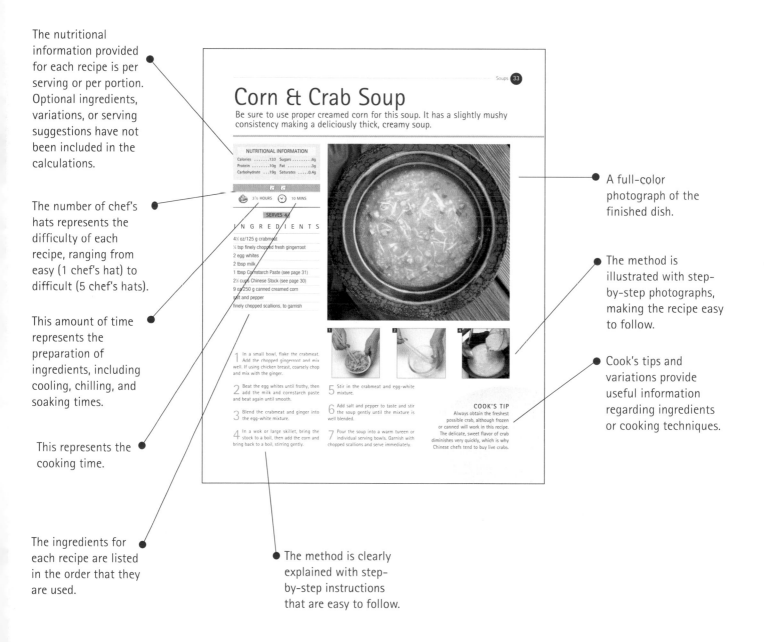

Soups 33

Corn & Crab Soup

Be sure to use proper creamed corn for this soup. It has a slightly mushy consistency making a deliciously thick, creamy soup.

NUTRITIONAL INFORMATION

Calories . . . . .133 Sugars 6g
Protein . . . . .10g Fat 3g
Carbohydrate . . .19g Saturates 0.4g

3½ HOURS   10 MINS

SERVES 4

INGREDIENTS

4½ oz/125 g crabmeat
¼ tsp finely chopped fresh gingerroot
2 egg whites
2 tbsp milk
1 tbsp Cornstarch Paste (see page 31)
2½ cups Chinese Stock (see page 30)
9 oz/250 g canned creamed corn
salt and pepper
finely chopped scallions, to garnish

1 In a small bowl, flake the crabmeat. Add the chopped gingerroot and mix well. If using chicken breast, coarsely chop and mix with the ginger.

2 Beat the egg whites until frothy, then add the milk and cornstarch paste and beat again until smooth.

3 Blend the crabmeat and ginger into the egg-white mixture.

4 In a wok or large skillet, bring the stock to a boil, then add the corn and bring back to a boil, stirring gently.

5 Stir in the crabmeat and egg-white mixture.

6 Add salt and pepper to taste and stir the soup gently until the mixture is well blended.

7 Pour the soup into a warm tureen or individual serving bowls. Garnish with chopped scallions and serve immediately.

COOK'S TIP
Always obtain the freshest possible crab, although frozen or canned will work in this recipe. The delicate, sweet flavor of crab diminishes very quickly, which is why Chinese chefs tend to buy live crabs.

A full-color photograph of the finished dish.

The method is illustrated with step-by-step photographs, making the recipe easy to follow.

Cook's tips and variations provide useful information regarding ingredients or cooking techniques.

The method is clearly explained with step-by-step instructions that are easy to follow.

Soups

Soup is an integral part of the Chinese meal but is rarely served as an appetizer as it is in the Western world. Instead, soup is usually served between courses to clear the palate and act as a beverage throughout the meal. The soup is usually presented in a large tureen in the center of the table for people to help themselves as the meal

progresses. The soups in this chapter combine a range of flavors and textures. There are thicker soups, thin clear consommés, and those which are served with wontons, dumplings, noodles, or even rice in them. Ideally the soup should be made with fresh stock, but this does require long preparation times. For quicker soup, you can use a stock cube. However, it is always worth making your own Chinese Stock (see page 30) if you have time.

Chicken & Corn Soup

A hint of chile and sherry flavors this soup while red bell pepper and tomato add color.

NUTRITIONAL INFORMATION

Calories 199	Sugars 8g
Protein 12g	Fat 8g
Carbohydrate ...19g	Saturates 1g

5 MINS   20 MINS

SERVES 4

I N G R E D I E N T S

1 skinless, boneless chicken breast,
  about 6 oz/175 g

2 tbsp corn oil

2–3 scallions, thinly sliced diagonally

1 small or ½ large red bell pepper,
  thinly sliced

1 garlic clove, crushed

4½ oz/125 g baby corn, thinly sliced

4 cups chicken stock

7 oz/200 g canned corn, well drained

2 tbsp sherry

2–3 tsp bottled sweet chile sauce

2–3 tsp cornstarch

2 tomatoes, cut into fourths
  and seeded, then sliced

salt and pepper

chopped fresh cilantro
  or parsley, to garnish

1 Cut the chicken breast into 4 strips lengthwise, then cut each strip into narrow slices across the grain.

2 Heat the oil in a wok or skillet, swirling it around until it is really hot.

3 Add the chicken and stir-fry for 3–4 minutes, moving it around the wok until it is well sealed all over and almost cooked through.

4 Add the scallions, bell pepper, and garlic, and stir-fry for 2–3 minutes. Add the baby corn and stock and bring to a boil.

5 Add the canned corn, sherry, sweet chile sauce, and salt to taste, and simmer for 5 minutes, stirring from time to time.

6 Blend the cornstarch with a little cold water. Add to the soup and bring to a boil, stirring until the sauce is thickened. Add the tomato slices, then season to taste and simmer for 1–2 minutes.

7 Serve the chicken and corn soup hot, sprinkled with chopped cilantro or parsley.

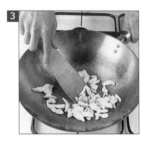

Corn & Crab Soup

Be sure to use proper creamed corn for this soup. It has a slightly mushy consistency making a deliciously thick, creamy soup.

NUTRITIONAL INFORMATION

Calories 133	Sugars 6g	
Protein 10g	Fat 3g	
Carbohydrate ...19g	Saturates 0.4g	

3½ HOURS   10 MINS

SERVES 4

I N G R E D I E N T S

4½ oz/125 g crabmeat

¼ tsp finely chopped fresh gingerroot

2 egg whites

2 tbsp milk

1 tbsp Cornstarch Paste (see page 31)

2½ cups Chinese Stock (see page 30)

9 oz/250 g canned creamed corn

salt and pepper

finely chopped scallions, to garnish

1 In a small bowl, flake the crabmeat. Add the chopped gingerroot and mix well. If using chicken breast, coarsely chop and mix with the ginger.

2 Beat the egg whites until frothy, then add the milk and cornstarch paste and beat again until smooth.

3 Blend the crabmeat and ginger into the egg-white mixture.

4 In a wok or large skillet, bring the stock to a boil, then add the corn and bring back to a boil, stirring gently.

5 Stir in the crabmeat and egg-white mixture.

6 Add salt and pepper to taste and stir the soup gently until the mixture is well blended.

7 Pour the soup into a warm tureen or individual serving bowls. Garnish with chopped scallions and serve immediately.

COOK'S TIP

Always obtain the freshest possible crab, although frozen or canned will work in this recipe. The delicate, sweet flavor of crab diminishes very quickly, which is why Chinese chefs tend to buy live crabs.

Spicy Shrimp Soup

Lime leaves are used as a flavoring in this soup to add tartness.

NUTRITIONAL INFORMATION

Calories . . . . .217 Sugars 16g
Protein . . . . .16g Fat 4g
Carbohydrate . . .31g Saturates 1g

10 MINS 20 MINS

SERVES 4

INGREDIENTS

2 tbsp tamarind paste

4 red chiles, very finely chopped

2 garlic cloves, crushed

1-inch/2.5-cm piece Thai ginger, peeled and very finely chopped

4 tbsp fish sauce

2 tbsp palm sugar or superfine sugar

5 cups fish stock

8 lime leaves

3½ oz/100 g carrots, very thinly sliced

12 oz/350 g sweet potato, diced

1 cup baby corn cobs, halved

3 tbsp fresh cilantro, roughly chopped

3½ oz/100 g cherry tomatoes, halved

8 oz/225 g fan-tail shrimp

1 Place the tamarind paste, red chiles, garlic, ginger, fish sauce, sugar, and fish stock in a preheated wok or large, heavy skillet. Roughly tear the lime leaves and add to the wok. Bring to a boil, stirring constantly to blend the flavors.

2 Reduce the heat and add the carrot, sweet potato, and baby corn cobs to the mixture in the wok.

3 Leave the soup to simmer, uncovered, for 10 minutes, or until the vegetables are just tender.

4 Stir the cilantro, cherry tomatoes, and shrimp into the soup and heat through for 5 minutes.

5 Transfer the soup to a warm soup tureen or individual serving bowls and serve hot.

COOK'S TIP

Thai ginger or galangal is a member of the ginger family, but it is yellow in color with pink sprouts. The flavor is aromatic and less pungent than ginger.

Hot & Sour Soup

This well-known soup from Peking is unusual in that it is thickened.
The "hot" flavor is achieved by the addition of plenty of black pepper.

NUTRITIONAL INFORMATION

Calories 124   Sugars 1g
Protein ....5g   Fat 8g
Carbohydrate ....8g   Saturates 1g

3½ HOURS   25 MINS

SERVES 4

INGREDIENTS

2 tbsp cornstarch

4 tbsp water

2 tbsp light soy sauce

3 tbsp rice wine vinegar

½ tsp ground black pepper

1 small fresh red chile

1 egg

2 tbsp vegetable oil

1 onion, chopped

3¾ cups chicken or beef consommé

1 open-cup mushroom, sliced

1¾ oz/50 g skinless chicken breast, cut into very thin strips

1 tsp sesame oil

1 In a mixing bowl, blend the cornstarch with the water to form a smooth paste.

2 Add the soy sauce, rice wine vinegar, and black pepper.

3 Finely chop the red chile and add to the ingredients in the bowl. Mix well.

4 Break the egg into a separate bowl and beat well. Set aside while you cook the other ingredients.

5 Heat the oil in a preheated wok and fry the onion for 1–2 minutes until softened.

6 Stir in the consommé, mushroom, and chicken and bring to a boil. Cook for 15 minutes, or until the chicken is tender.

7 Gradually pour the cornstarch mixture into the soup and cook, stirring constantly, until it thickens.

8 As you are stirring, gradually drizzle the egg into the soup, to create threads of egg.

9 Pour the hot and sour soup into a warm tureen or individual serving bowls, then sprinkle with the sesame oil and serve immediately.

Lamb & Rice Soup

This is a very filling soup, as it contains rice and tender pieces of lamb. Serve before a light main course.

NUTRITIONAL INFORMATION

Calories . . . . .116 Sugars 0.2g
Protein . . . . .9g Fat 4g
Carbohydrate . . .12g Saturates 2g

5 MINS   35 MINS

SERVES 4

INGREDIENTS

5½ oz/150 g lean lamb

¼ cup rice

3¾ cups lamb stock

1 leek, sliced

1 garlic clove, thinly sliced

2 tsp light soy sauce

1 tsp rice wine vinegar

1 medium open-cup mushroom,
    thinly sliced

salt

1 Using a sharp knife, trim any fat from the lamb and cut the meat into thin strips. Set aside until required.

2 Bring a large pan of lightly salted water to a boil and add the rice. Bring back to a boil, stir once, then reduce the heat and cook for 10–15 minutes, until tender.

3 Drain the rice and rinse under cold running water, then drain again and set aside until required.

4 Meanwhile, put the lamb stock in a large pan and bring to a boil.

5 Add the lamb strips, leek, garlic, soy sauce, and rice wine vinegar to the stock in the pan. Reduce the heat, then cover and leave to simmer for 10 minutes, or until the lamb is tender and cooked through.

6 Add the mushroom slices and the rice to the pan and cook for an additional 2–3 minutes, or until the mushroom is completely cooked through.

7 Ladle the soup into 4 individual warmed soup bowls and serve immediately.

VARIATION

Use a few dried Chinese mushrooms, rehydrated according to the package instructions and chopped, as an alternative to the open-cup mushroom. Add the Chinese mushrooms with the lamb in step 4.

Noodle & Mushroom Soup

This soup is very quickly and easily put together, and is cooked so that each ingredient can still be tasted in the finished dish.

NUTRITIONAL INFORMATION

Calories 74   Sugars 1g
Protein . . . . .13g   Fat 3g
Carbohydrate . . . .9g   Saturates 0.4g

4 HOURS   10 MINS

SERVES 4

I N G R E D I E N T S

¼ cup dried Chinese mushrooms or
   1⅓ cups portobello or cremino
   mushrooms

4 cups hot Fresh Vegetable Stock (page 30)

4½ oz/125 g thread egg noodles

2 tsp corn oil

3 garlic cloves, crushed

1-inch/2.5-cm piece ginger,
   shredded finely

½ tsp mushroom ketchup

1 tsp light soy sauce

2 cups bean sprouts

cilantro leaves, to garnish

1 Soak the dried Chinese mushrooms, if using, for at least 30 minutes in 1¼ cups of the hot vegetable stock. Remove the stems and discard, then slice the mushrooms. Reserve the stock.

2 Cook the noodles for 2–3 minutes in boiling water. Drain, then rinse and set aside until required.

3 Heat the oil over high heat in a wok or large, heavy skillet. Add the garlic and ginger, stir and add the mushrooms. Stir over high heat for 2 minutes.

4 Add the remaining vegetable stock with the reserved stock and bring to a boil. Add the mushroom ketchup and soy sauce and mix well.

5 Stir in the bean sprouts and cook until tender. Serve over the noodles, garnished with cilantro leaves.

COOK'S TIP

Dried mushrooms are highly fragrant and add a special flavor to Chinese dishes. There are many different varieties but shiitake are the best. Although not cheap, a small amount will go a long way and they will keep indefinitely in an airtight jar.

Wonton Soup

The recipe for the wonton skins makes 24, but the soup requires only half this quantity. The other half can be frozen, ready for another time.

NUTRITIONAL INFORMATION

Calories ....278 Sugars 2g
Protein ....10g Fat 5g
Carbohydrate ...50g Saturates 1g

45 MINS   5 MINS

SERVES 4

INGREDIENTS

WONTON SKINS

1 egg

6 tbsp water

scant 2 cups all-purpose flour, plus extra for dusting

FILLING

½ cup frozen chopped spinach, defrosted

1 tbsp pine nuts, toasted and chopped

¼ cup minced Quorn (TVP)

salt

SOUP

2½ cups vegetable stock

1 tbsp dry sherry

1 tbsp light soy sauce

2 scallions, chopped

1 To make the wonton skins, beat the egg lightly in a bowl and mix with the water. Stir in the flour to form a stiff dough. Knead lightly, then cover with a damp cloth and leave to rest for 30 minutes.

2 Roll the dough out into a large sheet about ¹⁄₁₆ inch/1.5 mm thick. Cut out 24 x 3-inch/7-cm squares. Dust each one lightly with flour. Only 12 squares are required for the soup so freeze the remainder to use on another occasion.

3 To make the filling, squeeze out the excess water from the spinach. Mix the spinach with the prepared pine nuts and Quorn until thoroughly combined. Season with salt.

4 Divide the mixture into 12 equal portions. Using a teaspoon, place one portion in the center of each square. Seal the wontons by bringing the opposite corners of each square together and squeezing well.

5 To make the soup, bring the vegetable stock, sherry, and soy sauce to a boil, add the wontons and boil rapidly for 2–3 minutes. Add the scallions and serve in warmed bowls immediately.

Spicy Chicken Noodle Soup

This filling soup is packed with spicy flavors and bright colors for a really attractive and hearty dish.

NUTRITIONAL INFORMATION

Calories	 286	Sugars	.... 21g
Protein	.... 22g	Fat	.... 6g
Carbohydrate	... 37g	Saturates	.... 1g

15 MINS   20 MINS

SERVES 4

INGREDIENTS

2 tbsp tamarind paste

4 red chiles, finely chopped

2 garlic cloves, crushed

2.5 cm/1-inch piece Thai ginger, peeled and very finely chopped

4 tbsp fish sauce

2 tbsp palm sugar or superfine sugar

8 lime leaves, roughly torn

5 cups chicken stock

12 oz/350 g boneless chicken breast

3½ oz/100 g carrots, very thinly sliced

12 oz/350 g sweet potato, diced

3½ oz/100 g baby corn cobs, halved

3 tbsp fresh cilantro, coarsely chopped

3½ oz/100 g cherry tomatoes, halved

5½ oz/150 g flat rice noodles

fresh cilantro, chopped, to garnish

1 Preheat a large wok or skillet. Place the tamarind paste, chiles, garlic, ginger, fish sauce, sugar, lime leaves, and chicken stock in the wok and bring to a boil, stirring constantly. Reduce the heat and cook for 5 minutes.

2 Using a sharp knife, thinly slice the chicken. Add the chicken to the wok and cook for an additional 5 minutes, stirring the mixture well.

3 Reduce the heat and add the carrots, sweet potato, and baby corn cobs to the wok. Leave to simmer, uncovered, for 5 minutes, or until the vegetables are just tender and the chicken is completely cooked through.

4 Stir in the chopped fresh cilantro, cherry tomatoes, and flat rice noodles.

5 Leave the soup to simmer for 5 minutes, or until the noodles are tender.

6 Garnish the spicy chicken noodle soup with chopped fresh cilantro and serve hot.

Beef & Vegetable Noodle Soup

Thin strips of beef are marinated in soy sauce and garlic to form the basis of this delicious soup. Served with noodles, it is both filling and delicious.

NUTRITIONAL INFORMATION

Calories	186	Sugars	.........1g
Protein	........17g	Fat	...........5g
Carbohydrate	...20g	Saturates	.......1g

35 MINS   20 MINS

SERVES 4

I N G R E D I E N T S

8 oz/225 g lean beef

1 garlic clove, crushed

2 scallions, chopped

3 tbsp soy sauce

1 tsp sesame oil

8 oz/225 g egg noodles

3¾ cups beef stock

3 baby corn cobs, sliced

½ leek, shredded

4½ oz/125 g broccoli, cut into florets

pinch of chili powder

1 Using a sharp knife, cut the beef into thin strips and place in a bowl with the crushed garlic, scallions, soy sauce, and sesame oil.

2 Mix together the ingredients in the bowl, turning the beef to coat. Cover and leave to marinate in the refrigerator for 30 minutes.

3 Cook the noodles in a pan of boiling water for 3–4 minutes. Drain the noodles thoroughly and set aside.

4 Put the beef stock in a large pan and bring to a boil. Add the beef, together with the marinade, the baby corn, leek, and broccoli. Cover and leave to simmer over low heat for 7–10 minutes, or until the beef and vegetables are tender and cooked through.

5 Stir in the noodles and chile powder. Cook for an additional 2–3 minutes.

6 Transfer the soup to bowls and serve immediately.

VARIATION

Use other vegetables, such as cauliflower and carrot, instead of leek and broccoli.

If preferred, use a few drops of chile sauce instead of chili powder, but remember it is very hot!

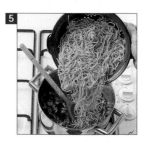

Corn & Lentil Soup

This pale-colored soup is made with corn and green lentils, and is similar in style to the traditional crab and corn soup.

NUTRITIONAL INFORMATION

Calories 171	Sugars 9g	
Protein 5g	Fat 2g	
Carbohydrate . . .30g	Saturates 0.3g	

🍲 5 MINS   🕐 30 MINS

SERVES 4

INGREDIENTS

2 tbsp green lentils

4 cups vegetable stock

½-inch/1-cm piece fresh gingerroot, chopped finely

2 tsp soy sauce

1 tsp sugar

1 tbsp cornstarch

3 tbsp dry sherry

11½ oz/325 g canned corn

1 egg white

1 tsp sesame oil

salt and pepper

TO GARNISH

scallion, cut into strips

red chile, cut into strips

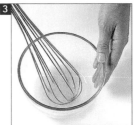

1 Wash the lentils in a strainer. Place in a pan with the stock, gingerroot, soy sauce and sugar. Bring to a boil and boil rapidly, uncovered, for 10 minutes. Skim off any froth on the surface. Reduce the heat, then cover and simmer for 15 minutes.

2 Mix the cornstarch with the sherry in a small bowl. Add the corn with the liquid from the can and cornstarch mixture to the pan. Simmer for 2 minutes.

3 Whisk the egg white lightly with the sesame oil. Pour the egg mixture into the soup in a thin stream, then remove from the heat and stir. The egg white will form white strands. Season with salt and pepper to taste.

4 Pour into 4 warmed soup bowls and garnish with strips of scallion and red chile. Serve the soup immediately.

COOK'S TIP

To save time use 15 oz/425 g canned green lentils instead of dried ones. Place the lentils and corn in a large pan with the stock and flavorings. Bring to a boil and simmer for 2 minutes, then continue with the recipe as given from step 2.

Chinese Potato & Pork Broth

In this recipe the pork is seasoned with traditional Chinese flavorings—soy sauce, rice wine vinegar, and a dash of sesame oil.

NUTRITIONAL INFORMATION

Calories	166	Sugars	.........2g
Protein	........10g	Fat	...........5g
Carbohydrate	...26g	Saturates	.......1g

5 MINS   20 MINS

SERVES 4

INGREDIENTS

4 cups chicken stock

2 large potatoes, diced

2 tbsp rice wine vinegar

2 tbsp cornstarch

4 tbsp water

4½ oz/125 g pork fillet, sliced

1 tbsp light soy sauce

1 tsp sesame oil

1 carrot, cut into very thin strips

1 tsp fresh gingerroot, chopped

3 scallions, sliced thinly

1 red bell pepper, sliced

8 oz/225 g canned bamboo shoots, drained

VARIATION

For extra heat, add 1 chopped red chile or 1 tsp of chili powder to the soup in step 5.

1 Add the chicken stock, diced potatoes, and 1 tablespoon of the rice wine vinegar to a pan and bring to a boil. Reduce the heat until the stock is just simmering.

2 Mix the cornstarch with the water, then stir into the hot stock.

3 Bring the stock back to a boil, stirring until thickened, then reduce the heat until it is just simmering again.

4 Place the pork slices in a dish and season with the remaining rice wine vinegar, the soy sauce, and sesame oil.

5 Add the pork slices, carrot strips, and ginger to the stock and cook for 10 minutes. Stir in the scallions, red bell pepper, and bamboo shoots. Cook for an additional 5 minutes. Pour the soup into warmed bowls and serve immediately.

Lettuce & Tofu Soup

This is a delicate, clear soup of shredded lettuce and small chunks of tofu with sliced carrots and scallions.

NUTRITIONAL INFORMATION

Calories 113	Sugars 2g
Protein 5g	Fat 8g
Carbohydrate 3g	Saturates 1g

5 MINS   15 MINS

SERVES 4

I N G R E D I E N T S

7 oz/200 g tofu

2 tbsp vegetable oil

1 carrot, sliced thinly

½-inch/1-cm piece fresh gingerroot, cut into thin shreds

3 scallions, sliced diagonally

5 cups vegetable stock

2 tbsp soy sauce

2 tbsp dry sherry

1 tsp sugar

1½ cups shredded romaine lettuce

salt and pepper

1 Using a sharp knife, cut the tofu into small cubes.

2 Heat the vegetable oil in a preheated wok or large pan, then add the tofu and stir-fry until browned. Remove with a perforated spoon and drain on paper towels.

3 Add the carrot, gingerroot, and scallions to the wok or pan and stir-fry for 2 minutes.

4 Add the vegetable stock, soy sauce, sherry, and sugar. Stir well to mix all the ingredients. Bring to a boil and simmer for 1 minute.

5 Add the romaine lettuce to the wok or pan and stir until it has just wilted.

6 Return the tofu to the pan to reheat. Season with salt and pepper to taste and serve the soup immediately in warmed bowls.

COOK'S TIP

For a prettier effect, score grooves along the length of the carrot with a sharp knife before slicing. This will create a flower effect as the carrot is cut into rounds. You could also try slicing the carrot on the diagonal to make longer slices.

Chile Fish Soup

Chinese mushrooms add an intense flavor to this soup which is unique.
If they are unavailable, use open-cup mushrooms, sliced.

NUTRITIONAL INFORMATION

Calories	166	Sugars	.........1g
Protein	........23g	Fat	...........7g
Carbohydrate	....4g	Saturates	.......1g

15 MINS   15 MINS

SERVES 4

INGREDIENTS

½ oz/15 g Chinese dried mushrooms

2 tbsp corn oil

1 onion, sliced

1 cup snow peas

1 cup bamboo shoots

3 tbsp sweet chile sauce

5 cups fish or vegetable stock

3 tbsp light soy sauce

2 tbsp fresh cilantro, plus extra to garnish

1 lb/450 g cod fillet, skinned and cubed

COOK'S TIP

Cod is used in this recipe as it is a meaty white fish. For real luxury, use monkfish tail instead.

There are many different varieties of dried mushrooms, but shiitake are best. They are not cheap, but a small amount will go a long way.

1 Place the mushrooms in a large bowl. Pour over enough boiling water to cover and leave to stand for 5 minutes. Drain the mushrooms thoroughly in a colander. Using a sharp knife, coarsely chop the mushrooms.

2 Heat the corn oil in a preheated wok or large skillet. Add the sliced onion to the wok and stir-fry for 5 minutes, or until softened.

3 Add the snow peas, bamboo shoots, chile sauce, stock and soy sauce to the wok and bring to a boil.

4 Add the cilantro and cod and leave to simmer for 5 minutes or until the fish is cooked through.

5 Transfer the soup to warm bowls, garnish with extra cilantro, if wished, and serve hot.

Shrimp Soup

This soup is an interesting mix of colors and textures. The egg may be made into a flat omelet and added as thin strips if preferred.

NUTRITIONAL INFORMATION

Calories 123   Sugars 0.2g
Protein ....13g   Fat 8g
Carbohydrate ....1g   Saturates 1g

5 MINS   20 MINS

SERVES 4

INGREDIENTS

2 tbsp corn oil

2 scallions, thinly sliced diagonally

1 carrot, coarsely grated

4½ oz/125 g large closed-cup mushrooms, thinly sliced

4 cups fish or vegetable stock

½ tsp Chinese five-spice powder

1 tbsp light soy sauce

4½ oz/125 g large shelled shrimp or peeled tiger shrimp, defrosted if frozen

½ bunch watercress or arugula, trimmed and coarsely chopped

1 egg, well beaten

salt and pepper

4 large shrimp in shells, to garnish (optional)

1 Heat the oil in a wok, swirling it around until really hot. Add the scallions and stir-fry for a minute, then add the carrots and mushrooms and continue to cook for about 2 minutes.

2 Add the stock and bring to a boil, then season to taste with salt and pepper, five-spice powder, and soy sauce and simmer for 5 minutes.

3 If the shrimp are really large, cut them in half before adding to the wok and simmer for 3-4 minutes.

4 Add the watercress to the wok and mix well, then slowly pour in the beaten egg in a circular movement so that it cooks in threads in the soup. Adjust the seasoning and serve each portion topped with a whole shrimp.

COOK'S TIP

The large open mushrooms with black gills give the best flavor but they tend to spoil the color of the soup, making it very dark. Oyster mushrooms can also be used.

Chicken Noodle Soup

Quick to make, this hot and spicy soup is hearty and warming. If you like your food really fiery, add a chopped dried or fresh chile with its seeds.

NUTRITIONAL INFORMATION

Calories 196	Sugars 4g
Protein 16g	Fat 11g
Carbohydrate 8g	Saturates 2g

10 MINS   25 MINS

SERVES 4–6

INGREDIENTS

1 sheet of dried egg noodles
   from a 9 oz/250 g package

1 tbsp oil

4 skinless, boneless chicken thighs, diced

1 bunch scallions, sliced

2 garlic cloves, chopped

¾-inch/2-cm piece fresh
   gingerroot, finely chopped

3¾ cups chicken stock

generous ¾ cup coconut milk

3 tsp red curry paste

3 tbsp peanut butter

2 tbsp light soy sauce

1 small red bell pepper, chopped

½ cup frozen peas

salt and pepper

VARIATION

Green curry paste can be
used instead of red curry paste
for a less fiery flavor.

1 Put the noodles in a shallow dish and soak in boiling water as the package directs.

2 Heat the oil in a large preheated pan or wok.

3 Add the diced chicken to the pan or wok and stir-fry for 5 minutes, stirring until lightly browned.

4 Add the white part of the scallions, the garlic, and ginger and stir-fry for 2 minutes, stirring.

5 Stir in the chicken stock, coconut milk, red curry paste, peanut butter, and soy sauce.

6 Season with salt and pepper to taste. Bring to a boil, stirring, then simmer for 8 minutes, stirring occasionally.

7 Add the red bell pepper, peas, and green scallion tops and cook for 2 minutes.

8 Add the drained noodles and heat through. Spoon the chicken noodle soup into warmed bowls and serve with a spoon and fork.

Spinach & Tofu Soup

This is a very colorful and delicious soup. If spinach is not in season, arugula or lettuce can be used instead.

NUTRITIONAL INFORMATION

Calories	33	Sugar	.........1g
Protein	.........4g	Fat	..........2g
Carbohydrate	....1g	Saturates	.....0.2g

3½ HOURS   10 MINS

SERVES 4

I N G R E D I E N T S

1 cake tofu

4½ oz/125 g spinach leaves

3 cups Chinese Stock (see page 30) or water

1 tbsp light soy sauce

salt and pepper

1 Using a sharp knife, cut the tofu into small pieces about ¼ inch/ 5 mm thick.

2 Wash the spinach leaves thoroughly under cold, running water and drain thoroughly.

3 Cut the spinach leaves into small pieces or shreds, discarding any discolored leaves and tough stems. (If possible, use fresh young spinach leaves, which have not yet developed tough ribs. Otherwise, it is important to cut out all the ribs and stems for this soup.) Set the spinach aside until required.

4 In a preheated wok or large skillet, bring the Chinese stock or water to a rolling boil.

5 Add the tofu cubes and light soy sauce, then bring back to a boil and simmer for 2 minutes over medium heat.

6 Add the shredded spinach leaves and simmer for 1 more minute, stirring gently. Skim the surface of the soup to make it clear, adjust the seasoning to taste.

7 Transfer the spinach and tofu soup to a warm soup tureen or individual serving bowls and serve with chopsticks, to pick up the pieces of food and a broad, shallow spoon for drinking the soup.

COOK'S TIP

Soup is an integral part of a Chinese meal; it is usually presented in a large bowl placed in the center of the table, and consumed as the meal progresses. It serves as a refresher between different dishes and as a beverage throughout the meal.

Peking Duck Soup

This is a hearty and robustly flavored soup, containing pieces of duck and vegetables cooked in a rich stock.

NUTRITIONAL INFORMATION

Calories	92	Sugars	.........3g
Protein	.........8g	Fat	...........5g
Carbohydrate	....3g	Saturates	.......1g

5 MINS   35 MINS

SERVES 4

INGREDIENTS

4½ oz/125 g lean duck breast meat

8 oz/225 g Napa Cabbage

3¾ cups chicken or duck stock

1 tbsp dry sherry or rice wine

1 tbsp light soy sauce

2 garlic cloves, crushed

pinch of ground star anise

1 tbsp sesame seeds

1 tsp sesame oil

1 tbsp chopped fresh parsley

1 Remove the skin from the duck breast and finely dice the flesh.

2 Using a sharp knife, shred the Napa cabbage.

3 Put the stock in a large pan and bring to a boil. Add the sherry, soy sauce, diced duck meat, and shredded Napa cabbage, and stir to mix thoroughly. Reduce the heat and leave to simmer gently for 15 minutes.

4 Stir in the garlic and star anise and cook over low heat for an additional 10–15 minutes, or until the duck is tender.

5 Meanwhile, dry-fry the sesame seeds in a preheated, heavy-based skillet or wok, stirring constantly.

6 Remove the sesame seeds from the skillet or wok and stir them into the soup, together with the sesame oil and chopped fresh parsley.

7 Spoon the soup into warm bowls and serve immediately.

VARIATION

If Napa cabbage is unavailable, use leafy green cabbage instead. You may wish to adjust the quantity to taste, as Western cabbage has a stronger flavor and odor than Napa cabbage.

Curried Chicken & Corn Soup

Tender cooked chicken strips and baby corn cobs are the main flavors in this delicious clear soup, with just a hint of ginger.

NUTRITIONAL INFORMATION

Calories 206	Sugars 5g	
Protein 29g	Fat 5g	
Carbohydrate . . .13g	Saturates 1g	

5 MINS   30 MINS

SERVES 4

INGREDIENTS

6 oz/175 g canned corn, drained

3¾ cups chicken stock

12 oz/350 g cooked, lean chicken, cut into strips

16 baby corn cobs

1 tsp Chinese curry powder

½-inch/1-cm piece fresh gingerroot, grated

3 tbsp light soy sauce

2 tbsp chopped chives

1 Place the canned corn in a food processor, together with ⅔ cup of the chicken stock and process until the mixture forms a smooth purée.

2 Pass the corn purée through a fine strainer, pressing with the back of a spoon to remove any husks.

3 Pour the remaining chicken stock into a large pan and add the strips of cooked chicken. Stir in the corn purée.

4 Add the baby corn cobs and bring the soup to a boil. Boil the soup for 10 minutes.

5 Add the Chinese curry powder, grated fresh gingerroot, and light soy sauce and stir well to combine. Cook for an additional 10–15 minutes.

6 Stir the chopped chives into the soup.

7 Transfer the curried chicken and corn soup to warm soup bowls and serve immediately.

COOK'S TIP

Prepare the soup up to 24 hours in advance without adding the chicken. Cool, then cover and store in the refrigerator. Add the chicken and heat the soup through thoroughly before serving.

Fish & Vegetable Soup

A chunky fish soup with strips of vegetables, all flavored with ginger and lemon, makes a meal in itself.

NUTRITIONAL INFORMATION

Calories	88	Sugars	.........1g
Protein	........12g	Fat	...........3g
Carbohydrate	....3g	Saturates	.....0.5g

🥖 🥖 🥖

🍲 40 MINS   🕐 20 MINS

SERVES 4

INGREDIENTS

9 oz/250 g white fish fillets (cod, halibut, haddock, sole, etc)

½ tsp ground ginger

½ tsp salt

1 small leek, trimmed

2–4 crab sticks, defrosted if frozen (optional)

1 tbsp corn oil

1 large carrot, cut into julienne strips

8 canned water chestnuts, thinly sliced

5 cups fish or vegetable stock

1 tbsp lemon juice

1 tbsp light soy sauce

1 large zucchini, cut into julienne strips

black pepper

1 Remove any skin from the fish and cut into cubes, about 1-inch/2.5-cm. Combine the ground ginger and salt and use to rub into the pieces of fish. Leave to marinate for at least 30 minutes.

2 Meanwhile, divide the green and white parts of the leek. Cut each part into 1-inch/2.5-cm lengths and then into julienne strips down the length of each piece, keeping the two parts separate. Slice the crab sticks into ½-inch/1-cm pieces.

3 Heat the oil in the wok, swirling it around so it is really hot. Add the white part of the leek and stir-fry for a couple of minutes, then add the carrots and water chestnuts and continue to cook for 1-2 minutes, stirring thoroughly.

4 Add the stock and bring to a boil, then add the lemon juice and soy sauce and simmer for 2 minutes.

5 Add the fish and continue to cook for about 5 minutes until the fish begins to break up a little, then add the green part of the leek and the zucchini and simmer for 1 minute. Add the sliced crab sticks, if using, and season to taste with black pepper. Simmer for an additional minute or so and serve piping hot.

COOK'S TIP

To skin fish, place the fillet skin-side down and insert a sharp, flexible knife at one end between the flesh and the skin. Hold the skin tightly at the end and push the knife along, keeping the blade flat against the skin.

Chicken Wonton Soup

This Chinese-style soup is delicious as an appetizer for an Asian meal or as a light meal.

15 MINS   10 MINS

SERVES 4-6

INGREDIENTS

FILLING

12 oz/350 g ground chicken

1 tbsp soy sauce

1 tsp grated fresh gingerroot

1 garlic clove, crushed

2 tsp sherry

2 scallions, chopped

1 tsp sesame oil

1 egg white

½ tsp cornstarch

½ tsp sugar

about 35 wonton skins

SOUP

6 cups chicken stock

1 tbsp light soy sauce

1 scallion, shredded

1 small carrot, cut into very thin slices

1 Place all the ingredients for the filling in a large bowl and mix until thoroughly combined.

2 Place a small spoonful of the filling in the center of each wonton skin.

3 Dampen the edges and gather up the wonton skin to form a small pouch enclosing the filling.

4 Cook the filled wontons in boiling water for 1 minute, or until they float to the top. Remove with a slotted spoon and set aside.

5 Bring the chicken stock to a boil. Add the soy sauce, scallion, and carrot.

6 Add the wontons to the soup and simmer gently for 2 minutes. Serve.

COOK'S TIP

If you have too many wonton skins you can freeze those left over. Place small squares of baking parchment in between the skins, then place in a freezer bag and freeze. Defrost thoroughly before using.

Asian Fish Soup

This is a deliciously different fish soup which can be made quickly and easily in a microwave.

NUTRITIONAL INFORMATION

Calories	105	Sugars	1g
Protein	13g	Fat	5g
Carbohydrate	1g	Saturates	1g

20 MINS   10 MINS

SERVES 4

I N G R E D I E N T S

1 egg

1 tsp sesame seeds, toasted

1 celery stalk, chopped

1 carrot, cut into julienne strips

4 scallions, sliced on the diagonal

1 tbsp oil

1½ cups fresh spinach

3¾ cups hot vegetable stock

4 tsp light soy sauce

9 oz/250 g haddock, skinned and cut into
small chunks

salt and pepper

VARIATION

Instead of topping the soup
with omelet shreds, you could
pour the beaten egg, without the
sesame seeds, into the hot stock at
the end of the cooking time. The
egg will set in pretty strands to give
a flowery look.

1 Beat the egg with the sesame seeds and seasoning. Lightly oil a plate and pour on the egg mixture. Cook on High power for 1½ minutes until just setting in the center. Leave to stand for a few minutes, then remove from the plate. Roll up the egg and shred thinly.

2 Mix together the celery, carrot, scallions, and oil. Cover and cook on High power for 3 minutes.

3 Wash the spinach thoroughly under cold, running water. Cut off and discard any long stems and drain well. Shred the spinach finely.

4 Add the hot stock, soy sauce, haddock, and spinach to the vegetable mixture. Cover and cook on High power for 5 minutes. Stir the soup and season to taste. Serve in warmed bowls with the shredded egg scattered over.

Mushroom Noodle Soup

A light, refreshing clear soup of mushrooms, cucumber, and small pieces of rice noodles, flavored with soy sauce and a touch of garlic.

NUTRITIONAL INFORMATION

Calories	84	Sugars	.........1g
Protein	.........1g	Fat	...........8g
Carbohydrate	....3g	Saturates	.......1g

5 MINS   10 MINS

SERVES 4

I N G R E D I E N T S

4½ oz/125 g flat or open-cup mushrooms

½ cucumber

2 scallions

1 garlic clove

2 tbsp vegetable oil

¼ cup Chinese rice noodles

¾ tsp salt

1 tbsp soy sauce

1 Wash the mushrooms and pat dry on paper towels. Slice thinly. Do not remove the peel as this adds more flavor.

2 Halve the cucumber lengthwise. Scoop out the seeds, using a teaspoon, and slice the cucumber thinly.

3 Chop the scallions finely and cut the garlic clove into thin strips.

4 Heat the vegetable oil in a large pan or wok.

5 Add the scallions and garlic to the pan or wok and stir-fry for 30 seconds. Add the mushrooms and stir-fry for 2–3 minutes.

6 Stir in 2½ cups water. Break the noodles into short lengths and add to the soup. Bring to a boil, stirring occasionally.

7 Add the cucumber slices, salt, and soy sauce, and simmer for 2–3 minutes.

8 Serve the mushroom noodle soup in warmed bowls, distributing the noodles and vegetables evenly.

COOK'S TIP

Scooping the seeds out from the cucumber gives it a prettier effect when sliced, and also helps to reduce any bitterness, but if you prefer, you can leave them in.

Fish Soup with Wontons

This soup is topped with small wontons filled with shrimp, making it both very tasty and satisfying.

NUTRITIONAL INFORMATION

Calories	115	Sugars	.........0g
Protein	........16g	Fat	...........5g
Carbohydrate	....1g	Saturates	.......1g

10 MINS   15 MINS

SERVES 4

I N G R E D I E N T S

4½ oz/125 g large, cooked, shelled shrimp

1 tsp chopped chives

1 small garlic clove, finely chopped

1 tbsp vegetable oil

12 wonton skins

1 small egg, beaten

3¾ cups fish stock

6 oz/175 g white fish fillet, diced

dash of chile sauce

sliced fresh red chile and chives,
   to garnish

1 Coarsely chop one fourth of the shrimp and mix together with the chopped chives and garlic.

2 Heat the oil in a preheated wok or large skillet until it is really hot.

3 Stir-fry the shrimp mixture for 1–2 minutes. Remove from the heat and set aside to cool completely.

4 Spread out the wonton skins on a counter. Spoon a little of the shrimp filling into the center of each wrapper. Brush the edges of the wrappers with beaten egg and press the edges together, scrunching them to form a "moneybag" shape. Set aside while you are preparing the soup.

5 Pour the fish stock into a large pan and bring to a boil. Add the diced white fish and the remaining shrimp and cook for 5 minutes.

6 Season to taste with the chile sauce. Add the wontons and cook for an additional 5 minutes.

7 Spoon into warmed serving bowls, then garnish with sliced red chile and chives and serve immediately.

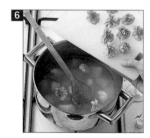

VARIATION

Replace the shrimp with cooked crabmeat for an alternative flavor.

Pork & Szechuan Vegetable

Sold in cans, Szechuan preserved vegetable is pickled mustard root, which is quite hot and salty, so rinse in water before use.

NUTRITIONAL INFORMATION

Calories 135	Sugars 1g	
Protein 14g	Fat 7g	
Carbohydrate 3g	Saturates 2g	

5 MINS   5 MINS

SERVES 4

I N G R E D I E N T S

9 oz/250 g pork fillet

2 tsp Cornstarch Paste (see page 31)

4½ oz/125 g Szechuan preserved vegetable

3 cups Chinese Stock (see page 30) or water

salt and pepper

a few drops sesame oil (optional)

2–3 scallions, sliced, to garnish

1 Preheat a wok or large, heavy-based skillet.

2 Using a sharp knife, cut the pork across the grain into thin shreds.

3 Mix the pork with the cornstarch paste until the pork is completely coated in the mixture.

4 Thoroughly wash and rinse the Szechuan preserved vegetable, then pat dry on absorbent paper towels. Cut the Szechuan preserved vegetable into thin shreds the same size as the pork.

5 Pour the Chinese stock into the wok or skillet and bring to a rolling boil. Add the pork to the wok and stir to separate the shreds. Return to a boil, continuing to stir.

6 Add the shredded Szechuan preserved vegetable and bring back to a boil once more.

7 Adjust the seasoning to taste and sprinkle with sesame oil. Serve hot, garnished with scallions.

COOK'S TIP

Szechuan preserved vegetable is actually mustard green root, pickled in salt and chiles. Available in cans from specialist Chinese supermarkets, it has a crunchy texture and spicy taste. Rinse in cold water before use and store in the refrigerator.

Crab & Ginger Soup

Two classic ingredients in Chinese cooking are blended together in this recipe for a special soup.

NUTRITIONAL INFORMATION

Calories . . . . .32 Sugars 1g
Protein . . . . .6g Fat 0.4g
Carbohydrate . . . .1g Saturates 0g

10 MINS   25 MINS

SERVES 4

INGREDIENTS

1 carrot

1 leek

1 bay leaf

3¾ cups fish stock

2 medium-sized cooked crabs

1-inch/2.5-cm piece fresh gingerroot, grated

1 tsp light soy sauce

½ tsp ground star anise

salt and pepper

1 Using a sharp knife, chop the carrot and leek into small pieces and place in a large pan with the bay leaf and fish stock.

2 Bring the mixture in the pan to a boil.

3 Reduce the heat, then cover and leave to simmer for 10 minutes, or until the vegetables are nearly tender.

4 Remove all of the meat from the cooked crabs. Break off and reserve the claws, break the joints and remove the meat, using a fork or skewer.

5 Add the crabmeat to the pan of fish stock, together with the ginger, soy sauce, and star anise, then bring to a boil. Leave to simmer for 10 minutes, or until the vegetables are tender and the crab is heated through.

6 Season the soup, then ladle into a warmed soup tureen or individual serving bowls and garnish with crab claws. Serve immediately.

VARIATION

If fresh crabmeat is unavailable, use drained canned crabmeat or thawed frozen crabmeat instead.

Crab & Corn Soup

Crab and corn are classic ingredients in Chinese cooking. Here egg noodles are added for a filling dish.

NUTRITIONAL INFORMATION

Calories	324	Sugars	.........6g
Protein	........27g	Fat	...........8g
Carbohydrate	...39g	Saturates	.......2g

5 MINS   20 MINS

SERVES 4

I N G R E D I E N T S

1 tbsp corn oil

1 tsp Chinese five-spice powder

8 oz/225 g carrots, cut into sticks

1½ cups canned or frozen corn

¾ cup peas

6 scallions, trimmed and sliced

1 red chile, seeded and very thinly sliced

14 oz/400 g canned white crabmeat

6 oz/175 g egg noodles

7½ cups fish stock

3 tbsp soy sauce

1 Heat the corn oil in a large preheated wok or heavy-based skillet.

2 Add the Chinese five-spice powder, carrots, corn, peas, scallions, and red chile to the wok and cook for 5 minutes, stirring constantly.

3 Add the crabmeat to the wok and stir-fry the mixture for 1 minute, distributing the crabmeat evenly.

4 Coarsely break up the egg noodles and add to the wok.

5 Pour the fish stock and soy sauce into the mixture in the wok and bring to a boil.

6 Cover the wok or skillet and leave the soup to simmer briskly for 5 minutes.

7 Stir once more, then transfer the soup to a warm soup tureen or individual serving bowls and serve at once.

COOK'S TIP

Chinese five-spice powder is a mixture of star anise, fennel, cloves, cinnamon, and Szechuan pepper. It has an unmistakable flavor. Use it sparingly, as it is very pungent.

Hot & Sour Mushroom Soup

Hot and sour soups are found across Southeast Asia in different forms. Reduce the number of chiles added if you prefer a milder dish.

NUTRITIONAL INFORMATION

Calories 87	Sugars 7g	
Protein 4g	Fat 5g	
Carbohydrate 8g	Saturates 1g	

10 MINS   20 MINS

SERVES 4

INGREDIENTS

2 tbsp tamarind paste

4 red chiles, very finely chopped

2 garlic cloves, crushed

1-inch/2.5-cm piece Thai ginger, peeled and very finely chopped

4 tbsp fish sauce

2 tbsp palm sugar or superfine sugar

8 lime leaves, coarsely torn

5 cups vegetable stock

3½ oz/100 g carrots, very thinly sliced

8 oz/225 g button mushrooms, halved

12 oz/350 g white cabbage, shredded

3½ oz/100 g fine green beans, halved

3 tbsp fresh cilantro, coarsely chopped

3½ oz/100 g cherry tomatoes, halved

COOK'S TIP

Tamarind is the dried fruit of the tamarind tree. Sold as a pulp or paste, it is used to give a special sweet and sour flavor to Asian dishes.

1 Place the tamarind paste, red chiles, garlic, Thai ginger, fish sauce, palm sugar, lime leaves, and vegetable stock in a large preheated wok or heavy-based skillet. Bring the mixture to a boil, stirring occasionally.

2 Reduce the heat and add the carrots, mushrooms, white cabbage, and green beans to the wok. Stir well, and leave the soup to simmer, uncovered, for 10 minutes, or until the vegetables are just tender.

3 Stir the fresh cilantro and cherry tomatoes into the mixture in the wok and heat through for an additional 5 minutes.

4 Transfer the soup to a warm tureen or individual serving bowls and serve immediately.

Chinese Cabbage Soup

This is a piquant soup, which is slightly sweet and sour in flavor.
It can be served as a hearty meal or appetizer.

NUTRITIONAL INFORMATION

Calories 65	Sugars 7g	
Protein 3g	Fat 0.5g	
Carbohydrate 11g	Saturates 0.1g	

5 MINS   30 MINS

SERVES 4

INGREDIENTS

1 lb/450 g bok choy

2½ cups vegetable stock

1 tbsp rice wine vinegar

1 tbsp light soy sauce

1 tbsp superfine sugar

1 tbsp dry sherry

1 fresh red chile, thinly sliced

1 tbsp cornstarch

2 tbsp water

1 Wash the bok choy thoroughly under cold running water, then rinse and drain. Pat dry on paper towels.

2 Trim the stems of the bok choy and shred the leaves.

3 Heat the vegetable stock in a large pan. Add the bok choy and cook for 10–15 minutes.

4 Mix together the rice wine vinegar, soy sauce, superfine sugar, and sherry in a small bowl. Add this mixture to the stock, together with the sliced chile.

5 Bring to a boil, then lower the heat and cook for 2–3 minutes.

6 Blend the cornstarch with the water to form a smooth paste.

7 Gradually stir the cornstarch mixture into the soup. Cook, stirring constantly, until it thickens. Cook for an additional 4–5 minutes.

8 Ladle the Chinese cabbage soup into individual warm serving bowls and serve immediately.

COOK'S TIP

Bok choy, also known as pak choi or spoon cabbage, has long, white leaf stems and fleshy, spoon-shaped, shiny green leaves. There are a number of varieties available, which differ mainly in size rather than flavor.

Mixed Vegetable Soup

Select 3 or 4 vegetables for this soup: the Chinese like to blend different colors, flavors, and textures to create harmony as well as contrast.

NUTRITIONAL INFORMATION

Calories	38	Sugars	.........3g
Protein	.........3g	Fat	..........2g
Carbohydrate	....4g	Saturates	.....0.2g

3½ HOURS   5 MINS

SERVES 4

INGREDIENTS

about 1–2 oz/25–55 g each of
   carrots, baby corn, asparagus,
   mushrooms, Napa cabbage, tofu,
   spinach, lettuce, snow peas, bamboo
   shoots, cucumber, tomatoes, etc.

2½ cups Chinese Stock (see page 30)

1 tbsp light soy sauce

a few drops sesame oil (optional)

salt and pepper

finely chopped scallions,
   to garnish

1 Preheat a wok or large heavy-based skillet.

2 Using a sharp knife or cleaver, cut your selection of vegetables into coarsely uniform shapes and sizes (slices, shreds, or cubes).

3 Pour the Chinese stock into the wok or skillet and bring to a rolling boil.

4 Add the vegetables, bearing in mind that some require a longer cooking time than others: add carrots and baby corn first, cook for 2 minutes, then add asparagus, mushrooms, Napa cabbage, tofu, and cook for another minute.

5 The spinach, lettuce, snow peas, bamboo shoots, cucumber, and tomato are added last. Stir, and bring the soup back to a boil.

6 Add the soy sauce and the sesame oil, if wished, and adjust the seasoning to taste.

7 Transfer the mixed vegetable soup to warm serving bowls and serve hot, garnished with scallions.

COOK'S TIP

Sesame oil is a low-saturate oil widely used for its nutty, aromatic flavor. Made from toasted sesame seeds, it is used as a seasoning, not as a cooking oil. Thick and dark, it burns easily, so it should be added at the last moment.

Chile & Watercress Soup

This delicious soup is a wonderful blend of colors and flavors. It is very hot, so if you prefer a milder taste, omit the seeds from the chiles.

NUTRITIONAL INFORMATION

Calories	90	Sugars	.....1g
Protein	.....7g	Fat	.....6g
Carbohydrate	...2g	Saturates	.....1g

10 MINS   15 MINS

SERVES 4

INGREDIENTS

1 tbsp corn oil

9 oz/250 g smoked tofu, sliced

1½ cups sliced shiitake mushrooms

2 tbsp chopped fresh cilantro

2 cups watercress or arugula

1 red chile, sliced finely, to garnish

STOCK

1 tbsp tamarind pulp

2 dried red chiles, chopped

2 kaffir lime leaves, torn in half

1-inch/2.5-cm piece fresh gingerroot, chopped

2-inch/5-cm piece Thai ginger, chopped

1 stem lemon grass, chopped

1 onion, cut into fourths

4 cups cold water

1 Put all the ingredients for the stock into a pan and bring to a boil.

2 Simmer the stock for 5 minutes. Remove from the heat and strain, reserving the stock.

3 Heat the corn oil in a wok or large, heavy skillet and cook the tofu over high heat for about 2 minutes, stirring constantly so that the tofu cooks evenly on both sides. Add the strained stock.

4 Add the mushrooms and cilantro, and boil for 3 minutes.

5 Add the watercress or arugula and boil for 1 minute.

6 Serve immediately, garnished with red chile slices.

VARIATION

You might like to try a mixture of different types of mushroom. Oyster, white, and straw mushrooms are all suitable.

Appetizers

Appetizers are often served at the start of a Chinese meal. This chapter contains a range of old favorites and traditional Chinese dishes, and there is sure to be something to suit every occasion. One of the advantages of these dishes is that they can be prepared well in advance. The Chinese usually serve a selection of

appetizers together as an assorted hors d'oeuvres. Remember not to have more than one type of the same food. The ingredients should be chosen for their harmony and balance in color, aroma, texture, and flavor. A suitable selection might contain Crispy Seaweed, Sesame Shrimp Toasts, Deep-Fried Spare Ribs, and Spring Rolls. Many of these dishes would also make an attractive addition to a buffet —for example, Filled Cucumber Cups and Money Bags.

Spicy Salt & Pepper Shrimp

For best results, use raw tiger shrimp in their shells. They are 3–4 inches/7–10 cm long, and you should get 18–20 per 1 lb 2 oz/500 g.

NUTRITIONAL INFORMATION

Calories 160	Sugars 0.2g
Protein 17g	Fat 10g
Carbohydrate ...0.5g	Saturates 1g

35 MINS   20 MINS

SERVES 4

INGREDIENTS

9–10½ oz/250–300 g raw shrimp in their shells, defrosted if frozen

1 tbsp light soy sauce

1 tsp Chinese rice wine or dry sherry

2 tsp cornstarch

vegetable oil, for deep-frying

2–3 scallions, to garnish

SPICY SALT AND PEPPER

1 tbsp salt

1 tsp ground Szechuan peppercorns

1 tsp five-spice powder

1 Pull the soft legs off the shrimp, but keep the body shell on. Dry well on absorbent paper towels.

2 Place the shrimp in a bowl with the soy sauce, rice wine, and cornstarch. Turn the shrimp to coat thoroughly in the mixture and leave to marinate for 25–30 minutes.

3 To make the Spicy Salt and Pepper, mix the salt, ground Szechuan peppercorns, and five-spice powder together. Place in a dry skillet and stir-fry for 3–4 minutes over low heat, stirring constantly to prevent the spices burning on the bottom of the pan. Remove the skillet from the heat and leave to cool.

4 Heat the vegetable oil in a preheated wok or large skillet until smoking, then deep-fry the shrimp in batches until golden brown. Remove the shrimp from the wok with a slotted spoon and drain on paper towels.

5 Place the scallions in a bowl, pour on 1 tablespoon of the hot oil and leave for 30 seconds. Serve the shrimp garnished with the scallions, and with the Spicy Salt and Pepper as a dip.

COOK'S TIP

The roasted spice mixture made with Szechuan peppercorns is used throughout China as a dip for deep-fried food. The peppercorns are sometimes roasted first and then ground. Dry-frying is a way of releasing the flavors of the spices.

Stuffed Zucchini

Hollow out some zucchini, fill them with a spicy beef mixture and bake them in the oven for a delicious side dish.

NUTRITIONAL INFORMATION

Calories	208	Sugars	.........3g
Protein	........12g	Fat	...........9g
Carbohydrate	...20g	Saturates	.......4g

45 MINS   35 MINS

SERVES 4

I N G R E D I E N T S

8 medium zucchini

1 tbsp sesame or vegetable oil

1 garlic clove, crushed

2 shallots, chopped finely

1 small red chile, seeded and chopped finely

9 oz/250 g lean ground beef

1 tbsp fish sauce or mushroom ketchup

1 tbsp chopped fresh cilantro or basil

2 tsp cornstarch, blended with a little cold water

1¼ cups cooked long-grain rice

salt and pepper

TO GARNISH

sprigs of fresh cilantro or basil

carrot slices

1 Slice the zucchini in half horizontally and scoop out a channel down the middle, discarding all the seeds. Sprinkle with salt and set aside for 15 minutes.

2 Heat the oil in a wok or skillet and add the garlic, shallots, and chile. Stir-fry for 2 minutes, until golden. Add the ground beef and stir-fry briskly for 5 minutes. Stir in the fish sauce, the chopped cilantro, and the blended cornstarch, and cook for 2 minutes, stirring until thickened. Season with salt and pepper, then remove from the heat.

3 Rinse the zucchini in cold water and arrange them in a greased shallow ovenproof dish, cut side uppermost. Mix the cooked rice into the ground beef, then use this mixture to stuff the zucchini.

4 Cover with foil and bake in a preheated oven at 375°F/190°C for 20–25 minutes, removing the foil for the last 5 minutes of cooking time.

5 Serve at once, garnished with sprigs of fresh cilantro and carrot slices.

Spring Rolls

This classic Chinese dish is very popular in the West. Serve hot or chilled with a soy sauce or hoisin dip.

NUTRITIONAL INFORMATION

Calories	442	Sugars	.........4g
Protein	........23g	Fat	..........21g
Carbohydrate	...42g	Saturates	.......3g

45 MINS   45 MINS

SERVES 4

INGREDIENTS

6 oz/175 g cooked pork, chopped

2¾ oz/75 g cooked chicken, chopped

1 tsp light soy sauce

1 tsp light brown sugar

1 tsp sesame oil

1 tsp vegetable oil

8 oz/225 g bean sprouts

⅓ cup canned bamboo shoots, drained, rinsed, and chopped

1 green bell pepper, seeded and chopped

2 scallions, sliced

1 tsp cornstarch

2 tsp water

vegetable oil, for deep-frying

SKINS

scant 1 cup all-purpose flour

5 tbsp cornstarch

1¾ cups water

3 tbsp vegetable oil

1 Mix the pork, chicken, soy sauce, sugar, and sesame oil. Cover and marinate for 30 minutes.

2 Heat the vegetable oil in a preheated wok. Add the bean sprouts, bamboo shoots, bell pepper, and scallions to the wok and stir-fry for 2–3 minutes. Add the meat and the marinade to the wok and stir-fry for 2–3 minutes.

3 Blend the cornstarch with the water and stir the mixture into the wok. Set aside to cool completely.

4 To make the skins, mix the flour and cornstarch and gradually stir in the water, to make a smooth batter.

5 Heat a small, oiled skillet. Swirl one-eighth of the batter over the base and cook for 2–3 minutes. Repeat with the remaining batter. Cover the skins with a damp dish cloth while frying the remaining skins.

6 Spread out the skins and spoon one-eighth of the filling along the center of each. Brush the edges with water and fold in the sides, then roll up.

7 Heat the oil for deep-frying in a wok to 350°F/180°C. Cook the spring rolls, in batches, for 2–3 minutes, until golden and crisp. Remove from the oil with a slotted spoon, then drain and serve immediately.

Filled Cucumber Cups

These attractive little cups would make an impressive appetizer at a dinner party.

NUTRITIONAL INFORMATION

Calories ....256 Sugars 7g
Protein ....10g Fat 21g
Carbohydrate ....8g Saturates 4g

10 MINS   0 MINS

SERVES 4

INGREDIENTS

1 cucumber

4 scallions, chopped finely

4 tbsp lime juice

2 small red chiles, seeded and chopped finely

3 tsp sugar

1¼ cups ground roasted peanuts

¼ tsp salt

3 shallots, sliced finely and deep-fried, to garnish

1 Wash the cucumber thoroughly and pat dry with absorbent paper towels.

2 To make the cucumber cups, cut the ends off the cucumber, and divide it into 3 equal lengths. Mark a line around the center of each one as a guide.

3 Make a zigzag cut all the way around the centre of each section, always pointing the knife towards the center of the cucumber.

4 Pull apart the two halves. Scoop out the center of each cup with a melon baller or teaspoon, leaving a base on the bottom of each cup.

5 Put the scallions, lime juice, red chiles, sugar, ground roasted peanuts, and salt in a bowl and mix well to combine.

6 Divide the filling evenly between the 6 cucumber cups and arrange on a serving plate.

7 Garnish the cucumber cups with the deep-fried shallots and serve.

COOK'S TIP

Cherry tomatoes can also be hollowed out very simply with a melon baller and filled with this mixture. The two look very pretty arranged together on a serving dish.

Pancake Rolls

This classic *dim sum* dish is adaptable to almost any filling of your choice. Here the traditional mixture of pork and bok choy is used.

NUTRITIONAL INFORMATION

Calories 488   Sugars 19g
Protein ....16g   Fat 24g
Carbohydrate ...55g   Saturates 4g

20 MINS   20 MINS

SERVES 4

INGREDIENTS

4 tsp vegetable oil

1–2 garlic cloves, crushed

8 oz/225 g ground pork

8 oz/225 g bok choy, shredded

4½ tsp light soy sauce

½ tsp sesame oil

8 spring roll skins, 10 inches/25 cm square, thawed if frozen

oil, for deep-frying

CHILE SAUCE

¼ cup superfine sugar

¼ cup rice vinegar

2 tbsp water

2 red chiles, finely chopped

1 Heat the oil in a preheated wok. Add the garlic and stir-fry for 30 seconds. Add the pork and stir-fry for 2–3 minutes, until lightly coloured.

2 Add the bok choy, soy sauce, and sesame oil to the wok and stir-fry for 2–3 minutes. Remove from the heat and set aside to cool.

3 Spread out the spring roll skins on a counter and spoon 2 tablespoons of the pork mixture along one edge of each. Roll the skin over once and fold in the sides. Roll up completely to make a sausage shape, brushing the edges with a little water to seal. Set the pancake rolls aside for 10 minutes to seal firmly.

4 To make the chile sauce, heat the sugar, vinegar, and water in a small pan, stirring until the sugar dissolves. Bring the mixture to a boil and boil rapidly until a light syrup forms. Remove from the heat and stir in the chopped red chiles.

Leave the sauce to cool and transfer to a bowl before serving.

5 Heat the oil for deep-frying in a wok until almost smoking. Reduce the heat slightly and fry the pancake rolls, in batches if necessary, for 3–4 minutes, until golden brown. Remove from the oil with a slotted spoon and drain on absorbent paper towels. Serve with the chile sauce.

Pot Sticker Dumplings

These dumplings obtain their name from the fact that they would stick to the pot when steamed if they were not fried crisply enough initially.

NUTRITIONAL INFORMATION

Calories	345	Sugar	.........3g
Protein	........13g	Fat	..........17g
Carbohydrate	...36g	Saturates	.......2g

50 MINS   25 MINS

SERVES 4

I N G R E D I E N T S

DUMPLINGS

scant 1¼ cups all-purpose flour

pinch of salt

3 tbsp vegetable oil

6–8 tbsp boiling water

oil, for deep-frying

½ cup water, for steaming

sliced scallions and chives, to garnish

soy sauce or hoisin sauce, to serve

FILLING

5½ oz/150 g lean chicken, very finely chopped

25 g/1 oz canned bamboo shoots, drained and chopped

2 scallions, finely chopped

½ small red bell pepper, seeded and finely chopped

½ tsp Chinese curry powder

1 tbsp light soy sauce

1 tsp superfine sugar

1 tsp sesame oil

1 To make the dumplings, mix together the flour and salt in a bowl. Make a well in the center, then add the oil and water and mix well to form a soft dough. Knead the dough on a lightly floured counter, then wrap in plastic wrap and let stand for 30 minutes. Meanwhile, mix all of the filling ingredients together in a large bowl.

2 Divide the dough into 12 equal-size pieces and roll each piece into a 5-inch/12.5-cm round. Spoon a portion of the filling on to one half of each round. Fold the dough over the filling to form a "pasty," pressing the edges together to seal.

3 Pour a little oil into a skillet and cook the dumplings, in batches, until browned and slightly crisp.

4 Return all of the dumplings to the pan and add about ½ cup water. Cover and steam for 5 minutes, until the dumplings are cooked through. Remove with a slotted spoon and garnish with scallions and chives. Serve with soy sauce or hoisin sauce.

Butterfly Shrimp

Use unshelled, raw jumbo shrimp, which are about 3–4 inches/ 7–10cm long.

NUTRITIONAL INFORMATION

Calories	157	Sugars	.......0.3g
Protein	.........8g	Fat	...........9g
Carbohydrate	....11g	Saturates	.......2g

🍲 25 MINS 🕐 10 MINS

SERVES 4

INGREDIENTS

12 raw jumbo shrimp
  in their shells

2 tbsp light soy sauce

1 tbsp Chinese rice wine or dry sherry

1 tbsp cornstarch

vegetable oil, for deep-frying

2 eggs, lightly beaten

8–10 tbsp dry bread crumbs

salt and pepper

shredded lettuce leaves, to serve

chopped scallions, either raw or soaked for
  about 30 seconds in hot oil, to garnish

1 Shell and devein the shrimp, leaving the tails on. Split them in half from the underbelly about halfway along, leaving the tails still firmly attached. Mix together the salt, pepper, soy sauce, wine, and cornstarch, then add the shrimp and turn to coat. Leave to marinate for 10-15 minutes.

2 Heat the oil in a preheated wok. Pick up each shrimp by the tail and dip it in the beaten egg, then roll it in the bread crumbs to coat well.

3 Deep-fry the shrimp in batches until golden brown. Remove them with a slotted spoon and drain on paper towels.

4 To serve, arrange the shrimp neatly on a bed of lettuce leaves and garnish with scallions.

COOK'S TIP

To devein shrimp, first remove the shell. Make a shallow cut about three-fourths of the way along the back of each shrimp, then pull out and discard the black intestinal vein.

Honeyed Chicken Wings

Chicken wings are ideal for an appetizer as they are small and perfect for eating with the fingers.

NUTRITIONAL INFORMATION

Calories	131	Sugars	.........4g
Protein	........10g	Fat	...........8g
Carbohydrate	....4g	Saturates	.......2g

5 MINS   40 MINS

SERVES 4

I N G R E D I E N T S

1 lb/450 g chicken wings

2 tbsp peanut oil

2 tbsp light soy sauce

2 tbsp hoisin sauce

2 tbsp clear honey

2 garlic cloves, crushed

1 tsp sesame seeds

M A R I N A D E

1 dried red chile

½-1 tsp chile powder

½-1 tsp ground ginger

finely grated rind of 1 lime

1 To make the marinade, crush the dried chile in a pestle and mortar. Mix together the crushed dried chile, chile powder, ground ginger, and lime rind in a small mixing bowl.

2 Thoroughly rub the spice mixture into the chicken wings with your fingertips. Set aside for at least 2 hours to let the flavors penetrate the chicken wings.

3 Heat the peanut oil in a large wok or skillet.

4 Add the chicken wings and fry, turning frequently, for 10–12 minutes, until golden and crisp. Drain off any excess oil.

5 Add the soy sauce, hoisin sauce, honey, garlic, and sesame seeds to the wok, turning the chicken wings to coat.

6 Reduce the heat and cook for 20–25 minutes, turning the chicken wings frequently, until completely cooked through. Serve hot.

COOK'S TIP

Make the dish in advance and freeze the chicken wings. Defrost thoroughly, then cover with foil and heat right through in a moderate oven.

Chile Fish Cakes

These small fish cakes are quick to make and are delicious served with a chile dip.

NUTRITIONAL INFORMATION

Calories 164	Sugars 1g	
Protein 23g	Fat 6g	
Carbohydrate 6g	Saturates 1g	

🍴 5 MINS   🕐 40 MINS

SERVES 4

INGREDIENTS

1 lb/450 g cod fillets, skinned

2 tbsp fish sauce

2 red chiles, seeded and very finely chopped

2 garlic cloves, crushed

10 lime leaves, very finely chopped

2 tbsp fresh cilantro, chopped

1 large egg

scant ¼ cup all-purpose flour

3½ oz/100 g fine green beans, very finely sliced

peanut oil, for frying

chile dip, to serve

1 Using a sharp knife, coarsely cut the cod fillets into bite-size pieces.

2 Place the cod in a food processor together with the fish sauce, chiles, garlic, lime leaves, cilantro, egg, and flour. Process until finely chopped and turn out into a large mixing bowl.

3 Add the green beans to the cod mixture and combine.

4 Divide the mixture into small balls. Flatten the balls between the palms of your hands to form rounds.

5 Heat a little oil in a preheated wok or large skillet. Fry the fish cakes on both sides until brown and crispy on the outside.

6 Transfer the fish cakes to serving plates and serve hot with a chile dip.

VARIATION

Almost any kind of fish fillets and seafood can used in this recipe: try haddock, crab meat, or lobster.

Bang-Bang Chicken

The cooked chicken meat is tenderized by being beaten with a rolling pin, hence the name for this very popular Szechuan dish.

NUTRITIONAL INFORMATION

Calories	82	Sugars	.........1g
Protein	........13g	Fat	..........3g
Carbohydrate	....2g	Saturates	.......1g

1¼ HOURS   40 MINS

SERVES 4

INGREDIENTS

4 cups water

2 chicken pieces (breast half and leg)

1 cucumber, cut into short thin sticks

SAUCE

2 tbsp light soy sauce

1 tsp sugar

1 tbsp finely chopped scallions, plus extra to garnish

1 tsp red chile oil

¼ tsp pepper

1 tsp sesame seeds, plus extra to garnish

2 tbsp peanut butter, creamed with a little sesame oil

1 Bring the water to a rolling boil in a wok or a large pan. Add the chicken pieces, then reduce the heat and cook, covered, for 30-35 minutes.

2 Remove the chicken from the wok or pan and immerse in a bowl of cold water for at least 1 hour to cool it, ready for shredding.

3 Remove the chicken pieces, then drain and dry on absorbent paper towels. Take the meat off the bone.

4 On a flat surface, pound the chicken with a rolling pin, then tear the meat

into shreds with 2 forks. Mix the chicken with the shredded cucumber and arrange in a serving dish.

5 To serve, mix together all the sauce ingredients until thoroughly combined and pour over the chicken and cucumber in the serving dish. Sprinkle some sesame seeds and chopped scallions over the sauce and serve.

COOK'S TIP

Take the time to tear the chicken meat into similar-sized shreds, to make an elegant-looking dish. You can do this quite efficiently with 2 forks, although Chinese cooks would do it with their fingers.

Small Shrimp Rolls

This variation of a spring roll is made with shrimps, stir-fried with shallots, carrot, cucumber, bamboo shoots, and rice.

NUTRITIONAL INFORMATION

Calories 388	Sugars 2g
Protein 9g	Fat 25g
Carbohydrate . . .33g	Saturates 6g

🍂 🍂

🥗 10 MINS   🕐 15 MINS

SERVES 4

I N G R E D I E N T S

2 tbsp vegetable oil

3 shallots, chopped very finely

1 carrot, cut into short thin sticks

3-inch/7-cm piece of cucumber, cut into short thin sticks

½ cup bamboo shoots, shredded finely

½ cup shelled small shrimp

generous ½ cup cooked long-grain rice

1 tbsp fish sauce or light soy sauce

1 tsp sugar

2 tsp cornstarch, blended in 2 tbsp cold water

8 × 10-inch/25-cm spring roll skins

oil for deep-frying

salt and pepper

plum sauce, to serve

TO GARNISH

scallion tassels

sprigs of fresh cilantro

1 Heat the oil in a wok and add the shallots, carrot, cucumber, and bamboo shoots. Stir-fry briskly for 2–3 minutes. Add the shrimp and cooked rice, and cook for an additional 2 minutes. Season.

2 Mix together the fish sauce, sugar, and blended cornstarch. Add to the stir-fry and cook, stirring constantly, for 1 minute, until thickened. Leave to cool slightly.

3 Place spoonfuls of the shrimp and vegetable mixture on the spring roll skins. Dampen the edges and roll them up to enclose the filling completely.

4 Heat the oil for deep-frying and fry the spring rolls until crisp and golden brown. Drain on paper towels. Serve the rolls garnished with scallion tassels and fresh cilantro and accompanied by the plum sauce.

Spinach Meatballs

Balls of pork mixture are coated in spinach and steamed before being served with a sesame and soy sauce dip.

NUTRITIONAL INFORMATION

Calories	137	Sugars	.........2g
Protein	........13g	Fat	...........7g
Carbohydrate	....6g	Saturates	.......2g

🍖 🍖 🍖

🍲 20 MINS   🕐 25 MINS

SERVES 4

I N G R E D I E N T S

4½ oz/125 g pork

1 small egg

½-inch/1-cm piece fresh gingerroot, chopped

1 small onion, finely chopped

1 tbsp boiling water

¼ cup canned bamboo shoots, drained, rinsed, and chopped

2 slices smoked ham, chopped

2 tsp cornstarch

1 lb/450 g fresh spinach

2 tsp sesame seeds

S A U C E

⅔ cup vegetable stock

½ tsp cornstarch

1 tsp cold water

1 tsp light soy sauce

½ tsp sesame oil

1 tbsp chopped chives

1 Grind the pork very finely in a food processor. Lightly beat the egg in a bowl and stir into the pork.

2 Put the ginger and onion in a separate bowl, then add boiling water and let stand for 5 minutes. Drain and add to the pork mixture with the bamboo shoots, ham, and cornstarch. Mix thoroughly and roll into 12 balls.

3 Wash the spinach and remove the stalks. Blanch in boiling water for 10 seconds. Drain well, then slice into very thin strips and mix with the sesame seeds. Roll the meatballs in the mixture to coat.

4 Place the meatballs on a heatproof plate in the base of a steamer. Cover and steam for 8–10 minutes, until cooked through and tender.

5 Meanwhile, make the sauce. Put the stock in a pan and bring to a boil. Mix together the cornstarch and water to a smooth paste and stir it into the stock. Stir in the soy sauce, sesame oil, and chives. Transfer the cooked meatballs to a warm plate and serve with the sauce.

Rice Paper Pockets

These special rice paper skins are available in Chinese supermarkets and health shops. Do not use the rice paper sold for making cakes.

NUTRITIONAL INFORMATION

Calories	133	Sugars	.........2g
Protein	........10g	Fat	..........8g
Carbohydrate	....5g	Saturates	.......1g

5 MINS   15 MINS

SERVES 4

INGREDIENTS

1 egg white

2 tsp cornstarch

2 tsp dry sherry

1 tsp superfine sugar

2 tsp hoisin sauce

8 oz/225 g peeled, cooked shrimp

4 scallions, sliced

1 oz/25 g canned water chestnuts, drained, rinsed, and chopped

8 Chinese rice paper skins

vegetable oil, for deep-frying

hoisin sauce or plum sauce, to serve

1 Lightly beat the egg white in a bowl. Mix in the cornstarch, dry sherry, sugar and hoisin sauce. Add the shrimp, scallions and water chestnuts, mixing thoroughly.

COOK'S TIP

Use this filling inside wonton skins (see page 42) if the rice paper skins are unavailable.

2 Soften the rice papers first by dipping them in a bowl of water one at a time. Spread them out on a clean counter.

3 Using a dessert spoon, place a little of the shrimp mixture into the center of each rice paper. Carefully wrap the rice paper around the filling to make a secure parcel. Repeat to make 8 parcels.

4 Heat the oil in a wok until it is almost smoking. Reduce the heat slightly, add the parcels, in batches if necessary, and deep-fry for 4–5 minutes, until crisp. Remove from the oil with a slotted spoon and drain on absorbent paper towels.

5 Transfer the parcels to a warmed serving dish and serve immediately with a little hoisin or plum sauce.

Crispy Wontons

Mushroom-filled crispy wontons are served on skewers with a dipping sauce flavored with chiles.

NUTRITIONAL INFORMATION

Calories	302	Sugars	.........1g
Protein	.........3g	Fat	25
Carbohydrate	...15g	Saturates	.......6g

45 MINS   20 MINS

SERVES 4

I N G R E D I E N T S

8 wooden skewers, soaked in cold water for 30 minutes

1 tbsp vegetable oil

1 tbsp chopped onion

1 small garlic clove, chopped

½ tsp chopped fresh gingerroot

½ cup chopped flat mushrooms

16 wonton skins (see page 42)

vegetable oil, for deep-frying

salt

S A U C E

2 tbsp vegetable oil

2 scallions, shredded thinly

1 red and 1 green chile, seeded and shredded thinly

3 tbsp light soy sauce

1 tbsp vinegar

1 tbsp dry sherry

pinch of sugar

1 Heat the vegetable oil in a preheated wok or skillet.

2 Add the onion, garlic, and gingerroot to the wok or pan and stir-fry for 2 minutes. Stir in the mushrooms and fry

for an additional 2 minutes. Season well with salt and leave to cool.

3 Place 1 teaspoon of the cooled mushroom filling in the center of each wonton skin.

4 Bring two opposite corners of each wonton skin together to cover the mixture and pinch together to seal. Repeat with the remaining corners.

5 Thread 2 wontons onto each skewer. Heat enough oil in a large pan to deep-fry the wontons in batches until golden and crisp. Do not overheat the oil, or the wontons will brown on the outside before they are properly cooked inside. Remove the wontons with a perforated spoon and drain on absorbent paper towels.

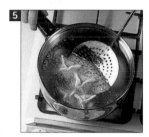

6 To make the sauce, heat the vegetable oil in a small pan until quite hot—until a small cube of bread dropped in the oil browns in a few seconds. Put the scallions and chiles in a bowl and pour the hot oil slowly on top. Mix in the remaining ingredients.

7 Transfer the crispy wontons to a serving dish and serve with the dipping sauce.

Salt & Pepper Shrimp

Szechuan peppercorns are very hot, adding heat and a red color to the shrimp. They are effectively offset by the sugar in this recipe.

NUTRITIONAL INFORMATION

Calories	 174	Sugars	.... 1g
Protein	.... 25g	Fat	.... 8g
Carbohydrate	.... 1g	Saturates	.... 1g

5 MINS   10 MINS

SERVES 4

INGREDIENTS

2 tsp salt

1 tsp black pepper

2 tsp Szechuan peppercorns

1 tsp sugar

1 lb/450 g shelled raw jumbo shrimp

2 tbsp peanut oil

1 red chile, seeded and finely chopped

1 tsp grated fresh gingerroot

3 garlic cloves, crushed

scallions, sliced, to garnish

shrimp crackers, to serve

1 Grind the salt, black pepper, and Szechuan peppercorns in a pestle and mortar.

2 Mix the salt and pepper mixture with the sugar and set aside until required.

3 Rinse the jumbo shrimp under cold running water and pat dry with absorbent paper towels.

4 Heat the oil in a preheated wok or large skillet.

5 Add the shrimp, chopped red chile, ginger and garlic to the wok or skillet and stir-fry for 4–5 minutes, until the shrimp are cooked through.

6 Add the salt and pepper mixture to the wok and stir-fry for 1 minute, stirring constantly so it does not burn on the base of the wok.

7 Transfer the shrimp to warm serving bowls and garnish with scallions. Serve hot with shrimp crackers.

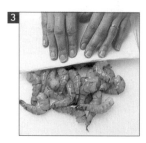

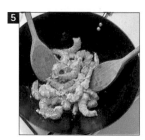

COOK'S TIP

Jumbo shrimp are widely available and have a lovely meaty texture. If using cooked tiger shrimp, add them with the salt and pepper mixture in step 5 —if the cooked shrimp are added, any earlier they will toughen up and be inedible.

Tofu Tempura

Crispy coated vegetables and tofu accompanied by a sweet, spicy dip give a real taste of Asia in this Japanese-style dish.

NUTRITIONAL INFORMATION

Calories	582	Sugars	........10g
Protein	........16g	Fat	.........27g
Carbohydrate	...65g	Saturates	.......4g

🍲

🥘 15 MINS 🕐 20 MINS

SERVES 4

I N G R E D I E N T S

4½ oz/125 g baby zucchini

4½ oz/125 g baby carrots

4½ oz/125 g baby corn cobs

4½ oz/125 g baby leeks

2 baby eggplants

8 oz/225 g tofu

vegetable oil, for deep-frying

julienne strips of carrot, gingerroot, and
    baby leek, to garnish

noodles, to serve

B A T T E R

2 egg yolks

1¼ cups water

2½ cups all-purpose flour

D I P P I N G   S A U C E

5 tbsp mirin or dry sherry

5 tbsp Japanese soy sauce

2 tsp clear honey

1 garlic clove, crushed

1 tsp grated fresh gingerroot

1 Slice the zucchini and carrots in half lengthwise. Trim the corn. Trim the leeks at both ends. Cut the eggplants into fourths. Cut the tofu into 1-inch/2.5-cm cubes.

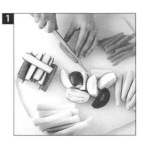

2 To make the batter, mix the egg yolks with the water. Sift in scant 1¼ cups of the flour and beat with a balloon whisk to form a thick batter. Don't worry if there are any lumps. Heat the oil for deep-frying to 350°F/180°C, or until a cube of bread browns in 30 seconds.

3 Place the remaining flour on a large plate and toss the vegetables and tofu until lightly coated.

4 Dip the tofu in the batter and deep-fry for 2–3 minutes, until lightly golden. Drain on paper towels and keep warm.

5 Dip the vegetables in the batter and deep fry, a few at a time, for 3–4 minutes, until golden. Drain and place on a warmed serving plate.

6 To make the dipping sauce, mix all the ingredients together. Serve with the vegetables and tofu, accompanied with noodles and garnished with julienne strips of vegetables.

Steamed Cabbage Rolls

These small cabbage pockets are quick and easy to prepare and cook.
They are ideal for a speedy appetizer.

NUTRITIONAL INFORMATION

Calories 162   Sugars 0.3g
Protein . . . . .24g   Fat 7g
Carbohydrates . . . .2g   Saturates 1g

5 MINS   20 MINS

SERVES 4

INGREDIENTS

8 cabbage leaves, trimmed

8 oz/225 g skinless, boneless
  chicken

6 oz/175 g shelled raw or cooked
  shrimp

1 tsp cornstarch

½ tsp chile powder

1 egg, lightly beaten

1 tbsp vegetable oil

1 leek, sliced

1 garlic clove, thinly sliced

sliced fresh red chile, to garnish

1 Blanch the cabbage for 2 minutes.
  Drain and pat dry with absorbent
paper towels.

2 Grind the chicken and shrimp in a
  food processor. Place in a bowl with
the cornstarch, chile powder, and egg. Mix
well to combine all the ingredients.

3 Place 2 tablespoons of the chicken
  and shrimp mixture toward one end
of each cabbage leaf. Fold the sides of the
cabbage leaf around the filling and roll up.

4 Arrange the parcels, seam-side down,
  in a single layer on a heatproof plate
and cook in a steamer for 10 minutes.

5 Meanwhile, sauté the leek and garlic
  in the oil for 1–2 minutes.

6 Transfer the cabbage pockets to
  warmed individual serving plates and
garnish with red chile slices. Serve with
the leek and garlic sauté.

COOK'S TIP

Use Napa cabbage or savoy
cabbage for this recipe, choosing
leaves of a similar size for the
pockets.

Pork Dim Sum

These small steamed pockets are traditionally served as an appetizer and are very adaptable to your favorite fillings.

NUTRITIONAL INFORMATION

Calories 478	Sugars 3g	
Protein 33g	Fat 29g	
Carbohydrate ...21g	Saturates 9g	

🥟 🥟

🥟 10 MINS   🕐 15 MINS

SERVES 4

INGREDIENTS

14 oz/400 g ground pork

2 scallions, chopped

⅓ cup canned bamboo shoots, drained, rinsed and chopped

1 tbsp light soy sauce

1 tbsp dry sherry

2 tsp sesame oil

2 tsp superfine sugar

1 egg white, lightly beaten

4½ tsp cornstarch

24 wonton skins

1 Place the ground pork, scallions, bamboo shoots, soy sauce, dry sherry, sesame oil, superfine sugar, and beaten egg white in a large mixing bowl and mix until all the ingredients are thoroughly combined.

2 Stir in the cornstarch, mixing until thoroughly incorporated with the other ingredients.

3 Spread out the wonton skins on a counter. Place a spoonful of the pork and vegetable mixture in the center of each wonton skin and lightly brush the edges of the skins with water.

4 Bring the sides of the skins together in the center of the filling, pinching firmly together.

5 Line a steamer with a clean, damp dish cloth and arrange the wontons inside.

6 Cover and steam for 5–7 minutes, until the dim sum are cooked through. Serve immediately.

COOK'S TIP

Bamboo steamers are designed to rest on the sloping sides of a wok above the water. They are available in a range of sizes.

Sesame Shrimp Toasts

These are one of the most popular appetizers in Chinese restaurants in the Western world. They are also quick and easy to make.

NUTRITIONAL INFORMATION

Calories ....237 Sugars 1g
Protein ....18g Fat 12g
Carbohydrate ...15g Saturates 2g

5 MINS   10 MINS

SERVES 4

INGREDIENTS

4 thick slices white bread

8 oz/225 g cooked shelled shrimp

1 tbsp soy sauce

2 garlic cloves, crushed

1 tbsp sesame oil

1 egg

2 tbsp sesame seeds

oil, for deep-frying

sweet chile sauce, to serve

1 Remove the crusts from the bread, if desired, then set aside until required.

2 Place the shelled shrimp, soy sauce, crushed garlic, sesame oil, and egg into a food processor and blend until a smooth paste has formed.

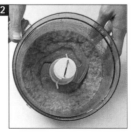

VARIATION

Add 2 chopped scallions to the mixture in step 2 for added flavor and crunch.

3 Spread the shrimp paste evenly over the 4 slices of bread. Sprinkle the sesame seeds evenly over the top of the shrimp mixture and then press the seeds down with your hands so that they stick to the mixture. Cut each slice in half and in half again to form 4 triangles.

4 Heat the oil in a large wok or skillet and deep-fry the toasts, sesame seed-

side up, for 4–5 minutes, until golden and crispy.

5 Remove the toasts with a slotted spoon and transfer to absorbent paper towels and leave to drain thoroughly.

6 Serve the sesame shrimp toasts warm with sweet chile sauce for dipping.

Chile & Peanut Shrimp

Peanut flavors are widely used in Far Eastern and Southeast Asian cooking and complement many ingredients.

NUTRITIONAL INFORMATION

Calories 478   Sugars 2g
Protein ....32g   Fat 30g
Carbohydrate ...19g   Saturates 11g

15 MINS   10 MINS

SERVES 4

INGREDIENTS

1 lb/450 g jumbo shrimp, shelled apart from tail end

3 tbsp crunchy peanut butter

1 tbsp chile sauce

10 sheets phyllo pastry

2 tbsp butter, melted

1¾ oz/50 g fine egg noodles

oil, for frying

1 Using a sharp knife, make a small horizontal slit across the back of each shrimp. Press down on the shrimps so that they lie flat.

2 Mix together the peanut butter and chile sauce in a small bowl until well blended. Using a pastry brush, spread a little of the sauce onto each shrimp so they are evenly coated.

3 Cut each pastry sheet in half and brush with melted butter.

4 Wrap each shrimp in a piece of pastry, tucking the edges under to fully enclose the shrimp.

5 Place the fine egg noodles in a bowl, pour over enough boiling water to cover and leave to stand for 5 minutes. Drain the noodles thoroughly. Use 2–3 cooked noodles to tie around each shrimp pocket.

6 Heat the oil in a preheated wok. Cook the shrimp for 3–4 minutes, until golden and crispy.

7 Remove the shrimp with a slotted spoon, then transfer to absorbent kitchen paper and leave to drain. Transfer to serving plates and serve warm.

COOK'S TIP

When using phyllo pastry, keep any unused pastry covered to prevent it drying out and becoming brittle.

Red Curry Fishcakes

You can use almost any kind of fish fillets or seafood for these delicious fishcakes, which can be eaten as an appetizer or a light meal.

NUTRITIONAL INFORMATION

Calories	203	Sugars	.........1g
Protein	........32g	Fat	..........8g
Carbohydrate	....1g	Saturates	.......1g

15 MINS   15 MINS

SERVES 6

INGREDIENTS

1 kg/2 lb 4 oz fish fillets or prepared seafood, such as cod, haddock, shrimp, crab meat, or lobster

1 egg, beaten

2 tbsp chopped fresh cilantro

Red Curry Paste (see page 148)

1 bunch scallions, finely chopped

vegetable oil, for deep-frying

chile flowers, to garnish

CUCUMBER SALAD

1 large cucumber, peeled and grated

2 shallots, peeled and grated

2 red chiles, seeded and very finely chopped

2 tbsp fish sauce

2 tbsp dried powdered shrimp

1½-2 tbsp lime juice

COOK'S TIP

To save time, Red Curry Paste can be bought ready-made in jars from Chinese grocery stores or large supermarkets.

1 Place the fish in a blender or food processor with the egg, cilantro, and curry paste and purée until smooth and well blended.

2 Turn the mixture into a bowl, then add the scallions and mix well to combine.

3 Taking 2 tablespoons of the fish mixture at a time, shape into balls, then flatten them slightly with your fingers to make fishcakes.

4 Heat the vegetable oil in a preheated wok or skillet until hot.

5 Add a few of the fishcakes to the wok or pan and deep-fry for a few minutes until brown and cooked through. Remove with a slotted spoon and drain on absorbent paper towels. Keep warm while cooking the remaining fishcakes.

6 Meanwhile, to make the cucumber salad, mix the cucumber with the shallots, chiles, fish sauce, dried shrimp, and lime juice.

7 Serve the cucumber salad immediately, with the warm fishcakes.

Vegetable Spring Rolls

There are many different versions of spring rolls throughout the Far East,
a vegetable filling being the classic.

NUTRITIONAL INFORMATION

Calories	189	Sugars	.........4g
Protein	.........2g	Fat	..........16g
Carbohydrate	....11g	Saturates	.......5g

10 MINS   15 MINS

SERVES 4

INGREDIENTS

8 oz/225 g carrots

1 red bell pepper

1 tbsp corn oil, plus extra for frying

¾ cup bean sprouts

finely grated zest and juice of 1 lime

1 red chile, seeded and very finely chopped

1 tbsp soy sauce

½ tsp arrowroot

2 tbsp chopped fresh cilantro

8 sheets phyllo pastry

2 tbsp butter

2 tsp sesame oil

TO SERVE

chile sauce

scallion tassels

1 Using a sharp knife, cut the carrots into thin sticks. Seed the bell pepper and cut into thin slices.

2 Heat the corn oil in a large preheated wok.

3 Add the carrot, red bell pepper, and bean sprouts and cook, stirring, for 2 minutes, until softened. Remove the wok from the heat and toss in the lime zest and juice, and the red chile.

4 Mix the soy sauce with the arrowroot. Stir the mixture into the wok, then return to the heat and cook for 2 minutes until the juices thicken.

5 Add the chopped fresh cilantro to the wok and mix well.

6 Lay the sheets of phyllo pastry out on a board. Melt the butter and sesame oil and brush each sheet with the mixture.

7 Spoon a little of the vegetable filling at the top of each sheet, then fold over each long side and roll up.

8 Add a little oil to the wok and cook the spring rolls in batches, for 2–3 minutes, until crisp and golden.

9 Transfer the spring rolls to a serving dish, then garnish with scallion tassels and serve hot with chile sauce.

Crispy Seaweed

This tasty Chinese appetizer is not all that it seems—the "seaweed" is in fact bok choy, which is then fried, salted, and tossed with pine nuts.

NUTRITIONAL INFORMATION

Calories 214	Sugars 14g
Protein 6g	Fat 15g
Carbohydrate ...15g	Saturates 2g

10 MINS   5 MINS

SERVES 4

INGREDIENTS

2 lb 4 oz/1 kg bok choy

peanut oil, for deep-frying (about 3¾ cups)

1 tsp salt

1 tbsp superfine sugar

2 tbsp toasted pine nuts

1 Rinse the bok choy leaves under cold running water and then pat dry thoroughly with absorbent paper towels.

2 Discarding any tough outer leaves, roll each bok choy leaf up, then slice through thinly so that the leaves are finely

shredded. Alternatively, use a food processor to shred the bok choy.

3 Heat the peanut oil in a large wok or heavy-based skillet.

4 Carefully add the shredded bok choy leaves to the wok or skillet and fry for 30 seconds until they shrivel up and become crispy (you will probably need to do this in several batches, depending on

the size of the wok).

5 Remove the crispy seaweed from the wok with a slotted spoon and drain on absorbent paper towels.

6 Transfer the crispy seaweed to a large bowl and toss with the salt, sugar and pine nuts. Serve immediately.

COOK'S TIPS

The tough, outer leaves of bok choy are discarded, as these will spoil the overall taste and texture of the dish.

Use savoy cabbage instead of the bok choy if it is unavailable, drying the leaves thoroughly before frying.

Money Bags

These traditional steamed dumplings can be eaten on their own or dipped in a mixture of soy sauce, sherry, and slivers of gingerroot.

NUTRITIONAL INFORMATION

Calories 315	Sugars 3g	
Protein 8g	Fat 8g	
Carbohydrate . . .56g	Saturates 1g	

45 MINS   20 MINS

SERVES 4

INGREDIENTS

3 Chinese dried mushrooms
(if unavailable, use thinly sliced
open-cup mushrooms)

1⅔ cups all-purpose flour

1 egg, beaten

scant ⅓ cup water

1 tsp baking powder

¾ tsp salt

2 tbsp vegetable oil

2 scallions, chopped

½ cup corn kernels

½ red chile, seeded and chopped

1 tbsp brown bean sauce

1 Place the dried mushrooms in a small bowl, then cover with warm water and leave to soak for 20–25 minutes.

2 To make the skins, sift the all-purpose flour into a bowl. Add the beaten egg and mix in lightly. Stir in the water, baking powder, and salt. Mix to make a soft dough.

3 Knead the dough lightly on a floured board. Cover with a damp dish cloth and set aside for 5–6 minutes. This gives the baking powder time to activate, so that the dumplings swell when steaming.

4 Drain the mushrooms, squeezing them dry. Remove the tough centers and chop the mushrooms.

5 Heat the vegetable oil in a wok or large skillet and stir-fry the mushrooms, scallions, corn, and chile for 2 minutes.

6 Stir in the brown bean sauce and remove from the heat.

7 Roll the dough into a large sausage and cut into 24 even-size pieces. Roll each piece out into a thin round and place a teaspoonful of the filling in the center. Gather up the edges to a point, pinch together and twist to seal.

8 Stand the dumplings in an oiled steaming basket. Place over a pan of simmering water, then cover and steam for 12–14 minutes before serving.

Vegetable Dim Sum

Dim sum are small Chinese pockets that may be filled with any variety of fillings, then steamed or fried and served with a dipping sauce.

NUTRITIONAL INFORMATION

Calories 295	Sugars 1g	
Protein 5g	Fat 22g	
Carbohydrate . . .20g	Saturates 6g	

15 MINS · 15 MINS

SERVES 4

INGREDIENTS

2 scallions, chopped

¼ cup green beans, chopped

½ small carrot, finely chopped

1 red chile, chopped

⅓ cup bean sprouts, chopped

½ cup chopped white mushrooms

¼ cup unsalted cashew nuts, chopped

1 small egg, beaten

2 tbsp cornstarch

1 tsp light soy sauce

1 tsp hoisin sauce

1 tsp sesame oil

32 wonton skins

oil, for deep-frying

1 tbsp sesame seeds

soy or plum dipping sauce, to serve

1 Mix all of the vegetables together in a bowl. Add the nuts, egg, cornstarch, soy sauce, hoisin sauce, and sesame oil to the bowl. Mix well.

2 Lay the wonton skins out on a cutting board and spoon small quantities of the mixture into the center of each. Gather the skin around the filling at the top, to make little pockets, but leave the tops open.

3 Heat the oil for deep-frying in a wok to 350°F/180°C until a cube of bread browns in 30 seconds. Fry the wontons, in batches, for 1–2 minutes until golden brown. Drain on paper towels and keep warm whilst frying the remaining wontons.

4 Sprinkle the sesame seeds over the wontons. Serve the vegetable dim sum with a soy or plum dipping sauce.

COOK'S TIP

If preferred, arrange the wontons on a heatproof plate and then cook in a steamer for 5–7 minutes for a healthier cooking method.

Crispy Crab Wontons

These delicious wontons are a superb appetizer. Deep-fried until crisp and golden, they are delicious with a chile dipping sauce.

NUTRITIONAL INFORMATION

Calories 266	Sugars 0.4g	
Protein 10g	Fat 17g	
Carbohydrate ...18g	Saturates 5g	

10 MINS   15 MINS

SERVES 4

INGREDIENTS

6 oz/175 g white crabmeat, flaked

1¾ oz/50 g canned water chestnuts, drained, rinsed, and chopped

1 small fresh red chile, chopped

1 scallion, chopped

1 tbsp cornstarch

1 tsp dry sherry

1 tsp light soy sauce

½ tsp lime juice

24 wonton skins

vegetable oil, for deep-frying

sliced lime, to garnish

1 To make the filling, mix together the crabmeat, water chestnuts, chile, scallion, cornstarch, sherry, soy sauce, and lime juice.

2 Spread out the wonton skins on a counter and spoon one portion of the filling into the center of each wonton skin.

3 Dampen the edges of the wonton skins with a little water and fold them in half to form triangles. Fold the two pointed ends in toward the center, then moisten with a little water to secure and pinch together to seal.

4 Heat the oil for deep-frying in a wok or deep-fryer to 350°–375°F/180°–190°C, or until a cube of bread browns in 30 seconds. Fry the wontons, in batches, for 2–3 minutes, until golden brown and crisp. Remove the wontons from the oil and leave to drain on paper towels.

5 Serve the wontons hot, garnished with slices of lime.

COOK'S TIP

Handle wonton skins carefully as they can be easily damaged. Make sure that the wontons are sealed well and secured before deep-frying to prevent the filling coming out and the wontons unwrapping.

Eggplant Satay

Eggplants and mushrooms are grilled on skewers and served with a tasty satay dipping sauce.

NUTRITIONAL INFORMATION

Calories	155	Sugars	.........2g
Protein	.........4g	Fat	..........14g
Carbohydrate	....3g	Saturates	.......3g

🍴 🍴 🍴

🍲 2¼ HOURS   🕐 25 MINS

SERVES 4

I N G R E D I E N T S

2 eggplants, cut into 1-inch/2.5-cm pieces

6 oz/175 g small chestnut mushrooms

M A R I N A D E

1 tsp cumin seeds

1 tsp coriander seeds

1-inch/2.5-cm piece gingerroot, grated

2 garlic cloves, crushed lightly

½ stalk lemon grass, chopped coarsely

4 tbsp light soy sauce

8 tbsp corn oil

2 tbsp lemon juice

P E A N U T S A U C E

½ tsp cumin seeds

½ tsp coriander seeds

3 garlic cloves

1 small onion, puréed in a food processor or chopped very finely by hand

1 tbsp lemon juice

1 tsp salt

½ red chile, seeded and sliced

½ cup coconut milk

generous 1 cup crunchy peanut butter

1 cup water

1 Thread the vegetables onto eight metal or pre-soaked wooden skewers.

2 For the marinade, grind the cumin and coriander seeds, ginger, garlic, and lemon grass. Stir-fry over high heat until fragrant. Remove from the heat and add the remaining marinade ingredients. Place the skewers in a dish and spoon the marinade over. Leave to marinate for at least 2 hours and up to 8 hours.

3 To make the peanut sauce, grind the cumin and coriander seeds with the garlic. Add all the ingredients except the water. Transfer to a pan and stir in the water. Bring to a boil and cook until thick.

4 Cook the skewers under a preheated very hot broiler for 15–20 minutes. Brush with the marinade frequently during the cooking time and turn once. Serve with the peanut sauce.

Spicy Corn Fritters

Cornmeal can be found in most supermarkets or health food stores. Yellow in color, it acts as a binding agent in this recipe.

NUTRITIONAL INFORMATION

Calories	213	Sugars	.........6g
Protein	.........5g	Fat	...........8g
Carbohydrate	...30g	Saturates	.......1g

5 MINS   15 MINS

SERVES 4

INGREDIENTS

2 cups canned or frozen corn

2 red chiles, seeded and very finely chopped

2 garlic cloves, crushed

10 lime leaves, very finely chopped

2 tbsp fresh cilantro, chopped

1 large egg

½ cup cornmeal

3½ oz/100 g fine green beans, very finely sliced

peanut oil, for frying

1 Place the corn, chiles, garlic, lime leaves, cilantro, egg, and cornmeal in a large mixing bowl, and stir to combine.

2 Add the green beans to the ingredients in the bowl and mix well, using a wooden spoon.

3 Divide the mixture into small, evenly sized balls. Flatten the balls of mixture between the palms of your hands to form rounds.

4 Heat a little peanut oil in a preheated wok or large skillet until really hot. Cook the fritters, in batches, until brown and crispy on the outside, turning occasionally.

5 Leave the fritters to drain on absorbent paper towels while frying the remaining fritters.

6 Transfer the fritters to warm serving plates and serve immediately.

COOK'S TIP

Kaffir lime leaves are dark green, glossy leaves that have a lemony-lime flavor. They can be bought from specialist Asian stores either fresh or dried. Fresh leaves impart the most delicious flavor.

Steamed Duck Buns

The dough used in this recipe may also be wrapped around chicken, pork, or shrimp, or sweet fillings as an alternative.

🍞 🍞 🍞 🍞

1½ HOURS   🕐 1 HOUR

SERVES 4

INGREDIENTS

DUMPLING DOUGH

2 cups all-purpose flour

½ oz/15 g active dry yeast

1 tsp superfine sugar

2 tbsp warm water

¾ cup warm milk

FILLING

10½ oz/300 g duck breast

1 tbsp light brown sugar

1 tbsp light soy sauce

2 tbsp clear honey

1 tbsp hoisin sauce

1 tbsp vegetable oil

1 leek, finely chopped

1 garlic clove, crushed

½-inch/1-cm piece fresh gingerroot, grated

1 Place the duck breast in a large bowl. Mix together the light brown sugar, soy sauce, honey, and hoisin sauce. Pour the mixture over the duck and marinate for 20 minutes.

2 Remove the duck from the marinade and cook on a rack set over a roasting pan in a preheated oven, at 400°F/200°C, for 35–40 minutes, until cooked through.

Leave to cool, then remove the meat from the bones and cut into small cubes.

3 Heat the vegetable oil in a preheated wok or skillet until really hot.

4 Add the leek, garlic, and ginger to the wok and fry for 3 minutes. Mix with the duck meat.

5 Sift the all-purpose flour into a large bowl. Mix the yeast, superfine sugar, and warm water in a separate bowl and leave in a warm place for 15 minutes.

6 Pour the yeast mixture into the flour, together with the warm milk, mixing to form a firm dough. Knead the dough on a floured counter for 5 minutes. Roll into a sausage shape, 1-inch/2.5-cm in diameter. Cut into 16 pieces, then cover and let stand for 20–25 minutes.

7 Flatten the dough pieces into 4-inch/10-cm rounds. Place a spoonful of filling in the center of each, draw up the sides to form a "moneybag" shape and twist to seal.

8 Place the dumplings on a clean, damp dish cloth in the base of a steamer, then cover and steam for 20 minutes. Serve immediately.

Barbecue Pork (Char Siu)

Also called honey-roasted pork, these are the strips of reddish meat sometimes seen hanging in the windows of Cantonese restaurants.

NUTRITIONAL INFORMATION

Calories 250	Sugar 8g
Protein 27g	Fat 10g
Carbohydrate 9g	Saturates 3g

🍲 4¼ HOURS   🕐 30 MINS

SERVES 4

I N G R E D I E N T S

1 lb 2 oz/500 g pork fillet

⅔ cup boiling water

1 tbsp honey, dissolved with a little hot water

M A R I N A D E

1 tbsp sugar

1 tbsp crushed yellow bean sauce

1 tbsp light soy sauce

1 tbsp hoisin sauce

1 tbsp oyster sauce

½ tsp chile sauce

1 tbsp brandy or rum

1 tsp sesame oil

shredded lettuce, to serve

1 Using a sharp knife or meat cleaver, cut the pork into strips about 1-inch/2.5-cm thick and 7-8 inches/ 18-20 cm long and place in a large shallow dish. Mix the marinade ingredients together and pour over the pork, turning until well coated. Cover, and leave to marinate for at least 3-4 hours, turning occasionally.

2 Remove the pork strips from the dish with a slotted spoon, reserving the marinade. Arrange the pork strips on a rack over a baking pan. Place the pan in a preheated oven and pour in the boiling water. Roast the pork for about 10-15 minutes.

3 Lower the oven temperature. Baste the pork strips with the reserved marinade and turn over using metal tongs. Roast for an additional 10 minutes.

4 Remove the pork from the oven, then brush with the honey syrup and lightly brown under a medium hot broiler for 3-4 minutes, turning once or twice.

5 To serve, let the pork cool slightly before cutting it. Cut across the grain into thin slices and arrange neatly on a bed of shredded lettuce. Make a sauce by boiling the marinade and the drippings in the baking pan for a few minutes, then strain and pour over the pork.

Pork Satay

Small pieces of tender pork are skewered on bamboo satay sticks, broiled or barbecued, then served with a delicious peanut sauce.

NUTRITIONAL INFORMATION

Calories 397	Sugars 8g	
Protein 35g	Fat 24g	
Carbohydrate 11g	Saturates 6g	

10 MINS   15 MINS

SERVES 4

INGREDIENTS

8 bamboo satay sticks, soaked in warm water

1 lb 2 oz/500 g pork tenderloin

SAUCE

1 cup unsalted peanuts

2 tsp hot chile sauce

¾ cup coconut milk

2 tbsp soy sauce

1 tbsp ground coriander

pinch of ground turmeric

1 tbsp dark muscovado sugar

salt

TO GARNISH

fresh flat-leaf parsley or cilantro

cucumber leaves (see Cook's Tip)

red chiles

1 To make the sauce, scatter the peanuts on a cookie sheet and toast under a preheated broiler until golden brown, turning them once or twice. Leave to cool, then grind them in a food processor, blender, or food mill. Alternatively, chop the peanuts very finely.

2 Put the ground peanuts into a small pan with the hot chile sauce, coconut milk, soy sauce, coriander, turmeric, sugar, and salt. Heat gently, stirring constantly and taking care not to burn the sauce on the bottom of the pan. Reduce the heat to very low and cook gently for 5 minutes.

3 Meanwhile, trim any fat from the pork. Cut the pork into small cubes and thread it onto the bamboo satay sticks. Place the kabobs on a rack covered with foil in a broiler pan.

4 Put half the peanut sauce into a small serving bowl. Brush the skewered pork with the remaining satay sauce and place under a preheated broiler for 10 minutes, turning and basting frequently, until cooked.

5 Serve the pork satay sticks with the reserved peanut sauce and garnish with flat-leaf parsley, cucumber leaves, and red chiles.

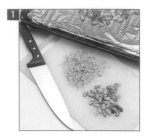

COOK'S TIP

To make cucumber leaves, slice a thick chunk from the side of a cucumber, and cut to shape. Cut grooves in the cucumber flesh in the shape of leaf veins.

Sweet & Sour Pork Ribs

This recipe uses the spare rib, the traditional Chinese-style rib. Baby back ribs and loin ribs are also suitable.

NUTRITIONAL INFORMATION

Calories 565   Sugars 29g
Protein . . . . .24g   Fat 37g
Carbohydrate . . .32g   Saturates 14g

2¼ HOURS   50 MINS

SERVES 4

INGREDIENTS

2 garlic cloves, crushed

2-inch/5-cm piece fresh gingerroot, grated

⅔ cup soy sauce

2 tbsp sugar

4 tbsp sweet sherry

4 tbsp tomato paste

2 cups cubed pineapple

4 lb 8 oz/2 kg pork spare ribs

3 tbsp clear honey

5 pineapple rings, fresh or canned, to serve

1 Mix together the garlic, ginger, soy sauce, sugar, sherry, tomato paste, and cubed pineapple in a non-porous dish.

2 Put the spare ribs into the dish and make sure that they are coated completely with the marinade.

3 Cover the dish with plastic wrap.

4 Leave the ribs to marinate at room temperature for 2 hours only.

5 Cook the ribs over a medium grill for 30–40 minutes, brushing with the honey after 20–30 minutes.

6 Baste the spare ribs with the reserved marinade frequently until cooked.

7 Cook the pineapple rings over the grill for 10 minutes, turning once.

8 Transfer the sweet & sour ribs to a serving dish and serve with the grilled pineapple rings on the side.

COOK'S TIP

If a marinade contains soy sauce, the marinating time should be limited, usually to 2 hours. If left to marinate for too long, the meat will dry out and become tough.

Lentil Balls with Sauce

Crisp golden lentil balls are served in a sweet and sour sauce with bell pepper and pineapple chunks.

NUTRITIONAL INFORMATION

Calories 384	Sugars 15g
Protein 17g	Fat 14g
Carbohydrate ...49g	Saturates 2g

15 MINS   35 MINS

SERVES 4

INGREDIENTS

1 cup red lentils

generous 1¾ cups water

½ green chile, seeded and chopped

4 scallions, chopped finely

1 garlic clove, crushed

1 tsp salt

4 tbsp pineapple juice from can (see below)

1 egg, beaten

½ red bell pepper, cut into chunks

½ green bell pepper, cut into chunks

2 canned pineapple rings, cut into chunks

vegetable oil for deep-frying

rice or noodles, to serve

SAUCE

3 tbsp white wine vinegar

2 tbsp sugar

2 tbsp tomato paste

1 tsp sesame oil

1 tsp cornstarch

½ tsp salt

6 tbsp water

2 tbsp vegetable oil

1 Wash the lentils, then place in a pan with the water and bring to a boil. Skim and boil rapidly for 10 minutes, uncovered. Reduce the heat and simmer for 5 minutes until you have a fairly dry mixture, stirring occasionally.

2 Remove from the heat and stir in the chile, scallions, garlic, salt, and pineapple juice. Leave to cool for 10 minutes.

3 To make the sauce, mix together the vinegar, sugar, tomato paste, sesame oil, cornstarch, salt, and water, and set aside.

4 Add the beaten egg to the lentil mixture. Heat the oil in a large pan or wok and deep-fry tablespoonfuls of the mixture in batches until crisp and golden. Remove with a perforated spoon and drain on paper towels.

5 Heat the 2 tablespoons of oil in a wok or skillet. Stir-fry the bell pepper for 2 minutes. Add the sauce mixture with the pineapple chunks. Bring to a boil, then reduce the heat and simmer for 1 minute, stirring constantly, until the sauce has thickened. Add the lentil balls and heat thoroughly, taking care not to break them up. Serve with rice or noodles.

Shrimp Omelet

This is called *Foo Yong* in China and is a classic dish that may be flavored with any ingredients you have to hand.

NUTRITIONAL INFORMATION

Calories	320	Sugars	.........1g
Protein	........31g	Fat	..........18g
Carbohydrate	....8g	Saturates	.......4g

🍠 5 MINS   🕐 10 MINS

SERVES 4

I N G R E D I E N T S

3 tbsp corn oil

2 leeks, trimmed and sliced

12 oz/350 g raw jumbo shrimp

4 tbsp cornstarch

1 tsp salt

3 cups sliced mushrooms

scant 1¼ cups bean sprouts

6 eggs

deep-fried leeks, to garnish (optional)

1 Heat the corn oil in a preheated wok or large skillet. Add the sliced leeks and stir-fry for 3 minutes.

2 Rinse the shrimp under cold running water and then pat dry with absorbent paper towels.

3 Mix together the cornstarch and salt in a large bowl.

4 Add the shrimp to the cornstarch and salt mixture and toss to coat all over.

5 Add the shrimp to the wok or skillet and stir-fry for 2 minutes, until the shrimp are almost cooked through.

6 Add the mushrooms and bean sprouts and stir-fry for 2 minutes more.

7 Beat the eggs with 3 tablespoons of cold water. Pour the egg mixture into the wok and cook until the egg sets, carefully turning over once. Turn the omelet out on to a clean board, then divide into 4 and serve hot, garnished with deep-fried leeks (if using).

VARIATION

If liked, divide the mixture into 4 once the initial cooking has taken place in step 6 and cook 4 individual omelets.

Chicken or Beef Satay

In this dish, strips of chicken or beef are threaded onto skewers and broiled, then served with a spicy peanut sauce.

NUTRITIONAL INFORMATION

Calories 314   Sugars 8g
Protein . . . . .32g   Fat 16g
Carbohydrate . . .10g   Saturates 4g

2¼ HOURS   15 MINS

SERVES 6

INGREDIENTS

4 boneless, skinned chicken breasts or
   1 lb 10 oz/750 g rump steak, trimmed

MARINADE

1 small onion, finely chopped

1 garlic clove, crushed

1-inch/2.5-cm piece fresh gingerroot,
   peeled and grated

2 tbsp dark soy sauce

2 tsp chile powder

1 tsp ground coriander

2 tsp dark brown sugar

1 tbsp lemon or lime juice

1 tbsp vegetable oil

SAUCE

1¼ cups coconut milk

4 tbsp crunchy peanut butter

1 tbsp fish sauce

1 tsp lemon or lime juice

salt and pepper

1 Using a sharp knife, trim any fat from the chicken or beef, then cut into thin strips, about 3 inches/7 cm long.

2 To make the marinade, place all the ingredients in a shallow dish and mix well. Add the chicken or beef strips and turn in the marinade until well coated.

Cover with plastic wrap and leave to marinate for 2 hours or overnight in the refrigerator.

3 Remove the meat from the marinade and thread the pieces, concertina style, on pre-soaked bamboo or thin wooden skewers.

4 Broil the chicken and beef satays for 8-10 minutes, turning and brushing

occasionally with the marinade, until cooked through.

5 Meanwhile, to make the sauce, mix the coconut milk with the peanut butter, fish sauce, and lemon juice in a pan. Bring to a boil and cook for 3 minutes. Season to taste.

6 Transfer the sauce to a serving bowl and serve with the cooked satays.

Vegetable Rolls

In this recipe a mixed vegetable stuffing is wrapped in Napa cabbage and steamed until tender.

NUTRITIONAL INFORMATION

Calories	69	Sugars	.........1g
Protein	.........2g	Fat	...........5g
Carbohydrate	....3g	Saturates	.......1g

10 MINS   20 MINS

SERVES 4

I N G R E D I E N T S

8 large Napa cabbage leaves

FILLING

2 baby corn cobs, sliced

1 carrot, finely chopped

1 celery stalk, chopped

4 scallions, chopped

4 water chestnuts, chopped

2 tbsp unsalted cashews, chopped

1 garlic clove, chopped

1 tsp grated fresh gingerroot

¼ cup canned bamboo shoots, drained, rinsed, and chopped

1 tsp sesame oil

2 tsp soy sauce

soy or chile sauce, to serve

1 Place the Napa cabbage leaves in a large bowl and pour over boiling water to soften them. Leave to stand for 1 minute and drain thoroughly.

2 Mix together the baby corn cobs, chopped carrot, celery, scallions, water chestnuts, cashews, garlic, ginger, and bamboo shoots in a large bowl.

3 In a separate bowl, mix together the sesame oil and soy sauce. Add this mixture to the vegetables, mixing well until the vegetables are thoroughly coated in the mixture.

4 Spread out the Napa cabbage leaves on a cutting board and spoon an equal quantity of the filling mixture on to each leaf.

5 Roll the Napa cabbage leaves up, folding in the sides, to make neat parcels. Secure with toothpicks.

6 Place the filled rolls in a small heatproof dish in a steamer, then cover and cook for 15–20 minutes, until the pockets are cooked.

7 Transfer the vegetable rolls to a warm serving dish and serve with a soy or chile sauce.

Chicken Wontons

These deliciously crispy nibbles make an ideal introduction to a Chinese meal. Here they are filled with a chicken and mushroom mixture.

NUTRITIONAL INFORMATION

Calories 285	Sugars 1g
Protein 16g	Fat 19g
Carbohydrate ...14g	Saturates 5g

20 MINS   35 MINS

SERVES 4

INGREDIENTS

9 oz/250 g boneless chicken breast, skinned

1 cup mushrooms

1 garlic clove

2 shallots

1 tbsp fish sauce or mushroom ketchup

1 tbsp chopped fresh cilantro

2 tbsp vegetable oil

about 50 wonton skins

oil, for deep-frying

salt and pepper

sliced scallion, to garnish

sweet chile sauce, to serve

1 Put the chicken, mushrooms, garlic, shallots, fish sauce, and cilantro into a blender or food processor. Blend for 10–15 seconds. Alternatively, chop all the ingredients finely and mix together well.

2 Heat the vegetable oil in a wok or skillet and add the chicken mixture. Stir-fry for about 8 minutes, breaking up the mixture as it cooks, until it browns. Transfer to a bowl and leave to cool for 10–15 minutes.

3 Place the wonton skins on a clean, damp dish cloth. Layering 2 skins together at a time, place teaspoonfuls of

the chicken mixture into the middle. Dampen the edges with water, then make small pouches, pressing the edges together to seal. Repeat with the remaining skins until all the mixture has been used.

4 Heat the oil for deep-frying in a wok or deep fat fryer. Fry the wontons, a few at a time, for 2–3 minutes until golden brown. Remove the wontons

from the oil with a perforated spoon and drain on paper towels. Keep warm while frying the remaining wontons.

5 Transfer the wontons to a warmed serving platter and garnish with the sliced scallion. Serve at once, accompanied by some sweet chile sauce.

Deep-Fried Spare Ribs

The spare ribs should be chopped into small bite-size pieces before or after cooking.

NUTRITIONAL INFORMATION

Calories	177	Sugars	.......0.2g
Protein	.........6g	Fat	..........14g
Carbohydrate	....6g	Saturates	.......4g

2¼ HOURS   5 MINS

SERVES 4

INGREDIENTS

8–10 finger spare ribs

1 tsp five-spice powder or 1 tbsp mild curry powder

1 tbsp rice wine or dry sherry

1 egg

2 tbsp all-purpose flour

vegetable oil, for deep-frying

1 tsp finely shredded scallions

1 tsp finely shredded fresh green or red hot chiles, seeded

salt and pepper

Spicy Salt and Pepper (see page 68), to serve

1 Chop the ribs into 3-4 small pieces. Place the ribs in a bowl with salt, pepper, five-spice powder, and the wine. Turn to coat the ribs in the spices and leave to marinate for 1-2 hours.

2 Mix the egg and flour together to make a batter. Dip the ribs in the batter one by one to coat well.

3 Heat the oil in a preheated wok until smoking. Deep-fry the ribs for 4-5 minutes, then remove with chopsticks or a slotted spoon and drain them on paper towels.

4 Reheat the oil over high heat and deep-fry the ribs once more for another minute. Remove and drain again on paper towels.

5 Pour 1 tablespoon of the hot oil over the scallions and chiles and leave for 30-40 seconds. Serve the ribs with Spicy Salt and Pepper, garnished with the shredded scallions and chiles.

COOK'S TIP

To make finger ribs, cut the sheet of spare ribs into individual ribs down each side of the bones. These ribs are then chopped into bite-size pieces for deep-frying.

Crab Ravioli

These small pockets are made from wonton skins, filled with mixed vegetables and crabmeat for a melt-in-the-mouth appetizer.

20 MINS   25 MINS

SERVES 4

INGREDIENTS

1 lb/450 g crabmeat (fresh or canned and drained)

½ red bell pepper, seeded and finely diced

4½ oz/125 g Napa cabbage, shredded

⅓ cup bean sprouts, coarsely chopped

1 tbsp light soy sauce

1 tsp lime juice

16 wonton skins

1 small egg, beaten

2 tbsp peanut oil

1 tsp sesame oil

salt and pepper

1 Mix together the crabmeat, bell pepper, Napa cabbage, bean sprouts, soy sauce, and lime juice. Season and leave to stand for 15 minutes.

2 Spread out the wonton skins on a counter. Spoon a little of the crabmeat mixture into the center of each skin. Brush the edges with egg and fold in half, pushing out any air. Press the edges together to seal.

3 Heat the peanut oil in a preheated wok or skillet. Cook the ravioli, in batches, for 3–4 minutes, turning, until browned. Remove with a slotted spoon and drain on paper towels.

4 Heat any remaining filling in the wok or skillet over a gentle heat until hot. Serve the ravioli with the hot filling and sprinkled with sesame oil.

COOK'S TIP

Make sure that the edges of the ravioli are sealed well and that all of the air is pressed out to prevent them from opening during cooking.

Pork Sesame Toasts

This classic Chinese appetizer is also a great nibble for serving at parties —but be sure to make plenty!

NUTRITIONAL INFORMATION

Calories	674	Sugars	.........2g
Protein	........33g	Fat	..........46g
Carbohydrate	...33g	Saturates	.......7g

🍖 5 MINS 🕐 35 MINS

SERVES 4

INGREDIENTS

9 oz/250 g lean pork

9 oz/250 g uncooked shelled shrimp, deveined

4 scallions, trimmed

1 garlic clove, crushed

1 tbsp chopped fresh cilantro leaves and stems

1 tbsp fish sauce

1 egg

8–10 thick slices of white bread

3 tbsp sesame seeds

⅔ cup vegetable oil

salt and pepper

TO GARNISH

sprigs of fresh cilantro

red bell pepper, sliced finely

1 Put the pork, shrimp, scallions, garlic, cilantro, fish sauce, egg, and seasoning into a food processor or blender. Process for a few seconds until the ingredients are finely chopped. Transfer the mixture to a bowl. Alternatively, chop the pork, shrimp, and scallions very finely, then mix with the garlic, cilantro, fish sauce, beaten egg, and seasoning until all the ingredients are well combined.

2 Spread the pork and shrimp mixture thickly over the bread so that it reaches right up to the edges. Cut off the crusts and slice each piece of bread into 4 squares or triangles.

3 Sprinkle the topping liberally with sesame seeds. Heat the oil in a wok or skillet. Cook a few pieces of the bread, topping side down first so that it sets the egg, for about 2 minutes until golden brown. Turn the pieces over to cook on the other side, about 1 minute.

4 Drain the pork and shrimp toasts and place them on paper towels. Cook the remaining pieces. Serve garnished with sprigs of fresh cilantro and strips of red bell pepper.

Seven-Spice Eggplants

This is a really simple dish of deep-fried eggplant slices and is perfect served with a chile dip.

NUTRITIONAL INFORMATION

Calories ....169 Sugars 2g
Protein ....2g Fat 12g
Carbohydrate ...15g Saturates 1g

35 MINS   20 MINS

SERVES 4

I N G R E D I E N T S

1 lb/450 g eggplants, wiped

1 egg white

3½ tbsp cornstarch

1 tsp salt

1 tbsp seven-spice seasoning

oil, for deep-frying

2 Rinse the eggplant thoroughly and pat dry with absorbent paper towels.

3 Place the egg white in a small bowl and whip until light and foamy.

4 Using a spoon, mix together the cornstarch, salt, and seven spice powder on a large plate.

5 Heat the oil for deep-frying in a large preheated wok or heavy-based skillet.

6 Dip the eggplant slices into the egg white, and then into the cornstarch and seven spice mixture to coat evenly.

7 Deep-fry the coated eggplant slices, in batches, for 5 minutes, until pale golden and crispy.

8 Transfer the eggplants to absorbent paper towels and leave to drain. Transfer the seven spice eggplants to serving plates and serve hot.

1 Using a sharp knife, thinly slice the eggplants. Place the eggplant in a colander, sprinkle with salt and leave to stand for 30 minutes. This will remove all the bitter juices.

COOK'S TIP

The best oil to use for deep-frying is peanut oil, which has a high smoke point and mild flavor, so it will neither burn nor taint the food. About 2½ cups oil is sufficient.

Chinese Potato Sticks

These potato sticks are a variation of the great Western favorite, being flavored with soy sauce and chile.

NUTRITIONAL INFORMATION

Calories	326	Sugars	.........1g
Protein	.........4g	Fat	..........22g
Carbohydrate	...29g	Saturates	.......3g

10 MINS   15 MINS

SERVES 4

INGREDIENTS

1 lb 7 oz/650 g medium-size potatoes

8 tbsp vegetable oil

1 fresh red chile, halved

1 small onion, cut into fourths

2 garlic cloves, halved

2 tbsp soy sauce

pinch of salt

1 tsp wine vinegar

1 tbsp coarse sea salt

pinch of chile powder

1 Peel the potatoes and cut into thin slices along their length. Cut the slices into short thin sticks.

2 Bring a pan of water to a boil and blanch the potato sticks for 2 minutes and drain, then rinse under cold water and drain well again. Pat the potato sticks thoroughly dry with absorbent paper towels.

3 Heat the oil in a preheated wok until it is almost smoking. Add the chile, onion, and garlic and stir-fry for 30 seconds. Remove and discard the chile, onion, and garlic.

4 Add the potato sticks to the oil and stir-fry for 3–4 minutes, until golden.

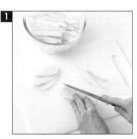  

5 Add the soy sauce, salt, and vinegar to the wok, reduce the heat and cook for 1 minute, until the potatoes are crisp.

6 Remove the potatoes with a slotted spoon and leave to drain on absorbent paper towels.

7 Transfer the potato sticks to a serving dish, then sprinkle with the sea salt and chile powder and serve.

VARIATION

Sprinkle other flavorings over the cooked potato sticks, such as curry powder, or serve with a chile dip.

Sesame Ginger Chicken

Chunks of chicken breast are marinated in a mixture of lime juice, garlic, sesame oil, and fresh ginger to give them a great flavor.

NUTRITIONAL INFORMATION

Calories 204	Sugars 0g	
Protein 28g	Fat 10g	
Carbohydrate 1g	Saturates 2g	

2¼ HOURS   10 MINS

SERVES 4

INGREDIENTS

1 lb 2 oz/500 g boneless chicken
   breasts

4 wooden satay sticks, soaked in
   warm water

sprigs of fresh mint, to garnish

MARINADE

1 garlic clove, crushed

1 shallot, chopped very finely

2 tbsp sesame oil

1 tbsp fish sauce or light soy sauce

finely grated rind of 1 lime or
   ½ lemon

2 tbsp lime juice or lemon juice

1 tsp sesame seeds

2 tsp finely grated fresh gingerroot

2 tsp chopped fresh mint

salt and pepper

1 To make the marinade, put the crushed garlic, chopped shallot, sesame oil, fish sauce, lime or lemon rind and juice, sesame seeds, grated gingerroot, and chopped mint into a large non-metallic bowl. Season with a little salt and pepper and mix together until all the ingredients are thoroughly combined.

2 Remove the skin from the chicken breasts and cut the flesh into chunks.

3 Add the chicken to the marinade, stirring to coat the chicken completely in the mixture. Cover with plastic wrap and chill in the refrigerator for at least 2 hours so that the flavors are absorbed.

4 Thread the chicken onto wooden satay sticks. Place them on the rack of a broiler pan and baste with the marinade.

5 Place the kabobs under a preheated broiler for 8–10 minutes. Turn them frequently, basting them with the remaining marinade.

6 Serve the chicken skewers at once, garnished with sprigs of fresh mint.

COOK'S TIP

The kabobs taste delicious if dipped into an accompanying bowl of hot chile sauce.

Sweet & Sour Shrimp

Shrimp are marinated in a soy sauce mixture, then coated in a light batter, fried, and served with a delicious sweet and sour dip.

🍗 🍗 🍗 🍗

🍲 40 MINS   🕐 20 MINS

SERVES 4

INGREDIENTS

16 large raw shrimp, peeled

1 tsp grated fresh gingerroot

1 garlic clove, crushed

2 scallions, sliced

2 tbsp dry sherry

2 tsp sesame oil

1 tbsp light soy sauce

vegetable oil, for deep-frying

shredded scallion, to garnish

BATTER

4 egg whites

4 tbsp cornstarch

2 tbsp all-purpose flour

SAUCE

2 tbsp tomato paste

3 tbsp white wine vinegar

4 tsp light soy sauce

2 tbsp lemon juice

3 tbsp light brown sugar

1 green bell pepper, seeded and cut into thin short sticks

½ tsp chile sauce

1¼ cups vegetable stock

2 tsp cornstarch

1 Using tweezers, devein the shrimp, then flatten them with a large knife.

2 Place the shrimp in a dish and add the ginger, garlic, scallions, dry sherry, sesame oil, and soy sauce. Cover with plastic wrap and leave to marinate for 30 minutes.

3 Make the batter by beating the egg whites until thick. Fold in the cornstarch and all-purpose flour to form a light batter.

4 Place all of the sauce ingredients in a pan and bring to a boil. Reduce the heat and leave to simmer for 10 minutes.

5 Remove the shrimp from the marinade and dip them into the batter to coat.

6 Heat the vegetable oil in a preheated wok or large skillet until almost smoking. Reduce the heat and fry the shrimp for 3–4 minutes, until crisp and golden brown.

7 Garnish the shrimp with shredded scallion and serve with the sauce.

Salads & Pickles

Vegetables play an important part in the Chinese diet and although salads as we know them in the West do not feature greatly on the Chinese menu, many lightly cooked

vegetable dishes can be classified as salads when they are left to cool and are lightly tossed in dressing. The freshest vegetables and brief cooking ensure the necessary balance of texture and flavor, while dressings add a touch of sharpness and acidity. Pickled vegetables are very popular in China. They are often served as snacks and appetizers, and can also be served with cold meat dishes. Once made, they will keep in the refrigerator for up to 2 weeks.

Shrimp Salad

Noodles and bean sprouts form the basis of this refreshing salad, which combines the flavors of fruit and shrimp.

NUTRITIONAL INFORMATION

Calories 359   Sugars 4g
Protein ....31g   Fat 15g
Carbohydrate ...25g   Saturates 2g

15 MINS   5 MINS

SERVES 4

INGREDIENTS

9 oz/250 g fine egg noodles

3 tbsp corn oil

1 tbsp sesame oil

1 tbsp sesame seeds

1 cup bean sprouts

1 ripe mango, sliced

6 scallions, sliced

2¾ oz/75 g radish, sliced

12 oz/350 g shelled cooked shrimp

2 tbsp light soy sauce

1 tbsp sherry

1 Place the egg noodles in a large bowl and pour over enough boiling water to cover. Leave to stand for 10 minutes.

2 Drain the noodles thoroughly and pat dry with paper towels.

COOK'S TIP

If fresh mango is unavailable, use canned mango slices, rinsed and drained, instead.

3 Heat the sunflower oil in a large wok or skillet and stir-fry the noodles for 5 minutes, tossing frequently.

4 Remove the wok from the heat and add the sesame oil, sesame seeds, and bean sprouts, tossing to mix well.

5 In a separate bowl, mix together the sliced mango, scallions, radish and shrimp. Stir in the light soy sauce and sherry and mix until thoroughly combined.

6 Toss the shrimp mixture with the noodles and transfer to a serving dish. Alternatively, arrange the noodles around the edge of a serving plate and pile the shrimp mixture into the center. Serve immediately as this salad is best eaten while still warm.

Sweet & Sour Tofu Salad

Tofu is a delicious, healthy alternative to meat. Mixed with crisp stir-fried vegetables it makes an ideal light meal or appetizer.

NUTRITIONAL INFORMATION

Calories 262	Sugars 15g	
Protein 16g	Fat 14g	
Carbohydrate ...19g	Saturates 2g	

🍖 🍖

🥗 10 MINS   🕐 15 MINS

SERVES 4

INGREDIENTS

2 tbsp vegetable oil

1 garlic clove, crushed

1 lb 2 oz/500 g tofu, cubed

1 onion, sliced

1 carrot, cut into julienne strips

1 stick celery, sliced

2 small red bell peppers, cored, seeded, and sliced

2½ cups snow peas, trimmed and halved

4½ oz/125 g broccoli, trimmed and divided into florets

4½ oz/125 g thin green beans, halved

2 tbsp oyster sauce

1 tbsp tamarind concentrate

1 tbsp fish sauce

1 tbsp tomato paste

1 tbsp light soy sauce

1 tbsp chile sauce

2 tbsp sugar

1 tbsp white vinegar

pinch of ground star anise

1 tsp cornstarch

1¼ cups water

1 Heat the vegetable oil in a large, heavy-based skillet or wok until hot.

2 Add the crushed garlic to the wok or skillet and cook for a few seconds.

3 Add the tofu, in batches, and stir-fry over gentle heat, until golden on all sides. Remove with a slotted spoon and keep warm.

4 Add the onion, carrot, celery, red bell pepper, snow peas, broccoli, and green beans to the pan and stir-fry for 2-3 minutes, or until tender-crisp.

5 Add the oyster sauce, tamarind concentrate, fish sauce, tomato paste, soy sauce, chile sauce, sugar, vinegar, and star anise, mixing well to blend. Stir-fry for an additional 2 minutes.

6 Mix the cornstarch with the water and add to the pan with the fried tofu. Stir-fry gently until the sauce boils and thickens slightly.

7 Transfer the sweet and sour tofu salad to warm serving plates and serve immediately.

Chicken & Noodle Salad

Strips of chicken are coated in a delicious spicy mixture, then stir-fried with noodles and served on a bed of salad.

NUTRITIONAL INFORMATION

Calories	217	Sugars	.........1g
Protein	........21g	Fat	...........11g
Carbohydrate	....9g	Saturates	.......2g

10 MINS   10 MINS

SERVES 4

I N G R E D I E N T S

1 tsp finely grated fresh gingerroot

½ tsp Chinese five-spice powder

1 tbsp all-purpose flour

½ tsp chile powder

12 oz/350 g boned chicken breast, skinned and sliced thinly

2 oz/55 g rice noodles

1½ cups finely shredded Napa cabbage or hard white cabbage

3-inch/7-cm piece of cucumber, sliced finely

1 large carrot, pared thinly

1 tbsp olive oil

2 tbsp lime or lemon juice

2 tbsp sesame oil

salt and pepper

TO GARNISH

lemon or lime slices

fresh cilantro leaves

1 Mix together the ginger, five-spice powder, flour, and chile powder in a shallow mixing bowl. Season with salt and pepper. Add the strips of chicken and roll in the mixture until well coated.

2 Put the noodles into a large bowl and cover with warm water. Leave to soak for about 5 minutes, then drain them well.

3 Mix together the Napa cabbage, cucumber, and carrot, and arrange in a salad bowl. Whisk together the olive oil and lime juice, then season with salt and pepper, and use to dress the salad.

4 Heat the sesame oil in a wok or skillet and add the chicken. Stir-fry for 5–6 minutes until well-browned and crispy on the outside. Remove from the

wok or skillet with a perforated spoon and drain on absorbent paper towels.

5 Add the noodles to the wok or skillet and stir-fry for 3–4 minutes until heated through. Remove from the wok, then mix with the chicken and pile the mixture on top of the salad. Serve garnished with lemon or lime slices and cilantro leaves.

Hot & Sour Duck Salad

This is a lovely tangy salad, drizzled with a lime juice and fish sauce dressing. It makes a splendid appetizer or light main course dish.

NUTRITIONAL INFORMATION

Calories	236	Sugars	.........3g
Protein	........27g	Fat	..........10g
Carbohydrate	...10g	Saturates	.......3g

40 MINS   5 MINS

SERVES 4

INGREDIENTS

2 heads crisp salad lettuce, washed and separated into leaves

2 shallots, thinly sliced

4 scallions, chopped

1 celery stalk, finely sliced into julienne strips

2-inch/5-cm piece cucumber, cut into julienne strips

scant 1 cup bean sprouts

7 oz/200 g canned water chestnuts, drained and sliced

4 duck breast fillets, roasted and sliced (see page 147)

orange slices, to serve

DRESSING

3 tbsp fish sauce

1½ tbsp lime juice

2 garlic cloves, crushed

1 red chile pepper, seeded and very finely chopped

1 green chile pepper, seeded and very finely chopped

1 tsp palm or raw sugar

1 Place the lettuce leaves into a large mixing bowl. Add the sliced shallots, chopped scallions, celery strips, cucumber strips, bean sprouts, and sliced water chestnuts. Toss well to mix. Place the mixture on a large serving platter.

2 Arrange the duck breast slices on top of the salad in an attractive overlapping pattern.

3 To make the dressing, put the fish sauce, lime juice, garlic, chiles, and sugar into a small pan. Heat gently, stirring constantly. Adjust the piquancy by adding more lime juice, or add more fish sauce to reduce the sharpness.

4 Drizzle the warm salad dressing over the duck salad and serve immediately with orange slices.

Asian Salad

This colorful crisp salad has a fresh orange dressing and is topped with crunchy vermicelli.

NUTRITIONAL INFORMATION

Calories	139	Sugars	.........8g
Protein	.........5g	Fat	...........7g
Carbohydrate	...15g	Saturates	.......1g

10 MINS   5 MINS

SERVES 4

INGREDIENTS

¼ cup dried vermicelli

½ head Napa cabbage

scant 1 cup bean sprouts

6 radishes

4½ oz/125 g snow peas

1 large carrot

4½ oz/125 g sprouting beans

DRESSING

juice of 1 orange

1 tbsp sesame seeds, toasted

1 tsp honey

1 tsp sesame oil

1 tbsp hazelnut oil

1 Break the vermicelli into small strands. Heat a wok and dry-fry the vermicelli until lightly golden.

COOK'S TIP

Make your own sprouting beans by soaking mung and adzuki beans overnight in cold water. Drain and rinse. Place in a large jar covered with cheesecloth. Lay the jar on its side in indirect light. For the next 3 days, rinse the beans once each day in cold water.

2 Remove from the pan with a slotted spoon and set aside until required.

3 Using a sharp knife or food processor, shred the Napa cabbage and wash with the bean sprouts. Drain thoroughly and place the leaves and bean sprouts in a large mixing bowl.

4 Thinly slice the radishes. Trim the snow peas and cut each into 3 pieces.

Cut the carrot into thin short sticks. Add the sprouting beans and prepared vegetables to the bowl.

5 Place all the dressing ingredients in a screw-top jar and shake until well-blended. Pour over the salad and toss.

6 Transfer the salad to a serving bowl and sprinkle over the reserved vermicelli before serving.

Papaya Salad

Choose firm papayas—or pawpaws as they are sometimes called—for this delicious salad.

NUTRITIONAL INFORMATION

Calories 193   Sugars 11g
Protein ....3g   Fat 15g
Carbohydrate ...12g   Saturates 2g

10 MINS   0 MINS

SERVES 4

INGREDIENTS

DRESSING

4 tbcp olive oil

1 tbsp fish sauce or light soy sauce

2 tbsp lime or lemon juice

1 tbsp dark muscovado sugar

1 tsp finely chopped fresh red or
  green chile

SALAD

1 crisp lettuce

¼ small white cabbage

2 papayas

2 tomatoes

¼ cup roasted peanuts, chopped coarsely

4 scallions, trimmed and sliced thinly

basil leaves, to garnish

1 To make the dressing, whisk together the oil, fish sauce, lime juice, sugar, and chile. Set aside, stirring occasionally to dissolve the sugar.

2 Shred the lettuce and white cabbage, then toss together and arrange on a large serving plate.

3 Peel the papayas and slice them in half. Scoop out the seeds, then slice the flesh thinly. Arrange on top of the lettuce and cabbage.

4 Soak the tomatoes in a bowl of boiling water for 1 minute, then lift out and peel. Remove the seeds and chop the flesh. Arrange on the salad leaves.

5 Scatter the peanuts and scallions over the top. Whisk the dressing and pour over the salad. Garnish with basil leaves and serve at once.

COOK'S TIP

Choose plain, unsalted peanuts and toast them under the broiler until golden to get the best flavor. Take care not to burn them, as they brown very quickly.

Potato & Chicken Salad

The spicy peanut dressing served with this salad may be prepared in advance and left to chill a day before required.

NUTRITIONAL INFORMATION

Calories 802   Sugars 15g
Protein ....35g   Fat 55g
Carbohydrate ...45g   Saturates 10g

5 MINS   15 MINS

SERVES 4

INGREDIENTS

4 large waxy potatoes

10½ oz/300 g fresh pineapple, diced

2 carrots, grated

6 oz/175 g bean sprouts

1 bunch scallions, sliced

1 large zucchini, cut into matchsticks

3 celery stalks, cut into matchsticks

generous 1 cup unsalted peanuts

2 cooked chicken breast fillets, about
　4½ oz/125 g each, sliced

DRESSING

6 tbsp crunchy peanut butter

6 tbsp olive oil

2 tbsp light soy sauce

1 red chile, chopped

2 tsp sesame oil

4 tsp lime juice

1 Using a sharp knife, cut the potatoes into small dice. Bring a pan of water to a boil.

2 Cook the diced potatoes in a pan of boiling water for 10 minutes, or until tender. Drain and leave to cool until required.

3 Transfer the cooled potatoes to a salad bowl.

4 Add the pineapple, carrots, bean sprouts, scallions, zucchini, celery, peanuts, and sliced chicken to the potatoes. Toss well to mix all the salad ingredients together.

5 To make the dressing, put the peanut butter in a small mixing bowl and gradually whisk in the olive oil and light soy sauce.

6 Stir in the chopped red chile, sesame oil, and lime juice. Mix until well combined.

7 Pour the spicy dressing over the salad and toss lightly to coat all of the ingredients. Serve the potato and chicken salad immediately.

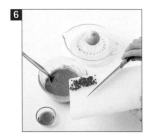

COOK'S TIP

Unsweetened canned pineapple may be used in place of the fresh pineapple for convenience. If only sweetened canned pineapple is available, drain it and rinse under cold running water before using.

Gado Gado Salad

The vegetables in this salad can either be arranged in individual piles on the serving platter or mixed together.

NUTRITIONAL INFORMATION

Calories	450	Sugars	........11g
Protein	........19g	Fat	..........28g
Carbohydrate	...29g	Saturates	.......6g

20 MINS 25 MINS

SERVES 4

I N G R E D I E N T S

9 oz/250 g new potatoes, scrubbed

1¼ cups green beans

4½ oz/125 g cauliflower, broken into small florets

1½ cups shredded white cabbage

1 carrot, cut into thin sticks

¼ cucumber, cut into chunks

scant 1 cup bean sprouts

2 hard-cooked eggs, shelled

S A U C E

6 tbsp crunchy peanut butter

1¼ cups cold water

1 garlic clove, crushed

1 fresh red chile, seeded and finely chopped

2 tbsp soy sauce

1 tbsp dry sherry

2 tsp sugar

1 tbsp lemon juice

1 Halve the potatoes and place in a pan of lightly salted water. Bring to a boil and then simmer for 12–15 minutes, or until cooked through.

2 Drain and plunge into cold water to cool. Set aside until required.

3 Bring another pan of lightly salted water to a boil. Add the green beans, cauliflower, and cabbage, and cook for 3 minutes. Drain and plunge the vegetables into cold water to cool and prevent any further cooking.

4 Drain the potatoes and other cooked vegetables. Arrange in piles on a large serving platter with the carrot, cucumber, and bean sprouts.

5 Cut the hard-cooked eggs into fourths and arrange on the salad. Cover and set aside.

6 To make the sauce, place the peanut butter in a bowl and blend in the water gradually, followed by the remaining ingredients.

7 Uncover the salad and drizzle some sauce over each serving.

Beef & Peanut Salad

This recipe looks stunning if you arrange the ingredients rather than toss them together.

NUTRITIONAL INFORMATION

Calories	194	Sugars	.........3g
Protein	........21g	Fat	..........10g
Carbohydrate	....5g	Saturates	.......3g

10 MINS   10 MINS

SERVES 4

INGREDIENTS

½ head Napa cabbage

1 large carrot

4 oz/115 g radishes

3½ oz/100 g baby corn cobs

1 tbsp peanut oil

1 red chile, seeded and chopped finely

1 garlic clove, chopped finely

12 oz/350 g lean beef (such as fillet, sirloin, or rump), trimmed and shredded finely

1 tbsp dark soy sauce

1 oz/25 g fresh peanuts (optional)

red chile, sliced, to garnish

DRESSING

1 tbsp smooth peanut butter

1 tsp superfine sugar

2 tbsp light soy sauce

1 tbsp sherry vinegar

salt and pepper

VARIATION

If preferred, use chicken, turkey, lean pork, or even strips of venison instead of beef in this recipe. Cut off all visible fat before you begin.

1 Finely shred the Napa cabbage and arrange on a platter.

2 Peel the carrot and cut into thin, short sticks. Wash and trim the radishes, then cut into fourths. Halve the baby corn lengthwise. Arrange these ingredients around the edge of the dish and set aside.

3 Heat the peanut oil in a non-stick wok or large skillet until really hot.

4 Add the red chile, garlic, and beef to the wok or skillet and stir-fry for 5 minutes.

5 Add the dark soy sauce and continue to stir-fry for an additional 1–2 minutes, until the beef is tender and just cooked through.

6 Meanwhile, make the dressing. Place all of the ingredients in a small bowl and blend them together until smooth.

7 Place the hot cooked beef in the center of the salad ingredients. Spoon over the dressing and sprinkle with a few peanuts, if using. Garnish with slices of red chile and serve immediately.

Broccoli & Almond Salad

This is a colorful, crunchy salad with a delicious dressing. It is better left overnight if possible for the flavors to mingle.

NUTRITIONAL INFORMATION

Calories 181   Sugars 7g
Protein . . . . .9g   Fat 12g
Carbohydrate . . . .9g   Saturates 2g

4½ HOURS   10 MINS

SERVES 4

INGREDIENTS

1 lb/450 g small broccoli florets

1¾ oz/50 g baby corn cobs, halved, lengthwise

1 red bell pepper, seeded and cut into thin strips

⅓ cup blanched almonds

DRESSING

1 tbsp sesame seeds

1 tbsp peanut oil

2 garlic cloves, crushed

2 tbsp light soy sauce

1 tbsp clear honey

2 tsp lemon juice

pepper

lemon zest, to garnish (optional)

1 Blanch the broccoli and baby corn cobs in boiling water for 5 minutes. Drain well, then rinse and drain again.

2 Transfer the broccoli and baby corn cobs to a large mixing bowl and add the bell pepper and almonds.

3 To make the dressing, heat a wok and add the sesame seeds. Dry-fry, stirring constantly, for 1 minute, or until the sesame seeds are lightly browned and are giving off a delicious aroma.

4 Mix the peanut oil, garlic, soy sauce, honey, lemon juice, and pepper to taste. Add the sesame seeds and mix well.

5 Pour the dressing over the salad, cover and set aside in the refrigerator for a minimum of 4 hours and preferably overnight.

6 Garnish the salad with lemon zest (if using) and serve.

COOK'S TIP

Take care when browning the sesame seeds, as they will quickly burn. Dry-fry over a low heat and stir constantly.

Cucumber Salad

This is a very refreshing accompaniment to any main dish and is an excellent "cooler" for curries.

NUTRITIONAL INFORMATION

Calories 33	Sugars 8g
Protein 0.2g	Fat 0g
Carbohydrate 9g	Saturates 0g

🍲 10 MINS   🕐 0 MINS

SERVES 4

INGREDIENTS

½ cucumber

1 tbsp rice vinegar

2 tbsp sugar

½ tsp salt

2 tbsp hot water

1 small shallot

1 Wash the cucumber thoroughly and pat dry with absorbent paper towels.

2 Peel the cucumber, halve it lengthwise, and seed it, using a teaspoon or a melon baller.

3 Using a sharp knife, slice the cucumber thinly.

4 Arrange the cucumber slices in an attractive pattern on a serving plate.

5 To make the dressing, mix together the rice vinegar, sugar, and salt in a bowl. Pour on the hot water and stir until the sugar has dissolved. Leave the dressing to cool slightly.

6 Pour the dressing evenly over the cucumber slices.

7 Using a sharp knife, thinly slice the shallot and sprinkle over the cucumber.

8 Cover the cucumber salad with plastic wrap and leave to chill in the refrigerator before serving. Serve as a cooling accompaniment to curries.

COOK'S TIP

Some people dislike the bitter taste that cucumbers can have—peeling off the skin and seeding the cucumber often eliminates this problem. Using a melon baller is the neatest method of seeding a cucumber.

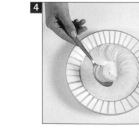

Hot & Sweet Salad

This salad is made by mixing fruit and vegetables with the sharp, sweet, and fishy flavors of the dressing.

NUTRITIONAL INFORMATION

Calories 169	Sugars 8g	
Protein 14g	Fat 8g	
Carbohydrate 11g	Saturates 1g	

15 MINS   0 MINS

SERVES 4

INGREDIENTS

9 oz/250 g white cabbage, finely shredded

2 tomatoes, skinned, seeded and chopped

9 oz/250 g cooked green beans, halved if large

4½ oz/125 g shelled shrimp

1 papaya, peeled, seeded, and chopped

1–2 fresh red chiles, seeded and very finely sliced

⅓ cup roasted salted peanuts, crushed

handful of lettuce or baby spinach leaves, shredded or torn into small pieces

DRESSING

4 tbsp lime juice

2 tbsp fish sauce

sugar, to taste

pepper

1 Mix the white cabbage with the tomatoes, green beans, shrimp, three-fourths of the papaya, and half of the chiles in a large mixing bowl.

2 Stir in two-thirds of the crushed peanuts and mix well.

3 Line the rim of a large serving plate with the lettuce leaves and pile the salad mixture into the center of the leaves.

4 To make the dressing, beat the lime juice with the fish sauce and add sugar and pepper to taste. Drizzle over the salad.

5 Scatter the top with the remaining papaya, chiles, and crushed peanuts. Serve at once.

COOK'S TIP

To skin tomatoes, make a cross at the base with a very sharp knife, then immerse in a bowl of boiling water for a few minutes. Remove with a slotted spoon and peel off the skin.

Hot Rice Salad

Nutty brown rice combines well with peanuts and a sweet and sour mixture of fruit and vegetables in this tangy salad dish.

NUTRITIONAL INFORMATION

Calories	464	Sugars	........17g
Protein	........15g	Fat	.........24g
Carbohydrate	...52g	Saturates	.......4g

5 MINS   30 MINS

SERVES 4

INGREDIENTS

1½ cups brown rice

1 bunch scallions

1 red bell pepper

4½ oz/125 g radishes

15 oz/425 g can pineapple pieces in natural juice, drained

scant 1 cup bean sprouts

3 oz/90 g/¾ cup dry-roasted peanuts

DRESSING

2 tbsp crunchy peanut butter

1 tbsp peanut oil

2 tbsp light soy sauce

2 tbsp white wine vinegar

2 tsp clear honey

1 tsp chile powder

½ tsp garlic salt

pepper

1 Put the rice in a pan and cover with water. Bring to a boil, then cover and simmer for 30 minutes until tender.

2 Meanwhile, chop the scallions, using a sharp knife. Seed and chop the red bell pepper and thinly slice the radishes.

3 To make the dressing, place the crunchy peanut butter, peanut oil, light soy sauce, white wine vinegar, honey, chile powder, garlic salt, and pepper in a small bowl and whisk to combine.

4 Drain the rice thoroughly and place in a heatproof bowl.

5 Heat the dressing in a small pan for 1 minute and then mix into the rice.

6 Working quickly, stir the pineapple pieces, scallions, bell pepper, bean sprouts, and peanuts into the mixture in the bowl.

7 Pile the hot rice salad into a warmed serving dish.

8 Arrange the radish slices around the outside of the salad and serve immediately.

Asian Chicken Salad

Mirin, soy sauce, and sesame oil give an Asian flavor to this delicious salad.

NUTRITIONAL INFORMATION

Calories	361	Sugars	.........2g
Protein	.......34g	Fat	..........16g
Carbohydrate	...17g	Saturates	.......3g

5 MINS   35 MINS

SERVES 4

INGREDIENTS

4 skinless, boneless chicken breasts

scant ⅓ cup mirin or sweet sherry

scant ⅓ cup light soy sauce

1 tbsp sesame oil

3 tbsp olive oil

1 tbsp red wine vinegar

1 tbsp Dijon mustard

9 oz/250 g egg noodles

9 oz/250 g bean sprouts

9 oz/250 g Napa cabbage, shredded

2 scallions, sliced

scant 2 cups sliced mushrooms

1 fresh red chile, finely sliced,
   to garnish

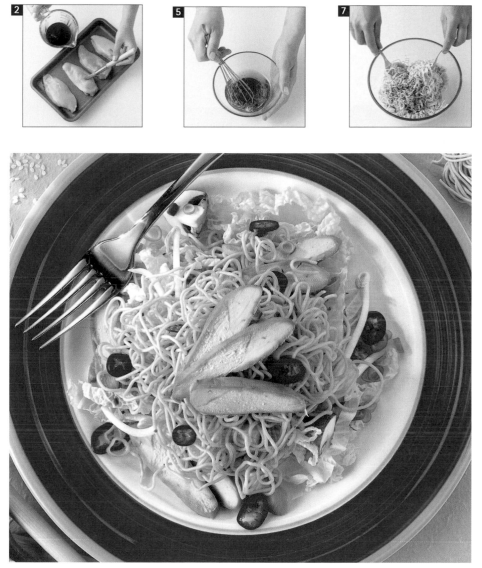

1 Pound the chicken breasts out to an even thickness between two sheets of plastic wrap with a rolling pin or the back of a heavy cleaver.

2 Put the chicken breasts in a roasting pan. Combine the mirin and soy sauce and brush over the chicken.

3 Place the chicken in a preheated oven, 400°F/200°C, for 20–30 minutes, basting often.

4 Remove the chicken from the oven and leave to cool slightly.

5 Whisk the sesame oil, olive oil, and red wine vinegar with the mustard.

6 Cook the noodles according to the instructions on the package. Rinse under cold running water, then drain.

7 Toss the noodles in the dressing until the noodles are completely coated.

8 Toss the bean sprouts, Napa cabbage, scallions, and mushrooms with the noodles.

9 Slice the cooked chicken very thinly and stir into the noodles. Garnish the salad with the chile slices and serve.

Mango Salad

This is an unusual combination but works well as long as the mango is very unripe. Papaya can be used instead, if you prefer.

NUTRITIONAL INFORMATION

Calories 26	Sugars 3g
Protein 1g	Fat 0.2g
Carbohydrate 6g	Saturates 0g

10 MINS   0 MINS

SERVES 4

INGREDIENTS

1 large unripe mango, peeled and cut into long thin shreds

1 small red chile, seeded and chopped finely

2 shallots, chopped finely

2 tbsp lemon juice

1 tbsp light soy sauce

6 roasted canned chestnuts, cut into fourths

1 watermelon, to serve

1 lollo biondo lettuce, or any crunchy lettuce

½ oz/15 g cilantro leaves

1 Soak the mango briefly in cold water, in order to remove any syrup. Meanwhile, combine the chile, shallots, lemon juice, and soy sauce. Drain the mango and combine with the chestnuts.

2 To make the melon basket, stand the watermelon on one end on a level surface. Holding a knife level and in one place, turn the watermelon on its axis so that the knife marks an even line all around the middle. Mark a 1-inch/2.5-cm wide handle across the top and through the center stem, joining the middle line at either end. (If you prefer a zigzag finish, mark the shape to be cut at this point before any cuts are made, to ensure even zigzags.)

3 Take a sharp knife and, following the marks made for the handle, make the first vertical cut. Then cut down the other side of the handle. Now follow the middle line and make your straight or zigzag cut, taking care that the knife is always pointing toward the center of the watermelon, and is level with the counter, as this ensures that when you reach the handle cuts, the cut out piece of melon will pull away cleanly.

4 Hollow out the flesh with a spoon, leaving a clean edge, and line with the lettuce and cilantro. Fill with the salad, then pour over the dressing and serve.

COOK'S TIP

A relative of the onion, though less pungent, shallots come in round and elongated varieties. When buying shallots, choose firm, dry-skinned ones that show no signs of wrinkling. Fresh shallots can be stored in the refrigerator for up to a week.

Chinese Salad Nests

Crisp fried potato nests are perfect as an edible salad bowl and delicious when filled with a colorful Chinese-style salad of vegetables and fruit.

NUTRITIONAL INFORMATION

Calories 272	Sugars 11g	
Protein 4g	Fat 4g	
Carbohydrate ...59g	Saturates 0.4g	

15 MINS   15 MINS

SERVES 4

INGREDIENTS

POTATO NESTS

1 lb/450 g meal potatoes, grated

scant 1 cup cornstarch

vegetable oil, for frying

fresh chives, to garnish

SALAD

4½ oz/125 g pineapple, cubed

1 green bell pepper, cut into strips

1 carrot, cut into thin strips

1¾ oz snow peas, sliced thickly

4 baby corn cobs, halved lengthwise

scant ⅓ cup bean sprouts

2 scallions, sliced

DRESSING

1 tbsp clear honey

1 tsp light soy sauce

1 garlic clove, crushed

1 tsp lemon juice

 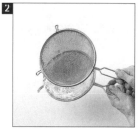 

1 To make the nests, rinse the potatoes several times in cold water. Drain well on paper towels so they are completely dry. This is to prevent the potatoes spitting when they are cooked in the fat. Place the potatoes in a mixing bowl. Add the cornstarch, mixing well to coat.

2 Half fill a wok with vegetable oil and heat until smoking. Line a 6-inch/15-cm diameter wire strainer with one fourth of the potato mixture and press another strainer of the same size on top.

3 Lower the strainers into the oil and cook for 2 minutes, until the potato nest is golden brown and crisp. Remove from the wok, draining off the excess oil.

4 Repeat 3 more times to use up all of the mixture and make a total of 4 nests. Leave to cool.

5 Mix the salad ingredients together then spoon into the potato baskets.

6 Mix the dressing ingredients together in a bowl. Pour the dressing over the salad, garnish with chives and serve.

Sweet & Sour Fish Salad

This refreshing blend of pink and white fish mixed with fresh pineapple and bell peppers would make an interesting appetizer or a light meal.

NUTRITIONAL INFORMATION

Calories	168	Sugars	.........5g
Protein	........24g	Fat	...........6g
Carbohydrate	....5g	Saturates	.......1g

25 MINS   10 MINS

SERVES 4

INGREDIENTS

8 oz/225 g trout fillets

8 oz/225 g white fish fillets (such as haddock or cod)

1¼ cups water

1 stalk lemon grass

2 lime leaves

1 large red chile

1 bunch scallions, trimmed and shredded

4 oz/115 g fresh pineapple flesh, diced

1 small red bell pepper, seeded and diced

1 bunch watercress or arugula, washed and trimmed

fresh snipped chives, to garnish

DRESSING

1 tbsp corn oil

1 tbsp rice wine vinegar

pinch of chile powder

1 tsp clear honey

salt and pepper

1 Rinse the fish, then place in a skillet and pour over the water.

2 Bend the lemon grass in half to bruise it and add to the pan with the lime leaves. Prick the chile with a fork and add to the pan. Bring to a boil and simmer for 7–8 minutes. Leave to cool.

3 Drain the fish, then flake the flesh away from the skin and place in a bowl. Gently stir in the scallions, pineapple, and bell pepper.

4 Arrange the washed watercress on 4 serving plates, then spoon the cooked fish mixture on top and set aside.

5 To make the dressing, mix all the ingredients together and season well. Spoon over the fish and serve garnished with chives.

Green Sesame Salad

A very elegant and light salad, which will complement rice and noodle dishes beautifully.

NUTRITIONAL INFORMATION

Calories 78   Sugars 8g
Protein ....3g   Fat 3g
Carbohydrate ....3g   Saturates 0.5g

10 MINS   0 MINS

SERVES 4

INGREDIENTS

1 cup bean sprouts

1½ tbsp chopped fresh cilantro

3 tbsp fresh lime juice

½ tsp mild chile powder

1 tsp sugar

½ tsp salt

3 celery stalks

1 large green bell pepper, seeded

1 large Granny Smith apple

2 tbsp toasted sesame seeds,
   to garnish

1 Soak the bean sprouts and drain thoroughly.

2 Place the bean sprouts in a bowl, removing any that seem a little brown or limp—it is essential that they are fresh and crunchy for this recipe.

3 To make the dressing, combine the cilantro, lime juice, chile powder, sugar, and salt in a small bowl and mix thoroughly.

4 Using a sharp knife, cut the celery into 1-inch/2.5-cm pieces. Cut the bell pepper into small pieces and the Granny Smith apple into small chunks.

5 Place the celery, bell pepper, and apple into the bowl containing the bean sprouts and stir gently to mix.

6 Just before serving, pour the dressing over the salad, tossing well to mix.

7 Garnish the green sesame salad with the toasted sesame seeds and serve with rice or noodle dishes.

COOK'S TIP

Keeping each ingredient as fresh and crunchy as possible will make all the difference to the appearance and taste of this elegant salad. To prevent the apples from going brown, soak the slices briefly in a little lemon juice and water as soon as you have cut them.

Sweet & Sour Cucumber

Chunks of cucumber are marinated in vinegar and sweetened with honey to make a sweet and sour appetizer.

NUTRITIONAL INFORMATION

Calories 45   Sugars 2g
Protein . . . . .1g   Fat 3g
Carbohydrate . . . .4g   Saturates 0.4g

50 MINS   0 MINS

SERVES 4

INGREDIENTS

1 cucumber

1 tsp salt

2 tsp honey

2 tbsp rice vinegar

3 tbsp chopped fresh cilantro

2 tsp sesame oil

¼ tsp crushed red peppercorns

strips of red and yellow bell pepper,
   to garnish

1 Peel thin strips off the cucumber, along the length, to give a pretty striped effect. Cut the cucumber in fourths lengthwise and then into 1-inch/2.5-cm

long pieces. Place in a colander. Sprinkle with salt and leave to stand for 30 minutes to let the salt draw out the excess water from the cucumber.

2 Wash the cucumber thoroughly to remove the salt, then drain and pat dry with paper towels.

3 Place the cucumber pieces in a large mixing bowl.

4 Combine the honey with the vinegar and pour over the cucumber. Mix together and marinate for 15 minutes.

5 Stir in the chopped fresh cilantro and sesame oil, and place the salad in a serving bowl.

6 Sprinkle over the crushed red peppercorns. Serve garnished with strips of red and yellow bell pepper.

COOK'S TIP

Rice vinegar is a common Chinese cooking ingredient. White rice vinegar is made from rice wine, whereas red rice vinegar is made from fermented rice. Both have a distinctive flavor, but the white version tends to be used more often, as it will not color the food.

Stir-Fried Chile Cucumber

Warm cucumbers are absolutely delicious, especially when combined with the heat of chile and the flavor of ginger.

NUTRITIONAL INFORMATION

Calories 67   Sugars 4g
Protein . . . . .1g   Fat 5g
Carbohydrate . . . .5g   Saturates 1g

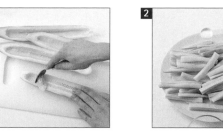

30 MINS   5 MINS

SERVES 4

I N G R E D I E N T S

2 medium cucumbers

2 tsp salt

1 tbsp vegetable oil

2 garlic cloves, crushed

½-inch/1-cm fresh gingerroot, grated

2 fresh red chiles, chopped

2 scallions, chopped

1 tsp yellow bean sauce

1 tbsp clear honey

½ cup water

1 tsp sesame oil

1 Peel the cucumbers and cut in half lengthwise. Scrape the seeds from the center with a teaspoon or melon baller and discard.

2 Cut the cucumber into strips and place on a plate. Sprinkle the salt over the cucumber strips and set aside for 20 minutes to bring out the juices. Rinse well under cold running water and pat dry with absorbent paper towels.

3 Heat the vegetable oil in a preheated wok or large skillet until it is almost smoking. Lower the heat slightly and add the garlic, ginger, chiles, and scallions and stir-fry for 30 seconds.

4 Add the cucumbers to the wok, together with the yellow bean sauce and honey and stir-fry for 30 seconds.

5 Add the water and cook the stir-fry over high heat until most of the water has evaporated.

6 Sprinkle the sesame oil over, transfer to a warm serving dish, and serve.

COOK'S TIP

The cucumber is sprinkled with salt and left to stand in order to draw out the excess water, thus preventing a soggy meal!

Poultry

Second to pork, poultry is one of the most popular foods throughout China. It also plays an important symbolic role in Chinese cooking. The cock symbolizes the male, positiveness, and aggression while the duck represents happiness and fidelity. Being uniformly tender, poultry is ideal for Chinese cooking methods, which rely on the rapid

cooking of small, even-size pieces of meat. Poultry can be cut into wafer-thin slices, thin short sticks or cubes, and can be quickly cooked without any loss of moisture or tenderness. This chapter contains dishes that are stir-fried, braised, steamed, and roasted and contains old favorites such as Lemon Chicken and Peking Duck, as well as more unusual dishes such as Duck with Lime & Kiwifruit and Honey & Soy Chicken.

Chicken Chop Suey

Chop suey is a well known and popular dish based on bean sprouts and soy sauce with a meat or vegetable flavoring.

NUTRITIONAL INFORMATION

Calories 337   Sugars 7g
Protein . . . . .32g   Fat 18g
Carbohydrate . . .14g   Saturates 3g

25 MINS   15 MINS

SERVES 4

I N G R E D I E N T S

4 tbsp light soy sauce

2 tsp light brown sugar

1 lb 2 oz/500 g skinless, boneless chicken breasts

3 tbsp vegetable oil

2 onions, cut into fourths

2 garlic cloves, crushed

12 oz/350 g bean sprouts

3 tsp sesame oil

1 tbsp cornstarch

3 tbsp water

scant 1¾ cups chicken stock

shredded leek, to garnish

VARIATION

This recipe may be made with strips of lean steak, pork, or with mixed vegetables. Change the type of stock accordingly.

1 Mix the soy sauce and sugar together, stirring until the sugar has dissolved.

2 Trim any fat from the chicken and cut into thin strips. Place the meat in a shallow dish and spoon the soy mixture over them, turning to coat. Marinate in the refrigerator for 20 minutes.

3 Heat the oil in a wok and stir-fry the chicken for 2–3 minutes, until golden brown. Add the onions and garlic and cook for an additional 2 minutes. Add the bean sprouts and cook for 4–5 minutes, then add the sesame oil.

4 Mix the cornstarch and water to form a smooth paste. Pour the stock into the wok, then add the cornstarch paste and bring to a boil, stirring until the sauce is thickened and clear. Serve, garnished with shredded leek.

Cashew Chicken

Yellow bean sauce is available from large supermarkets. Try to buy a chunky sauce rather than a smooth sauce for texture.

NUTRITIONAL INFORMATION

Calories 398   Sugars 2g
Protein . . . . .31g   Fat 27g
Carbohydrate . . . .8g   Saturates 4g

10 MINS   15 MINS

SERVES 4

I N G R E D I E N T S

1 lb/450 g boneless chicken breasts

2 tbsp vegetable oil

1 red onion, sliced

3 cups sliced flat mushrooms

⅔ cup cashew nuts

2¾ oz/75 g jar yellow bean sauce

fresh cilantro, to garnish

egg fried rice or plain boiled rice,
    to serve

1 Using a sharp knife, remove the excess skin from the chicken breasts, if desired. Cut the chicken into small, bite-size chunks.

2 Heat the vegetable oil in a preheated wok or skillet.

3 Add the chicken to the wok and stir-fry for 5 minutes.

4 Add the red onion and mushrooms to the wok and continue to stir-fry for an additional 5 minutes.

5 Spread out the cashew nuts on a cookie sheet and toast them under a preheated medium broiler until just browning—toasting nuts brings out their full flavor.

6 Toss the toasted cashew nuts into the wok together with the yellow bean sauce and heat through.

7 Allow the sauce to bubble for 2–3 minutes.

8 Transfer the cashew chicken to warm serving bowls and garnish with fresh cilantro. Serve hot with egg fried rice or plain boiled rice.

VARIATION

Chicken thighs could be used instead of the chicken breasts for a more economical dish.

Lemon Chicken

This is on everyone's list of favorite Chinese dishes, and it is so simple to make. Serve with stir-fried vegetables for a truly delicious meal.

NUTRITIONAL INFORMATION

Calories ....272 Sugars 1g
Protein ....36g Fat 11g
Carbohydrate ....5g Saturates 2g

5 MINS 15 MINS

SERVES 4

INGREDIENTS

vegetable oil, for deep-frying

1 lb 7 oz/650 g skinless, boneless chicken, cut into strips

lemon slices and shredded scallion, to garnish

SAUCE

1 tbsp cornstarch

6 tbsp cold water

3 tbsp fresh lemon juice

2 tbsp sweet sherry

½ tsp superfine sugar

1 Heat the oil for deep-frying in a preheated wok or skillet to 350°F/180°C or until a cube of bread browns in 30 seconds.

2 Reduce the heat and stir-fry the chicken strips for 3–4 minutes, until cooked through.

3 Remove the chicken with a slotted spoon, then set aside and keep warm. Drain the oil from the wok.

4 To make the sauce, mix the cornstarch with 2 tablespoons of the water to form a paste.

5 Pour the lemon juice and remaining water into the mixture in the wok.

6 Add the sweet sherry and superfine sugar and bring to a boil, stirring until the sugar has completely dissolved.

7 Stir in the cornstarch mixture and return to a boil. Reduce the heat and simmer, stirring constantly, for 2–3 minutes, until the sauce is thickened and clear.

8 Transfer the chicken to a warm serving plate and pour the sauce over the top.

9 Garnish the chicken with the lemon slices and shredded scallion and serve immediately.

COOK'S TIP

If you would prefer to use chicken portions rather than strips, cook them in the oil, covered, over low heat for about 30 minutes, or until cooked through.

Stir-Fried Ginger Chicken

The oranges add color and piquancy to this refreshing dish, which complements the chicken well.

NUTRITIONAL INFORMATION

Calories	289	Sugars	........15g
Protein	........20g	Fat	...........9g
Carbohydrate	...17g	Saturates	.......2g

5 MINS   20 MINS

SERVES 4

INGREDIENTS

2 tbsp corn oil

1 onion, sliced

6 oz/175 g carrots, cut into thin sticks

1 garlic clove, crushed

12 oz/350 g boneless skinless chicken breasts

2 tbsp grated fresh gingerroot

1 tsp ground ginger

4 tbsp sweet sherry

1 tbsp tomato paste

1 tbsp raw sugar

scant ½ cup orange juice

1 tsp cornstarch

1 orange, peeled and segmented

fresh snipped chives, to garnish

1 Heat the oil in a large preheated wok. Add the onion, carrots, and garlic and stir-fry over high heat for 3 minutes, until the vegetables begin to soften.

2 Slice the chicken into thin strips. Add to the wok with the fresh and ground ginger. Stir-fry for an additional 10 minutes, until the chicken is well cooked through and golden in color.

3 Mix together the sherry, tomato paste, sugar, orange juice, and cornstarch in a bowl. Stir the mixture into the wok and heat through until the mixture bubbles and the juices start to thicken.

4 Add the orange segments and carefully toss to mix.

5 Transfer the stir-fried chicken to warm serving bowls and garnish with freshly snipped chives. Serve immediately.

COOK'S TIP

Make sure that you do not continue cooking the dish once the orange segments have been added in step 4, otherwise they will break up.

Grilled Chicken Legs

Just the thing to put on the grill—chicken legs, coated with a spicy, curry-like butter, then grilled until crispy and golden.

NUTRITIONAL INFORMATION

Calories	660	Sugars	.........4g
Protein	........34g	Fat	..........57g
Carbohydrate	....4g	Saturates	......30g

🍲 5 MINS   🕐 20 MINS

SERVES 4

I N G R E D I E N T S

12 chicken drumsticks

S P I C E D   B U T T E R

¾ cup butter

2 garlic cloves, crushed

1 tsp grated fresh gingerroot

2 tsp ground turmeric

4 tsp cayenne pepper

2 tbsp lime juice

3 tbsp mango chutney

TO SERVE

crisp green seasonal salad

boiled rice

VARIATION

This spicy butter mixture would be equally effective on grilled chicken or turkey breast fillets. Skin before coating with the mixture.

1 To make the Spiced Butter mixture, beat the butter with the garlic, ginger, turmeric, cayenne pepper, lime juice, and chutney until well blended.

2 Using a sharp knife, slash each chicken leg to the bone 3–4 times.

3 Cook the drumsticks over a moderate grill for 12–15 minutes, until almost cooked. Alternatively, broil the chicken for 10–12 minutes, until almost cooked, turning halfway through.

4 Spread the chicken legs liberally with the butter mixture and continue to cook for an additional 5–6 minutes, turning and basting frequently with the butter until golden and crisp. Serve the chicken legs hot or cold with a crisp green salad and rice.

Braised Chicken

This is a delicious way to cook a whole chicken. It has a wonderful glaze, which is served as a sauce.

NUTRITIONAL INFORMATION

Calories	294	Sugars	.........9g
Protein	........31g	Fat	..........15g
Carbohydrate	...10g	Saturates	.......3g

5 MINS

1¼ HOURS

SERVES 4

INGREDIENTS

3 lb 5 oz/1.5 kg chicken

3 tbsp vegetable oil

1 tbsp peanut oil

2 tbsp dark brown sugar

5 tbsp dark soy sauce

⅔ cup water

2 garlic cloves, crushed

1 small onion, chopped

1 fresh red chile, chopped

celery leaves and chives,
    to garnish

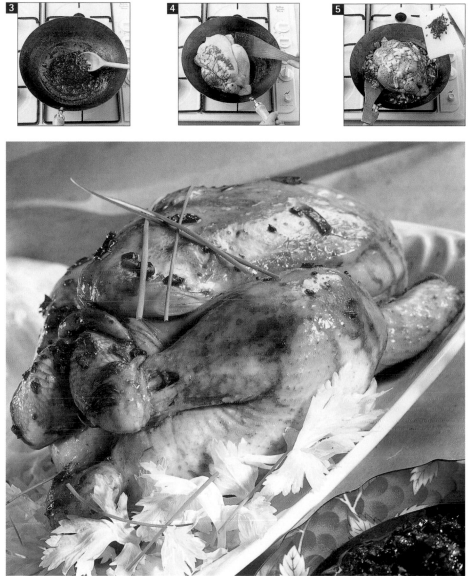

1 Preheat a large wok or large skillet.

2 Clean the chicken inside and out with damp paper towels.

3 Put the vegetable oil and peanut oil in the wok, then add the dark brown sugar and heat gently until the sugar caramelizes.

4 Stir the soy sauce into the wok. Add the chicken and turn it in the mixture to coat thoroughly on all sides.

5 Add the water, garlic, onion, and chile. Cover and simmer, turning the chicken occasionally, for 1 hour, or until

nicely browned and cooked through. Test by piercing a thigh with the point of a knife or a skewer—the juices will run clear when the chicken is cooked.

6 Remove the chicken from the wok and set aside. Increase the heat and reduce the sauce In the wok until thickened. Transfer the chicken to a serving plate. Garnish with celery leaves and chives and serve with the sauce.

COOK'S TIP

For a spicier sauce, add 1 tablespoon finely chopped fresh gingerroot and 1 tablespoon ground Szechuan peppercorns with the chile in step 5.

Yellow Bean Chicken

Ready-made yellow bean sauce is available from large supermarkets and Chinese food stores. It is made from yellow soybeans and is quite salty.

NUTRITIONAL INFORMATION

Calories 234   Sugars 1g
Protein ....26g   Fat 12g
Carbohydrate ....6g   Saturates 2g

25 MINS   10 MINS

SERVES 4

INGREDIENTS

1 lb/450 g skinless, boneless chicken
  breasts

1 egg white, beaten

1 tbsp cornstarch

1 tbsp rice wine vinegar

1 tbsp light soy sauce

1 tsp superfine sugar

3 tbsp vegetable oil

1 garlic clove, crushed

½-inch/1-cm piece fresh gingerroot,
  grated

1 green bell pepper, seeded
  and diced

2 large mushrooms, sliced

3 tbsp yellow bean sauce

yellow or green bell pepper strips,
  to garnish

1 Trim any fat from the chicken and cut the meat into 1-inch/2.5-cm cubes.

2 Mix the egg white and cornstarch in a shallow bowl. Add the chicken and turn in the mixture to coat. Set aside for 20 minutes.

3 Mix the rice wine vinegar, soy sauce, and superfine sugar in a bowl.

4 Remove the chicken from the egg white mixture.

5 Heat the oil in a preheated wok, then add the chicken and stir-fry for 3–4 minutes, until golden brown. Remove the chicken from the wok with a slotted spoon, then set aside and keep warm.

6 Add the garlic, ginger, bell pepper, and mushrooms to the wok and stir-fry for 1–2 minutes.

7 Add the yellow bean sauce and cook for 1 minute. Stir in the vinegar mixture and return the chicken to the wok. Cook for 1–2 minutes and serve hot, garnished with bell pepper strips.

VARIATION

Black bean sauce would work equally well with this recipe. Although this would affect the appearance of the dish, as it is much darker in color, the flavors would be compatible.

Kung Po Chicken

In this recipe, cashew nuts are used, but peanuts, walnuts, or almonds can be substituted, if preferred.

NUTRITIONAL INFORMATION

Calories 294   Sugars 3g
Protein ....21g   Fat 18g
Carbohydrate ...10g   Saturates 4g

10 MINS   5 MINS

SERVES 4

INGREDIENTS

9–10½ oz/250–300 g chicken meat, boned and skinned

¼ tsp salt

⅓ egg white

1 tsp Cornstarch Paste (see page 31)

1 medium green bell pepper, cored and seeded

4 tbsp vegetable oil

1 scallion, cut into short sections

a few small slices of fresh gingerroot

4-5 small dried red chiles, soaked, seeded, and shredded

2 tbsp crushed yellow bean sauce

1 tsp rice wine or dry sherry

scant 1 cup roasted cashew nuts

a few drops of sesame oil

boiled rice, to serve

1 Cut the chicken into small cubes about the size of sugar lumps. Place the chicken in a small bowl and mix with the salt, the egg white, and the Cornstarch Paste, in that order.

2 Cut the green bell pepper into cubes or triangles about the same size as the chicken pieces.

3 Heat the oil in a wok, add the chicken and stir-fry for 1 minute. Remove with a slotted spoon and keep warm.

4 Add the scallion, ginger, chiles, and green bell pepper. Stir-fry for 1 minute, then add the chicken with the yellow bean sauce and wine. Blend well and stir-fry for another minute. Finally stir in the cashew nuts and sesame oil. Serve hot with boiled rice.

VARIATION

Any nuts can be used in place of the cashew nuts, if preferred. The important point is the crunchy texture, which is very much a feature of Szechuan cooking.

Fruity Duck Stir-Fry

The pineapple and plum sauce add a sweetness and fruity flavor to this colorful vegetable mixture which blends well with the duck.

NUTRITIONAL INFORMATION

Calories	241	Sugars	.......7g
Protein	.....26g	Fat	...........8g
Carbohydrate	...16g	Saturates	.......2g

🕒 5 MINS   🕒 25 MINS

SERVES 4

INGREDIENTS

4 duck breasts

1 tsp Chinese five-spice powder

1 tbsp cornstarch

1 tbsp chile oil

8 oz/225 g pearl onions, peeled

2 garlic cloves, crushed

3½ oz/100 g baby corn cobs

1¼ cups canned pineapple chunks

6 scallions, sliced

⅔ cup bean sprouts

2 tbsp plum sauce

1 Remove any skin from the duck breasts. Cut the duck into thin slices.

2 Mix the five-spice powder and the cornstarch. Toss the duck in the mixture until well coated.

3 Heat the oil in a preheated wok. Stir-fry the duck for 10 minutes, or until just beginning to crispen around the edges. Remove and set aside.

4 Add the onions and garlic to the wok and stir-fry for 5 minutes, until softened. Add the baby corn cobs and stir-fry for an additional 5 minutes. Add the pineapple chunks, scallions and bean sprouts and stir-fry for 3–4 minutes. Stir in the plum sauce.

5 Return the cooked duck to the wok and toss until well mixed. Transfer to warm serving dishes and serve hot.

COOK'S TIP

Buy pineapple chunks in natural juice rather than syrup for a fresher flavor. If you can only obtain pineapple in syrup, rinse it in cold water and drain thoroughly before using.

Chile Coconut Chicken

This tasty dish combines the flavors of lime, peanut, coconut, and chile. You'll find coconut cream in most supermarkets or delicatessens.

NUTRITIONAL INFORMATION

Calories	348	Sugars	.........2g
Protein	........36g	Fat	..........21g
Carbohydrate	....3g	Saturates	.......8g

🥖 🥖 🥖

🥘 5 MINS   🕐 15 MINS

SERVES 4

I N G R E D I E N T S

⅔ cup hot chicken stock

⅓ cup coconut cream

I tbsp corn oil

8 skinless, boneless chicken thighs, cut into long, thin strips

1 small red chile, sliced thinly

4 scallions, sliced thinly

4 tbsp smooth or crunchy peanut butter

finely grated rind and juice of 1 lime

I fresh red chile and scallion tassel, to garnish

boiled rice, to serve

1 Pour the chicken stock into a measuring pitcher or small bowl. Crumble the coconut cream into the chicken stock and stir the mixture until the coconut cream dissolves.

2 Heat the oil in a preheated wok or large heavy skillet.

3 Add the chicken strips and cook, stirring, until the chicken turns a golden color.

4 Stir in the chopped red chile and scallion and cook gently for a few more minutes.

5 Add the peanut butter, coconut cream and chicken stock mixture, lime rind and lime juice and simmer, uncovered, for 5 minutes, stirring frequently to prevent the mixture sticking to the base of the wok or pan.

6 Transfer the chile coconut chicken to a warm serving dish, then garnish with the red chile and scallion tassel and serve with boiled rice.

COOK'S TIP

Serve jasmine rice with this spicy chicken. It has a fragrant aroma that is well-suited to the flavors in this dish.

Chicken with Black Bean Sauce

This tasty chicken stir-fry is quick and easy to make and is full of fresh flavors and crunchy vegetables.

NUTRITIONAL INFORMATION

Calories 205	Sugars 4g	
Protein 25g	Fat 9g	
Carbohydrate 6g	Saturates 2g	

40 MINS   10 MINS

SERVES 4

INGREDIENTS

15 oz /425 g chicken breasts, sliced thinly

pinch of salt

pinch of cornstarch

2 tbsp oil

1 garlic clove, crushed

1 tbsp black bean sauce

1 each small red and green bell pepper, cut into strips

1 red chile, chopped finely

1½ cups sliced mushrooms

1 onion, chopped

6 scallions, chopped

salt and pepper

SEASONING

½ tsp salt

½ tsp sugar

3 tbsp chicken stock

1 tbsp dark soy sauce

2 tbsp beef stock

2 tbsp rice wine

1 tsp cornstarch, blended with a little rice wine

1 Put the chicken strips in a bowl. Add a pinch of salt and a pinch of cornstarch and cover with water. Leave to stand for 30 minutes.

2 Heat 1 tablespoon of the oil in a wok or deep-sided skillet and stir-fry the chicken for 4 minutes.

3 Remove the chicken to a warm serving dish and clean the wok.

4 Add the remaining oil to the wok and add the garlic, black bean sauce, green and red bell peppers, chile, mushrooms, onion, and scallions. Stir-fry for 2 minutes, then return the chicken to the wok.

5 Add the seasoning ingredients and cook for 3 minutes, then thicken with a little of the cornstarch blend. Serve with fresh noodles.

Duck with Ginger & Lime

Just the thing for a lazy summer day—roasted duck sliced and served with a dressing made of ginger, lime juice, sesame oil, and fish sauce.

NUTRITIONAL INFORMATION

Calories	529	Sugars	.........3g
Protein	........38g	Fat	..........41g
Carbohydrate	....3g	Saturates	.......6g

20 MINS   25 MINS

SERVES 4

INGREDIENTS

3 boneless Barbary duck breasts, about
   9 oz/250 g each

salt

DRESSING

½ cup olive oil

2 tsp sesame oil

2 tbsp lime juice

grated rind and juice of 1 orange

2 tsp fish sauce

1 tbsp grated gingerroot

1 garlic clove, crushed

2 tsp light soy sauce

3 scallions, finely chopped

1 tsp sugar

about 9 oz/250 g assorted salad greens

orange slices, to garnish (optional)

1 Wash the duck breasts and dry on paper towels, then cut in half. Prick the skin all over with a fork and season well with salt. Place the duck pieces, skin-side down, on a wire rack or trivet over a roasting pan.

2 Cook the duck in a preheated oven, at 375°F/190°C, for 10 minutes, then turn over and cook for an additional 12-15 minutes, or until it is cooked, but still pink in the center, and the skin is crisp.

3 To make the dressing, beat the olive oil and sesame oil with the lime juice, orange rind and juice, fish sauce, grated gingerroot, garlic, light soy sauce, scallions, and sugar in a small bowl until well blended.

4 Remove the duck from the oven, and leave to cool. Using a sharp knife, cut the duck into thick slices.

5 Add a little of the dressing to moisten and coat the duck.

6 To serve, arrange assorted salad greens on a serving dish. Top with the sliced duck breasts and drizzle with the remaining salad dressing.

7 Garnish with orange slices, if using, then serve at once.

Red Chicken Curry

The chicken is cooked with a curry paste using red chiles. It is a fiery hot sauce—for a milder version, reduce the number of chiles used.

NUTRITIONAL INFORMATION

Calories . . . . .331 Sugars 5g
Protein . . . . .36g Fat 17g
Carbohydrate . . . .7g Saturates 3g

10 MINS   10 MINS

SERVES 4

INGREDIENTS

4 tbsp vegetable oil

2 garlic cloves, crushed

scant 1¾ cups coconut milk

6 chicken breast fillets, skinned and
   cut into bite-size pieces

½ cup chicken stock

2 tbsp fish sauce

sliced red and green chiles, lemon slices
   and chives, to garnish

boiled rice, to serve

RED CURRY PASTE

8 dried red chiles, seeded
   and chopped

1-inch/2.5-cm fresh Thai ginger or
   gingerroot, peeled and sliced

3 stalks lemon grass, chopped

1 garlic clove, peeled

2 tsp shrimp paste

1 kaffir lime leaf, chopped

1 tsp ground coriander

¾ tsp ground cumin

1 tbsp chopped fresh cilantro

1 tsp salt and black pepper

1 To make the red curry paste, place all the ingredients in a food processor or blender and process until smooth.

2 Heat the vegetable oil in a large, heavy-based pan or wok. Add the garlic and cook for 1 minute, until it turns golden.

3 Stir in the red curry paste and cook for 10-15 seconds.

4 Gradually add the coconut milk, stirring constantly (don't worry if the mixture starts to look curdled at this stage).

5 Add the chicken pieces and turn in the sauce mixture to coat. Cook gently for 3-5 minutes, until almost tender.

6 Stir in the chicken stock and fish sauce, mixing well, then cook for an additional 2 minutes.

7 Transfer the chicken curry to a warmed serving dish and garnish with sliced red and green chiles. Serve with rice.

Grilled Duckling

The sweet, spicy marinade used in this recipe gives the duckling a subtle flavor of Asia.

NUTRITIONAL INFORMATION

Calories 249   Sugars 20g
Protein ....27g   Fat 6g
Carbohydrate ...23g   Saturates 2g

6¼ HOURS   30 MINS

SERVES 4

INGREDIENTS

3 garlic cloves, crushed

⅔ cup light soy sauce

5 tbsp light muscovado sugar

1-inch/2.5-cm piece fresh gingerroot, grated

1 tbsp chopped fresh cilantro

1 tsp five-spice powder

4 duckling breasts

sprig of fresh cilantro,
    to garnish (optional)

1 To make the marinade, mix together the garlic, soy sauce, sugar, grated ginger, chopped cilantro and five-spice powder in a small bowl until well combined.

2 Place the duckling breasts in a shallow, non-metallic dish and pour over the marinade. Carefully turn over the duckling so that it is fully coated with the marinade on both sides.

3 Cover the bowl with plastic wrap and leave to marinate for 1-6 hours, turning the duckling once or twice so that the marinade is fully absorbed.

4 Remove the duckling from the marinade, reserving the marinade for basting.

5 Grill the duckling breasts over hot coals for 20–30 minutes, turning and basting frequently with the reserved marinade, using a pastry brush.

6 Cut the duckling into slices and transfer to warm serving plates. Serve the grilled duckling garnished with a sprig of fresh cilantro, if using.

COOK'S TIP

Duckling is quite a fatty meat so there is no need to add oil to the marinade. However, you must remember to oil the grill rack to prevent the duckling from sticking. Do this well away from the grill to avoid any danger of a flare-up.

Garlic & Lime Chicken

Garlic and cilantro flavor the chicken breasts, which are served with a caramelized sauce, sharpened with lime juice.

NUTRITIONAL INFORMATION

Calories 280   Sugars 7g
Protein ....26g   Fat 17g
Carbohydrate ....7g   Saturates 8g

10 MINS   25 MINS

SERVES 4

INGREDIENTS

4 large skinless, boneless
   chicken breasts

scant 4 tbsp garlic butter,
   softened

3 tbsp chopped fresh cilantro

1 tbsp corn oil

finely grated zest and juice of 2 limes,
   plus extra zest, to garnish

4 tbsp palm sugar or raw sugar

TO SERVE

boiled rice

lemon wedges

1 Place each chicken breast between 2 sheets of plastic wrap and pound with a rolling pin until flattened to about ½ inch/1 cm thick.

2 Mix together the garlic butter and cilantro and spread over each flattened chicken breast. Roll up like a jelly roll and secure with a toothpick.

3 Heat the corn oil in a preheated wok or heavy-based skillet.

4 Add the chicken rolls to the wok or skillet and cook, turning, for 15–20 minutes, until cooked through.

5 Remove the chicken from the wok and transfer to a board. Cut each chicken roll into slices.

6 Add the lime zest, juice, and sugar to the wok and heat gently, stirring, until the sugar has dissolved. Raise the heat and let bubble for 2 minutes.

7 Arrange the chicken on warmed serving plates and spoon the pan juices over to serve.

8 Garnish the garlic and lime chicken with lime zest, and serve with boiled rice and lemon wedges.

COOK'S TIP

Be sure to check that the chicken is cooked through before slicing and serving. Cook over gentle heat so as not to overcook the outside, while the inside is still cooking.

Peking Duck

No Chinese cook book would be complete without this famous recipe, in which crispy skinned duck is served with pancakes and a tangy sauce.

NUTRITIONAL INFORMATION

Calories ....357 Sugars 48g
Protein ....20g Fat 10g
Carbohydrate ...49g Saturates 2g

6¼ HOURS   1½ HOURS

SERVES 4

INGREDIENTS

4 lb/1.8 kg duck

7½ cups boiling water

4 tbsp clear honey

2 tsp dark soy sauce

2 tbsp sesame oil

½ cup hoisin sauce

generous ½ cup superfine sugar

½ cup water

carrot strips, to garnish

Chinese pancakes; short, thick
  cucumber sticks; and shredded scallions,
  to serve

1 Place the duck on a rack set over a roasting pan and pour 5 cups of the boiling water over it.

2 Remove the duck and rack and discard the water. Pat dry with absorbent paper towels, then replace the duck and the rack and set aside for several hours.

3 In a small bowl, mix together the clear honey, remaining boiling water, and dark soy sauce, until they are thoroughly combined.

4 Brush the mixture over the skin and inside the duck. Reserve the remaining glaze. Set the duck aside for 1 hour, until the glaze has dried.

5 Coat the duck with another layer of glaze. Let dry and repeat until all of the glaze is used.

6 Heat the sesame oil in a pan and add the hoisin sauce, superfine sugar, and water. Simmer for 2–3 minutes, until thickened. Leave to cool and then refrigerate until required.

7 Cook the duck in a preheated oven, at 375°F/190°C, for 30 minutes. Turn the duck over and cook for 20 minutes. Turn the duck again and cook for 20–30 minutes, until cooked through and the skin is crisp.

8 Remove the duck from the oven and set aside for 10 minutes.

9 Meanwhile, heat the pancakes in a steamer for 5–7 minutes or according to the instructions on the package. Cut the skin and duck meat into strips and garnish with the carrot strips, then serve with the pancakes, sauce, cucumber and scallion.

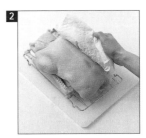

Szechuan Chile Chicken

In China, the chicken pieces are chopped through the bone for this dish, but if you do not possess a cleaver, use filleted chicken meat.

NUTRITIONAL INFORMATION

Calories 218   Sugars 4g
Protein . . . . .23g   Fat 9g
Carbohydrate . . . .8g   Saturates 2g

🌶 🌶

🍲 4 HOURS   🕙 15 MINS

SERVES 4

INGREDIENTS

1 lb 2 oz/500 g chicken thighs

¼ tsp pepper

1 tbsp sugar

2 tsp light soy sauce

1 tsp dark soy sauce

1 tbsp rice wine or dry sherry

2 tsp cornstarch

2–3 tbsp vegetable oil

1–2 garlic cloves, crushed

2 scallions, cut into short sections,
    with the white and green parts
    separated

4–6 small dried red chiles, soaked and
    seeded

2 tbsp crushed yellow bean sauce

about ⅔ cup Chinese Stock (see page 30)
    or water

1 Cut or chop the chicken thighs into bite-size pieces and marinate with the pepper, sugar, soy sauces, wine, and cornstarch for 25–30 minutes.

2 Heat the oil in a pre-heated wok and stir-fry the chicken for 1–2 minutes, until lightly brown. Remove with a slotted spoon, then transfer to a warm dish and reserve. Add the garlic, the white parts of the scallion, the chiles, and yellow bean sauce to the wok and stir-fry for about 30 seconds.

3 Return the chicken to the wok, stirring constantly for 1-2 minutes, then add the stock and bring to a boil. Cover and braise over medium heat for 5–6 minutes, stirring once or twice. Garnish with the green parts of the scallion and serve immediately.

COOK'S TIP

One of the striking features of Szechuan cooking is the quantity of chiles used. Food generally in this region is much hotter than elsewhere in China—people tend to keep a string of dry chiles hanging from the eaves of their houses.

Chicken with Mushrooms

Dried Chinese mushrooms (shiitake) should be used for this dish—
otherwise use black rather than white fresh mushrooms.

NUTRITIONAL INFORMATION

Calories 125   Sugars 0.3g
Protein . . . . .20g   Fat 3g
Carbohydrates . . . .3g   Saturates 1g

1¼ HOURS   20 MINS

SERVES 4

INGREDIENTS

10½–12 oz/300–350 g chicken, boned and skinned

½ tsp sugar

1 tbsp light soy sauce

1 tsp rice wine or dry sherry

2 tsp cornstarch

4–6 dried Chinese mushrooms, soaked in warm water

1 tbsp fresh gingerroot, finely shredded

salt and pepper

a few drops of sesame oil

cilantro leaves, to garnish

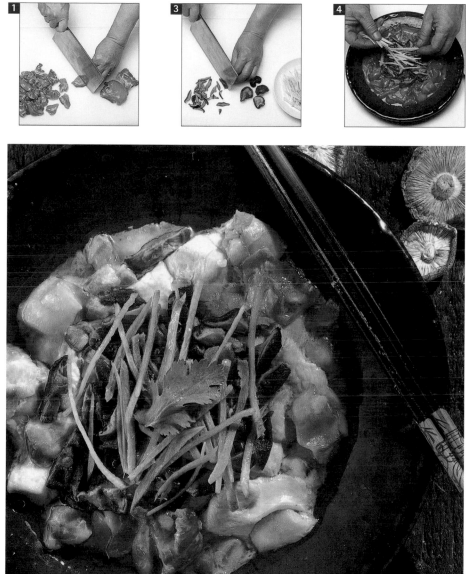

1 Using a sharp knife or meat cleaver, cut the chicken into small bite-sized pieces and place in a bowl.

2 Add the sugar, light soy sauce, wine, and cornstarch to the chicken, then toss to coat and leave to marinate for 25–30 minutes.

3 Drain the mushrooms and dry on absorbent paper towels. Slice the mushrooms into thin shreds, discarding any hard pieces of stem.

4 Place the chicken pieces on a heat-proof dish that will fit inside a bamboo steamer. Arrange the mushroom slices and ginger shreds on top of the chicken and sprinkle with salt, pepper, and sesame oil.

5 Place the dish on the rack inside a hot steamer or on a rack in a wok filled with hot water, then steam over high heat for 20 minutes.

6 Serve hot, garnished with cilantro leaves.

COOK'S TIP

Do not throw away the soaking water from the dried Chinese mushrooms. It is very useful, as it can be added to soups and stocks to give extra flavor.

Cumin-Spiced Chicken

Cumin seeds are more frequently associated with Indian cooking, but they are used in this Chinese recipe for their earthy flavor.

NUTRITIONAL INFORMATION

Calories 245	Sugars 9g
Protein 28g	Fat 10g
Carbohydrate 11g	Saturates 2g

5 MINS   15 MINS

SERVES 4

I N G R E D I E N T S

1 lb/450 g boneless, skinless chicken breasts

2 tbsp corn oil

1 clove garlic, crushed

1 tbsp cumin seeds

1 tbsp fresh gingerroot, grated

1 red chile, seeded and sliced

1 red bell pepper, seeded and sliced

1 green bell pepper, seeded and sliced

1 yellow bell pepper, seeded and sliced

⅔ cup bean sprouts

12 oz/350 g bok choy or other green leaves

2 tbsp sweet chile sauce

3 tbsp light soy sauce

deep-fried crispy ginger, to garnish (see Cook's Tip)

COOK'S TIP

To make the deep-fried ginger garnish, peel and thinly slice a large piece of gingerroot. Carefully lower the slices of ginger into a wok or small pan of hot oil and cook for 30 seconds. Transfer to paper towels and leave to drain thoroughly.

1 Using a sharp knife, slice the chicken breasts into thin strips.

2 Heat the oil in a large preheated wok.

3 Add the chicken to the wok and stir-fry for 5 minutes.

4 Add the garlic, cumin seeds, ginger, and chile to the wok, stirring to mix.

5 Add all the bell peppers to the wok and stir-fry for an additional 5 minutes.

6 Toss in the bean sprouts and bok choy together with the sweet chile sauce and soy sauce and continue to cook until the bok choy leaves start to wilt.

7 Transfer to warm serving bowls and garnish with deep-fried ginger (see Cook's Tip).

Spicy Peanut Chicken

This quick dish has many variations, but this version includes the classic combination of peanuts, chicken, and chiles.

NUTRITIONAL INFORMATION

Calories 342   Sugars 3g
Protein ....25g   Fat 24g
Carbohydrate ....6g   Saturates 5g

5 MINS   10 MINS

SERVES 4

INGREDIENTS

10½ oz/300 g skinless, boneless chicken breast

2 tbsp peanut oil

scant 1 cup shelled peanuts

1 fresh red chile, sliced

1 green bell pepper, seeded and cut into strips

fried rice, to serve

SAUCE

⅔ cup chicken stock

1 tbsp Chinese rice wine or dry sherry

1 tbsp light soy sauce

1½ tsp light brown sugar

2 garlic cloves, crushed

1 tsp fresh gingerroot, grated

1 tsp rice wine vinegar

1 tsp sesame oil

1 Trim any fat from the chicken and cut the meat into 1-inch/2.5-cm cubes. Set aside until required.

2 Heat the peanut oil in a preheated wok or skillet.

3 Add the peanuts to the wok and stir-fry for 1 minute. Remove the peanuts with a slotted spoon and set aside.

4 Add the chicken to the wok and cook for 1–2 minutes.

5 Stir in the chile and green bell pepper and cook for 1 minute. Remove from the wok with a slotted spoon and set aside.

6 Put half of the peanuts in a food processor and process until almost smooth. If necessary, add a little stock to form a softer paste. Alternatively, place them in a plastic bag and crush them with a rolling pin.

7 To make the sauce, add the chicken stock, Chinese rice wine, light soy sauce, light brown sugar, crushed garlic, grated fresh gingerroot, and rice wine vinegar to the wok.

8 Heat the sauce without boiling and stir in the peanut purée, remaining peanuts, chicken, sliced red chile, and green bell pepper strips. Mix well until all the ingredients are thoroughly combined.

9 Sprinkle the sesame oil into the wok, then stir and cook for 1 minute. Transfer the spicy peanut chicken to a warm serving dish and serve hot with fried rice.

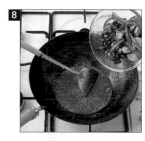

Duck with Leek & Cabbage

Duck is a strongly flavored meat that benefits from the added citrus peel to counteract this rich taste.

NUTRITIONAL INFORMATION

Calories	192	Sugars	.........5g
Protein	........26g	Fat	...........7g
Carbohydrate	....6g	Saturates	.......2g

10 MINS   40 MINS

SERVES 4

INGREDIENTS

4 duck breasts

12 oz/350 g green cabbage,
   thinly shredded

8 oz/225 g leeks, sliced

finely grated zest of 1 orange

⅓ cup oyster sauce

1 tsp toasted sesame seeds,
   to serve

1 Heat a large wok and dry-fry the duck breasts, with the skin on, for 5 minutes on each side (you may need to do this in 2 batches).

2 Remove the duck breasts from the wok and transfer to a clean board.

3 Using a sharp knife, cut the duck breasts into thin slices.

4 Remove all but 1 tablespoon of the fat from the duck left in the wok; discard the rest.

5 Using a sharp knife, thinly shred the green cabbage.

6 Add the leeks, green cabbage and orange zest to the wok and stir-fry for 5 minutes, until the vegetables have softened.

7 Return the duck to the wok and heat through for 2–3 minutes.

8 Drizzle the oyster sauce over the mixture in the wok and toss well until all the ingredients are combined, then heat through.

9 Scatter the stir-fry with toasted sesame seeds, then transfer to a warm serving dish and serve hot.

VARIATION

Use Napa cabbage for a lighter, sweeter flavor instead of the green cabbage, if you prefer.

Chicken & Corn Sauté

This quick and healthy dish is stir-fried, which means you need use only the minimum of fat.

NUTRITIONAL INFORMATION

Calories	280	Sugars 7g
Protein	........31g	Fat 11g
Carbohydrate	....9g	Saturates 2g

🥘 🥘

🍲 5 MINS   🕐 10 MINS

SERVES 4

I N G R E D I E N T S

4 skinless, boneless chicken breasts

9 oz/250 g baby corn cobs

9 oz/250 g snow peas

2 tbsp corn oil

1 tbsp sherry vinegar

1 tbsp honey

1 tbsp light soy sauce

1 tbsp corn seeds

pcpper

rice or Chinese egg noodles, to serve

1 Using a sharp knife, slice the chicken breasts into long, thin strips.

2 Cut the baby corn in half lengthwise and top and tail the snow peas.

3 Heat the corn oil in a preheated wok or a wide skillet.

4 Add the chicken breasts to the wok and stir-fry over a fairly high heat for 1 minute.

5 Add the baby corn and snow peas and stir-fry over moderate heat for 5–8 minutes, until evenly cooked. The vegetables should still be slightly crunchy.

6 Mix together the sherry vinegar, honey, and soy sauce in a small bowl.

7 Stir the vinegar mixture into the pan with the corn seeds.

8 Season well with pepper. Cook, stirring, for 1 minute.

9 Serve the chicken & corn sauté hot with rice or Chinese egg noodles.

VARIATION

Rice vinegar or balsamic vinegar makes a good substitute for the sherry vinegar.

Turkey with Cranberry Glaze

Traditional Christmas ingredients are given a Chinese twist in this stir-fry that contains cranberries, ginger, chestnuts, and soy sauce.

NUTRITIONAL INFORMATION

Calories 167   Sugars 11g
Protein . . . . .8g   Fat 7g
Carbohydrate . . .20g   Saturates 1g

🥩 5 MINS   🕐 15 MINS

SERVES 4

INGREDIENTS

1 turkey breast

2 tbsp corn oil

2 tbsp preserved ginger

½ cup fresh or frozen cranberries

½ cup canned chestnuts

4 tbsp cranberry sauce

3 tbsp light soy sauce

salt and pepper

1 Remove any skin from the turkey breast. Using a sharp knife, thinly slice the turkey breast.

2 Heat the corn oil in a large preheated wok or heavy-based skillet.

3 Add the turkey to the wok and stir-fry for 5 minutes, until cooked through.

4 Using a sharp knife, finely chop the preserved ginger.

5 Add the ginger and the cranberries to the wok or skillet and stir-fry for 2–3 minutes, until the cranberries have softened.

6 Add the chestnuts, cranberry sauce, and soy sauce, then season to taste with salt and pepper and leave to bubble for 2–3 minutes.

7 Transfer the turkey stir-fry to warm serving dishes and serve immediately.

COOK'S TIP

It is very important that the wok is very hot before you stir-fry. Test by by holding your hand flat about 3 inches/7.5 cm above the base of the interior—you should be able to feel the heat radiating from it.

Duck with Mangoes

Use fresh mangoes in this recipe for a terrific flavor and color. If they are unavailable, use canned mangoes and rinse them before using.

NUTRITIONAL INFORMATION

Calories	235	Sugars	.........6g
Protein	........23g	Fat	..........14g
Carbohydrate	....6g	Saturates	.......2g

5 MINS   35 MINS

SERVES 4

INGREDIENTS

2 medium-size ripe mangoes

1¼ cups chicken stock

2 garlic cloves, crushed

1 tsp grated fresh gingerroot

3 tbsp vegetable oil

2 large skinless duck breasts, about 8 oz/225 g each

1 tsp wine vinegar

1 tsp light soy sauce

1 leek, sliced

freshly chopped parsley, to garnish

1 Peel the mangoes and cut the flesh from each side of the pits. Cut the flesh into strips.

2 Put half of the mango pieces and the chicken stock in a food processor and process until smooth. Alternatively, press half of the mangoes through a fine strainer and mix with the stock.

3 Rub the garlic and ginger over the duck. Heat the vegetable oil in a preheated wok and cook the duck breasts, turning, until sealed. Reserve the oil in the wok and remove the duck.

4 Place the duck on a rack set over a roasting pan and cook in a preheated oven, at 425°F/220°C, for 20 minutes, until the duck is cooked through.

5 Meanwhile, place the mango and stock mixture in a pan and add the wine vinegar and light soy sauce.

6 Bring the mixture in the pan to a boil and cook over high heat, stirring, until reduced by half.

7 Heat the oil reserved in the wok and stir-fry the sliced leek and remaining mango for 1 minute. Remove from the wok, then transfer to a serving dish and keep warm until required.

8 Slice the cooked duck breasts and arrange the slices on top of the leek and mango mixture. Pour the sauce over the duck slices, then garnish and serve.

Duck with Broccoli & Peppers

This is a colorful dish using different colored bell peppers and broccoli to make it both tasty and appealing to the eye.

NUTRITIONAL INFORMATION

Calories . . . . .261 Sugars 3g
Protein . . . . .26g Fat 13g
Carbohydrate . . . .11g Saturates 2g

35 MINS   15 MINS

SERVES 4

INGREDIENTS

1 egg white

2 tbsp cornstarch

1 lb/450 g skinless, boneless duck meat

vegetable oil, for deep-frying

1 red bell pepper, seeded and diced

1 yellow bell pepper, seeded and diced

4½ oz/125 g small broccoli florets

1 garlic clove, crushed

2 tbsp light soy sauce

2 tsp Chinese rice wine or dry sherry

1 tsp light brown sugar

½ cup chicken stock

2 tsp sesame seeds

1 In a mixing bowl, beat together the egg white and cornstarch.

2 Using a sharp knife, cut the duck into 1-inch/2.5-cm cubes and stir into the egg white mixture. Leave to stand for 30 minutes.

3 Heat the oil for deep-frying in a preheated wok or heavy-based skillet until almost smoking.

4 Remove the duck from the egg white mixture, then add to the wok and fry in the oil for 4–5 minutes, until crisp.

Remove the duck from the oil with a slotted spoon and drain on paper towels.

5 Add the bell peppers and broccoli to the wok and stir-fry for 2–3 minutes. Remove with a slotted spoon and drain on paper towels.

6 Pour all but 2 tablespoons of the oil from the wok and return to the heat. Add the garlic and stir-fry for 30 seconds.

Stir in the soy sauce, Chinese rice wine, sugar, and chicken stock and bring rapidly to a boil.

7 Stir in the duck and reserved vegetables and cook for 1–2 minutes.

8 Carefully spoon the duck and vegetables onto a warmed serving dish and sprinkle with the sesame seeds. Serve immediately.

Honey & Soy Chicken

Clear honey is often added to Chinese recipes for sweetness. It combines well with the saltiness of the soy sauce.

NUTRITIONAL INFORMATION

Calories . . . . . . .279 Sugars 10g
Protein . . . . .38g Fat 8g
Carbohydrate . . .12g Saturates 2g

35 MINS   25 MINS

SERVES 4

INGREDIENTS

2 tbsp clear honey

3 tbsp light soy sauce

1 tsp Chinese five-spice powder

1 tbsp sweet sherry

1 garlic clove, crushed

8 chicken thighs

1 tbsp corn oil

1 red chile

3½ oz/100 g baby corn cobs, halved

8 scallion, sliced

1 cup bean sprouts

1 Mix together the honey, soy sauce, Chinese five-spice powder, sherry, and garlic in a large bowl.

2 Using a sharp knife, make 3 slashes in the skin of each chicken thigh. Brush the honey and soy marinade over the chicken thighs, then cover and leave to stand for at least 30 minutes.

3 Heat the oil in a large preheated wok. Add the chicken and cook over fairly high heat for 12–15 minutes, until the chicken browns and the skin begins to crispen. Remove the chicken with a slotted spoon and keep warm until required.

4 Using a sharp knife, seed and very finely chop the chile.

5 Add the chile, corn cobs, scallions, and bean sprouts to the wok and stir-fry for 5 minutes.

6 Return the chicken to the wok and mix all of the ingredients together until completely heated through. Transfer to serving plates and serve immediately.

COOK'S TIP

Chinese five-spice powder is found in most large supermarkets and is a blend of star anise, fennel seeds, cloves, cinnamon bark, and Szechuan pepper.

Duck with Lime & Kiwifruit

Tender breasts of duck served in thin slices, with a sweet but very tangy lime and wine sauce, full of pieces of kiwifruit.

NUTRITIONAL INFORMATION

Calories 264   Sugars 20g
Protein ....20g   Fat 10g
Carbohydrate ...21g   Saturates 2g

🍗 🍗 🍗 🍗

1¼ HOURS   15 MINS

SERVES 4

I N G R E D I E N T S

4 boneless or part-boned
  duck breasts

grated rind and juice of 2 large limes

2 tbsp corn oil

4 scallions, thinly
  sliced diagonally

4½ oz/125 g carrots, cut into
  thin short sticks

⅓ cup dry white wine

¼ cup white sugar

2 kiwifruit, peeled, halved and sliced

salt and pepper

parsley sprigs and lime halves tied in knots
  (see Cook's Tip), to garnish

1 Trim any fat from the duck, then prick the skin all over with a fork and lay in a shallow dish. Add half the grated lime and half the juice to the duck breasts, rubbing in thoroughly. Leave to stand in a cool place for at least 1 hour, turning the breasts at least once.

2 Drain the duck breasts, reserving the marinade. Heat 1 tablespoon of oil in a wok. Add the duck and cook quickly to seal all over, then lower the heat and continue to cook for 5 minutes, turning several times until just cooked through and well browned all over. Remove and keep warm.

3 Wipe the wok clean with paper towels and heat the remaining oil. Add the scallions and carrots and stir-fry for 1 minute, then add the remaining lime marinade, wine, and sugar. Bring to a boil and simmer for 2–3 minutes until slightly syrupy.

4 Add the duck breasts to the sauce, then season and add the kiwifruit. Stir-fry for a minute or until really hot and both the duck and kiwifruit are well coated in the sauce.

5 Cut each duck breast into slices, leaving a "hinge" at one end, then open out into a fan shape and arrange on plates. Spoon the sauce over the duck and sprinkle with the remaining pieces of lime rind. Garnish and serve.

COOK'S TIP

To make the garnish, trim a piece off the base of each lime half so they stand upright. Pare off a thin strip of rind from the top of the lime halves, about ¼ inch/5 mm thick, but do not detach it. Tie the strip into a knot with the end bending over the cut surface of the lime.

Peanut Sesame Chicken

Sesame seeds and peanuts give extra crunch and flavor to this stir-fry and the fruit juice glaze gives a lovely shiny coating to the sauce.

NUTRITIONAL INFORMATION

Calories 435	Sugars 10g	
Protein 38g	Fat 26g	
Carbohydrate ...14g	Saturates 4g	

 10 MINS   15 MINS

SERVES 4

INGREDIENTS

2 tbsp vegetable oil

2 tbsp sesame oil

1 lb 2 oz/500 g boneless, skinned chicken breasts, sliced into strips

9 oz/250 g broccoli, divided into small florets

9 oz/250 g baby or dwarf corn cobs, halved if large

1 small red bell pepper, cored, seeded, and sliced

2 tbsp soy sauce

1 cup orange juice

2 tsp cornstarch

2 tbsp toasted sesame seeds

generous ⅓ cup roasted, shelled, unsalted peanuts

rice or noodles, to serve

1 Heat the vegetable oil and sesame oil in a large, heavy-based skillet or wok until smoking. Add the chicken strips and stir-fry until browned, about 4-5 minutes.

2 Add the broccoli, corn, and red bell pepper and stir-fry for an additional 1-2 minutes.

3 Meanwhile, mix the soy sauce with the orange juice and cornstarch. Stir into the chicken and vegetable mixture, stirring constantly until the sauce has slightly thickened and a glaze develops.

4 Stir in the sesame seeds and peanuts, mixing well. Heat the stir-fry for an additional 3-4 minutes.

5 Transfer the stir-fry to a warm serving dish and serve with rice or noodles.

COOK'S TIP

Make sure you use the unsalted variety of peanuts or the dish will be too salty, as the soy sauce adds saltiness.

Chicken Foo Yong

Although commonly described as an omelet, a foo yong ("white lotus petals") should use egg whites only to create a very delicate texture.

NUTRITIONAL INFORMATION

Calories	220	Sugars	.........1g
Protein	........16g	Fat	..........14g
Carbohydrate	....7g	Saturates	.......3g

5 MINS   5 MINS

SERVES 4

INGREDIENTS

6 oz/175 g chicken breast fillet, skinned

½ tsp salt

pepper

1 tsp rice wine or dry sherry

1 tbsp cornstarch

3 eggs

½ tsp finely chopped scallion

3 tbsp vegetable oil

1¼ cups green peas

1 tsp light soy sauce

salt

few drops of sesame oil

1 Cut the chicken across the grain into very small, paper-thin slices, using a cleaver. Place the chicken slices in a shallow dish.

2 In a small bowl, mix together ½ teaspoon salt, pepper, rice wine, and cornstarch.

3 Pour the mixture over the chicken slices in the dish, turning the chicken until well coated.

4 Beat the eggs in a small bowl with a pinch of salt and the scallion.

5 Heat the vegetable oil in a preheated wok, then add the chicken slices and stir-fry for 1 minute, making sure that the slices are kept separated.

6 Pour the beaten eggs over the chicken, and lightly scramble until set. Do not stir too vigorously, or the mixture will break up in the oil. Stir the oil from the bottom of the wok so that the foo yong rises to the surface.

7 Add the peas, light soy sauce, and salt to taste and blend well. Transfer to warm serving dishes, then sprinkle with sesame oil and serve.

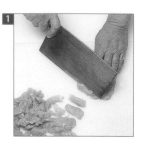

COOK'S TIP

If available, chicken *goujons* can be used for this dish: these are small, delicate strips of chicken that require no further cutting and are very tender.

Coconut Chicken Curry

Okra or ladies fingers are slightly bitter in flavor. The pineapple and coconut in this recipe offsets them in both color and flavor.

NUTRITIONAL INFORMATION

Calories 456	Sugars 21g	
Protein 29g	Fat 29g	
Carbohydrate ...22g	Saturates 17g	

5 MINS   45 MINS

SERVES 4

INGREDIENTS

2 tbsp corn oil

1 lb/450 g boneless, skinless chicken thighs or breasts

1 cup okra

1 large onion, sliced

2 garlic cloves, crushed

3 tbsp mild curry paste

1¼ cups chicken stock

1 tbsp fresh lemon juice

½ cup creamed coconut, coarsely grated

1¼ cups fresh or canned pineapple, cubed

⅔ cup thick, plain yogurt

2 tbsp chopped fresh cilantro

freshly boiled rice, to serve

TO GARNISH

lemon wedges

fresh cilantro sprigs

1 Heat the oil in a wok. Cut the chicken into bite-size pieces, then add to the wok and stir-fry until evenly browned.

2 Using a sharp knife, trim the okra. Add the onion, garlic, and okra to the wok and cook for an additional 2–3 minutes, stirring constantly.

3 Mix the curry paste with the chicken stock and lemon juice and pour into the wok. Bring to a boil, then cover and leave to simmer for 30 minutes.

4 Stir the grated coconut into the curry and cook for 5 minutes.

5 Add the pineapple, yogurt and cilantro and cook for 2 minutes, stirring. Garnish and serve.

COOK'S TIP

Score around the top of the okra with a knife before cooking to release the sticky gluelike substance, which is bitter in taste.

Red Chicken with Tomatoes

This is a really colorful dish, the red of the tomatoes perfectly complementing the orange sweet potato.

NUTRITIONAL INFORMATION

Calories	316	Sugars	.........5g
Protein	.........28g	Fat	..........19g
Carbohydrate	....8g	Saturates	.......3g

5 MINS   35 MINS

SERVES 4

INGREDIENTS

1 tbsp corn oil

1 lb/450 g boneless, skinless chicken

2 garlic cloves, crushed

2 tbsp red curry paste

2 tbsp fresh Thai ginger or
    gingerroot, grated

1 tbsp tamarind paste

4 lime leaves

8 oz/225 g sweet potato

2½ cups coconut milk

8 oz/225 g cherry tomatoes, halved

3 tbsp chopped fresh cilantro

cooked jasmine or fragrant rice,
    to serve

1 Heat the corn oil in a large preheated wok or heavy-based skillet.

COOK'S TIP

Fresh Thai ginger is a spice very similar to ginger but not as pungent. It can be bought fresh from Asian food stores but is also available dried and as a powder. The fresh root needs to be peeled before slicing to use.

2 Using a sharp knife, thinly slice the chicken. Add the chicken to the wok or skillet and stir-fry for 5 minutes, until lightly browned.

3 Add the garlic, curry paste, ginger, tamarind paste, and lime leaves to the wok and stir-fry for 1 minute.

4 Using a sharp knife, peel and dice the sweet potato.

5 Add the coconut milk and sweet potato to the mixture in the wok and bring to a boil. Leave to bubble over medium heat for 20 minutes, until the juices start to thicken and reduce.

6 Add the cherry tomatoes and cilantro to the curry and cook for an additional 5 minutes, stirring occasionally. Transfer to serving plates and serve hot with cooked jasmine or fragrant rice.

Honey-Glazed Duck

The honey and soy glaze gives a wonderful sheen and flavor to the duck skin. Such a simple recipe, yet the result is unutterably delicious.

NUTRITIONAL INFORMATION

Calories 176	Sugars 8g	
Protein 22g	Fat 5g	
Carbohydrate ...10g	Saturates 1g	

2¼ HOURS   30 MINS

SERVES 4

I N G R E D I E N T S

1 tsp dark soy sauce

2 tbsp clear honey

1 tsp garlic vinegar

2 garlic cloves, crushed

1 tsp ground star anise

2 tsp cornstarch

2 tsp water

2 large boneless duck breasts, about
    8 oz/225g each

celery leaves, cucumber wedges, and
    chives, to garnish

1 Mix together the soy sauce, honey, garlic vinegar, garlic, and star anise.

2 Blend the cornstarch with the water to form a smooth paste and stir it into the soy sauce mixture.

3 Place the duck breasts in a shallow ovenproof dish. Brush with the soy marinade, turning to coat them completely. Cover and leave to marinate in the refrigerator for at least 2 hours, or overnight if possible.

4 Remove the duck from the marinade and cook in a preheated oven, at 425°F/220°C, for 20–25 minutes, basting frequently with the glaze.

5 Remove the duck from the oven and transfer to a preheated broiler. Broil for 3–4 minutes to caramelize the top.

6 Remove the duck from the broiler pan and cut into thin slices. Arrange the duck slices in a warm serving dish, then garnish with celery leaves, cucumber wedges, and chives. Serve immediately.

COOK'S TIP

If the duck begins to burn slightly while it is cooking in the oven, cover with foil. Check that the duck breasts are cooked through by inserting the point of a sharp knife into the thickest part of the flesh—the juices should run clear.

Lemon & Sesame Chicken

Sesame seeds have a strong flavor that adds nuttiness to recipes. They are perfect for coating these thin chicken strips.

NUTRITIONAL INFORMATION

Calories 273	Sugars 5g	
Protein 29g	Fat 13g	
Carbohydrate 11g	Saturates 3g	

10 MINS   10 MINS

SERVES 4

INGREDIENTS

4 boneless, skinless chicken breasts

1 egg white

2 tbsp sesame seeds

2 tbsp vegetable oil

1 onion, sliced

1 tbsp raw sugar

finely grated zest and juice of
    1 lemon

3 tbsp lemon curd

1 cup canned water chestnuts,
    drained

lemon zest, to garnish

COOK'S TIP

Water chestnuts are commonly added to Chinese recipes for their crunchy texture as they do not have a great deal of flavor.

1 Place the chicken breasts between 2 sheets of plastic wrap and pound with a rolling pin to flatten. Slice the chicken into thin strips.

2 Whisk the egg white until light and foamy. Dip the chicken strips into the egg white, then coat in the sesame seeds.

3 Heat the oil in a wok and stir-fry the onion for 2 minutes until softened.

4 Add the chicken to the wok and stir-fry for 5 minutes, until the chicken turns golden.

5 Mix the sugar, lemon zest, lemon juice, and lemon curd and add to the wok. Let it bubble slightly.

6 Slice the water chestnuts thinly. Add to the wok and cook for 2 minutes. Garnish with lemon zest and serve hot.

Chicken with Chile & Basil

Chicken drumsticks are cooked in a delicious sauce and served with deep-fried basil for color and flavor.

NUTRITIONAL INFORMATION

Calories	196	Sugars	.........2g
Protein	........23g	Fat	..........10g
Carbohydrate	....3g	Saturates	.......2g

5 MINS   30 MINS

SERVES 4

INGREDIENTS

8 chicken drumsticks

2 tbsp soy sauce

1 tbsp corn oil

1 red chile

3½oz/100 g carrots, cut into thin sticks

6 celery stalks, cut into sticks

3 tbsp sweet chile sauce

oil, for frying

about 50 fresh basil leaves

1 Remove the skin from the chicken drumsticks if desired. Make 3 slashes in each drumstick. Brush the drumsticks with the soy sauce.

2 Heat the corn oil in a preheated wok and fry the drumsticks for 20 minutes, turning frequently, until they are cooked through.

3 Seed and finely chop the chile. Add the chile, carrots, and celery to the wok and cook for an additional 5 minutes. Stir in the chile sauce, then cover and let bubble gently while preparing the basil leaves.

4 Heat a little oil in a heavy based pan. Carefully add the basil leaves—stand well away from the pan and protect

your hand with a dish cloth as they may spit a little. Cook the basil leaves for about 30 seconds, until they begin to curl up but not brown. Leave the leaves to drain on absorbent paper towels.

5 Arrange the cooked chicken, vegetables and pan juices onto a warm serving plate. Garnish with the deep-fried crispy basil leaves and serve immediately.

COOK'S TIP

Basil has a very strong flavor, which is perfect with chicken and Chinese flavorings. You could use baby spinach instead of the basil, if you prefer.

Meat

Pork is the most popular meat in China because it is tender and suitable for all Chinese cooking methods. Lamb is popular in northern China, where religious laws forbid the eating of pork. Beef, although it is used in some dishes, is less popular than pork. This is partly because of economic and religious reasons, but also because it is less versatile in

cooking. One of the favorite cooking methods in China is stir-frying because it is a simple and easy way of preparing meat, as well as being healthy and economical. Stir-frying gives a dry, chewy texture, whereas braising and steaming, which are other popular cooking methods, ensure a tender result. This is also true of double-cooking in which the meat is first tenderized by long, slow simmering in water, followed by a quick crisping or stir-frying in a sauce.

Beef & Broccoli Stir-Fry

This is a great combination of ingredients in terms of color and flavor, and it is so simple to prepare.

NUTRITIONAL INFORMATION

Calories	232	Sugars	.........1g
Protein	........12g	Fat	..........19g
Carbohydrate	....4g	Saturates	.......6g

4¼ HOURS   15 MINS

SERVES 4

INGREDIENTS

8 oz/225 g lean steak, trimmed

2 garlic cloves, crushed

dash of chile oil

½-inch/1-cm piece fresh gingerroot, grated

½ tsp Chinese five-spice powder

2 tbsp dark soy sauce

2 tbsp vegetable oil

5½ oz/150 g broccoli florets

1 tbsp light soy sauce

⅔ cup beef stock

2 tsp cornstarch

4 tsp water

carrot strips, to garnish

1 Using a sharp knife, cut the steak into thin strips and place in a shallow glass dish.

2 Mix together the garlic, chile oil, grated ginger, Chinese five-spice powder, and dark soy sauce in a small bowl and pour over the beef, tossing to coat the strips evenly.

3 Cover the bowl and leave the meat to marinate in the refrigerator for several hours to let the flavours develop fully.

4 Heat 1 tablespoon of the vegetable oil in a preheated wok or skillet. Add the broccoli and stir-fry over medium heat for 4–5 minutes. Remove from the wok with a slotted spoon and set aside until required.

5 Heat the remaining oil in the wok. Add the steak together with the marinade, and stir-fry for 2-3 minutes, until the steak is browned and sealed.

6 Return the broccoli to the wok and stir in the light soy sauce and stock.

7 Blend the cornstarch with the water to form a smooth paste and stir into the wok. Bring to a boil, stirring, until thickened and clear. Cook for 1 minute. Transfer the beef & broccoli stir-fry to a warm serving dish, then arrange the carrot strips in a lattice on top and serve immediately.

Pork with Daikon

Pork and daikon are a perfect combination, especially with the added heat of the sweet chile sauce.

NUTRITIONAL INFORMATION

Calories	280	Sugars	.........1g
Protein	........25g	Fat	..........19g
Carbohydrate	....2g	Saturates	.......4g

🍞 🍞 🍞

🥗 10 MINS   🕐 15 MINS

SERVES 4

I N G R E D I E N T S

4 tbsp vegetable oil

1 lb/450 g pork tenderloin

1 eggplant

8 oz/225 g daikon

2 garlic cloves, crushed

3 tbsp soy sauce

2 tbsp sweet chile sauce

boiled rice or noodles, to serve

1 Heat 2 tablespoons of the vegetable oil in a large preheated wok or skillet.

2 Using a sharp knife, thinly slice the pork into even-size pieces.

3 Add the slices of pork to the wok or skillet and stir-fry for about 5 minutes.

4 Using a sharp knife, trim and dice the eggplant. Peel and slice the daikon.

5 Add the remaining vegetable oil to the wok.

6 Add the diced eggplant to the wok or skillet together with the garlic and stir-fry for 5 minutes.

7 Add the daikon to the wok and stir-fry for 2 minutes.

8 Stir the soy sauce and sweet chile sauce into the mixture in the wok and cook until heated through.

9 Transfer the pork and daikon to warm serving bowls and serve immediately with boiled rice or noodles.

COOK'S TIP

Daikon is a long white vegetable common in Chinese cooking. Usually grated, it has a milder flavor than red radish. It is generally available in most large supermarkets.

Beef with Bamboo Shoots

Tender beef, marinated in a soy and tomato sauce, is stir-fried with crisp bamboo shoots and snow peas in this simple recipe.

NUTRITIONAL INFORMATION

Calories	275	Sugars	.........3g
Protein	........21g	Fat	..........19g
Carbohydrate	....6g	Saturates	.......6g

1¼ HOURS   10 MINS

SERVES 4

INGREDIENTS

12 oz/350 g rump steak

3 tbsp dark soy sauce

1 tbsp tomato ketchup

2 garlic cloves, crushed

1 tbsp fresh lemon juice

1 tsp ground coriander

2 tbsp vegetable oil

1¾ cups snow peas

2 cups canned bamboo shoots

1 tsp sesame oil

COOK'S TIP

Leave the meat to marinate for at least 1 hour in order for the flavors to penetrate and increase the tenderness of the meat. If possible, leave for a little longer for a fuller flavor to develop.

1 Thinly slice the meat and place in a non metallic dish together with the dark soy sauce, tomato ketchup, garlic, lemon juice, and ground coriander. Mix well so that all of the meat is coated in the marinade, then cover and leave for at least 1 hour.

2 Heat the vegetable oil in a preheated wok. Add the meat to the wok and stir-fry for 2–4 minutes (depending on how well cooked you like your meat), until cooked through.

3 Add the snow peas and bamboo shoots to the mixture in the wok and stir-fry over high heat, tossing frequently, for an additional 5 minutes.

4 Drizzle with the sesame oil and toss well to combine. Transfer to serving dishes and serve hot.

Lamb with Garlic Sauce

This dish contains Szechuan pepper, which is quite hot and may be replaced with black pepper, if preferred.

NUTRITIONAL INFORMATION

Calories	320	Sugars	........2g
Protein	........25g	Fat	..........21g
Carbohydrate	....4g	Saturates	.......6g

🍖 35 MINS 🕐 10 MINS

SERVES 4

INGREDIENTS

1 lb/450 g lamb fillet or loin

2 tbsp dark soy sauce

2 tsp sesame oil

2 tbsp Chinese rice wine or dry sherry

½ tsp Szechuan pepper

4 tbsp vegetable oil

4 garlic cloves, crushed

¼ cup water chestnuts, cut into fourths

1 green bell pepper, seeded and sliced

1 tbsp wine vinegar

1 tbsp sesame oil

rice or noodles, to serve

1 Cut the lamb into 1-inch/2.5-cm pieces and place in a shallow dish.

2 Mix together 1 tablespoon of the soy sauce, the sesame oil, Chinese rice wine, and Szechuan pepper. Pour the mixture over the lamb, turning to coat, and leave to marinate for 30 minutes.

3 Heat the vegetable oil in a preheated wok. Remove the lamb from the marinade and add to the wok, together with the garlic. Stir-fry for 2–3 minutes.

4 Add the water chestnuts and bell pepper and stir-fry for 1 minute.

5 Add the remaining soy sauce and the wine vinegar, mixing together well.

6 Add the sesame oil and cook, stirring constantly, for 1–2 minutes, until the lamb is cooked through.

7 Transfer the lamb and garlic sauce to a warm serving dish and serve immediately with rice or noodles.

COOK'S TIPS

Chinese chives, also known as garlic chives, would make an appropriate garnish for this dish.

Sesame oil is used as a flavoring, rather than for frying, as it burns readily, hence it is added at the end of cooking.

Sweet & Sour Pork

In this classic Chinese dish, tender pork pieces are fried and served in a crunchy sauce. This dish is perfect served with plain rice.

NUTRITIONAL INFORMATION

Calories	357	Sugars	. . . . .25g
Protein	. . . . .28g	Fat	. . . . .14g
Carbohydrate	. . .30g	Saturates	. . . . . . .4g

10 MINS   20 MINS

SERVES 4

INGREDIENTS

1 lb/450 g pork tenderloin

2 tbsp corn oil

8 oz/225 g zucchini

1 red onion, cut into thin wedges

2 garlic cloves, crushed

8 oz/225 g carrots, cut into thin sticks

1 red bell pepper, seeded and sliced

1 cup baby corn cobs

scant 1 cup white mushrooms, halved

6 oz/175 g fresh pineapple, cubed

⅔ cup bean sprouts

⅔ cup pineapple juice

1 tbsp cornstarch

2 tbsp soy sauce

3 tbsp tomato ketchup

1 tbsp white wine vinegar

1 tbsp clear honey

1 Using a sharp knife, thinly slice the pork tenderloin into even-size pieces.

2 Heat the corn oil in a large preheated wok. Add the pork to the wok and stir-fry for 10 minutes, or until the pork is completely cooked through and beginning to turn crispy at the edges.

3 Meanwhile, cut the zucchini into thin sticks.

4 Add the onion, garlic, carrots, zucchini, bell pepper, corn cobs, and mushrooms to the wok and stir-fry for an additional 5 minutes.

5 Add the pineapple cubes and bean sprouts to the wok and stir-fry for 2 minutes.

6 Mix together the pineapple juice, cornstarch, soy sauce, tomato ketchup, white wine vinegar, and honey.

7 Pour the sweet and sour mixture into the wok and cook over high heat, tossing frequently, until the juices thicken. Transfer the sweet and sour pork to serving bowls and serve hot.

COOK'S TIP

If you prefer a crisper coating, toss the pork in a mixture of cornstarch and egg white and deep fry in the wok in step 2.

Lamb with Satay Sauce

This recipe demonstrates the classic serving of lamb satay—lamb marinated in chile and coconut and threaded onto wooden skewers.

NUTRITIONAL INFORMATION

Calories	.501	Sugars	.6g
Protein	.34g	Fat	.37g
Carbohydrate	.9g	Saturates	.10g

35 MINS   25 MINS

SERVES 4

INGREDIENTS

1 lb/450 g lamb loin fillet

1 tbsp mild curry paste

⅔ cup coconut milk

2 garlic cloves, crushed

½ tsp chile powder

½ tsp cumin

SATAY SAUCE

1 tbsp corn oil

1 onion, diced

6 tbsp crunchy peanut butter

1 tsp tomato paste

1 tsp fresh lime juice

scant ½ cup cold water

1 Using a sharp knife, thinly slice the lamb and place in a large dish.

2 Mix together the curry paste, coconut milk, garlic, chile powder, and cumin in a bowl. Pour over the lamb and toss well. Cover and marinate for 30 minutes.

3 To make the satay sauce. Heat the oil in a large wok and stir-fry the onion for 5 minutes, then reduce the heat and cook for 5 minutes.

4 Stir in the peanut butter, tomato paste, lime juice, and water.

5 Thread the lamb onto wooden skewers, reserving the marinade.

6 Broil the lamb skewers under a hot broiler for 6–8 minutes, turning once.

7 Add the reserved marinade to the wok, bring to a boil and cook for 5 minutes. Serve the lamb skewers with the satay sauce.

COOK'S TIP

Soak the wooden skewers in cold water for 30 minutes before broiling to prevent the skewers from burning.

Stir-Fried Beef & Vegetables

Fillet of beef is perfect for stir-frying as it is so tender and lends itself to quick cooking.

NUTRITIONAL INFORMATION

Calories	.521	Sugars	.7g
Protein	.31g	Fat	.35g
Carbohydrate	.18g	Saturates	.8g

10 MINS   20 MINS

SERVES 4

INGREDIENTS

2 tbsp corn oil

12 oz/350 g fillet of beef, sliced

1 red onion, sliced

6 oz/175 g zucchini

6 oz/175 g carrots, thinly sliced

1 red bell pepper, seeded and sliced

1 small head Napa cabbage, shredded

1 cup bean sprouts

generous 2 cups canned bamboo shoots, drained

scant 1 cup cashew nuts, toasted

SAUCE

3 tbsp medium sherry

3 tbsp light soy sauce

1 tsp ground ginger

1 garlic clove, crushed

1 tsp cornstarch

1 tbsp tomato paste

1 Heat the corn oil in a large preheated wok. Add the sliced beef and red onion to the wok and stir-fry for about 4–5 minutes or until the onion begins to soften and the meat is just beginning to brown.

2 Trim the zucchini and slice diagonally.

3 Add the carrots, bell pepper, and zucchini to the wok and stir-fry for 5 minutes.

4 Toss in the Napa cabbage, bean sprouts, and bamboo shoots and heat through for 2–3 minutes, until the leaves are just beginning to wilt.

5 Scatter the cashews nuts over the stir-fry and toss well to mix.

6 To make the sauce, mix together the sherry, soy sauce, ground ginger, garlic, cornstarch and tomato paste until well combined.

7 Pour the sauce over the stir-fry and toss to mix. Let the sauce bubble for 2–3 minutes, until the juices thicken.

8 Transfer to warm serving dishes and serve at once.

Twice-Cooked Pork

Twice-cooked is a popular way of cooking meat in China. The meat is first boiled to tenderize it, then cut into strips or slices and stir-fried.

NUTRITIONAL INFORMATION

Calories	199	Sugars	..3g
Protein	....15g	Fat	..13g
Carbohydrate	..4g	Saturates	..3g

3¼ HOURS   30 MINS

SERVES 4

INGREDIENTS

9–10½ oz/250–300 g shoulder or leg of pork, in one piece

1 small green bell pepper, cored and seeded

1 small red bell pepper, cored and seeded

4½ oz/125 g canned sliced bamboo shoots, rinsed and drained

3 tbsp vegetable oil

1 scallion, cut into short sections

1 tsp salt

½ tsp sugar

1 tbsp light soy sauce

1 tsp chile bean sauce

1 tsp rice wine or dry sherry

a few drops of sesame oil

1 Immerse the pork in a pot of boiling water to cover. Return to a boil and skim the surface. Reduce the heat, then cover and simmer for 15–20 minutes. Turn off the heat and leave the pork in the water to cool for at least 2–3 hours.

2 Remove the pork and drain well. Trim off any excess fat, then cut into small, thin slices. Cut the bell peppers into pieces about the same size as the pork and the sliced bamboo shoots.

3 Heat the vegetable oil in a preheated wok and add the vegetables together with the scallion. Stir-fry for 1 minute.

4 Add the pork, followed by the salt, sugar, light soy sauce, chile bean sauce, and wine. Blend well and continue stirring for another minute. Transfer the stir-fry to a warm serving dish, then sprinkle with sesame oil and serve.

COOK'S TIP

For ease of handling, buy a boned piece of meat, and roll into a compact shape. Tie securely with string before placing in the boiling water.

Lamb with Mushroom Sauce

Use a lean cut of lamb, such as fillet, for this recipe for both flavor and tenderness.

NUTRITIONAL INFORMATION

Calories 219   Sugars 1g
Protein . . . . .21g   Fat 14g
Carbohydrate . . . .4g   Saturates 4g

5 MINS   10 MINS

SERVES 4

INGREDIENTS

12 oz/350 g lean boneless lamb, such as
    fillet or loin

2 tbsp vegetable oil

3 garlic cloves, crushed

1 leek, sliced

3 cups sliced large mushrooms

½ tsp sesame oil

fresh red chiles, to garnish

SAUCE

1 tsp cornstarch

4 tbsp light soy sauce

3 tbsp Chinese rice wine or dry sherry

3 tbsp water

½ tsp chile sauce

1 Using a sharp knife or meat cleaver, cut the lamb into thin strips.

2 Heat the vegetable oil in a preheated wok or large skillet.

3 Add the lamb strips, garlic, and leek and stir-fry for 2–3 minutes.

4 To make the sauce, mix together the cornstarch, soy sauce, Chinese rice wine, water, and chile sauce, then set aside.

5 Add the sliced mushrooms to the wok and stir-fry for 1 minute.

6 Stir in the prepared sauce and cook for 2–3 minutes, or until the lamb is cooked through and tender.

7 Sprinkle the sesame oil over the top and transfer the lamb and mushrooms to a warm serving dish. Garnish with red chiles and serve immediately.

VARIATION

The lamb can be replaced with lean steak or pork tenderloin in this classic recipe from Beijing. You could also use 2–3 scallions, 1 shallot or 1 small onion instead of the leek, if you prefer.

Beef & Beans

The green of the beans complements the dark color of the beef, served in a rich sauce.

NUTRITIONAL INFORMATION

Calories	381	Sugars	. . . . .3g
Protein	. . . . .25g	Fat	. . . . .27g
Carbohydrate	. . .10g	Saturates	. . . . . . .8g

35 MINS   15 MINS

SERVES 4

INGREDIENTS

1 lb/450 g rump or fillet steak, cut into
    1-inch/2.5-cm pieces

MARINADE

2 tsp cornstarch

2 tbsp dark soy sauce

2 tsp peanut oil

SAUCE

2 tbsp vegetable oil

3 garlic cloves, crushed

1 small onion, cut into 8

8 oz/225 g thin green beans, halved

scant ¼ cup unsalted cashews

scant ¼ cup canned bamboo shoots,
    drained and rinsed

2 tsp dark soy sauce

2 tsp Chinese rice wine or dry sherry

½ cup beef stock

2 tsp cornstarch

4 tsp water

salt and pepper

1 To make the marinade for the beef, mix together the cornstarch, soy sauce, and peanut oil.

2 Place the steak in a shallow glass bowl. Pour the marinade over the steak and turn to coat thoroughly, then cover and leave to marinate in the refrigerator for at least 30 minutes.

3 To make the sauce, heat the oil in a preheated wok. Add the garlic, onion, beans, cashews, and bamboo shoots and stir-fry for 2–3 minutes.

4 Remove the steak from the marinade, and drain, then add to the wok and stir-fry for 3–4 minutes.

5 Mix the soy sauce, Chinese rice wine, and beef stock together. Blend the cornstarch with the water and add to the soy sauce mixture, mixing to combine.

6 Stir the mixture into the wok and bring the sauce to a boil, stirring until thickened and clear. Reduce the heat and leave to simmer for 2–3 minutes. Season to taste and serve immediately.

Beef & Bok Choy

In this recipe, a colorful selection of vegetables is stir-fried with tender strips of steak.

NUTRITIONAL INFORMATION

Calories 369	Sugars 9g
Protein 29g	Fat 23g
Carbohydrate ...12g	Saturates 8g

15 MINS   5 MINS

SERVES 4

INGREDIENTS

1 large head of bok choy, about
  9–9½ oz/250–275 g, torn into
  large pieces

2 tbsp vegetable oil

2 garlic cloves, crushed

1 lb 2 oz/500 g rump or fillet steak,
  cut into thin strips

5½ oz/150 g snow peas, trimmed

5½ oz/150 g baby corn cobs

6 scallions, chopped

2 red bell peppers, cored, seeded,
  and thinly sliced

2 tbsp oyster sauce

1 tbsp fish sauce

1 tbsp sugar

rice or noodles, to serve

1 Steam the bok choy over boiling water until just tender. Keep warm.

2 Heat the oil in a large, heavy-based skillet or wok, then add the garlic and steak strips and stir-fry until just browned, about 1-2 minutes.

3 Add the snow peas, baby corn, scallions, red bell pepper, oyster sauce, fish sauce, and sugar to the pan, mixing well. Stir-fry for an additional 2-3 minutes, until the vegetables are just tender, but still crisp.

4 Arrange the bok choy leaves in the base of a heated serving dish and spoon the beef and vegetable mixture into the center.

5 Serve the stir-fry immediately, with rice or noodles.

COOK'S TIP

Bok choy is one of the most important ingredients in this dish. If unavailable, use Napa cabbage, or kai choy (mustard leaves).

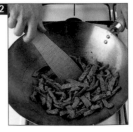

Sesame Lamb Stir-Fry

This is a very simple, but delicious dish, in which lean pieces of lamb are cooked in sugar and soy sauce and then sprinkled with sesame seeds.

NUTRITIONAL INFORMATION

Calories 276   Sugars 4g
Protein ....25g   Fat 18g
Carbohydrate ....5g   Saturates 6g

5 MINS   10 MINS

SERVES 4

INGREDIENTS

1 lb/450 g boneless lean lamb

2 tbsp peanut oil

2 leeks, sliced

1 carrot, cut into short, thin sticks

2 garlic cloves, crushed

scant ⅓ cup lamb or vegetable stock

2 tsp light brown sugar

1 tbsp dark soy sauce

4½ tsp sesame seeds

1 Using a sharp knife, cut the lamb into thin strips.

2 Heat the peanut oil in a preheated wok or large skillet until really hot.

3 Add the lamb and stir-fry for 2–3 minutes. Remove the lamb from the wok with a slotted spoon and set aside until required.

4 Add the leeks, carrot, and garlic to the wok or skillet and stir-fry in the remaining oil for 1–2 minutes.

5 Remove the vegetables from the wok with a slotted spoon and set aside.

6 Drain any remaining oil from the wok. Place the lamb or vegetable stock, light brown sugar, and dark soy sauce

in the wok and add the lamb. Cook, stirring constantly to coat the lamb, for 2–3 minutes.

7 Sprinkle the sesame seeds over the top, turning the lamb to coat.

8 Spoon the leek, carrot, and garlic mixture onto a warm serving dish and top with the lamb. Serve immediately.

COOK'S TIP

Be careful not to burn the sugar in the wok when heating and coating the meat, otherwise the flavor of the dish will be spoiled.

Beef & Black Bean Sauce

It is not necessary to use the expensive cuts of beef steak for this recipe: the meat will be tender as it is cut into small thin slices and marinated.

NUTRITIONAL INFORMATION

Calories ....392 Sugars 2g
Protein ....13g Fat 36g
Carbohydrate ....3g Saturates 7g

3¼ HOURS   10 MINS

SERVES 4

INGREDIENTS

9–10½ oz/250–300 g beef steak (such as rump)

1 small onion

1 small green bell pepper, cored and seeded

1¼ cups vegetable oil

1 scallion, cut into short sections

a few small slices of fresh gingerroot

1-2 small green or red chiles, seeded and sliced

2 tbsp crushed black bean sauce

MARINADE

½ tsp baking soda or baking powder

½ tsp sugar

1 tbsp light soy sauce

2 tsp rice wine or dry sherry

2 tsp Cornstarch Paste (see page 31)

2 tsp sesame oil

1 Using a sharp knife or meat cleaver, cut the beef into small, thin strips.

2 To make the marinade, mix together all the ingredients in a shallow dish. Add the beef strips, then turn to coat and leave to marinate for at least 2-3 hours.

3 Cut the onion and green bell pepper into small cubes.

4 Heat the vegetable oil in a pre-heated wok or large skillet. Add the beef strips and stir-fry for 1 minute, or until the color changes. Remove the beef strips with a slotted spoon and drain on absorbent paper towels. Keep warm and set aside until required.

5 Pour off the excess oil, leaving about 1 tablespoon in the wok. Add the scallion, ginger, chiles, onion, and green bell pepper and stir-fry for 1 minute.

6 Add the black bean sauce and stir until smooth. Return the beef strips to the wok, then blend well and stir-fry for another minute. Transfer the stir-fry to a warm serving dish and serve hot.

Spicy Pork & Rice

Pork is coated in a spicy mixture before being fried until crisp in this recipe and then stirred into a delicious egg rice for a very filling meal.

NUTRITIONAL INFORMATION

Calories 599	Sugars 11g	
Protein 30g	Fat 22g	
Carbohydrate . . .76g	Saturates 7g	

10 MINS   35 MINS

SERVES 4

INGREDIENTS

1⅓ cups long-grain white rice

2½ cups cold water

12 oz/350 g pork tenderloin

2 tsp Chinese five-spice powder

4 tbsp cornstarch

3 large eggs, beaten

2 tbsp raw sugar

2 tbsp corn oil

1 onion

2 garlic cloves, crushed

3½ oz/100 g carrots, diced

1 red bell pepper, seeded and diced

1 cup peas

2 tbsp butter

salt and pepper

1 Rinse the rice under cold running water. Place the rice in a large pan, then add the cold water and a pinch of salt. Bring to a boil and cover, then reduce the heat and leave to simmer for 9 minutes, or until all of the liquid has been absorbed and the rice is tender.

2 Meanwhile, slice the pork tenderloin into very thin even-size pieces, using a sharp knife or meat cleaver. Set the pork strips aside until required.

3 Whisk together the Chinese five-spice powder, cornstarch, 1 egg and the raw sugar. Toss the pork in the mixture until coated.

4 Heat the corn oil in a large wok or skillet. Add the pork and cook over high heat until the pork is cooked through and crispy. Remove the pork from the wok with a slotted spoon and set aside until required.

5 Using a sharp knife, cut the onion into dice.

6 Add the onion, garlic, carrots, bell pepper, and peas to the wok and stir-fry for 5 minutes.

7 Return the pork to the wok together with the cooked rice and stir-fry for 5 minutes.

8 Heat the butter in a skillet. Add the remaining beaten eggs and cook until set. Turn out onto a clean board and slice thinly. Toss the strips of egg into the rice mixture and serve immediately.

Fish-Flavored Pork

"Fish-flavored" is a Szechuan cooking term meaning that the dish is prepared with seasonings normally used in fish dishes.

NUTRITIONAL INFORMATION

Calories	183	Sugars	.......0.2g
Protein	........14g	Fat	..........13g
Carbohydrate	....3g	Saturates	.......3g

🌶 🌶 🌶

🍲 25 MINS   🕐 10 MINS

SERVES 4

INGREDIENTS

about 2 tbsp dried wood ears

9–10½ oz/250–300 g pork fillet

1 tsp salt

2 tsp Cornstarch Paste (see page 31)

3 tbsp vegetable oil

1 garlic clove, finely chopped

½ tsp fresh gingerroot, finely chopped

2 scallions, finely chopped, with the white and green parts separated

2 celery stalks, thinly sliced

½ tsp sugar

1 tbsp light soy sauce

1 tbsp chile bean sauce

2 tsp rice vinegar

1 tsp rice wine or dry sherry

a few drops of sesame oil

1 Soak the wood ears in warm water for 20 minutes, then rinse in cold water until the water is clear. Drain well, then cut into thin shreds.

2 Cut the pork into thin shreds, then mix in a bowl with a pinch of salt and about half the cornstarch paste until well coated.

3 Heat 1 tablespoon of vegetable oil in a preheated wok. Add the pork strips and stir-fry for 1 minute, until the color changes, then remove with a slotted spoon and set aside until required.

4 Heat the remaining oil in the wok. Add the garlic, ginger, the white parts of the scallions, the wood ears, and celery and stir-fry for about 1 minute.

5 Return the pork strips together with the salt, sugar, soy sauce, chile bean sauce, vinegar and wine. Blend well and continue stirring for another minute.

6 Finally add the green parts of the scallions and blend in the remaining cornstarch paste and sesame oil. Stir until the sauce has thickened. Transfer the fish-flavored pork to a warm serving dish and serve immediately.

COOK'S TIP

Also known as cloud ears, wood ears are a dried gray-black fungus widely used in Szechuan cooking. They are always soaked in warm water before using. Wood ears have a crunchy texture and a mild flavor.

Oyster Sauce Beef

As in Pork Fry with Vegetables (see page 201), the vegetables used in this recipe can be varied as you like.

NUTRITIONAL INFORMATION

Calories	462	Sugars	.........2g
Protein	........16g	Fat	..........42g
Carbohydrate	....4g	Saturates	.......8g

4 HOURS   10 MINS

SERVES 4

INGREDIENTS

10½ oz/300 g beef steak

1 tsp sugar

1 tbsp light soy sauce

1 tsp rice wine or dry sherry

1 tsp Cornstarch Paste (see page 31)

½ small carrot

½ cup snow peas

½ cup canned bamboo shoots, drained

¼ cup canned straw mushrooms, drained

1¼ cups vegetable oil

1 scallion, cut into short sections

2–3 small slices fresh gingerroot

½ tsp salt

2 tbsp oyster sauce

2–3 tbsp Chinese Stock (see page 30) or water

1 Cut the beef into small, thin slices with a sharp meat cleaver. Place in a shallow dish with the sugar, light soy sauce, rice wine or dry sherry, and cornstarch paste and leave to marinate for 25-30 minutes.

2 Slice the carrot, snow peas, bamboo shoots, and straw mushrooms into roughly the same size pieces as each other.

3 Heat the oil in a wok and add the beef slices. Stir-fry for 1 minute, then remove and keep warm.

4 Pour off the oil, leaving about 1 tablespoon in the wok. Add the sliced vegetables with the scallion and ginger and stir-fry for about 2 minutes. Add the salt, beef, and oyster sauce with stock or water. Blend well until heated through and serve.

VARIATION

You can use whatever vegetables are available for this dish, but it is important to get a good contrast of color—don't use all red or all green for example.

Spicy Pork Balls

These small meatballs are packed with flavor and cooked in a crunchy tomato sauce for a very quick dish.

NUTRITIONAL INFORMATION

Calories	299	Sugars	.........3g
Protein	........28g	Fat	..........15g
Carbohydrate	...14g	Saturates	.......4g

10 MINS   40 MINS

SERVES 4

I N G R E D I E N T S

1 lb/450 g ground pork

2 shallots, finely chopped

2 garlic cloves, crushed

1 tsp cumin seeds

½ tsp chile powder

½ cup fresh whole-wheat bread crumbs

1 egg, beaten

2 tbsp corn oil

14 oz/400 g canned chopped tomatoes, flavored with chile

2 tbsp soy sauce

7 oz /200 g canned water chestnuts, drained

3 tbsp chopped fresh cilantro

COOK'S TIP

Add a few teaspoons of chile sauce to a tin of chopped tomatoes, if you can't find the flavored variety.

1 Place the ground pork in a large mixing bowl. Add the shallots, crushed garlic cloves, cumin seeds, chile powder, bread crumbs, and beaten egg and mix together well.

2 Use your hands to form the mixture into balls.

3 Heat the oil in a large preheated wok. Add the pork balls and stir-fry, in batches, over high heat for 5 minutes, until sealed on all sides.

4 Add the tomatoes, soy sauce, and water chestnuts and bring to a boil. Return the pork balls to the wok, then reduce the heat and leave to simmer for 15 minutes.

5 Scatter with chopped fresh cilantro and serve hot.

Pork with Bell Peppers

This is a really simple yet colorful dish, the trio of bell peppers offsetting the pork and sauce wonderfully.

NUTRITIONAL INFORMATION

Calories 459	Sugars 5g	
Protein 19g	Fat 39g	
Carbohydrate 8g	Saturates 13g	

30 MINS   25 MINS

SERVES 4

I N G R E D I E N T S

½ oz/15 g Chinese dried mushrooms

1 lb/450 g pork leg steaks

2 tbsp vegetable oil

1 onion, sliced

1 red bell pepper, seeded and diced

1 green bell pepper, seeded and diced

1 yellow bell pepper, seeded and diced

4 tbsp oyster sauce

1 Place the mushrooms in a large bowl. Pour over enough boiling water to cover and leave to stand for 20 minutes.

2 Using a sharp knife, trim any excess fat from the pork steaks. Cut the pork into thin strips.

3 Bring a large pan of water to a boil. Add the pork to the boiling water and cook for 5 minutes.

4 Remove the pork from the pan with a slotted spoon and leave to drain thoroughly.

5 Heat the oil in a large preheated wok. Add the pork to the wok and stir-fry for about 5 minutes.

6 Remove the mushrooms from the water and leave to drain thoroughly. Coarsely chop the mushrooms.

7 Add the mushrooms, onion, and the bell peppers to the wok and stir-fry for 5 minutes.

8 Stir in the oyster sauce and cook for 2-3 minutes. Serve immediately.

COOK'S TIP

Use open-cup mushrooms, sliced, instead of Chinese mushrooms, if you prefer.

Lamb & Ginger Stir-Fry

Slices of lamb cooked with garlic, ginger, and shiitake mushrooms make a quick and easy supper. It is best served with Chinese egg noodles.

NUTRITIONAL INFORMATION

Calories	347	Sugars	.........2g
Protein	........31g	Fat	..........21g
Carbohydrate	....7g	Saturates	.......7g

10 MINS   5 MINS

SERVES 4

INGREDIENTS

1 lb 2 oz/500 g lamb tenderloin

2 tbsp corn oil

1 tbsp fresh gingerroot, chopped

2 garlic cloves, chopped

6 scallions, white and green parts diagonally sliced

3 cups sliced shiitake mushrooms

6 oz/175 g sugar snap peas

1 tsp cornstarch

2 tbsp dry sherry

1 tbsp light soy sauce

1 tsp sesame oil

1 tbsp sesame seeds, toasted

Chinese egg noodles, to serve

1 Using a sharp knife or meat cleaver, cut the lamb into ¼-inch/5-mm slices.

2 Heat the corn oil in a large preheated wok or skillet.

3 Add the lamb to the wok or skillet and stir-fry for 2 minutes.

4 Add the chopped gingerroot, chopped garlic cloves, sliced scallions, mushrooms, and sugar snap peas and stir-fry for 2 minutes.

5 Blend the cornstarch with the sherry and stir into the wok.

6 Add the light soy sauce and sesame oil and cook, stirring, for 1 minute, until thickened.

7 Sprinkle over the sesame seeds, then transfer the lamb and ginger stir-fry to a warm serving dish and serve the stir-fry with Chinese egg noodles.

COOK'S TIP

Shiitake mushrooms are much used in Chinese cooking. They have a slightly meaty flavor and can be bought both fresh and dried. Their powerful flavor will permeate more bland mushrooms. Cook them briefly or they begin to toughen.

Pork Ribs with Plum Sauce

Pork ribs are always very popular at grills, and you can flavor them with a number of spicy bastes.

NUTRITIONAL INFORMATION

Calories	590	Sugars	.........1g
Protein	........26g	Fat	..........51g
Carbohydrate	....3g	Saturates	......17g

35 MINS   45 MINS

SERVES 4

I N G R E D I E N T S

2 lb/900 g pork spare ribs

2 tbsp corn oil

1 tsp sesame oil

2 garlic cloves, crushed

1-inch/2.5-cm piece fresh gingerroot, grated

⅔ cup plum sauce

2 tbsp dry sherry

2 tbsp hoisin sauce

2 tbsp soy sauce

4–6 scallions, to garnish (optional)

1 To prepare the garnish, trim the scallions to about 3 inches/7.5 cm long. Slice both ends into thin strips, leaving the onion intact in the center.

2 Put the scallions into a bowl of iced water for at least 30 minutes until the ends start to curl up. Leave them in the water and set aside until required.

3 If you buy the spare ribs in a single piece, cut them into individual ribs. Bring a large pan of water to a boil and add the ribs. Cook for 5 minutes, then drain thoroughly.

4 Heat the oils in a pan, then add the garlic and ginger and cook gently for 1–2 minutes. Stir in the plum sauce, sherry, hoisin, and soy sauces and heat through.

5 Brush the sauce over the pork ribs. Grill over hot coals for 5–10 minutes, then move to a cooler part of the grill for an additional 15–20 minutes, basting with the remaining sauce. Garnish and serve hot.

COOK'S TIP

Par-cooking the ribs in boiling water removes excess fat, which helps prevent the ribs from spitting during cooking. Do not be put off by the large quantity—there is only a little meat on each, but they are quite cheap to buy.

Pork Satay Stir-Fry

Satay sauce is easy to make and is one of the most popular sauces in Asian cooking. It is perfect with beef, chicken, or pork.

NUTRITIONAL INFORMATION

Calories 506   Sugars 11g
Protein ....31g   Fat 36g
Carbohydrate ...15g   Saturates 8g

10 MINS   15 MINS

SERVES 4

INGREDIENTS

5½ oz/150 g carrots

2 tbsp corn oil

12 oz/350 g pork neck fillet, thinly sliced

1 onion, sliced

2 garlic cloves, crushed

1 yellow bell pepper, seeded and sliced

1½ cups snow peas

2¾ oz/75 g fine asparagus

chopped salted peanuts, to serve

SATAY SAUCE

6 tbsp crunchy peanut butter

6 tbsp coconut milk

1 tsp chile flakes

1 clove garlic, crushed

1 tsp tomato paste

COOK'S TIP

Cook the sauce just before serving as it tends to thicken very quickly and will not be spoonable if you cook it too far in advance.

1 Using a sharp knife, slice the carrots into thin sticks.

2 Heat the oil in a large, preheated wok. Add the pork, onion, and garlic and stir-fry for 5 minutes, until the lamb is cooked through.

3 Add the carrots, bell pepper, snow peas, and asparagus to the wok and stir-fry for 5 minutes.

4 To make the satay sauce, place the peanut butter, coconut milk, chile flakes, garlic and tomato paste in a small pan and heat gently, stirring, until well combined. Be careful not to let the sauce stick to the bottom of the pan.

5 Transfer the stir-fry to warm serving plates. Spoon the satay sauce over the stir-fry and scatter with chopped peanuts. Serve immediately.

Marinated Beef

This dish is quick to cook, but benefits from lengthy marinating, as this tenderizes and flavors the meat.

NUTRITIONAL INFORMATION

Calories	195	Sugars	.........1g
Protein	........12g	Fat	..........15g
Carbohydrate	....3g	Saturates	.......4g

1¼ HOURS   10 MINS

SERVES 4

INGREDIENTS

8 oz/225 g lean steak

1 tbsp light soy sauce

1 tsp sesame oil

2 tsp Chinese rice wine or dry sherry

1 tsp superfine sugar

2 tsp hoisin sauce

1 garlic clove, crushed

½ tsp cornstarch

green bell pepper slices, to garnish

rice or noodles, to serve

SAUCE

2 tbsp dark soy sauce

1 tsp superfine sugar

½ tsp cornstarch

3 tbsp oyster sauce

8 tbsp water

2 tbsp vegetable oil

3 garlic cloves, crushed

½-inch/1-cm piece fresh gingerroot, grated

8 baby corn cobs, halved lengthwise

½ green bell pepper, seeded and thinly sliced

1 oz/25 g bamboo shoots, drained and rinsed

1 Using a sharp knife or meat cleaver, cut the steak into 1-inch/2.5-cm cubes and place in a shallow dish.

2 Mix together the soy sauce, sesame oil, Chinese rice wine, superfine sugar, hoisin sauce, garlic, and cornstarch and pour over the steak, turning it to coat completely. Cover and marinate for at least 1 hour, or preferably overnight in the refrigerator for a fuller flavor.

3 Meanwhile, make the sauce. Mix together the dark soy sauce with the superfine sugar, cornstarch, oyster sauce, and water.

4 Heat the oil in a preheated wok. Add the steak, together with the marinade, and stir-fry for 2–3 minutes, until sealed and lightly browned.

5 Add the garlic, ginger, baby corn cobs, bell pepper, and bamboo shoots. Stir in the oyster sauce mixture and bring to a boil. Reduce the heat and cook for 2–3 minutes.

6 Transfer to a warm serving dish, then garnish with green bell pepper slices and serve immediately with rice or noodles.

Lamb Meatballs

These small meatballs are made with ground lamb and flavored with chile, garlic, parsley, and Chinese curry powder.

NUTRITIONAL INFORMATION

Calories	320	Sugars	.........1g
Protein	........28g	Fat	..........20g
Carbohydrate	....8g	Saturates	.......6g

5 MINS   20 MINS

SERVES 4

INGREDIENTS

1 lb/450 g ground lamb

3 garlic cloves, crushed

2 scallions, finely chopped

½ tsp chile powder

1 tsp Chinese curry powder

1 tbsp chopped fresh parsley

½ cup fresh white bread crumbs

1 egg, beaten

3 tbsp vegetable oil

4½ oz/125 g Napa cabbage, shredded

1 leek, sliced

1 tbsp cornstarch

2 tbsp water

1¼ cups lamb stock

1 tbsp dark soy sauce

shredded leek, to garnish

VARIATION

Use ground pork or beef instead of the lamb as an alternative.

1 Mix the lamb, garlic, scallions, chile powder, Chinese curry powder, parsley, and bread crumbs together in a bowl. Work the egg into the mixture, bringing it together to form a firm mixture. Roll into 16 small, even-size balls.

2 Heat the oil in a preheated wok. Add the Napa cabbage and leek and stir-fry for 1 minute. Remove from the wok with a slotted spoon and set aside.

3 Add the meatballs to the wok and fry in batches, turning gently, for 3-4 minutes, until golden brown all over.

4 Mix the cornstarch and water together to form a smooth paste and set aside. Pour the lamb stock and soy sauce into the wok and cook for 2–3 minutes. Stir in the cornstarch paste. Bring to a boil and cook, stirring constantly, until the sauce is thickened and clear.

5 Return the Napa cabbage and leek to the wok and cook for 1 minute, until heated through. Arrange the Napa cabbage and leek on a warm serving dish and top with the meatballs, then garnish with shredded leek and serve immediately.

Beef Teriyaki

This Japanese-style teriyaki sauce complements grilled beef, but it can also be used to accompany chicken or salmon.

NUTRITIONAL INFORMATION

Calories 184	Sugars 6g	
Protein 24g	Fat 5g	
Carbohydrate 8g	Saturates 2g	

🐷 🐷

🍲 2¼ HOURS   ⏱ 15 MINS

SERVES 4

INGREDIENTS

1 lb/450 g extra thin lean beef steaks

8 scallions, trimmed and cut into short lengths

1 yellow bell pepper, seeded and cut into chunks

green salad, to serve

SAUCE

1 tsp cornstarch

2 tbsp dry sherry

2 tbsp white wine vinegar

3 tbsp soy sauce

1 tbsp dark muscovado sugar

1 garlic clove, crushed

½ tsp ground cinnamon

½ tsp ground ginger

1 Place the meat in a shallow, non-metallic dish.

2 To make the sauce, combine the cornstarch with the sherry, then stir in the remaining sauce ingredients. Pour the sauce over the meat and leave to marinate for at least 2 hours.

3 Remove the meat from the sauce. Pour the sauce into a small pan.

4 Cut the meat into thin strips and thread these, concertina-style, on to pre-soaked wooden skewers, alternating each strip of meat with the prepared pieces of scallion and bell pepper.

5 Gently heat the sauce until it is just simmering, stirring occasionally.

6 Grill the kabobs over hot coals for 5–8 minutes, turning and basting the beef and vegetables occasionally with the reserved teriyaki sauce.

7 Arrange the skewers on serving plates and pour the remaining sauce over the kabobs. Serve with a green salad.

Red Spiced Beef

A spicy stir-fry flavored with paprika, chile, and tomato, with a crisp bite to it from the celery strips.

NUTRITIONAL INFORMATION

Calories 431	Sugars 0g
Protein 32g	Fat 28g
Carbohydrate . . .14g	Saturates 10g

40 MINS   10 MINS

SERVES 4

INGREDIENTS

1 lb 6 oz/625 g sirloin or rump steak

2 tbsp paprika

2–3 tsp mild chile powder

½ tsp salt

6 celery stalks

6 tbsp stock or water

2 tbsp tomato paste

2 tbsp clear honey

3 tbsp wine vinegar

1 tbsp Worcestershire sauce

2 tbsp corn oil

4 scallions, thinly sliced diagonally

4 tomatoes, peeled, seeded and sliced

1–2 garlic cloves, crushed

Chinese noodles, to serve

celery leaves, to garnish (optional)

1 Using a sharp knife or meat cleaver, cut the steak across the grain into narrow strips ½ inch/1 cm thick and place in a bowl.

2 Combine the paprika, chile powder, and salt, then add to the beef and mix thoroughly until the meat strips are evenly coated with the spices. Leave the beef to marinate in a cool place for at least 30 minutes.

3 Cut the celery into 2-inch/5-cm lengths, then cut the lengths into strips about ¼ inch/5 mm thick.

4 Combine the stock or water, tomato paste, honey, wine vinegar, and Worcestershire sauce and set aside.

5 Heat the oil in the wok until really hot. Add the scallions, celery, tomatoes, and garlic and stir-fry for 1 minute, until the vegetables are beginning

to soften, then add the steak strips. Stir-fry over high heat for 3-4 minutes, until the meat is well sealed.

6 Add the sauce to the wok and continue to stir-fry briskly until thoroughly coated and sizzling.

7 Serve with noodles and garnish with celery leaves, if liked.

Meat 197

Soy & Sesame Beef

Soy sauce and sesame seeds are classic ingredients in Chinese cooking. Use a dark soy sauce for fuller flavor and richness.

NUTRITIONAL INFORMATION

Calories	324	Sugars	.........2g
Protein	........25g	Fat	..........22g
Carbohydrate	....3g	Saturates	.......6g

🥘 5 MINS 🕐 10 MINS

SERVES 4

INGREDIENTS

2 tbsp sesame seeds

1 lb/450 g beef fillet

2 tbsp vegetable oil

1 green bell pepper, seeded and thinly sliced

4 garlic cloves, crushed

2 tbsp dry sherry

4 tbsp soy sauce

6 scallions, sliced

noodles, to serve

1 Heat a large wok or heavy-based skillet until it is very hot.

2 Add the sesame seeds to the wok or skillet and dry fry, stirring, for 1–2 minutes, until they just begin to brown. Remove the sesame seeds from the wok and set aside until required.

3 Using a sharp knife or meat cleaver, thinly slice the beef.

4 Heat the vegetable oil in the wok or skillet. Add the beef and stir-fry for 2–3 minutes, until sealed on all sides.

5 Add the sliced bell pepper and crushed garlic to the wok and continue stir-frying for 2 minutes.

6 Add the dry sherry and soy sauce to the wok together with the scallions. Let the mixture in the wok bubble, stirring occasionally, for 1 minute, but do not let the mixture burn.

7 Transfer the garlic beef stir-fry to warm serving bowls and scatter with the dry-fried sesame seeds. Serve hot with boiled noodles.

COOK'S TIP

You can spread the sesame seeds out on a cookie sheet and toast them under a preheated broiler until browned all over, if you prefer.

Five-Spice Lamb

Chinese five-spice powder is a blend of cinnamon, fennel, star anise, ginger, and cloves, all finely ground together.

NUTRITIONAL INFORMATION

Calories	361	Sugars	. . . . .3g
Protein	. . . . .35g	Fat	. . . . .22g
Carbohydrate	. . . .5g	Saturates	. . . . . . .8g

1¼ HOURS   10 MINS

SERVES 4

INGREDIENTS

1 lb 6 oz/625 g lean boneless lamb (leg or fillet)

2 tsp Chinese five-spice powder

3 tbsp corn oil

1 red bell pepper, cored, seeded, and thinly sliced

1 green bell pepper, cored, seeded, and thinly sliced

1 yellow or orange bell pepper, cored, seeded, and thinly sliced

4–6 scallions, thinly sliced diagonally

1 cup green or fine beans, cut into 1½-inch/4-cm lengths

2 tbsp soy sauce

4 tbsp sherry

salt and pepper

Chinese noodles, to serve

TO GARNISH

strips of red and yellow bell pepper

fresh cilantro leaves

1 Cut the lamb into narrow strips, about 1½ inches/4 cm long, across the grain. Place in a bowl, then add the five-spice powder and ¼ teaspoon salt. Mix well and leave to marinate, covered, in a cool place for at least an hour and up to 24 hours.

2 Heat half the oil in the wok, swirling it around until really hot. Add the lamb and stir-fry briskly for 3–4 minutes until almost cooked through. Remove from the pan and set aside.

3 Add the remaining oil to the wok and when hot add the bell peppers and scallions. Stir-fry for 2-3 minutes, then add the beans and stir for a minute or so.

4 Add the soy sauce and sherry to the wok and when hot return the lamb and any juices to the wok. Stir-fry for 1-2 minutes, until the lamb is really hot again and thoroughly coated in the sauce. Season to taste.

5 Serve with Chinese noodles, garnished with strips of red and green bell pepper and fresh cilantro.

Sweet & Sour Pork

This dish is a popular choice in Western diets, and must be one of the best known of Chinese recipes.

NUTRITIONAL INFORMATION

Calories 471   Sugars 47g
Protein . . . . .16g   Fat 13g
Carbohydrate . . .77g   Saturates 2g

10 MINS   20 MINS

SERVES 4

I N G R E D I E N T S

⅔ cup vegetable oil, for deep-frying

8 oz/225 g pork fillet (tenderloin), cut into
   ½-inch/1-cm cubes

1 onion, sliced

1 green bell pepper, seeded and sliced

8 oz/225 g pineapple pieces

1 small carrot, cut into thin strips

25 g/1 oz canned bamboo shoots,
   drained, rinsed and halved

rice or noodles, to serve

B A T T E R

scant 1 cup all-purpose flour

1 tbsp cornstarch

1½ tsp baking powder

1 tbsp vegetable oil

S A U C E

generous ½ cup light brown sugar

2 tbsp cornstarch

½ cup white wine vinegar

2 garlic cloves, crushed

4 tbsp tomato paste

6 tbsp pineapple juice

1 To make the batter, sift the all-purpose flour into a mixing bowl, together with the cornstarch and baking powder. Add the vegetable oil and stir in enough water to make a thick, smooth batter (about ¾ cup).

2 Pour the vegetable oil into a preheated wok and heat until almost smoking.

3 Dip the cubes of pork into the batter, and cook in the hot oil, in batches, until the pork is cooked through. Remove the pork from the wok with a slotted spoon and drain on absorbent paper towels. Set aside and keep warm until required.

4 Drain all but 1 tablespoon of oil from the wok and return it to the heat. Add the onion, bell pepper, pineapple pieces, carrot, and bamboo shoots and stir-fry for 1–2 minutes. Remove from the wok with a slotted spoon and set aside.

5 Mix all of the sauce ingredients together and pour into the wok. Bring to a boil, stirring until thickened and clear. Cook for 1 minute, then return the pork and vegetables to the wok. Cook for an additional 1–2 minutes, then transfer to a serving plate and serve at once with rice or noodles.

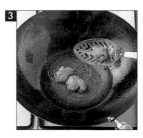

Sweet Potato & Coconut Beef

This is a truly aromatic dish, blending the heat of red curry paste with the aroma and flavor of the lime leaves and coconut.

NUTRITIONAL INFORMATION

Calories	322	Sugars	.........9g
Protein	........18g	Fat	..........18g
Carbohydrate	...24g	Saturates	.......6g

10 MINS   25 MINS

SERVES 4

INGREDIENTS

2 tbsp vegetable oil

2 garlic cloves

1 onion

12 oz/350 g rump steak

12 oz/350 g sweet potato

2 tbsp red curry paste

1¼ cups coconut milk

3 lime leaves

jasmine rice, to serve

1 Heat the vegetable oil in a large preheated wok or large heavy-based skillet.

2 Peel the garlic cloves and crush them in a pestle and mortar. Thinly slice the onions.

3 Using a sharp knife, thinly slice the beef. Add the beef to the wok and stir-fry for 2 minutes, until sealed on all sides.

4 Add the garlic and the onion to the wok and stir-fry for an additional 2 minutes.

5 Using a sharp knife, peel and dice the sweet potato.

6 Add the sweet potato to the wok with the red curry paste, coconut milk, and lime leaves and bring to a rapid boil. Reduce the heat, then cover and leave to simmer for 15 minutes, until the potatoes are tender.

7 Remove and discard the lime leaves and transfer the stir-fry to warm serving bowls. Serve hot, accompanied by jasmine rice.

VARIATION

If you cannot obtain lime leaves, use 1 teaspoon grated lime zest instead.

Pork Fry with Vegetables

This is a very simple dish that lends itself to almost any combination of vegetables that you have to hand.

NUTRITIONAL INFORMATION

Calories 216	Sugars 3g
Protein 19g	Fat 12g
Carbohydrate 5g	Saturates 3g

🍲 🍲 🍲

🧊 5 MINS   🕐 15 MINS

SERVES 4

INGREDIENTS

12 oz/350 g lean pork tenderloin

2 tbsp vegetable oil

2 garlic cloves, crushed

½-inch/1-cm piece fresh gingerroot, cut into slivers

1 carrot, cut into thin strips

1 red bell pepper, seeded and diced

1 fennel bulb, sliced

1 oz/25 g water chestnuts, halved

½ cup bean sprouts

2 tbsp Chinese rice wine

1¼ cups pork or chicken stock

pinch of dark brown sugar

1 tsp cornstarch

2 tsp water

1 Cut the pork into thin slices. Heat the oil in a preheated wok. Add the garlic, ginger, and pork and stir-fry for 1–2 minutes, until the meat is sealed.

2 Add the carrot, bell pepper, fennel, and water chestnuts to the wok and stir-fry for about 2-3 minutes.

3 Add the bean sprouts and stir-fry for 1 minute. Remove the pork and vegetables from the wok and keep warm.

4 Add the Chinese rice wine, pork stock, and sugar to the wok. Blend the cornstarch to a smooth paste with the water and stir it into the sauce. Bring to a boil, stirring constantly until thickened and clear.

5 Return the meat and vegetables to the wok and cook for 1–2 minutes, until heated through and coated with the sauce. Serve immediately.

VARIATION

Use dry sherry instead of the Chinese rice wine if you have difficulty obtaining it.

Lamb with Black Bean Sauce

Red onions add great color to recipes and are perfect in this dish, combining with the colors of the bell peppers.

NUTRITIONAL INFORMATION

Calories ....328 Sugars 5g
Protein ....26g Fat 20g
Carbohydrate ...12g Saturates 6g

🍲 10 MINS 🕐 15 MINS

SERVES 4

INGREDIENTS

1 lb/450 g lamb neck fillet or boneless
 leg of lamb chops

1 egg white, lightly beaten

4 tbsp cornstarch

1 tsp Chinese five-spice powder

3 tbsp corn oil

1 red onion

1 red bell pepper, seeded and sliced

1 green bell pepper, seeded and sliced

1 yellow or orange bell pepper, seeded
 and sliced

5 tbsp black bean sauce

boiled rice or noodles, to serve

1 Using a sharp knife, slice the lamb into very thin strips.

2 Mix together the egg white, cornstarch, and Chinese five-spice powder. Toss the lamb strips in the mixture until evenly coated.

3 Heat the oil in a wok and stir-fry the lamb over high heat for 5 minutes, until it crispens around the edges.

4 Slice the red onion. Add the onion and bell pepper slices to the wok and stir-fry for 5–6 minutes, until the vegetables just begin to soften.

5 Stir the black bean sauce into the mixture in the wok and heat through.

6 Transfer the lamb and sauce to warm serving plates and serve hot with freshly boiled rice or noodles.

COOK'S TIP

Take care when frying the lamb as the cornstarch mixture may cause it to stick to the wok. Move the lamb around the wok constantly during stir-frying.

Roast Red Pork

Pork tenderloin is given a marvellous flavor and distinctive red color in this excellent recipe.

NUTRITIONAL INFORMATION

Calories	305	Sugars	.........4g
Protein	........40g	Fat	..........13g
Carbohydrate	....5g	Saturates	.......5g

12¼ HOURS   40 MINS

SERVES 4

INGREDIENTS

1 lb 10 oz/750 g pork tenderloin

1 tsp red food coloring

4 garlic cloves, crushed

1 tsp Chinese five-spice powder

1 tbsp light soy sauce

1 tbsp fish sauce

1 tbsp dry sherry

1 tbsp dark muscovado sugar

1 tbsp sesame oil

1 tbsp finely fresh gingerroot, grated

TO GARNISH

lettuce

scallions, finely sliced

1 Rinse the pork and trim off any fat. Place in a large, clear plastic food bag or freezer bag and add the red food coloring. Roll the pork around in the bag to coat it in the coloring.

2 Mix all the remaining ingredients together and add the mixture to the pork in the plastic bag. Secure the opening and chill overnight, or for at least 12 hours, turning the bag over occasionally.

3 Place the pork on a rack over a roasting pan. Cook in a preheated oven at 425°F/220°C for 15 minutes.

Remove from the oven and baste with the remaining marinade.

4 Reduce the oven temperature to 350°F/180°C and roast the pork for an additional 25 minutes, basting with any remaining marinade. Leave to cool for at least 10 minutes before slicing.

5 Slice thinly and arrange on a serving platter, then garnish and serve.

COOK'S TIP

Putting the pork in a plastic bag helps to prevent your hands from turning red from the food coloring.

Curried Lamb with Potatoes

This dish is very filling, requiring only a simple vegetable accompaniment or bread.

NUTRITIONAL INFORMATION

Calories . . . . . . .375 Sugars 6g
Protein . . . . .26g Fat 19g
Carbohydrate . . .27g Saturates 6g

🍲 🍲

⏱ 10 MINS   🕐 1 HOUR

SERVES 4

I N G R E D I E N T S

1 lb/450 g potatoes, diced

1 lb/450 g lean lamb, cubed

2 tbsp medium hot curry paste

3 tbsp corn oil

1 onion, sliced

1 eggplant, diced

2 garlic cloves, crushed

1 tbsp fresh gingerroot, grated

⅔ cup lamb or beef stock

salt

2 tbsp chopped fresh cilantro,
   to garnish

1 Bring a large pan of lightly salted water to a boil. Add the potatoes and cook for 10 minutes. Remove the potatoes from the pan with a slotted spoon and drain thoroughly.

COOK'S TIP

The wok is an ancient Chinese invention, the name coming from the Cantonese, meaning a "cooking vessel."

2 Meanwhile, place the lamb cubes in a large mixing bowl. Add the curry paste and mix well until the lamb is evenly coated in the paste.

3 Heat the oil in a large preheated wok.

4 Add the onion, eggplant, garlic, and ginger to the wok and stir-fry for 5 minutes.

5 Add the lamb to the wok and stir-fry for an additional 5 minutes.

6 Add the stock and cooked potatoes to the wok. Bring to a boil and leave to simmer for 30 minutes, until the lamb is tender and cooked through.

7 Transfer the stir-fry to warm serving dishes and scatter with chopped fresh cilantro. Serve immediately.

Spicy Beef

In this recipe, beef is steeped in a tangy marinade and served with a spicy, chile-flavored sauce.

NUTRITIONAL INFORMATION

Calories	246	Sugars	.........2g
Protein	........21g	Fat	..........13g
Carbohydrate	...10g	Saturates	.......3g

1¼ HOURS   10 MINS

SERVES 4

INGREDIENTS

8 oz/225 g fillet steak

2 garlic cloves, crushed

1 tsp powdered star anise

1 tbsp dark soy sauce

grated lemon zest, to garnish

SAUCE

2 tbsp vegetable oil

1 bunch scallions, halved lengthwise

1 tbsp dark soy sauce

1 tbsp dry sherry

¼ tsp chile sauce

⅔ cup water

2 tsp cornstarch

4 tsp water

1 Cut the steak into thin strips and place in a shallow dish.

2 Mix together the garlic, star anise, and dark soy sauce in a bowl.

3 Pour the sauce mixture over the steak strips, turning them to coat thoroughly. Cover and leave to marinate in the refrigerator for at least 1 hour.

4 To make the sauce, heat the oil in a preheated wok or large skillet. Reduce the heat and stir-fry the scallions for 1-2 minutes.

5 Remove the scallions from the wok with a slotted spoon, then drain on absorbent paper towels and set aside until required.

6 Add the beef to the wok, together with the marinade, and stir-fry for 3-4 minutes. Return the scallions to the wok and add the soy sauce, sherry, chile sauce, and the water from the cup.

7 Blend the cornstarch with the remaining water and stir into the wok. Bring to a boil, stirring until the sauce thickens and clears.

8 Transfer to a warm serving dish. Garnish and serve immediately.

Fish & Seafood

China's many miles of coastline, rivers, and lakes offer an enormous variety of fresh and salt-water fish and seafood. Among the most popular are carp, bass, bream, clams, crab,

crawfish, and shrimp. Dishes that include shark's fins, abalone, squid, and edible seaweed are also common. When buying fish and seafood for Chinese cooking, freshness is imperative to flavor, so be sure to buy it when really fresh and use as soon as possible, preferably the same day. Chinese chefs buy live fish, which are kept alive until just before cooking. Favorite cooking methods for fish are steaming and quick poaching in boiling water or broth.

Small Shrimp Foo Yong

The classic ingredients of this popular dish are eggs, carrots, and small shrimp. Add extra ingredients such as peas or crabmeat, if desired.

NUTRITIONAL INFORMATION

Calories	240	Sugars	.........1g
Protein	........22g	Fat	..........16g
Carbohydrate	....1g	Saturates	.......3g

5 MINS   10 MINS

SERVES 4

INGREDIENTS

2 tbsp vegetable oil

1 carrot, grated

5 eggs, beaten

8 oz/225 g raw small shrimp, shelled

1 tbsp light soy sauce

pinch of Chinese five-spice powder

2 scallions, chopped

2 tsp sesame seeds

1 tsp sesame oil

COOK'S TIP

If only cooked shrimp are available, add them just before the end of cooking, but make sure they are fully incorporated into the foo yong. They require only heating through. Overcooking will make them chewy and tasteless.

1 Heat the vegetable oil in a preheated wok or skillet, swirling it around until the oil is really hot.

2 Add the grated carrot and stir–fry for 1–2 minutes.

3 Push the carrot to one side of the wok or skillet and add the beaten eggs. Cook, stirring gently, for 1–2 minutes.

4 Stir the small shrimp, light soy sauce, and five-spice powder into the mixture in the wok. Stir-fry the mixture for 2–3 minutes, or until the small shrimps change color from gray to pink and the mixture is almost dry.

5 Turn the small shrimp foo yong out onto a warm plate and sprinkle the scallions, sesame seeds, and sesame oil on top. Serve immediately.

Fried Shrimp with Cashews

Cashew nuts are delicious as part of a stir-fry with almost any other ingredient. Use the unsalted variety in cooking.

NUTRITIONAL INFORMATION

Calories	406	Sugar	.........3g
Protein	........31g	Fat	..........25g
Carbohydrate	...13g	Saturates	.......4g

5 MINS

5 MINS

SERVES 4

I N G R E D I E N T S

2 garlic cloves, crushed

1 tbsp cornstarch

pinch of superfine sugar

1 lb/450 g raw jumbo shrimp

4 tbsp vegetable oil

1 leek, sliced

4½ oz/125 g broccoli florets

1 orange bell pepper, seeded and diced

½ cup unsalted cashew nuts

S A U C E

¾ cup fish stock

1 tbsp cornstarch

dash of chile sauce

2 tsp sesame oil

1 tbsp Chinese rice wine

1 Mix together the garlic, cornstarch, and sugar in a bowl.

2 Peel and devein the shrimp. Stir the shrimp into the mixture to coat thoroughly.

3 Heat the vegetable oil in a preheated wok and add the shrimp mixture. Stir-fry over high heat for 20–30 seconds until the shrimp turn pink. Remove the shrimp from the wok with a slotted spoon, drain on absorbent paper towels and set aside until required.

4 Add the leek, broccoli, and bell pepper to the wok and stir-fry for 2 minutes.

5 To make the sauce, place the fish stock, cornstarch, chile sauce to taste, the sesame oil, and Chinese rice wine in a small glass bowl. Mix together until thoroughly blended.

6 Add the sauce to the wok, together with the cashew nuts. Return the shrimp to the wok and cook for 1 minute to heat through.

7 Transfer the shrimp stir-fry to a warm serving dish and serve immediately.

Stir-Fried Salmon with Leeks

Salmon is marinated in a deliciously rich, sweet sauce, then stir-fried and served on a bed of crispy leeks.

NUTRITIONAL INFORMATION

Calories	360	Sugars	.........9g
Protein	........24g	Fat	25
Carbohydrate	....11g	Saturates	.......4g

35 MINS   15 MINS

SERVES 4

INGREDIENTS

1 lb/450 g salmon fillet, skinned

2 tbsp sweet soy sauce

2 tbsp tomato ketchup

1 tsp rice wine vinegar

1 tbsp raw sugar

1 garlic clove, crushed

4 tbsp corn oil

1 lb/450 g leeks, thinly shredded

finely chopped red chiles,
    to garnish

1 Using a sharp knife, cut the salmon into slices. Place the slices of salmon in a shallow non-metallic dish.

2 Mix together the soy sauce, tomato ketchup, rice wine vinegar, sugar, and garlic.

3 Pour the mixture over the salmon, then toss well and leave to marinate for about 30 minutes.

4 Meanwhile, heat 3 tablespoons of the corn oil in a large preheated wok.

5 Add the leeks to the wok and stir-fry over medium-high heat for 10 minutes, until the leeks become crispy and tender.

6 Using a slotted spoon, carefully remove the leeks from the wok and transfer to warmed serving plates.

7 Add the remaining oil to the wok. Add the salmon and the marinade to the wok and cook for 2 minutes.

8 Remove the salmon from the wok and spoon over the leeks, then garnish with finely chopped red chiles and serve immediately.

VARIATION

This recipe works well with beef fillet instead of salmon, when you prefer a meat dish.

Fish with Black Bean Sauce

Steaming is one of the preferred methods of cooking whole fish in China as it maintains both the flavor and the texture.

NUTRITIONAL INFORMATION

Calories	292	Sugars	.........3g
Protein	........44g	Fat	...........7g
Carbohydrate	....6g	Saturates	.....0.4g

10 MINS   10 MINS

SERVES 4

INGREDIENTS

2 lb/900 g whole snapper, cleaned and scaled

3 garlic cloves, crushed

2 tbsp black bean sauce

1 tsp cornstarch

2 tsp sesame oil

2 tbsp light soy sauce

2 tsp superfine sugar

2 tbsp dry sherry

1 small leek, shredded

1 small red bell pepper, seeded and cut into thin strips

shredded leek and lemon wedges, to garnish

boiled rice or noodles, to serve

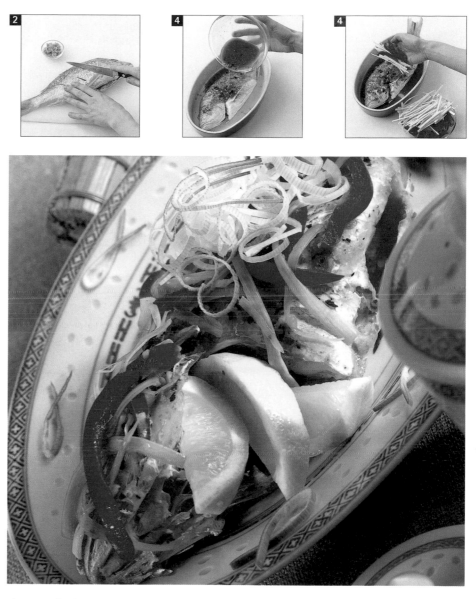

1 Rinse the fish inside and out with cold running water and pat dry with paper towels.

2 Make 2–3 diagonal slashes in the flesh on each side of the fish, using a sharp knife. Rub the garlic into the fish.

3 Mix together the black bean sauce, cornstarch, sesame oil, light soy sauce, sugar, and dry sherry.

4 Place the fish in a shallow heatproof dish and pour the sauce mixture over the top. Sprinkle the shredded leek and bell pepper strips on top of the sauce.

5 Place the dish in the top of a steamer, cover and steam for 10 minutes, until the fish is cooked through.

6 Transfer the fish to a serving dish, then garnish with shredded leek and lemon wedges and serve with boiled rice or noodles.

COOK'S TIP

Insert the point of a sharp knife into the fish to test if it is cooked. The fish is cooked through if the knife goes into the flesh easily.

Fried Squid Flowers

The addition of green bell pepper and black bean sauce to the squid makes a colorful and delicious dish from the Cantonese school.

NUTRITIONAL INFORMATION

Calories	172	Sugars	.........1g
Protein	........13g	Fat	..........13g
Carbohydrate	....2g	Saturates	.......1g

10 MINS   5 MINS

SERVES 4

I N G R E D I E N T S

12–14 oz/350–400 g prepared and cleaned squid (see Cook's Tip, below)

1 medium green bell pepper, cored and seeded

3–4 tbsp vegetable oil

1 garlic clove, finely chopped

¼ tsp finely chopped fresh gingerroot

2 tsp finely chopped scallions

½ tsp salt

2 tbsp crushed black bean sauce

1 tsp Chinese rice wine or dry sherry

a few drops sesame oil

boiled rice, to serve

1 If ready-prepared squid is not available, prepare as instructed in the Cook's Tip, below.

2 Open up the squid and, using a meat cleaver or sharp knife, score the inside in a criss-cross pattern.

3 Cut the squid into pieces about the size of an oblong postage stamp.

4 Blanch the squid pieces in a bowl of boiling water for a few seconds. Remove and drain; dry well on absorbent paper towels.

5 Cut the bell pepper into small triangular pieces. Heat the oil in a preheated wok or large skillet and stir-fry the bell pepper for about 1 minute.

6 Add the garlic, ginger, scallions, salt, and squid. Continue stirring for another minute.

7 Finally add the black bean sauce and Chinese rice wine, and blend well.

8 Transfer the squid flowers to a serving dish, then sprinkle with sesame oil and serve with boiled rice.

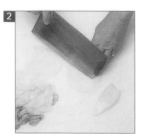

COOK'S TIP

Clean the squid by first cutting off the head. Cut off the tentacles and reserve. Remove the small soft bone at the base of the tentacles and the transparent backbone, as well as the ink bag. Peel off the thin skin, then wash and dry well.

Sweet & Sour Shrimp

Use raw shrimp for this dish if possible. Omit steps 1 and 2 if ready-cooked ones are used.

NUTRITIONAL INFORMATION

Calories 373   Sugars 11g
Protein ....13g   Fat 26g
Carbohydrate ...19g   Saturates 3g

3½ HOURS   10 MINS

SERVES 4

INGREDIENTS

6–9 oz/175–250 g shelled raw jumbo shrimp

pinch of salt

1 tsp egg white

1 tsp Cornstarch Paste (see page 31)

1¼ cups vegetable oil

SAUCE

1 tbsp vegetable oil

½ small green bell pepper, cored, seeded, and thinly sliced

½ small carrot, thinly sliced

4½ oz/125 g canned water chestnuts, drained and sliced

½ tsp salt

1 tbsp light soy sauce

2 tbsp sugar

3 tbsp rice or sherry vinegar

1 tsp rice wine or dry sherry

1 tbsp tomato sauce

½ tsp chile sauce

3–4 tbsp Chinese Stock (see page 30) or water

2 tsp Cornstarch Paste (see page 31)

a few drops sesame oil

1 Mix together the shrimp with the salt, egg white, and Cornstarch Paste.

2 Heat the oil in a preheated wok and stir-fry the shrimp for 30-40 seconds only. Remove and drain on paper towels.

3 Pour off the oil and wipe the wok clean with paper towels. To make the sauce, first heat the tablespoon of oil. Add the vegetables and stir-fry for 1 minute, then add the seasonings with the stock and bring to a boil.

4 Add the shrimp and stir until blended well. Thicken the sauce with the Cornstarch Paste and stir until smooth. Sprinkle with sesame oil and serve hot.

Sesame Salmon with Cream

Salmon fillet holds its shape when tossed in sesame seeds and stir-fried. It is served in a creamy sauce of diced zucchini.

NUTRITIONAL INFORMATION

Calories	550	Sugars	.........1g
Protein	........35g	Fat	..........45g
Carbohydrate	....2g	Saturates	......12g

🕑 5 MINS 🕐 10 MINS

SERVES 4

INGREDIENTS

1 lb 6 oz–1 lb 10 oz/625–750 g
   salmon or pink trout fillets

2 tbsp light soy sauce

3 tbsp sesame seeds

3 tbsp corn oil

4 scallions, thinly sliced diagonally

2 large zucchini, diced, or 5-inch/13-cm
   piece cucumber, diced

grated rind of ½ lemon

1 tbsp lemon juice

½ tsp turmeric

6 tbsp fish stock or water

3 tbsp heavy cream or mascarpone

salt and pepper

curly endive, to garnish

1 Skin the fish (see Cook's Tip, below) and cut into strips about 1½ x ¾ inches/4 x 2 cm. Pat dry on paper towels. Season lightly, then brush with soy sauce and sprinkle all over with sesame seeds.

2 Heat 2 tablespoons of oil in the wok. Add the pieces of fish and stir-fry for 3-4 minutes until lightly browned all over. Remove with a spatula, then drain on paper towels and keep warm.

3 Heat the remaining oil in the wok and add the scallions and zucchini or cucumber and stir-fry for 1-2 minutes. Add the lemon rind and juice, turmeric, stock, and seasoning and bring to a boil for 1 minute. Stir in the cream.

4 Return the fish pieces to the wok and toss gently in the sauce until they are really hot. Garnish and serve.

COOK'S TIP

To skin, lay the fillet skin-side down. Insert a sharp, flexible knife at one end between the flesh and the skin. Hold the skin tightly at the end and push the knife along, keeping the knife blade as flat as possible against the skin.

Baked Crab with Ginger

In Chinese restaurants, only live crabs are used, but ready-cooked ones can be used at home quite successfully.

NUTRITIONAL INFORMATION

Calories	261	Sugars	0.5g
Protein	18g	Fat	17g
Carbohydrate	5g	Saturates	2g

3¾ HOURS   10 MINS

SERVES 4

INGREDIENTS

1 large or 2 medium crabs, weighing about 1 lb 10 oz/750 g in total

2 tbsp Chinese rice wine or dry sherry

1 egg, lightly beaten

1 tbsp cornstarch

3-4 tbsp vegetable oil

1 tbsp finely chopped fresh gingerroot

3–4 scallions, cut into sections

2 tbsp light soy sauce

1 tsp sugar

scant ⅓ cup Chinese Stock (see page 30) or water

½ tsp sesame oil

cilantro leaves, to garnish

1 Cut the crab in half from the underbelly. Break off the claws and crack them with the back of a cleaver or a large kitchen knife.

2 Discard the legs and crack the shell, breaking it into several pieces. Discard the feathery gills and the stomach sac. Place the crabmeat in a bowl.

3 Mix together the wine, egg, and cornstarch. Pour the mixture over the crab and leave to marinate for 10-15 minutes.

4 Heat the vegetable oil in a preheated wok and stir-fry the crab with the chopped ginger and scallions for 2-3 minutes.

5 Add the soy sauce, sugar, and Chinese stock, then blend well and bring to a boil. Cover and cook for 3-4 minutes, then remove the lid and sprinkle with sesame oil. Serve, garnished with fresh cilantro leaves.

COOK'S TIP

Crabs are almost always sold ready-cooked. The crab should feel heavy for its size, and when it is shaken, there should be no sound of water inside. A good medium-sized crab should yield about 1 lb 2 oz/500 g meat, enough for 3-4 people.

Braised Fish Fillets

Any white fish, such as lemon sole or plaice, is ideal for this delicious dish.

NUTRITIONAL INFORMATION

Calories	107	Sugars	. . . . .2g
Protein	. . . . .17g	Fat	. . . . .2g
Carbohydrate	. . . .6g	Saturates	. . . . .0.3g

4 HOURS   10 MINS

SERVES 4

INGREDIENTS

3-4 small Chinese dried mushrooms

10½–12 oz/300–350 g fish fillets

1 tsp salt

½ egg white, lightly beaten

1 tsp Cornstarch Paste (see page 31)

2½ cups vegetable oil

1 tsp finely chopped fresh gingerroot

2 scallions, finely chopped

1 garlic clove, finely chopped

½ small green bell pepper, seeded
   and cut into small cubes

½ small carrot, thinly sliced

½ cup canned sliced bamboo shoots,
   rinsed and drained

½ tsp sugar

1 tbsp light soy sauce

1 tsp rice wine or dry sherry

1 tbsp chile bean sauce

2–3 tbsp Chinese Stock (see page 30)
   or water

a few drops of sesame oil

1 Soak the dried mushrooms in a bowl of warm water for 30 minutes. Drain thoroughly on paper towels, reserving the soaking water for stock or soup. Squeeze the mushrooms to extract all of the moisture, then cut off and discard any hard stems and slice thinly.

2 Cut the fish into bite-size pieces, then place in a shallow dish and mix with a pinch of salt, the egg white, and Cornstarch Paste, turning the fish to coat well.

3 Heat the oil in a preheated wok. Add the fish pieces to the wok and deep-fry for 1 minute. Remove the fish pieces with a slotted spoon and leave to drain on paper towels.

4 Pour off the excess oil, leaving about 1 tablespoon in the wok. Add the ginger, scallions, and garlic to flavor the oil for a few seconds, then add the bell pepper, carrot, and bamboo shoots and stir-fry for 1 minute.

5 Add the sugar, soy sauce, wine, chile bean sauce, stock, and the remaining salt and bring to a boil. Add the fish pieces, stirring to coat with the sauce, and braise for 1 minute. Sprinkle with sesame oil and serve.

Tuna & Vegetable Stir-Fry

Fresh tuna is a dark, meaty fish and is now widely available at fresh fish counters. It lends itself perfectly to the rich flavors in this recipe.

NUTRITIONAL INFORMATION

Calories 245	Sugars 11g
Protein 30g	Fat 7g
Carbohydrate . . .14g	Saturates 1g

10 MINS   10 MINS

SERVES 4

I N G R E D I E N T S

8 oz/225 g carrots

1 onion

6 oz/175 g baby corn cobs

2 tbsp corn oil

1¾ cups snow peas

1 lb/450 g fresh tuna

2 tbsp fish sauce

1 tbsp palm sugar

finely grated zest and juice of 1 orange

2 tbsp sherry

1 tsp cornstarch

rice or noodles, to serve

1 Using a sharp knife, cut the carrots into thin sticks, slice the onion and halve the baby corn cobs.

2 Heat the corn oil in a large preheated wok or skillet.

3 Add the onion, carrots, snow peas, and baby corn cobs to the wok or skillet and stir-fry for 5 minutes.

4 Using a sharp knife, thinly slice the fresh tuna.

5 Add the tuna slices to the wok or skillet and stir-fry for 2–3 minutes, until the tuna turns opaque.

6 Mix together the fish sauce, palm sugar, orange zest and juice, sherry, and cornstarch.

7 Pour the mixture over the tuna and vegetables and cook for 2 minutes, until the juices thicken. Serve the stir-fry with rice or noodles.

VARIATION

Try using swordfish steaks instead of the tuna. Swordfish steaks are now widely available and are similar in texture to tuna.

Mullet with Ginger

Ginger is used widely in Chinese cooking for its strong, pungent flavor.
Although fresh ginger is best, ground ginger may be used instead.

NUTRITIONAL INFORMATION

Calories	...... .195	Sugars	....6g
Protein	.... .31g	Fat	....3g
Carbohydrate	....9g	Saturates	.... .0g

10 MINS   15 MINS

SERVES 4

INGREDIENTS

1 whole mullet, cleaned and scaled

2 scallions, chopped

1 tsp grated fresh gingerroot

½ cup garlic wine vinegar

½ cup light soy sauce

3 tsp superfine sugar

dash of chile sauce

½ cup fish stock

1 green bell pepper, seeded and
   thinly sliced

1 large tomato, skinned, seeded, and cut
   into thin strips

salt and pepper

sliced tomato, to garnish

1 Rinse the fish inside and out and pat dry with paper towels.

2 Make 3 diagonal slits in the flesh on each side of the fish. Season the fish with salt and pepper inside and out, according to taste.

3 Place the fish on a heatproof plate and scatter the chopped scallions and grated ginger over the top. Cover and steam for 10 minutes, until the fish is cooked through.

4 Meanwhile, place the garlic wine vinegar, light soy sauce, superfine sugar, chile sauce, fish stock, bell pepper, and tomato in a pan and bring to a boil, stirring occasionally.

5 Cook the sauce over high heat until the sauce has slightly reduced and thickened.

6 Remove the fish from the steamer and transfer to a warm serving dish. Pour the sauce over the fish, then garnish with tomato slices and serve immediately.

VARIATION

Use fillets of fish for this
recipe if preferred, and reduce
the cooking time to 5–7 minutes.

Squid with Oyster Sauce

Squid is a delicious fish, which if prepared and cooked correctly, is a fast-cooking, attractive, and tasty ingredient.

NUTRITIONAL INFORMATION

Calories 320	Sugars 1g	
Protein 18g	Fat 26g	
Carbohydrate 2g	Saturates 3g	

5 MINS   15 MINS

SERVES 4

I N G R E D I E N T S

1 lb/450 g squid

⅔ cup vegetable oil

½–inch/1–cm piece fresh gingerroot, grated

2 oz/55 g snow peas

5 tbsp hot fish stock

red bell pepper triangles, to garnish

S A U C E

1 tbsp oyster sauce

1 tbsp light soy sauce

pinch of superfine sugar

1 garlic clove, crushed

1 To prepare the squid, cut down the center of the body lengthwise. Flatten the squid out, inside uppermost, and score a lattice design deep into the flesh, using a sharp knife.

2 To make the sauce, combine the oyster sauce, soy sauce, sugar, and garlic in a small bowl. Stir to dissolve the sugar and set aside until required.

3 Heat the oil in a preheated wok until almost smoking. Lower the heat slightly, then add the squid and stir-fry until they curl up. Remove with a slotted spoon and drain thoroughly on absorbent paper towels.

4 Pour off all but 2 tablespoons of the oil and return the wok to the heat. Add the ginger and snow peas and stir-fry for 1 minute.

5 Return the squid to the wok and pour in the sauce and hot fish stock. Leave to simmer for 3 minutes until thickened. Transfer to a warm serving dish, then garnish with bell pepper triangles and serve immediately.

COOK'S TIP

Take care not to overcook the squid, otherwise it will be rubbery and unappetizing.

Shrimp Omelet

This really is a meal in minutes, combining many Chinese ingredients for a truly tasty dish.

NUTRITIONAL INFORMATION

Calories	.270	Sugars	.1g
Protein	.30g	Fat	.15g
Carbohydrate	.3g	Saturates	.3g

5 MINS   10 MINS

SERVES 4

INGREDIENTS

2 tbsp corn oil

4 scallions

12 oz/350 g peeled shrimp

⅔ cup bean sprouts

1 tsp cornstarch

1 tbsp light soy sauce

6 eggs

3 tbsp cold water

1 Heat the corn oil in a large preheated wok or skillet.

2 Using a sharp knife, trim the scallions and cut into slices.

3 Add the shrimp, scallions, and bean sprouts to the wok and stir-fry for 2 minutes.

4 In a small bowl, mix together the cornstarch and soy sauce until well combined.

5 In a separate bowl, beat the eggs with the water, using a metal fork, and then blend with the cornstarch and soy mixture.

6 Add the egg mixture to the wok and cook for 5–6 minutes, until the mixture sets.

7 Transfer the omelet to a warm serving plate and cut into quarters to serve.

COOK'S TIP

It is important to use fresh bean sprouts for this dish as the canned ones don't have the necessary crunchy texture.

Spiced Scallops

Scallops are available both fresh and frozen. Make sure they are completely defrosted before cooking.

NUTRITIONAL INFORMATION

Calories 276   Sugar 6g
Protein ....25g   Fat 15g
Carbohydrate ....8g   Saturates 2g

10 MINS   10 MINS

SERVES 4

I N G R E D I E N T S

12 large scallops with coral attached,
  defrosted if frozen, or 12 oz/
  350 g small scallops without
  coral, defrosted

4 tbsp corn oil

4–6 scallions, thinly sliced diagonally

1 garlic clove, crushed

1-inch/2.5-cm fresh gingerroot,
  finely chopped

2½ cups snow peas

generous 2 cups sliced white or closed-cup
  mushrooms

2 tbsp sherry

2 tbsp soy sauce

1 tbsp clear honey

¼ tsp ground allspice

salt and pepper

1 tbsp sesame seeds, toasted

1 Wash and dry the scallops, discarding any black pieces and detach the corals, if using.

2 Slice each scallop into 3–4 pieces and if the corals are large, halve them.

3 Heat 2 tablespoons of the corn oil in a preheated wok or large, heavy-based skillet, swirling it around until really hot.

4 Add the scallions, garlic, and ginger to the wok or skillet and stir-fry for 1 minute.

5 Add the snow peas to the wok and continue to cook for an additional 2-3 minutes, stirring continuously. Remove to a bowl and set aside.

6 Add the remaining corn oil to the wok and when really hot add the scallops and corals and stir-fry for a couple of minutes.

7 Add the mushrooms and continue to cook for an additional minute or so.

8 Add the sherry, soy sauce, honey, and allspice to the wok, with salt and pepper to taste. Mix thoroughly, then return the snow pea mixture to the wok.

9 Season well with salt and pepper and toss together over high heat for a minute or so until piping hot. Serve the scallops and vegetables immediately, sprinkled with sesame seeds.

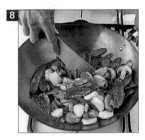

Szechuan Shrimp

Raw shrimp should be used if possible, otherwise add the ready-cooked shrimp at the beginning of step 3.

NUTRITIONAL INFORMATION

Calories	.315	Sugars	.1g
Protein	16g	Fat	.27g
Carbohydrate	.3g	Saturates	.3g

3½ HOURS   10 MINS

SERVES 4

INGREDIENTS

9–10½ oz/250–300 g raw jumbo shrimp

pinch of salt

½ egg white, lightly beaten

1 tsp Cornstarch Paste (see page 31)

2½ cups vegetable oil

fresh cilantro leaves, to garnish

SAUCE

1 tsp finely chopped fresh gingerroot

2 scallions, finely
    chopped

1 garlic clove, finely chopped

3–4 small dried red chiles, seeded and
    chopped

1 tbsp light soy sauce

1 tsp rice wine or dry sherry

1 tbsp tomato paste

1 tbsp oyster sauce

2–3 tbsp Chinese Stock (see page 30) or
    water

a few drops sesame oil

1 Peel the raw shrimp, then mix with the salt, egg white, and Cornstarch Paste until the shrimp are well coated.

2 Heat the oil in a preheated wok or large skillet until it is smoking, then deep-fry the shrimp in hot oil for 1 minute. Remove with a slotted spoon and drain on paper towels.

3 Pour off the oil, leaving about 1 tablespoon in the wok. Add all the ingredients for the sauce, in the order listed, then bring to a boil and stir until smooth and well blended.

4 Add the shrimp to the sauce and stir until well blended.

5 Serve the shrimp garnished with fresh cilantro leaves.

Squid with Black Bean Sauce

Squid really is wonderful if quickly cooked as in this recipe, and contrary to popular belief, it is not tough and rubbery unless it is overcooked.

NUTRITIONAL INFORMATION

Calories	180	Sugars	.........2g
Protein	........19g	Fat	...........7g
Carbohydrate	...10g	Saturates	.......1g

5 MINS   20 MINS

SERVES 4

I N G R E D I E N T S

1 lb/450 g squid rings

2 tbsp all-purpose flour

½ tsp salt

1 green bell pepper, seeded

2 tbsp peanut oil

1 red onion, sliced

5¾ oz/160 g jar black bean sauce

1 Rinse the squid rings under cold running water and pat dry thoroughly with absorbent paper towels.

2 Mix the all-purpose flour and salt in a bowl. Add the squid rings and toss until they are evenly coated.

3 Using a sharp knife, slice the bell pepper into thin strips.

4 Heat the peanut oil in a large preheated wok or heavy-based skillet, swirling the oil around the base of the wok until it is really hot.

5 Add the bell pepper slices and red onion to the wok or skillet and stir-fry for 2 minutes, or until the vegetables are just beginning to soften.

6 Add the squid rings to the wok or skillet and cook for an additional 5 minutes, until the squid is cooked through. Be careful not to overcook the squid.

7 Add the black bean sauce to the wok and heat through until the juices are bubbling. Transfer the squid stir-fry to warm serving bowls and serve immediately.

COOK'S TIP

Serve this recipe with fried rice or noodles tossed in soy sauce, if you wish.

Seared Scallops

Scallops have a terrific, subtle flavor that is complemented in this dish by the buttery sauce.

NUTRITIONAL INFORMATION

Calories	272	Sugars	.........0g
Protein	........28g	Fat	..........17g
Carbohydrate	....2g	Saturates	.......8g

5 MINS   10 MINS

SERVES 4

INGREDIENTS

1 lb/450 g fresh scallops, without roe, or the same amount of frozen scallops, defrosted thoroughly

6 scallions

2 tbsp vegetable oil

1 green chile, seeded and sliced

3 tbsp sweet soy sauce

2 tbsp butter, cubed

1 Rinse the scallops thoroughly under cold running water, then drain and pat the scallops dry with absorbent paper towels.

2 Using a sharp knife, slice each scallop in half horizontally.

3 Using a sharp knife, trim and slice the scallions.

4 Heat the vegetable oil in a large preheated wok or heavy-based skillet, swirling the oil around the base of the wok until it is really hot.

5 Add the sliced green chile, scallions and scallops to the wok and stir-fry over high heat for 4–5 minutes, until the scallops are just cooked through. If using frozen scallops, be sure not to overcook them as they will easily disintegrate.

6 Add the soy sauce and butter to the scallop stir-fry and heat through until the butter melts.

7 Transfer to warm serving bowls and serve hot.

COOK'S TIP

If you buy scallops on the shell, slide a knife underneath the membrane to loosen it and cut off the tough muscle that holds the scallop to the shell. Discard the black stomach sac and intestinal vein.

Fish in Szechuan Hot Sauce

This is a classic Szechuan recipe, in which the fish is quickly fried and served with a characteristic sauce.

NUTRITIONAL INFORMATION

Calories	.470	Sugar	.3g
Protein	.45g	Fat	.29g
Carbohydrate	.7g	Saturates	.4g

3¾ HOURS   15 MINS

SERVES 4

INGREDIENTS

1 carp, bream, sea bass, trout, grouper or gray mullet, about 1 lb 10 oz/750g, gutted

1 tbsp light soy sauce

1 tbsp Chinese rice wine or dry sherry

vegetable oil, for deep-frying

flat-leaf parsley or cilantro sprigs, to garnish

SAUCE

2 garlic cloves, finely chopped

2–3 scallions, finely chopped

1 tsp finely chopped fresh gingerroot

2 tbsp chile bean sauce

1 tbsp tomato paste

2 tsp sugar

1 tbsp rice vinegar

½ cup Chinese Stock (see page 30) or water

1 tbsp Cornstarch Paste (see page 31)

½ tsp sesame oil

3 Rub the fish with the soy sauce and rice wine on both sides. Transfer the fish to a plate, then cover with plastic wrap and leave to marinate in the refrigerator for 10-15 minutes.

4 Heat the oil in a preheated wok or large skillet until smoking.

5 Deep-fry the fish in the hot oil for 3-4 minutes on both sides, or until golden brown.

6 Pour off the oil, leaving about 1 tablespoon in the wok. Push the fish to one side of the wok and add the garlic, white parts of the scallions, ginger, chile bean sauce, tomato paste, sugar, vinegar, and Chinese Stock.

7 Bring the mixture in the wok to a boil and braise the fish in the sauce for 4–5 minutes, turning it over once.

8 Add the green parts of the scallions and stir in the Cornstarch Paste to thicken the sauce.

9 Sprinkle with sesame oil and serve immediately, garnished with fresh parsley or cilantro.

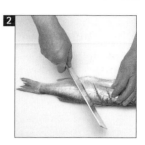

1 Wash the fish and dry well on absorbent paper towels.

2 Score both sides of the fish to the bone with a sharp knife, making diagonal cuts at intervals of 1 inch/2.5 cm.

Shrimp with Vegetables

This colorful and delicious dish is cooked with vegetables: vary them according to seasonal availability.

NUTRITIONAL INFORMATION

Calories	298	Sugars	.........1g
Protein	........13g	Fat	..........26g
Carbohydrate	....3g	Saturates	.......3g

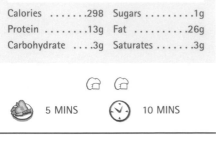

5 MINS   10 MINS

SERVES 4

I N G R E D I E N T S

½ cup snow peas

½ small carrot

2 oz/55 g baby corn cobs

½ cup straw mushrooms

6–9 oz/175–250 g raw jumbo shrimp, shelled

1 tsp salt

½ egg white, lightly beaten

1 tsp Cornstarch Paste (see page 31)

about 1¼ cups vegetable oil

1 scallion, cut into short sections

4 slices fresh gingerroot, peeled and finely chopped

½ tsp sugar

1 tbsp light soy sauce

1 tsp Chinese rice wine or dry sherry

a few drops sesame oil

lemon slices and chopped fresh chives, to garnish

1 Using a sharp knife, top and tail the snow peas; cut the carrot into the same size as the snow peas; halve the baby corn and straw mushrooms.

2 Mix the shrimp with a pinch of the salt, the egg white, and Cornstarch Paste until the shrimp are evenly coated.

3 Preheat a wok over high heat for 2-3 minutes, then add the vegetable oil and heat to medium-hot.

4 Add the shrimp to the wok, stirring to separate them. Remove the shrimp with a slotted spoon as soon as the color changes.

5 Pour off the oil, leaving about 1 tablespoon in the wok. Add the snow peas, carrot, corn cobs, mushrooms, and scallions.

6 Add the shrimp together with the ginger, sugar, soy sauce, and wine, blending well.

7 Sprinkle with the sesame oil and serve hot, garnished with lemon slices and chopped fresh chives.

Fish & Ginger Stir-Fry

This delicious and spicy recipe is a really quick fish dish, ideal for midweek family meals or light lunches at weekends.

NUTRITIONAL INFORMATION

Calories 280   Sugars 2g
Protein . . . . .31g   Fat 10g
Carbohydrate . . .17g   Saturates 2g

5 MINS   15 MINS

SERVES 4

INGREDIENTS

4 tbsp cornstarch

½ tsp ground ginger

1 lb 8 oz/675 g firm white fish fillets, skinned and cubed

3 tbsp peanut oil

1 inch/2.5 cm fresh gingerroot, grated

1 leek, thinly sliced

1 tbsp white wine vinegar

2 tbsp Chinese rice wine or dry sherry

3 tbsp dark soy sauce

1 tsp superfine sugar

2 tbsp lemon juice

finely shredded leek, to garnish

1 Mix the cornstarch and ground ginger in a bowl.

2 Add the cubes of fish, in batches, to the cornstarch mixture, turning to coat the fish thoroughly in the mixture.

3 Heat the peanut oil in a preheated wok or large, heavy-based skillet, swirling the oil around the base of the wok until it is really hot.

4 Add the grated fresh ginger and sliced leek to the wok or skillet and stir-fry for 1 minute.

5 Add the coated fish to the wok and cook for an additional 5 minutes, until browned, stirring to prevent the fish from sticking to the base of the wok.

6 Add the remaining ingredients and cook over low heat for 3–4 minutes, until the fish is cooked through.

7 Transfer the fish and ginger stir-fry to a serving dish and serve immediately.

VARIATION

Use any firm white fish which will hold its shape, such as cod, haddock, or monkfish.

Stir-Fried Cod with Mango

Fish and fruit are a classic combination, and in this recipe a tropical flavor is added which gives a great scented taste to the dish.

NUTRITIONAL INFORMATION

Calories	200	Sugars	........12g
Protein	........21g	Fat	...........7g
Carbohydrate	...14g	Saturates	.......1g

🥘 10 MINS   🕐 15 MINS

SERVES 4

I N G R E D I E N T S

6 oz/175 g carrots

2 tbsp vegetable oil

1 red onion, sliced

1 red bell pepper, seeded and sliced

1 green bell pepper, seeded and sliced

1 lb/450 g skinless cod fillet

1 ripe mango

1 tsp cornstarch

1 tbsp soy sauce

scant ½ cup tropical fruit juice

1 tbsp lime juice

1 tbsp chopped fresh cilantro, to garnish

1 Using a sharp knife, slice the carrots into thin sticks.

2 Heat the oil in a preheated wok and stir-fry the onion, carrots, and bell peppers for 5 minutes.

3 Using a sharp knife, cut the cod into small cubes. Peel the mango, then carefully remove the flesh from the center stone. Cut the flesh into thin slices.

4 Add the cod and mango to the wok and stir-fry for an additional 4–5 minutes, until the fish is cooked through. Be careful not to break the fish up.

5 Mix together the cornstarch, soy sauce, fruit juice, and lime juice. Pour the mixture into the wok and stir until the mixture bubbles and the juices thicken. Scatter with cilantro and serve immediately.

VARIATION

You can use papaya as an alternative to the mango, if you prefer.

Fish with Coconut & Basil

Fish curries are sensational and this is no exception. Red curry and coconut are fantastic flavors with the fried fish.

NUTRITIONAL INFORMATION

Calories	209	Sugars	........10g
Protein	........21g	Fat	...........8g
Carbohydrate	...15g	Saturates	.......1g

5 MINS   15 MINS

SERVES 4

I N G R E D I E N T S

2 tbsp vegetable oil

1 lb/450 g skinless cod fillet

scant ¼ cup seasoned flour

1 garlic clove, crushed

2 tbsp red curry paste

1 tbsp fish sauce

1¼ cups coconut milk

6 oz/175 g cherry tomatoes, halved

20 fresh basil leaves

fragrant rice, to serve

1 Heat the vegetable oil in a large preheated wok.

2 Using a sharp knife, cut the fish into large cubes, removing any bones with a pair of clean tweezers.

3 Place the seasoned flour in a bowl. Add the cubes of fish and mix until well coated.

4 Add the coated fish to the wok and stir-fry over high heat for 3–4 minutes, until the fish just begins to brown at the edges.

5 In a small bowl, mix together the garlic, curry paste, fish sauce, and coconut milk. Pour the mixture over the fish and bring to a boil.

6 Add the tomatoes to the mixture in the wok and leave to simmer for 5 minutes.

7 Roughly chop or tear the fresh basil leaves. Add the basil to the wok, then stir carefully to combine, taking care not to break up the cubes of fish.

8 Transfer to serving plates and serve hot with fragrant rice.

COOK'S TIP

Take care not to overcook the dish once the tomatoes are added, otherwise they will break down and the skins will come away.

Crispy Fried Squid

Squid tubes are classically used in Chinese cooking and are most attractive when presented as in the following recipe.

NUTRITIONAL INFORMATION	
Calories 156	Sugars 0g
Protein 17g	Fat 6g
Carbohydrate 7g	Saturates 8g

10 MINS   10 MINS

SERVES 4

INGREDIENTS

1 lb/450 g squid, cleaned

4 tbsp cornstarch

1 tsp salt

1 tsp freshly ground black pepper

1 tsp chile flakes

peanut oil, for frying

dipping sauce, to serve

1 Using a sharp knife, remove the tentacles from the squid and trim. Slice the bodies down one side and open out to give a flat piece.

2 Score the flat pieces with a criss-cross pattern, then cut each piece into 4.

3 Mix together the cornstarch, salt, pepper, and chile flakes.

COOK'S TIP

Squid tubes may be purchased frozen if they are not available fresh. They are usually ready-cleaned and are easy to use. Ensure that they are completely defrosted before cooking.

4 Place the salt and pepper mixture in a large plastic bag. Add the squid pieces and shake the bag thoroughly to coat the squid in the flour mixture.

5 Heat about 2 inches/5 cm of peanut oil in a large preheated wok.

6 Add the squid pieces to the wok and stir-fry, in batches, for 2 minutes, until the squid pieces start to curl up.

Do not overcook, or the squid will become tough.

7 Remove the squid pieces with a slotted spoon, then transfer to absorbent paper towels and leave to drain thoroughly.

8 Transfer the fried squid pieces to serving plates and serve immediately with a dipping sauce.

Cantonese Shrimp

This shrimp dish is very simple and is ideal for supper or lunch when time is short.

NUTRITIONAL INFORMATION

Calories	460	Sugar	.........3g
Protein	........53g	Fat	24
Carbohydrate	....6g	Saturates	.......5g

🦐 🦐 🦐

10 MINS   20 MINS

SERVES 4

I N G R E D I E N T S

5 tbsp vegetable oil

4 garlic cloves, crushed

1 lb 8 oz/675 g raw shrimp, shelled and deveined

2–inch/5–cm piece fresh gingerroot, chopped

6 oz/175 g lean pork, diced

1 leek, sliced

3 eggs, beaten

shredded leek and red bell pepper matchsticks, to garnish

rice, to serve

S A U C E

2 tbsp Chinese rice wine or dry sherry

2 tbsp light soy sauce

2 tsp superfine sugar

⅔ cup fish stock

4½ tsp cornstarch

3 tbsp water

1 Heat 2 tablespoons of the vegetable oil in a preheated wok.

2 Add the garlic to the wok and stir-fry for 30 seconds.

3 Add the shrimp to the wok and stir-fry for 5 minutes, until they change

color. Remove the shrimp from the wok or skillet with a slotted spoon, set aside and keep warm.

4 Add the remaining oil to the wok and heat, swirling the oil around the base of the wok until it is really hot.

5 Add the ginger, diced pork, and leek to the wok and stir-fry over medium heat for 4-5 minutes, until the pork is lightly colored and sealed.

6 To make the sauce, add the rice wine, soy sauce, superfine sugar, and fish stock to the wok and stir to blend.

7 In a small bowl, blend the cornstarch with the water to form a smooth paste and stir it into the wok. Cook, stirring, until the sauce thickens and clears.

8 Return the shrimp to the wok and add the beaten eggs. Cook for 5–6 minutes, gently stirring occasionally, until the eggs set.

9 Transfer to a warm serving dish, then garnish with shredded leek and bell pepper matchsticks and serve immediately with rice.

Gingered Monkfish

This dish is a real treat and is perfect for special occasions. Monkfish has a delicate flavor that is ideal with asparagus, chile, and ginger.

NUTRITIONAL INFORMATION

Calories	133	Sugars	.........0g
Protein	........21g	Fat	...........5g
Carbohydrate	....1g	Saturates	.......1g

5 MINS   10 MINS

SERVES 4

INGREDIENTS

1 lb/450 g monkfish

1 tbsp grated fresh gingerroot

2 tbsp sweet chile sauce

1 tbsp corn oil

3½ oz/100 g fine asparagus

3 scallions, sliced

1 tsp sesame oil

1 Using a sharp knife, slice the monkfish into thin flat rounds. Set aside until required.

2 Mix together the grated gingerroot and the sweet chile sauce in a small bowl, stirring until thoroughly blended. Brush the ginger and chile sauce mixture over all sides of the monkfish pieces, using a pastry brush.

3 Heat the corn oil in a large preheated wok or heavy-based skillet.

4 Add the monkfish pieces, asparagus and chopped scallions to the wok or skillet and cook for 5 minutes, stirring gently so the fish pieces do not break up.

5 Remove the wok or skillet from the heat, then drizzle the sesame oil over the stir-fry and toss well to combine.

6 Transfer the stir-fried gingered monkfish to warm serving plates and serve immediately.

COOK'S TIP

Monkfish is quite expensive, but it is well worth using as it has a wonderful flavor and texture. At a push, you could use cubes of chunky cod fillet instead.

Mussels with Lettuce

Mussels require careful preparation but very little cooking. They are available fresh or in vacuum packs when out of season.

NUTRITIONAL INFORMATION

Calories . . . . .205 Sugars 0.3g
Protein . . . . .31g Fat 9g
Carbohydrate . . . .1g Saturates 4g

15 MINS   5 MINS

SERVES 4

INGREDIENTS

2 lb 4 oz/1 kg mussels in their shells, scrubbed

2 stalks lemon grass

1 iceberg lettuce

2 tbsp lemon juice

scant ½ cup water

2 tbsp butter

finely grated zest of 1 lemon

2 tbsp oyster sauce

1 Place the scrubbed mussels in a large pan.

2 Using a sharp knife, thinly slice the lemon grass and shred the lettuce.

3 Add the lemon grass, lemon juice, and water to the pan of mussels, cover with a tight-fitting lid and cook for 5 minutes, until the mussels have opened. Discard any that do not open.

4 Carefully remove the cooked mussels from their shells, using a fork and set aside until required.

5 Heat the butter in a large preheated wok or skillet. Add the lettuce and finely grated lemon zest to the wok or skillet and stir-fry for 2 minutes, until the lettuce begins to wilt.

6 Add the oyster sauce to the wok and heat through, stirring well until the sauce is thoroughly incorporated in the mixture. Stir in the reserved mussels and heat through.

7 Transfer the mixture in the wok to a warm serving dish and then serve immediately.

COOK'S TIP

When using fresh mussels, be sure to discard any opened mussels before scrubbing and any unopened mussels after cooking.

Seafood Omelet

This delicious omelet is filled with a mixture of fresh vegetables, sliced squid and shrimp.

NUTRITIONAL INFORMATION

Calories	.216	Sugars	.2g
Protein	.20g	Fat	.13g
Carbohydrate	.4g	Saturates	.4g

5 MINS   10 MINS

SERVES 4

INGREDIENTS

4 eggs

3 tbsp milk

1 tbsp fish sauce or light soy sauce

1 tbsp sesame oil

3 shallots, sliced finely

1 small red bell pepper, cored, seeded, and sliced very finely

1 small leek, trimmed and cut into short, thin sticks

4½ oz/125 g squid rings

4½ oz/125 g cooked shelled shrimp

1 tbsp chopped fresh basil

1 tbsp butter

salt and pepper

sprigs of fresh basil, to garnish

VARIATIONS

Chopped cooked chicken makes a delicious alternative to the squid.

Use fresh cilantro instead of the basil, if desired.

1 Beat the eggs, milk and fish sauce or soy sauce together.

2 Heat the sesame oil in a wok or large skillet and add the shallots, bell pepper and leek. Stir-fry briskly for 2–3 minutes.

3 Add the squid rings, shrimp and chopped basil to the wok or skillet. Stir-fry for an additional 2–3 minutes, until the squid looks opaque.

4 Season the mixture in the wok with salt and pepper to taste. Transfer to a warmed plate and keep warm until required.

5 Melt the butter in a large omelette pan or skillet and add the beaten egg mixture. Cook over a medium-high heat until just set.

6 Spoon the vegetable and seafood mixture in a line down the middle of the omelette, then fold each side of the omelette over.

7 Transfer the omelette to a warmed serving dish and cut into 4 portions. Garnish with sprigs of fresh basil and serve at once.

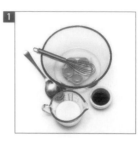

Mussels with Lemon Grass

Give fresh mussels a Far-Eastern flavor by using some Kaffir lime leaves, garlic and lemon grass in the stock used for steaming them.

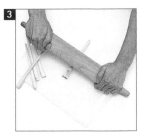

NUTRITIONAL INFORMATION

Calories 194	Sugar 0g
Protein 33g	Fat 7g
Carbohydrate 1g	Saturates 1g

10 MINS   10 MINS

SERVES 4

I N G R E D I E N T S

1 lb 10 oz/750 g live mussels

1 tbsp sesame oil

3 shallots, chopped finely

2 garlic cloves, chopped finely

1 stalk lemon grass

2 Kaffir lime leaves

2 tbsp chopped fresh cilantro

finely grated rind of 1 lime

2 tbsp lime juice

1¼ cups hot vegetable stock

crusty bread, to serve

fresh cilantro and lime wedges, to garnish

1 Using a small sharp knife, scrape the beards off the mussels under cold running water. Scrub them well, discarding any that are damaged or remain open when tapped. Keep rinsing until there is no trace of sand.

2 Heat the sesame oil in a large pan and fry the shallots and garlic gently for about 2 minutes, until they are just softened.

3 Bruise the lemon grass, using a meat mallet or rolling pin, and add to the pan with the Kaffir lime leaves, cilantro, lime rind and juice, mussels and stock. Put the lid on the pan and cook over a moderate heat for 3–5 minutes. Shake the pan from time to time.

4 Lift the mussels out into 4 warmed soup plates, discarding any that remain shut. Boil the remaining liquid rapidly to reduce slightly. Remove the lemon grass and lime leaves, then pour the liquid over the mussels.

5 Garnish with cilantro and lime wedges, and serve at once.

COOK'S TIP

Mussels are now farmed, so they should be available from good fishmongers throughout the year.

Mussels in Black Bean Sauce

This dish looks so impressive, the combination of colors making it look almost too good to eat.

NUTRITIONAL INFORMATION

Calories	174	Sugars 4g
Protein	........19g	Fat 8g
Carbohydrate	....6g	Saturates 1g

5 MINS   10 MINS

SERVES 4

INGREDIENTS

12 oz/350 g leeks

12 oz/350 g cooked green-lipped mussels, shelled

1 tsp cumin seeds

2 tbsp vegetable oil

2 garlic cloves, crushed

1 red bell pepper, seeded and sliced

½ cup canned bamboo shoots, drained

6 oz/175 g baby spinach

5¾ oz/160 g jar black bean sauce

1 Using a sharp knife, trim the leeks and shred them.

2 Place the cooked green-lipped mussels in a large bowl, then sprinkle with the cumin seeds and toss well to coat all over. Set aside until required.

3 Heat the vegetable oil in a preheated wok, swirling the oil around the base of the wok until it is really hot.

4 Add the shredded leeks, garlic, and sliced red bell pepper to the wok and stir-fry for 5 minutes, until the vegetables are tender.

5 Add the bamboo shoots, baby spinach leaves, and cooked green-lipped mussels to the wok and stir-fry for 2 minutes.

6 Pour the black bean sauce over the ingredients in the wok, then toss well to coat all the ingredients in the sauce and leave to simmer for a few seconds, stirring occasionally.

7 Transfer the stir-fry to warm serving bowls and serve immediately.

COOK'S TIP

If fresh green-lipped mussels are not available, they can be bought shelled in cans and jars from most large supermarkets.

Fish with Ginger Butter

Whole mackerel or trout are stuffed with herbs and wrapped in baking parchment, then baked and served drizzled with a fresh ginger butter.

NUTRITIONAL INFORMATION

Calories 328	Sugar 0g
Protein 24g	Fat 25g
Carbohydrate 1g	Saturates 13g

10 MINS · 30 MINS

SERVES 4

INGREDIENTS

4 x 9 oz/250 g whole trout or mackerel, gutted

4 tbsp chopped fresh cilantro

5 garlic cloves, crushed

2 tsp grated lemon or lime zest

2 tsp vegetable oil

banana leaves, for wrapping (optional)

generous ⅓ cup butter

1 tbsp grated fresh gingerroot

1 tbsp light soy sauce

salt and pepper

cilantro sprigs and lemon or lime wedges, to garnish

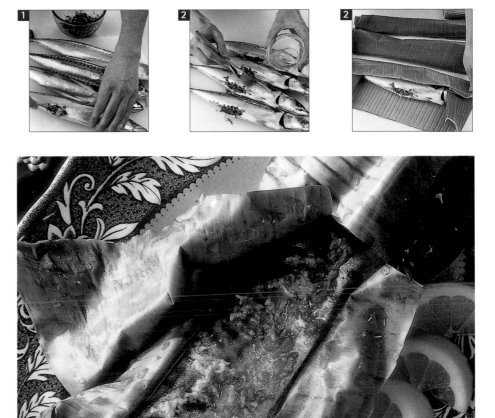

1 Wash and dry the fish. Mix the cilantro with the garlic, lemon zest, and salt and pepper to taste. Spoon into the fish cavities.

2 Brush the fish with a little oil and season well, then place each fish on a double thickness sheet of baking parchment or foil and wrap up well to enclose. Alternatively, wrap in banana leaves (see right).

3 Place on a cookie sheet and bake in a preheated oven for 25 minutes, until the flesh will flake easily.

4 Meanwhile, melt the butter in a small pan. Add the ginger and mix well.

5 Stir the light soy sauce into the pan.

6 To serve, unwrap the fish packages, then drizzle over the ginger butter and garnish with cilantro and lemon wedges.

COOK'S TIP

For a really authentic touch, wrap the fish in banana leaves, which can be ordered from specialist Asian supermarkets. They are not edible, but impart a delicate flavor to the fish.

Chile Shrimp

Large shrimp are marinated in a chile mixture, then stir-fried with cashews. Serve with a fluffy rice and braised vegetables.

NUTRITIONAL INFORMATION

Calories	435	Sugars	.........2g
Protein	........4.2g	Fat	23
Carbohydrate	...10g	Saturates	.......4g

2¼ HOURS   5 MINS

SERVES 4

I N G R E D I E N T S

5 tbsp soy sauce

5 tbsp dry sherry

3 dried red chiles, seeded and chopped

2 garlic cloves, crushed

2 tsp grated fresh gingerroot

5 tbsp water

1 lb 6 oz/625 g shelled jumbo shrimp

1 large bunch scallions, chopped

⅔ cup salted cashew nuts

3 tbsp vegetable oil

2 tsp cornstarch

1 Mix the soy sauce, sherry, chiles, garlic, ginger, and water in a bowl.

2 Add the jumbo shrimp, scallions, and cashews and mix well. Cover tightly and leave to marinate for at least 2 hours, stirring occasionally.

3 Heat the oil in a large wok. Remove the shrimp, scallions, and cashews from the marinade with a slotted spoon and add to the wok, reserving the marinade. Stir-fry over high heat for 1-2 minutes.

4 Mix the reserved marinade with the cornstarch, then add to the wok and stir-fry for 30 seconds, until the marinade forms a slightly thickened shiny glaze over the shrimp mixture. Serve immediately.

COOK'S TIP

For an attractive presentation, serve this dish on mixed wild rice and basmati rice. Start cooking the wild rice in boiling water. After 10 minutes, add the basmati rice or other rice and continue boiling until all grains are tender. Drain well and adjust the seasoning.

Shrimp Stir-Fry

A very quick and tasty stir-fry using shrimp and cucumber, cooked with lemon grass, chile, and ginger.

NUTRITIONAL INFORMATION

Calories	178	Sugars	.........1g
Protein	........22g	Fat	...........7g
Carbohydrate	....3g	Saturates	.......1g

5 MINS   5 MINS

SERVES 4

INGREDIENTS

½ cucumber

2 tbsp corn oil

6 scallions, halved lengthwise and cut into 1½-inch/4-cm lengths

1 stalk lemon grass, sliced thinly

1 garlic clove, chopped

1 tsp chopped fresh red chile

2 cups oyster mushrooms

1 tsp chopped fresh gingerroot

12 oz/350 g cooked shelled shrimp

2 tsp cornstarch

2 tbsp water

1 tbsp dark soy sauce

½ tsp fish sauce

2 tbsp dry sherry or rice wine

boiled rice, to serve

1 Cut the cucumber into strips about ¼ x 1¾ inches/5 mm x 4 cm.

2 Heat the corn oil in a wok or large skillet.

3 Add the scallions, cucumber, lemon grass, garlic, chile, oyster mushrooms, and ginger to the wok or skillet and stir-fry for 2 minutes.

4 Add the shrimp and stir-fry for an additional minute.

5 Mix together the cornstarch, water, soy sauce, and fish sauce until smooth.

6 Stir the cornstarch mixture and sherry into the wok and heat through, stirring, until the sauce has thickened. Serve with rice.

COOK'S TIP

The white part of the lemon grass stem can be thinly sliced and left in the cooked dish. If using the whole stem, remove it before serving. You can buy lemon grass chopped and dried, or preserved in jars, but neither has the fragrance or delicacy of the fresh variety.

Hot & Sweet Shrimp

Uncooked shrimp are speared on skewers and brushed with a sesame oil, lime juice, and cilantro baste and then grilled.

NUTRITIONAL INFORMATION

Calories 239   Sugars 8g
Protein . . . . .28g   Fat 11g
Carbohydrate . . . .8g   Saturates 2g

1 HOUR   10 MINS

SERVES 4

INGREDIENTS

wooden skewers soaked in warm water for 20 minutes

1 lb 2 oz/500 g uncooked shrimp

3 tbsp sesame oil

2 tbsp lime juice

1 tbsp chopped fresh cilantro

SAUCE

4 tbsp light malt vinegar

2 tbsp fish sauce or light soy sauce

2 tbsp water

2 tbsp light muscovado sugar

2 garlic cloves, crushed

2 tsp grated fresh gingerroot

1 red chile, seeded and chopped finely

2 tbsp chopped fresh cilantro

salt

1 Peel the shrimp, leaving the tails intact. Remove the vein that runs along the back of each one, then skewer the shrimp on to the wooden skewers.

2 Mix together the sesame oil, lime juice, and chopped cilantro in a shallow bowl. Lay the skewered shrimp in this mixture. Cover and chill in the refrigerator for 30 minutes, turning once, so that the shrimp absorb the marinade.

3 Meanwhile, make the sauce. Heat the light malt vinegar, fish sauce or soy sauce, water, sugar, and salt to taste until boiling. Remove from the heat and leave to cool.

4 Mix together the crushed garlic, grated ginger, red chile, and cilantro in a small serving bowl. Add the cooled vinegar mixture and stir until well combined.

5 Place the shrimp on a foil-lined broiler pan under a preheated broiler for 6 minutes, turning once and basting often with the marinade, until cooked.

6 Transfer to a warmed serving platter and serve with the dipping sauce.

Crab with Napa Cabbage

The delicate flavor of Napa cabbage and crabmeat are enhanced by the coconut milk in this recipe.

NUTRITIONAL INFORMATION

Calories	109	Sugars	1g
Protein	11g	Fat	6g
Carbohydrate	2g	Saturates	1g

5 MINS   10 MINS

SERVES 4

INGREDIENTS

2 cups shiitake mushrooms

2 tbsp vegetable oil

2 garlic cloves, crushed

6 scallions, sliccd

1 head Napa cabbage, shredded

1 tbsp mild curry paste

6 tbsp coconut milk

7 oz/200 g canned white crabmeat, drained

1 tsp chile flakes

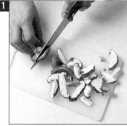

1 Using a sharp knife, cut the mushrooms into slices.

2 Heat the vegetable oil in a large preheated wok or heavy-based skillet.

3 Add the mushrooms and garlic to the wok or skillet and stir-fry for 3 minutes, until the mushrooms have softened.

4 Add the scallions and shredded Napa cabbage to the wok and stir-fry until the leaves have wilted.

5 Mix together the mild curry paste and coconut milk in a small bowl.

6 Add the curry paste and coconut milk mixture to the wok, together with the crabmeat and chile flakes. Mix together until well combined.

7 Heat the mixture in the wok until the juices start to bubble.

8 Transfer the crab and vegetable stir-fry to warm serving bowls and serve.

COOK'S TIP

Shiitake mushrooms are now readily available in the fresh vegetable section of most large supermarkets.

Coconut Shrimp

Fan-tail shrimp make any meal a special occasion, especially when cooked in such a delicious crispy coating.

NUTRITIONAL INFORMATION

Calories	236	Sugars	.........1g
Protein	........27g	Fat	..........13g
Carbohydrate	....3g	Saturates	.......7g

5 MINS   10 MINS

SERVES 4

INGREDIENTS

½ cup dry unsweetened coconut

½ cup fresh white bread crumbs

1 tsp Chinese five-spice powder

½ tsp salt

finely grated zest of 1 lime

1 egg white

1 lb/450 g fan-tail shrimp

corn oil, for frying

lemon wedges, to garnish

soy or chile sauce, to serve

1 Mix together the shredded coconut, white bread crumbs, Chinese five-spice powder, salt, and finely grated lime zest in a bowl.

2 Lightly whisk the egg white in a separate bowl.

3 Rinse the shrimp under cold running water, and pat dry with paper towels.

4 Dip the shrimp into the egg white, then into the coconut and bread crumb mixture, so that they are evenly coated.

5 Heat about 2 inches/5 cm of corn oil in a large preheated wok.

6 Add the shrimp to the wok and stir-fry for 5 minutes, until golden and crispy.

7 Remove the shrimp with a slotted spoon and leave to drain on paper towels.

8 Transfer the coconut shrimp to warm serving dishes and garnish with lemon wedges. Serve immediately with a soy or chile sauce.

COOK'S TIP

Chinese five-spice powder is a mixture of star anise, fennel seeds, cloves, cinnamon bark, and Szechuan pepper. It is very pungent, so should be used sparingly. It will keep indefinitely in an airtight container

Crabmeat Cakes

Make these tasty crabmeat cakes to serve as a snack or appetizer, or as an accompaniment to a main meal.

NUTRITIONAL INFORMATION

Calories	262	Sugars	.........4g
Protein	........13g	Fat	..........17g
Carbohydrate	...14g	Saturates	.......3g

20 MINS · 55 MINS

SERVES 4

INGREDIENTS

scant ½ cup cup long-grain rice

1 tbsp sesame oil

1 small onion, chopped finely

1 large garlic clove, crushed

2 tbsp chopped fresh cilantro

7 oz/200 g canned crabmeat, drained

1 tbsp fish sauce or light soy sauce

1 cup coconut milk

2 eggs

4 tbsp vegetable oil

salt and pepper

sliced scallions, to garnish

1 Cook the rice in plenty of boiling, lightly salted water until just tender, about 12 minutes. Rinse with cold water and drain well.

2 Heat the sesame oil in a small skillet and cook the onion and garlic gently for 5 minutes, until softened and golden brown.

3 Combine the rice, onion, garlic, cilantro, crabmeat, fish sauce, and coconut milk. Season. Beat the eggs and add to the mixture. Divide the mixture between 8 greased ramekin dishes or teacups and place them in a baking dish

or roasting pan with enough warm water to come halfway up their sides. Place in a preheated oven at 350°F/180°C for 25 minutes, until set. Leave to cool.

4 Turn the crab cakes out of the ramekin dishes . Heat the oil in a wok or skillet and fry the crab cakes in the oil until golden brown. Drain on paper towels, then garnish and serve.

COOK'S TIP

If you want, you can prepare these crab cakes up to the point where they have been baked. Cool them, then cover and chill, ready for frying when needed.

Vegetables

The Chinese eat far more vegetables than meat or poultry. This is partly because of widespread poverty, which means that many people cannot afford meat, and also because of religious reasons. Vegetables are used extensively in all meals; even meat and poultry dishes include some kind of vegetable as a supplementary ingredient in order to give

the dish a harmonious balance of color, aroma, flavor, and texture. The Chinese like their vegetables crisp so they are cooked for only a very short time, thus preserving their bright colors as well as valuable nutrients. As with most ingredients in Chinese cooking, it is important to choose the freshest vegetables available to ensure maximum flavor and crispness. As well as side dishes, this chapter also contains deliciously filling main meals.

Green Bean Stir-Fry

These beans are simply cooked in a spicy, hot sauce for a tasty and very easy recipe.

NUTRITIONAL INFORMATION

Calories 86	Sugars 4g
Protein 2g	Fat 6g
Carbohydrates 6g	Saturates 1g

🂠 🂠

 5 MINS   🕐 5 MINS

SERVES 4

I N G R E D I E N T S

1 lb/450 g thin green beans

2 fresh red chiles

2 tbsp peanut oil

½ tsp ground star anise

1 garlic clove, crushed

2 tbsp light soy sauce

2 tsp clear honey

½ tsp sesame oil

1 Using a sharp knife, cut the green beans in half.

2 Slice the fresh chiles, removing the seeds first if you prefer a milder dish.

3 Heat the peanut oil in a preheated wok or large, heavy-based skillet until the oil is almost smoking.

4 Lower the heat slightly, then add the halved green beans to the wok and stir-fry for 1 minute.

5 Add the sliced red chiles, star anise, and garlic to the wok and stir-fry for an additional 30 seconds.

6 Mix together the soy sauce, honey, and sesame oil in a small bowl.

7 Stir the sauce mixture into the wok. Cook for 2 minutes, tossing the beans to ensure that they are thoroughly coated in the sauce.

8 Transfer the mixture in the wok or pan to a warm serving dish and serve immediately.

VARIATION

This recipe is surprisingly delicious made with Brussels sprouts instead of green beans. Trim the sprouts, then shred them finely. Stir-fry the sprouts in hot oil for 2 minutes, then proceed with the recipe from step 4.

Bean Sprouts & Vegetables

This dish is served cold as a salad or appetizer and is very easy to make. It is a form of cold chop suey.

NUTRITIONAL INFORMATION

Calories . . . . .56 Sugars 5g
Protein . . . . .4g Fat 1g
Carbohydrate . . . .9g Saturates 0.2g

3¼ HOURS   0 MINS

SERVES 4

INGREDIENTS

1 lb/450 g bean sprouts

2 fresh red chiles, seeded and finely chopped

1 red bell pepper, seeded and thinly sliced

1 green bell pepper, seeded and thinly sliced

¼ cup water chestnuts, cut into fourths

1 celery stalk, sliced

Chinese roasted meats and noodles, to serve

MARINADE

3 tbsp rice wine vinegar

2 tbsp light soy sauce

2 tbsp chopped chives

1 garlic clove, crushed

pinch of Chinese curry powder

1 Place the bean sprouts, chopped red chiles, red and green bell peppers, water chestnuts, and celery in a large bowl and mix well to combine all the ingredients.

2 To make the marinade, mix together the rice wine vinegar, light soy sauce, chopped chives, crushed garlic, and Chinese curry powder in a bowl.

3 Pour the marinade over the prepared vegetables. Toss to mix the vegetables thoroughly in the marinade.

4 Cover the salad with plastic wrap and leave to chill in the refrigerator for at least 3 hours.

5 Drain the vegetables thoroughly, then transfer to a serving dish and serve with Chinese roasted meats or noodles.

COOK'S TIP

There are hundreds of varieties of chiles and it is not always possible to tell how hot they are going to be. As a general rule, dark green chiles are hotter than light green and red chiles. Thin, pointed chiles are usually hotter than fatter, blunter chiles.

Honey-Fried Napa Cabbage

Napa cabbage are rather similar to lettuce in that the leaves are delicate with a sweet flavor.

NUTRITIONAL INFORMATION

Calories	121	Sugars	....6g
Protein	....5g	Fat	....7g
Carbohydrate	...10g	Saturates	....1g

5 MINS   10 MINS

SERVES 4

INGREDIENTS

1 lb/450 g Napa cabbage

1 tbsp peanut oil

½-inch/1-cm piece fresh gingerroot, grated

2 garlic cloves, crushed

1 fresh red chile, sliced

1 tbsp Chinese rice wine or dry sherry

4½ tsp light soy sauce

1 tbsp clear honey

½ cup orange juice

1 tbsp sesame oil

2 tsp sesame seeds

orange zest, to garnish

COOK'S TIP

Single-flower honey has a better, more individual flavor than blended honey. Acacia honey is typically Chinese, but you could also try clover, lemon blossom, lime flower, or orange blossom.

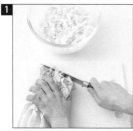  

1 Separate the Napa cabbage and shred them finely, using a sharp knife.

2 Heat the peanut oil in a preheated wok. Add the ginger, garlic, and chile to the wok and stir-fry the mixture for 30 seconds.

3 Add the Napa cabbage, Chinese rice wine, soy sauce, honey, and orange juice to the wok. Reduce the heat and leave to simmer for 5 minutes.

4 Add the sesame oil to the wok, then sprinkle the sesame seeds on top and mix to combine.

5 Transfer to a warm serving dish Garnish with the orange zest and serve immediately.

Vegetable Sesame Stir-Fry

Sesame seeds add a delicious flavor to any recipe and are particularly good with vegetables in this soy and rice wine or sherry sauce.

NUTRITIONAL INFORMATION

Calories 118	Sugars 2g
Protein 3g	Fat 9g
Carbohydrate 5g	Saturates 1g

5 MINS   10 MINS

SERVES 4

I N G R E D I E N T S

2 tbsp vegetable oil

3 garlic cloves, crushed

1 tbsp sesame seeds,
    plus extra to garnish

2 celery stalks, sliced

2 baby corn cobs, sliced

½ cup white mushrooms

1 leek, sliced

1 zucchini, sliced

1 small red bell pepper, sliced

1 fresh green chile, sliced

2 oz/55 g Napa cabbage, shredded

rice or noodles, to serve

S A U C E

½ tsp Chinese curry powder

2 tbsp light soy sauce

1 tbsp Chinese rice wine or dry sherry

1 tsp sesame oil

1 tsp cornstarch

4 tbsp water

1 Heat the vegetable oil in a preheated wok or heavy-based skillet, swirling the oil around the base of the wok until it is almost smoking.

2 Lower the heat slightly, then add the garlic and sesame seeds and stir-fry for 30 seconds.

3 Add the celery, baby corn cobs, mushrooms, leek, zucchini, bell pepper, chile, and Napa cabbage and stir-fry for 4–5 minutes, until the vegetables are beginning to soften.

4 To make the sauce, mix together the Chinese curry powder, light soy sauce, Chinese rice wine, sesame oil, cornstarch, and water.

5 Stir the sauce mixture into the wok until well combined with the other ingredients.

6 Bring to a boil and cook, stirring constantly, until the sauce thickens and clears.

7 Cook for 1 minute, then spoon into a warm serving dish and garnish with sesame seeds. Serve the vegetable sesame stir-fry immediately with rice or noodles.

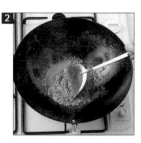

Bok Choy with Cashew Nuts

Plum sauce is readily available in jars and has a terrific, sweet flavor which complements the vegetables.

NUTRITIONAL INFORMATION

Calories	241	Sugars	.........7g
Protein	.........7g	Fat	..........19g
Carbohydrate	....11g	Saturates	.......4g

5 MINS   15 MINS

SERVES 4

INGREDIENTS

2 red onions

6 oz/175 g red cabbage

2 tbsp peanut oil

8 oz/225 g bok choy

2 tbsp plum sauce

⅔ cup roasted cashew nuts

1 Using a sharp knife, cut the red onions into thin wedges and thinly shred the red cabbage.

2 Heat the peanut oil in a large preheated wok or heavy-based skillet until the oil is really hot.

3 Add the onion wedges to the wok or skillet and stir-fry for 5 minutes, until the onions are just beginning to brown.

4 Add the red cabbage to the wok and stir-fry for an additional 2–3 minutes.

5 Add the bok choy leaves to the wok or skillet and stir-fry for 5 minutes, until the leaves have just wilted.

6 Drizzle the plum sauce over the vegetables, then toss together until well combined and heat until the liquid is bubbling.

7 Scatter with the roasted cashew nuts and transfer to warm serving bowls.

VARIATION

Use unsalted peanuts instead of the cashew nuts, if you prefer.

Bamboo with Cucumber

A simple stir-fried side dish of canned bamboo shoots and sliced cucumber is the perfect accompaniment to a Chinese main meal.

NUTRITIONAL INFORMATION

Calories	101	Sugars	.......0.2g
Protein	.........3g	Fat	..........7g
Carbohydrate	....7g	Saturates	.......1g

20 MINS   10 MINS

SERVES 4

I N G R E D I E N T S

½ cucumber

2 tbsp sesame oil

4 shallots, chopped finely

1 garlic clove, sliced finely

12 oz/350 g canned bamboo shoots, drained

1 tbsp dry sherry

1 tbsp soy sauce

2 tsp cornstarch

1 tsp sesame seeds

salt

TO GARNISH

2 red chile flowers, sliced scallions

1 Slice the cucumber thinly and sprinkle with salt. Leave for 10–15 minutes, then rinse with cold water. Prepare the chile and scallion garnish.

2 Heat the sesame oil in a wok or skillet and add the shallots and garlic. Stir-fry for 2 minutes, until golden.

3 Add the bamboo shoots and cucumber to the wok or skillet and stir-fry for 2–3 minutes.

4 Blend together the dry sherry, soy sauce, and cornstarch. Add to the

bamboo shoots and cucumber, stirring well to combine.

5 Cook for 1–2 minutes to thicken slightly, then add the sesame seeds and stir through.

6 Transfer the vegetables to a warmed serving dish. Garnish with the chile flowers and chopped scallion. Serve at once.

COOK'S TIPS

Salting the cucumber before it is stir-fried draws out some of its moisture so that it stays crisp.

Add some very finely sliced carrot to this dish to give some extra color, if you like.

Bamboo with Spinach

In this recipe, spinach is fried with spices and then braised in a soy-flavored sauce with bamboo shoots for a rich, delicious dish.

NUTRITIONAL INFORMATION

Calories . . . . .105 Sugars 1g
Protein . . . . .3g Fat 9g
Carbohydrate . . . .3g Saturates 2g

5 MINS   10 MINS

SERVES 4

INGREDIENTS

3 tbsp peanut oil

8 oz/225 g spinach, chopped

6 oz/175 g canned bamboo shoots, drained and rinsed

1 garlic clove, crushed

2 fresh red chiles, sliced

pinch of ground cinnamon

1¼ cups vegetable stock

pinch of sugar

pinch of salt

1 tbsp light soy sauce

COOK'S TIP

Fresh bamboo shoots are rarely available in the West and, in any case, are extremely time-consuming to prepare. Canned bamboo shoots are quite satisfactory, as they are used to provide a crunchy texture, rather than for their flavor, which is fairly insipid.

1 Heat the peanut oil in a preheated wok or large skillet, swirling the oil around the base of the wok until it is really hot.

2 Add the spinach and bamboo shoots to the wok and stir-fry for 1 minute.

3 Add the garlic, chiles, and cinnamon to the mixture in the wok and stir-fry for an additional 30 seconds.

4 Stir in the stock, sugar, salt, and light soy sauce, then cover and cook over medium heat for 5 minutes, or until the vegetables are cooked through and the sauce has reduced. If there is too much cooking liquid, blend a little cornstarch with double the quantity of cold water and stir into the sauce.

5 Transfer the bamboo shoots and spinach to a serving dish and serve.

Gingered Broccoli

Ginger and broccoli are a perfect combination of flavors and make an exceptionally tasty side dish.

NUTRITIONAL INFORMATION

Calories	118	Sugars	.........3g
Protein	.........8g	Fat	...........7g
Carbohydrate	....6g	Saturates	.......1g

5 MINS   15 MINS

SERVES 4

I N G R E D I E N T S

2-inch/5-cm piece fresh gingerroot

2 tbsp peanut oil

1 garlic clove, crushed

1 lb 8 oz/675 g broccoli florets

1 leek, sliced

scant ½ cup water chestnuts, halved

½ tsp superfine sugar

½ cup vegetable stock

1 tsp dark soy sauce

1 tsp cornstarch

2 tsp water

1 Using a sharp knife, finely chop the ginger. (Alternatively, cut the ginger into larger strips, to be discarded later, for a slightly milder ginger flavor.)

2 Heat the peanut oil in a preheated wok. Add the garlic and ginger and stir-fry for 30 seconds.

3 Add the broccoli, leek, and water chestnuts and stir-fry for an additional 3–4 minutes.

4 Add the superfine sugar, vegetable stock, and dark soy sauce to the wok, then reduce the heat and simmer for 4–5 minutes, until the broccoli is almost cooked but still crisp.

5 Blend the cornstarch with the water to form a smooth paste and stir it into the wok. Bring to a boil and cook, stirring constantly, for 1 minute, until thickened.

6 If using larger strips of ginger, remove from the wok and discard.

7 Transfer the vegetables to a serving dish and serve immediately.

VARIATION

Use spinach instead of the broccoli, if you prefer. Trim the woody ends and cut the remainder into 2-inch/5-cm lengths, keeping the stems and leaves separate. Add the stems with the leek in step 3 and add the leaves 2 minutes later. Reduce the cooking time in step 4 to 3–4 minutes.

Deep-Fried Zucchini

These zucchini fritters are irresistible and could be served as a starter or snack with a chile dip.

NUTRITIONAL INFORMATION

Calories	117	Sugars	.........2g
Protein	.........3g	Fat	...........6g
Carbohydrate	...14g	Saturates	.......1g

5 MINS • 20 MINS

SERVES 4

INGREDIENTS

1 lb/450 g zucchini

1 egg white

⅓ cup cornstarch

1 tsp salt

1 tsp Chinese five-spice powder

oil, for deep-frying

chile dip, to serve

1 Using a sharp knife, slice the zucchini into rings or chunky sticks.

2 Place the egg white in a small mixing bowl. Lightly whip the egg white until foamy, using a fork.

3 Mix the cornstarch, salt, and Chinese five-spice powder together and sprinkle onto a large plate.

4 Heat the oil for deep-frying in a large preheated wok or heavy-based skillet.

5 Dip each piece of zucchini into the beaten egg white, then coat in the cornstarch and five-spice mixture.

6 Deep-fry the zucchini, in batches, for 5 minutes, until pale golden and crispy. Repeat with the remaining zucchini.

7 Remove the zucchini with a slotted spoon and leave to drain on absorbent paper towels while deep-frying the remainder.

8 Transfer the zucchini to serving plates and serve with a chile dip.

VARIATION

Alter the seasoning by using chile powder or curry powder instead of the Chinese five-spice powder, if you prefer.

Stuffed Napa Cabbage

Mushrooms, scallions, celery, and rice are flavored with five-spice powder and wrapped in Napa cabbage.

25 MINS   45 MINS

SERVES 4

I N G R E D I E N T S

8 large Napa cabbage leaves

scant ⅓ cup long-grain rice

½ vegetable stock cube

¼ cup butter

1 bunch scallions, trimmed and chopped finely

1 celery stalk, chopped finely

generous 2 cups sliced white mushrooms

1 tsp Chinese five-spice powder

1¼ cups strained tomatoes

salt and pepper

fresh chives, to garnish

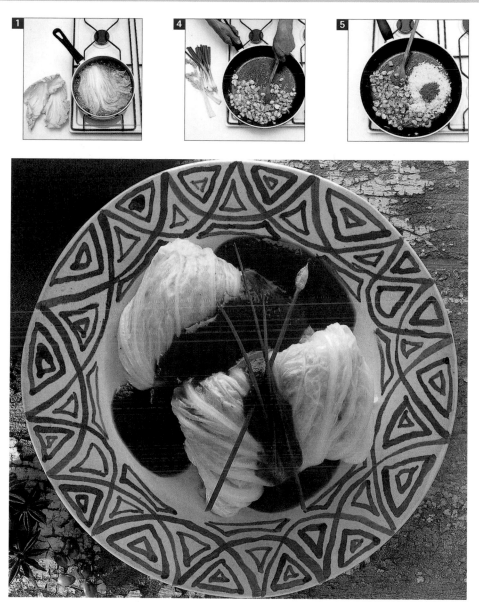

1 Blanch the Napa cabbage in boiling water for 1 minute. Refresh them under cold running water and drain well. Be careful not to tear them.

2 Cook the rice in plenty of boiling water, with the stock cube, until just tender. Drain well and set aside until required.

3 Meanwhile, melt the butter in a skillet and fry the scallions and celery gently for 3–4 minutes, until softened but not browned.

4 Add the mushrooms to the wok or skillet and cook for an additional 3–4 minutes, stirring frequently.

5 Add the cooked rice to the pan with the five-spice powder. Season with salt and pepper and stir well to combine the ingredients.

6 Lay out the Napa cabbage on a counter and divide the rice mixture between them. Roll each leaf into a neat pocket to enclose the stuffing. Place them, seam-side down, in a greased ovenproof dish. Pour the strained tomatoes over them and cover with foil. Bake in a preheated oven, 375°F/190°C, for 25–30 minutes.

7 Serve the stuffed Napa cabbage immediately, garnished with a few fresh chives.

Bell Peppers with Chestnuts

This is a colorful recipe, topped with crisp-fried, shredded leeks for both flavor and color.

NUTRITIONAL INFORMATION

Calories	192	Sugars	.........5g
Protein	.........3g	Fat	..........14g
Carbohydrate	...13g	Saturates	......13g

5 MINS   15 MINS

SERVES 4

INGREDIENTS

8 oz/225 g leeks

oil, for deep-frying

3 tbsp peanut oil

1 yellow bell pepper, seeded and diced

1 green bell pepper, seeded and diced

1 red bell pepper, seeded and diced

7 oz/200 g canned water chestnuts, drained and sliced

2 garlic cloves, crushed

3 tbsp light soy sauce

1 To make the garnish, finely slice the leeks into thin strips, using a sharp knife.

2 Heat the oil for deep-frying in a wok or large, heavy-based skillet.

3 Add the sliced leeks to the wok or skillet and cook for 2–3 minutes, until crispy. Set aside until required.

4 Heat the 3 tablespoons of peanut oil in the wok or skillet.

5 Add the yellow, green, and red bell peppers to the wok and stir-fry over high heat for 5 minutes, until they are just beginning to brown at the edges and to soften.

6 Add the sliced water chestnuts, garlic, and light soy sauce to the wok and stir-fry all of the vegetables for an additional 2–3 minutes.

7 Spoon the bell pepper stir-fry onto warm serving plates, then garnish with the crispy leeks and serve.

COOK'S TIP

Add 1 tablespoon of hoisin sauce with the soy sauce in step 6 for extra flavor and spice.

Sherry & Soy Vegetables

This is a simple, yet tasty side dish that is just as delicious served as a snack or main course.

NUTRITIONAL INFORMATION

Calories	374	Sugars	........10g
Protein	........14g	Fat	..........25g
Carbohydrate	...20g	Saturates	.......5g

10 MINS   15 MINS

SERVES 4

INGREDIENTS

2 tbsp corn oil

1 red onion, sliced

6 oz/175 g carrots, thinly sliced

6 oz/175 g zucchini, sliced diagonally

1 red bell pepper, seeded and sliced

1 small head Napa cabbage, shredded

1 cup bean sprouts

8 oz/225 g canned bamboo shoots, drained

⅓ cup cashew nuts, toasted

SAUCE

3 tbsp medium sherry

3 tbsp light soy sauce

1 tsp ground ginger

1 garlic clove, crushed

1 tsp cornstarch

1 tbsp tomato paste

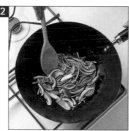
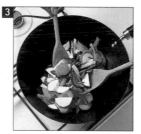

4 Add the Napa cabbage, bean sprouts, and bamboo shoots and heat through for 2–3 minutes, until the leaves begin to wilt. Stir in the cashews.

1 Heat the corn oil in a preheated wok.

2 Add the red onion and stir-fry for 2–3 minutes, until softened.

3 Add the carrots, zucchini, and bell pepper slices to the wok and stir-fry for an additional 5 minutes.

5 Combine the sherry, soy sauce, ginger, garlic, cornstarch, and tomato paste. Pour over the vegetables and toss well. Leave to simmer for 2–3 minutes, until the juices start to thicken. Serve immediately.

VARIATION

Use any mixture of fresh vegetables that you have to hand in this very versatile dish.

Broccoli in Oyster Sauce

Some Cantonese restaurants use only the stems of the broccoli for this dish, for the crunchy texture.

NUTRITIONAL INFORMATION

Calories	100	Sugars	1g
Protein	3g	Fat	9g
Carbohydrate	2g	Saturates	1g

3½ HOURS   5 MINS

SERVES 4

INGREDIENTS

9–10½ oz/250–300 g broccoli

3 tbsp vegetable oil

3-4 small slices fresh gingerroot

½ tsp salt

½ tsp sugar

3–4 tbsp Chinese Stock (see page 30) or water

1 tbsp oyster sauce

COOK'S TIP

The broccoli stems have to be peeled and cut diagonally to ensure that they will cook evenly. If they are thin stalks, the pieces can be added to the wok at the same time as the florets, but otherwise add the stems first, to ensure that they will be tender.

1 Using a sharp knife, cut the broccoli spears into small florets. Trim the stems and peel off the rough skin, then cut the stems diagonally into diamond-shaped chunks.

2 Heat the vegetable oil in a preheated wok until really hot.

3 Add the pieces of broccoli stem and the slices of gingerroot to the wok and stir-fry for half a minute, then add the florets and continue to stir-fry for another 2 minutes.

4 Add the salt, sugar, and Chinese stock, and continue stirring for another minute or so.

5 Blend in the oyster sauce. Transfer the broccoli to a serving dish and serve hot or cold.

Eight-Jewel Vegetables

This recipe, as the title suggests, is a colorful mixture of eight vegetables, cooked in a black bean and soy sauce.

NUTRITIONAL INFORMATION

Calories 110	Sugars 3g
Protein 4g	Fat 8g
Carbohydrate 7g	Saturates 1g

5 MINS   10 MINS

SERVES 4

INGREDIENTS

2 tbsp peanut oil

6 scallions, sliced

3 garlic cloves, crushed

1 green bell pepper, seeded and diced

1 red bell pepper, seeded and diced

1 fresh red chile, sliced

2 tbsp chopped water chestnuts

1 zucchini, chopped

1 cup oyster mushrooms

3 tbsp black bean sauce

2 tsp Chinese rice wine or dry sherry

4 tbsp dark soy sauce

1 tsp dark brown sugar

2 tbsp water

1 tsp sesame oil

1 Heat the peanut oil in a preheated wok or large skillet until it is almost smoking.

2 Lower the heat slightly, then add the scallions and garlic and stir-fry for about 30 seconds.

3 Add the green and red bell peppers, fresh red chile, water chestnuts, and zucchini to the wok or skillet and stir-fry for 2–3 minutes, until the vegetables are just beginning to soften.

4 Add the oyster mushrooms, black bean sauce, Chinese rice wine, dark soy sauce, dark brown sugar, and water to the wok and stir-fry for an additional 4 minutes.

5 Sprinkle the stir-fry with sesame oil and serve immediately.

COOK'S TIP

Eight jewels or treasures form a traditional part of the Chinese New Year celebrations, which start in the last week of the old year. The Kitchen God, an important figure, is sent to give a report to heaven, returning on New Year's Eve in time for the feasting.

Spicy Mushrooms

A mixture of mushrooms common in Western cooking have been used in this recipe for a richly flavored dish.

NUTRITIONAL INFORMATION

Calories	103	Sugars	.........4g
Protein	.........3g	Fat	...........8g
Carbohydrate	....5g	Saturates	.......2g

5 MINS   10 MINS

SERVES 4

INGREDIENTS

2 tbsp peanut oil

2 garlic cloves, crushed

3 scallions, chopped

2½ cups white mushrooms

2 large open-cup mushrooms, sliced

generous 1 cup oyster mushrooms

1 tsp chile sauce

1 tbsp dark soy sauce

1 tbsp hoisin sauce

1 tbsp wine vinegar

½ tsp ground Szechuan pepper

1 tbsp dark brown sugar

1 tsp sesame oil

chopped parsley, to garnish

1 Heat the peanut oil in a preheated wok or large, heavy-based skillet until almost smoking.

2 Reduce the heat slightly, then add the crushed garlic cloves and scallions to the wok or skillet and stir-fry for 30 seconds.

3 Add all the mushrooms to the wok, together with the chile sauce, dark soy sauce, hoisin sauce, wine vinegar, ground Szechuan pepper, and dark brown sugar and stir-fry for 4–5 minutes, until the mushrooms are cooked through. Stir constantly to prevent the mixture sticking to the base of the wok.

4 Sprinkle the sesame oil on top of the mixture in the wok. Transfer to a warm serving dish, garnish with parsley and serve immediately.

COOK'S TIP

If Chinese dried mushrooms are available, add a small quantity to this dish for texture. Wood ears are widely used and are available dried from Chinese food stores. They should be rinsed, then soaked in warm water for 20 minutes and rinsed again before use.

Golden Needles with Bamboo

Golden needles are the dried flower buds of the tiger lily and have a unique musky flavor. They are available, dried, from Chinese stores.

NUTRITIONAL INFORMATION

Calories	178	Sugars	.........3g
Protein	.........4g	Fat	...........9g
Carbohydrate	...22g	Saturates	.......1g

35 MINS　　　25 MINS

SERVES 4

I N G R E D I E N T S

¼ cup dried lily flowers

1 lb/450 g canned bamboo shoots, drained

½ cup cornstarch

vegetable oil, for deep-frying

1 tbsp vegetable oil

scant 2 cups vegetable stock

1 tbsp dark soy sauce

1 tbsp dry sherry

1 tsp sugar

1 large garlic clove, sliced

½ red bell pepper

½ green bell pepper

½ yellow bell pepper

1 Soak the lily flowers in hot water for 30 minutes.

2 Coat the bamboo shoots in cornstarch. Heat enough oil in a large heavy-based pan to deep-fry the bamboo shoots in batches until just beginning to color. Remove with a perforated spoon and drain on absorbent paper towels.

3 Drain the lily flowers and trim off the hard ends. Heat 1 tablespoon of oil in a wok or large skillet. Add the lily flowers, bamboo shoots, stock, soy sauce, sherry, sugar, and garlic.

4 Slice the bell peppers thinly and add to the wok or skillet. Bring to a boil, stirring constantly, then reduce the heat and simmer for 5 minutes. Add extra water or stock if necessary.

5 Transfer the mixture in the wok to warm serving dishes and serve.

COOK'S TIP

To coat the bamboo shoots easily with cornstarch, place the cornstarch in a plastic bag, then add the bamboo shoots in batches and shake well.

Cantonese Garden Vegetables

This dish tastes as fresh as it looks. Try to get hold of baby vegetables as they look and taste so much better in this dish.

NUTRITIONAL INFORMATION

Calories	 130	Sugars	.... 8g
Protein	.... 6g	Fat	.... 8g
Carbohydrate	.... 8g	Saturates	.... 1g

5 MINS   10 MINS

SERVES 4

INGREDIENTS

2 tbsp peanut oil

1 tsp Chinese five-spice powder

2¾ oz/75 g baby carrots, halved

2 celery stalks, sliced

2 baby leeks, sliced

½ cup snow peas

4 baby zucchini, halved lengthwise

8 baby corn cobs

8 oz/225 g firm marinated tofu, cubed

4 tbsp fresh orange juice

1 tbsp clear honey

celery leaves and orange zest,
   to garnish

cooked rice or noodles, to serve

VARIATION

Lemon juice would be just as delicious as the orange juice in this recipe, but use 3 tablespoons instead of 4 tablespoons.

1 Heat the peanut oil in a preheated wok or large, heavy-based skillet until almost smoking.

2 Add the Chinese five-spice powder, carrots, celery, leeks, snow peas, zucchini, and corn cobs and stir-fry for 3–4 minutes.

3 Add the bean curd to the wok or skillet and cook for an additional 2 minutes, stirring gently so the tofu does not break up.

4 Stir the fresh orange juice and clear honey into the wok or skillet, then reduce the heat and cook for 1–2 minutes.

5 Transfer the stir-fry to a serving dish. Garnish with celery leaves and orange zest and serve with rice or noodles.

Fish Eggplant

Like Fish-Flavored Pork (see page 186), there is no fish involved in this dish, and the meat can be omitted without affecting the flavor.

NUTRITIONAL INFORMATION

Calories ....130 Sugars 3g
Protein ....8g Fat 8g
Carbohydrate ....6g Saturates 2g

35 MINS   15 MINS

SERVES 4

I N G R E D I E N T S

1 lb 2 oz/500 g eggplant

vegetable oil, for deep-frying

1 garlic clove, finely chopped

½ tsp finely chopped fresh gingerroot

2 scallions, finely chopped, with the white and green parts separated

4½ oz/125 g pork, thinly shredded (optional)

1 tbsp light soy sauce

2 tsp rice wine or dry sherry

1 tbsp chile bean sauce

½ tsp sugar

1 tbsp rice vinegar

2 tsp cornstarch paste (see page 31)

a few drops sesame oil

salt

1 Using a sharp knife, cut the eggplant into rounds and then into thin strips about the size of potato chips—the skin can either be peeled or left on. Place the eggplant strips into a colander, then sprinkle with salt and leave to stand for 30 minutes. Rinse thoroughly and pat dry on paper towels. This process removes the bitter juices from the eggplant.

2 Heat the vegetable oil in a preheated wok or large skillet until smoking.

3 Add the eggplant chips and deep-fry for 3–4 minutes, until soft. Remove and drain on absorbent paper towels.

4 Pour off the hot oil, leaving about 1 tablespoon in the wok. Add the garlic, ginger, and the white parts of the scallions, followed by the pork (if using). Stir-fry for 1 minute, or until the color of the meat changes, then add the light soy sauce, rice wine, and chile bean sauce, blending well.

5 Return the eggplant chips to the wok or skillet together with the sugar, ½ teaspoon salt, and the rice vinegar.

6 Continue stirring the mixture in the wok for another minute or so, then add the cornstarch paste and stir until the sauce has thickened.

7 Add the green parts of the scallions to the wok and toss to combine. Sprinkle on the sesame oil and serve immediately.

Bamboo with Bell Peppers

This dish has a wonderfully strong ginger flavor, which is integral to Chinese cooking. The mixed bell peppers give the dish a burst of color.

NUTRITIONAL INFORMATION

Calories	101	Sugars	. . . . .5g
Protein	. . . . .3g	Fat	. . . . .6g
Carbohydrate	. . . .9g	Saturates	. . . . . . .1g

5 MINS   15 MINS

SERVES 4

INGREDIENTS

2 tbsp peanut oil

8 oz/225 g canned bamboo shoots, drained and rinsed

1-inch/2.5-cm piece fresh gingerroot, finely chopped

1 small red bell pepper, seeded and thinly sliced

1 small green bell pepper, seeded and thinly sliced

1 small yellow bell pepper, seeded and thinly sliced

1 leek, sliced

½ cup vegetable stock

1 tbsp light soy sauce

2 tsp light brown sugar

2 tsp Chinese rice wine or dry sherry

1 tsp cornstarch

2 tsp water

1 tsp sesame oil

1. Heat the peanut oil in a preheated wok or large skillet, swirling the oil around the base of the wok or pan until it is really hot.

2. Add the bamboo shoots, ginger, bell peppers, and leek to the wok and stir-fry for 2–3 minutes.

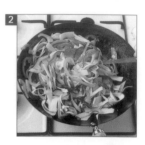

3. Stir in the vegetable stock, soy sauce, light brown sugar, and Chinese rice wine, then bring to a boil, stirring constantly.

4. Reduce the heat and simmer for 4–5 minutes, until the vegetables begin to soften.

5. Blend the cornstarch with the water, stirring to form a smooth paste.

6. Stir the cornstarch paste into the wok. Bring to a boil and cook, stirring constantly, until the sauce thickens and clears.

7. Sprinkle the sesame oil over the vegetables and cook for 1 minute. Transfer to a warm serving dish and serve immediately.

COOK'S TIP

Add a chopped fresh red chile or a few drops of chile sauce for a spicier dish.

Braised Vegetables

This colorful selection of braised vegetables makes a splendid accompaniment to a main dish.

NUTRITIONAL INFORMATION

Calories ....170 Sugars 8g
Protein ....7g Fat 10g
Carbohydrate ...14g Saturates 1g

🦪 🦪 🦪

🍲 10 MINS   🕐 10 MINS

SERVES 4

INGREDIENTS

3 tbsp corn oil

1 garlic clove, crushed

1 Chinese cabbage, thickly shredded

2 onions, peeled and cut into wedges

9 oz/250 g broccoli florets

2 large carrots, peeled and cut into thin julienne strips

12 baby corn cobs, halved if large

½ cup snow peas, halved

1½ cups sliced Chinese or oyster mushrooms

1 tbsp grated fresh gingerroot

¾ cup vegetable stock

2 tbsp light soy sauce

1 tbsp cornstarch

salt and pepper

½ tsp sugar

1 Heat the oil in a wok. Add the garlic, cabbage, onions, broccoli, carrots, corn, snow peas, mushrooms, and ginger and stir-fry for 2 minutes.

2 Add the stock, then cover and cook for an additional 2-3 minutes.

3 Blend the soy sauce with the cornstarch and season with salt and pepper to taste.

4 Remove the braised vegetables from the pan with a slotted spoon and keep warm. Add the soy sauce mixture to the pan juices, mixing well. Bring to a boil, stirring constantly, until the mixture thickens slightly. Stir in the sugar.

5 Return the vegetables to the pan and toss in the slightly thickened sauce. Cook gently to just heat through, then serve immediately.

COOK'S TIP

This dish also makes an ideal vegetarian main meal. Double the quantities, to serve 4-6, and serve with noodles or Green-Fried Rice (see page 318).

Stir-Fried Seasonal Vegetables

When selecting different fresh vegetables for this dish, bear in mind that there should always be a contrast in color as well as texture.

NUTRITIONAL INFORMATION

Calories 108	Sugars 3g
Protein 3g	Fat 9g
Carbohydrate 4g	Saturates 1g

3½ HOURS   10 MINS

SERVES 4

I N G R E D I E N T S

1 medium red bell pepper, cored
  and seeded

4½ oz/125 g zucchini

4½ oz/125 g cauliflower

4½ oz/125 g green beans

3 tbsp vegetable oil

a few small slices gingerroot

½ tsp salt

½ tsp sugar

Chinese Stock (see page 30) or
  water

1 tbsp light soy sauce

a few drops of sesame oil (optional)

1 Using a sharp knife or cleaver, cut the red bell pepper into small squares. Thinly slice the zucchini. Trim the cauliflower and divide into small florets, discarding any thick stems. Make sure the vegetables are cut into roughly similar shapes and sizes to ensure even cooking.

2 Top and tail the green beans, then cut them in half.

3 Heat the vegetable oil in a pre-heated wok or large, heavy-based skillet.

4 Add the prepared vegetables to the wok and stir-fry with the ginger for 2 minutes.

5 Add the salt and sugar to the wok or skillet, and continue to stir-fry for 1-2 minutes, adding a little Chinese Stock or water if the vegetables appear to be too dry. Do not add liquid unless necessary.

6 Add the light soy sauce and sesame oil (if using) and stir well to lightly coat the vegetables.

7 Transfer the stir-fried vegetables to a warm serving dish and serve immediately.

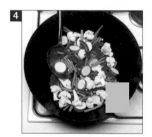

VARIATION

Almost any vegetables could
be used in this dish but make sure
there is a good variety of color,
and always include several crisp
vegetables, such as carrots or
snow peas.

Vegetable Chop Suey

Make sure that the vegetables are all cut into pieces of a similar size in this recipe, so that they cook within the same amount of time.

NUTRITIONAL INFORMATION

Calories 155	Sugars 6g	
Protein 4g	Fat 12g	
Carbohydrate 9g	Saturates 2g	

🍲 5 MINS   🕐 5 MINS

SERVES 4

INGREDIENTS

1 yellow bell pepper, seeded

1 red bell pepper, seeded

1 carrot

1 zucchini

1 fennel bulb

1 onion

½ cup snow peas

2 tbsp peanut oil

3 cloves garlic, crushed

1 tsp grated fresh fresh gingerroot

scant 1 cup bean sprouts

2 tsp light brown sugar

2 tbsp light soy sauce

½ cup vegetable stock

1 Cut the bell peppers, carrot, zucchini, and fennel into thin slices. Cut the onion into fourths and then cut each piece in half. Slice the snow peas diagonally to create the maximum surface area.

2 Heat the oil in a preheated wok, then add the garlic and ginger and stir-fry for 30 seconds. Add the onion and stir-fry for an additional 30 seconds.

3 Add the bell peppers, carrot, zucchini, fennel, and snow peas to the wok and stir-fry for 2 minutes.

4 Add the bean sprouts to the wok and stir in the sugar, soy sauce, and stock. Reduce the heat to low and simmer for 1–2 minutes, until the vegetables are tender and coated in the sauce.

5 Transfer the vegetables and sauce to a serving dish and serve immediately.

VARIATION

Use any combination of colorful vegetables that you have to hand to make this versatile dish.

Sweet & Sour Cauliflower

Although sweet and sour flavorings are mainly associated with pork, they are ideal for flavoring vegetables as in this tasty recipe.

NUTRITIONAL INFORMATION

Calories 154   Sugars 16g
Protein ....6g   Fat 7g
Carbohydrate ...17g   Saturates 1g

5 MINS   20 MINS

SERVES 4

INGREDIENTS

1 lb/450 g cauliflower florets

2 tbsp corn oil

1 onion, sliced

scant 1¾ cups sliced carrots

1 cup snow peas

1 ripe mango, sliced

⅔ cup bean sprouts

3 tbsp chopped fresh cilantro

3 tbsp fresh lime juice

1 tbsp clear honey

6 tbsp coconut milk

1 Bring a large pan of water to a boil. Add the cauliflower to the pan and cook for 2 minutes. Drain the cauliflower thoroughly.

2 Heat the corn oil in a large preheated wok.

3 Add the onion and carrots to the wok and stir-fry together for 5 minutes.

4 Add the drained cauliflower and snow peas to the wok and stir-fry for 2–3 minutes.

5 Add the mango and bean sprouts to the wok and stir-fry for 2 minutes.

6 Mix together the cilantro, lime juice, honey, and coconut milk in a bowl.

7 Add the cilantro and coconut mixture to the wok and stir-fry for 2 minutes, until the juices are bubbling.

8 Transfer the sweet and sour cauliflower stir-fry to serving dishes and serve immediately.

VARIATION

Use broccoli instead of the cauliflower as an alternative, if you prefer.

Potato Stir-Fry

In this sweet and sour dish, tender vegetables are simply stir-fried with spices and coconut milk, and flavored with lime.

NUTRITIONAL INFORMATION

Calories 138   Sugars 5g
Protein ....2g   Fat 6g
Carbohydrate ...20g   Saturates 1g

10 MINS   20 MINS

SERVES 4

I N G R E D I E N T S

4 waxy potatoes

2 tbsp vegetable oil

1 yellow bell pepper, diced

1 red bell pepper, diced

1 carrot, cut into short thin sticks

1 zucchini, cut into short thin sticks

2 garlic cloves, crushed

1 red chile, sliced

1 bunch scallions, halved lengthwise

8 tbsp coconut milk

1 tsp chopped lemon grass

2 tsp lime juice

finely grated rind of 1 lime

1 tbsp chopped fresh cilantro

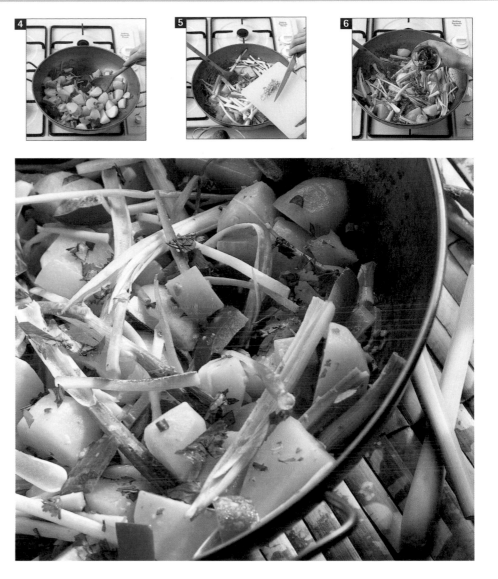

1 Using a sharp knife, cut the potatoes into small dice.

2 Bring a large pan of water to a boil and cook the diced potatoes for 5 minutes. Drain thoroughly.

3 Heat the vegetable oil in a wok or large skillet, swirling the oil around the base of the wok until it is really hot.

4 Add the potatoes, diced bell peppers, carrot, zucchini, garlic, and chile to the wok and stir-fry the vegetables for 2-3 minutes.

5 Stir in the scallions, coconut milk, chopped lemon grass, and lime juice and stir-fry the mixture for an additional 5 minutes.

6 Add the lime rind and cilantro and stir-fry for 1 minute. Serve hot.

COOK'S TIP

Check that the potatoes are not overcooked in step 2, otherwise the potato pieces will disintegrate when they are stir-fried in the wok.

Leeks with Yellow Bean Sauce

This is a simple side dish that is ideal with other main meal vegetarian dishes.

NUTRITIONAL INFORMATION

Calories . . . . .131 Sugars 3g
Protein . . . . .6g Fat 9g
Carbohydrate . . . .7g Saturates 2g

5 MINS   10 MINS

SERVES 4

I N G R E D I E N T S

1 lb/450 g leeks

6 oz/175 g baby corn cobs

6 scallions

3 tbsp peanut oil

8 oz/225 g Napa cabbage, shredded

4 tbsp yellow bean sauce

1 Using a sharp knife, slice the leeks, halve the baby corn cobs and thinly slice the scallions.

2 Heat the peanut oil in a large preheated wok or skillet until it is smoking hot.

3 Add the leeks, shredded Napa cabbage and baby corn cobs to the wok or skillet.

4 Stir-fry the vegetables over high heat for 5 minutes, until the edges of the vegetables are slightly brown.

5 Add the scallions to the wok or skillet, stirring to combine.

6 Add the yellow bean sauce to the wok or skillet.

7 Stir-fry the mixture in the wok for an additional 2 minutes, until heated through and the vegetables are thoroughly coated in the sauce.

8 Transfer the vegetables and sauce to warm serving dishes and serve immediately.

COOK'S TIP

Yellow bean sauce adds an authentic Chinese flavor to stir-fries. It is made from crushed salted soybeans mixed with flour and spices to make a thick paste. It is mild in flavor and is excellent with a range of vegetables.

Winter Vegetable Stir-Fry

Ordinary winter vegetables are given extraordinary treatment in this lively stir-fry, which is just the thing for perking up jaded palates.

NUTRITIONAL INFORMATION

Calories 175   Sugars 7g
Protein ....6g   Fat 13g
Carbohydrate ....9g   Saturates 2g

🥘 5 MINS   🕐 10 MINS

SERVES 4

INGREDIENTS

3 tbsp sesame oil

scant ¼ cup blanched almonds

1 large carrot, cut into thin strips

1 large turnip, cut into thin strips

1 onion, sliced finely

1 garlic clove, crushed

3 celery stalks, sliced finely

4½ oz/125 g Brussels sprouts, trimmed and halved

4½ oz/125 g cauliflower, broken into florets

4½ oz/125 g white cabbage, shredded

2 tsp sesame seeds

1 tsp grated fresh gingerroot

½ tsp medium chile powder

1 tbsp chopped fresh cilantro

1 tbsp light soy sauce

salt and pepper

sprigs of fresh cilantro, to garnish

1 Heat the oil in a wok or large skillet. Stir-fry the almonds until lightly browned, then lift them out and drain on paper towels.

2 Add all the vegetables to the wok or skillet, except for the cabbage. Stir-fry the vegetables briskly for 3–4 minutes.

3 Add the cabbage, sesame seeds, ginger, and chile powder and cook, stirring, for 2 minutes. Season to taste.

4 Add the chopped cilantro, soy sauce, and almonds, stirring gently to mix. Serve the vegetables, garnished with cilantro sprigs.

COOK'S TIP

As well as adding protein, vitamins, and useful fats to the diet, nuts and seeds add important flavor and texture to vegetarian meals. Sesame seeds are also a good source of vitamin E.

Carrot & Orange Stir-Fry

Carrots and oranges have long been combined in Asian cooking, the orange juice bringing out the sweetness of the carrots.

NUTRITIONAL INFORMATION

Calories	341	Sugars	........26g
Protein	.........10g	Fat	..........21g
Carbohydrate	...28g	Saturates	.......4g

10 MINS   10 MINS

SERVES 4

INGREDIENTS

2 tbsp corn oil

1 lb/450 g carrots, grated

8 oz/225 g leeks, shredded

2 oranges, peeled and segmented

2 tbsp tomato ketchup

1 tbsp raw sugar

2 tbsp light soy sauce

⅔ cup chopped peanuts

VARIATION

You could use pineapple instead of orange, if you prefer. If using canned pineapple, make sure that it is in natural juice not syrup which would spoil the fresh taste of this dish.

1 Heat the corn oil in a preheated wok.

2 Add the grated carrot and leeks to the wok and stir-fry for 2–3 minutes, until the vegetables have just softened.

3 Add the orange segments to the wok and heat through gently, ensuring that you do not break up the orange segments as you stir the mixture.

4 Mix the tomato ketchup, raw sugar, and light soy sauce together in a small mixing bowl.

5 Add the tomato and sugar mixture to the wok and stir-fry for an additional 2 minutes.

6 Transfer the stir-fry to warm serving bowls and scatter with the chopped peanuts. Serve immediately.

Ginger & Orange Broccoli

Thinly sliced broccoli florets are lightly stir-fried and served in a ginger and orange sauce.

NUTRITIONAL INFORMATION

Calories 133   Sugars 6g
Protein ....9g   Fat 7g
Carbohydrate ...10g   Saturates 1g

5 MINS   10 MINS

SERVES 4

INGREDIENTS

1 lb 10 oz/750 g broccoli

2 thin slices fresh gingerroot

2 garlic cloves

1 orange

2 tsp cornstarch

1 tbsp light soy sauce

½ tsp sugar

2 tbsp vegetable oil

1 Divide the broccoli into small florets. Peel the stems, using a vegetable peeler, and then cut the stems into thin slices, using a sharp knife.

2 Cut the gingerroot into matchsticks and slice the garlic.

3 Peel 2 long strips of zest from the orange and cut into thin strips. Place the strips in a bowl, then cover with cold water and set aside.

4 Squeeze the juice from the orange and mix with the cornstarch, light soy sauce, sugar, and 4 tablespoons water.

5 Heat the vegetable oil in a wok or large skillet. Add the broccoli stem slices and stir-fry for 2 minutes.

6 Add the gingerroot slices, garlic, and broccoli florets, and stir-fry for an additional 3 minutes.

7 Stir the orange sauce mixture into the wok and cook, stirring constantly, until the sauce has thickened and coated the broccoli.

8 Drain the reserved orange rind and stir into the wok before serving.

VARIATION

This dish could be made with cauliflower, if you prefer, or a mixture of cauliflower and broccoli.

Honey-Fried Spinach

This stir-fry is the perfect accompaniment to bean curd dishes, and it is so quick and simple to make.

NUTRITIONAL INFORMATION

Calories	146	Sugars	.........9g
Protein	.........4g	Fat	...........9g
Carbohydrate	...10g	Saturates	.......2g

🍲 🍲

🥢 5 MINS   🕑 15 MINS

SERVES 4

INGREDIENTS

4 scallions

3 tbsp peanut oil

12 oz/350 g shiitake mushrooms, sliced

2 garlic cloves, crushed

12 oz/350 g baby leaf spinach

2 tbsp dry sherry

2 tbsp clear honey

1 Using a sharp knife, slice the scallions.

2 Heat the peanut oil in a large preheated wok or heavy-based skillet.

3 Add the shiitake mushrooms to the wok and stir-fry for 5 minutes, until the mushrooms have softened.

COOK'S TIP

Single-flower honey has a better, more individual flavor than blended honey. Acacia honey is typically Chinese, but you could also try clover, lemon blossom, lime flower, or orange blossom.

4 Stir the crushed garlic into the wok or heavy-based skillet.

5 Add the baby leaf spinach to the wok or skillet and stir-fry for an additional 2–3 minutes, until the spinach leaves have just wilted.

6 Mix together the dry sherry and clear honey in a small bowl until well combined. Drizzle the sherry and honey mixture over the spinach and heat through, stirring to coat the spinach leaves thoroughly in the mixture.

7 Transfer the stir-fry to warm serving dishes, then scatter with the chopped scallions and serve immediately.

Spinach with Mushrooms

For best results, use straw mushrooms, available in cans from Asian stores. If these are unavailable, use white mushrooms instead.

NUTRITIONAL INFORMATION

Calories	201	Sugars	. . . . .8g
Protein	. . . . .7g	Fat	. . . . .15g
Carbohydrate	. . .10g	Saturates	. . . . . . .2g

5 MINS   10 MINS

SERVES 4

INGREDIENTS

¼ cup pine nuts

1 lb 2 oz/500 g fresh spinach leaves

1 red onion

2 garlic cloves

3 tbsp vegetable oil

15 oz/425 g canned straw mushrooms, drained

3 tbsp raisins

2 tbsp soy sauce

salt

1 Heat a wok or large, heavy-based skillet.

2 Dry-fry the pine nuts in the wok until lightly browned. Remove with a perforated spoon and set aside.

3 Wash the spinach thoroughly, picking the leaves over and removing long stalks. Drain thoroughly and pat dry with absorbent paper towels.

4 Using a sharp knife, slice the red onion and the garlic.

5 Heat the vegetable oil in the wok or skillet. Add the onion and garlic slices and stir-fry for 1 minute, until slightly softened.

6 Add the spinach and mushrooms, and continue to stir-fry until the leaves have wilted. Drain off any excess liquid.

7 Stir in the raisins, reserved pine nuts and soy sauce. Stir-fry until thoroughly heated and all the ingredients are well combined.

8 Season to taste with salt. Transfer to a warm serving dish and serve.

COOK'S TIP

Soak the raisins in 2 tablespoons dry sherry before using. This helps to plump them up as well as adding extra flavor to the stir-fry.

Broccoli & Black Bean Sauce

Broccoli works well with the black bean sauce in this recipe, while the almonds add extra crunch and flavor.

NUTRITIONAL INFORMATION

Calories	139	Sugars	.........3g
Protein	.........7g	Fat	..........10g
Carbohydrate	....5g	Saturates	.......1g

5 MINS   15 MINS

SERVES 4

I N G R E D I E N T S

1 lb/450 g broccoli florets

2 tbsp corn oil

1 onion, sliced

2 cloves garlic, thinly sliced

¼ cup slivered almonds

1 head Napa cabbage, shredded

4 tbsp black bean sauce

1 Bring a large pan of water to a boil.

2 Add the broccoli florets to the pan and cook for 1 minute. Drain the broccoli thoroughly.

3 Meanwhile, heat the corn oil in a large preheated wok.

4 Add the onion and garlic slices to the wok and stir-fry until just beginning to brown.

5 Add the drained broccoli florets and the slivered almonds to the mixture in the wok and stir-fry for an additional 2–3 minutes.

6 Add the shredded Napa cabbage to the wok and stir-fry for an additional 2 minutes, stirring the leaves briskly around the wok.

7 Stir the black bean sauce into the vegetables in the wok, tossing to coat the vegetables thoroughly in the sauce and cook until the juices are just beginning to bubble.

8 Transfer the vegetables to warm serving bowls and serve immediately.

VARIATION

Use unsalted cashew nuts instead of the almonds, if preferred.

Vegetable & Nut Stir-Fry

A colorful selection of vegetables are stir-fried in a creamy peanut sauce and sprinkled with nuts to serve.

10 MINS   15 MINS

SERVES 4

INGREDIENTS

3 tbsp crunchy peanut butter

⅔ cup water

1 tbsp soy sauce

1 tsp sugar

1 carrot

½ red onion

4 baby zucchini

1 red bell pepper

9 oz/250 g egg thread noodles

scant ¼ cup peanuts, chopped roughly

2 tbsp vegetable oil

1 tsp sesame oil

1 small green chile, seeded and sliced thinly

1 garlic clove, sliced thinly

8 oz/225 g canned water chestnuts, drained and sliced

generous 1 cup bean sprouts

salt

1 Gradually blend the peanut butter with the water in a small bowl. Stir in the soy sauce and sugar. Set aside.

2 Cut the carrot into thin, short sticks and slice the red onion. Slice the zucchini on the diagonal and cut the bell pepper into chunks.

3 Bring a large pan of water to a boil and add the egg noodles. Remove from the heat immediately and leave to stand for 4 minutes, stirring occasionally to separate the noodles.

4 Heat a wok or large skillet, then add the peanuts and dry-fry until they are beginning to brown. Remove with a perforated spoon and set aside until required.

5 Add the oils to the pan and heat. Add the carrot, onion, zucchini, bell pepper, chile, and garlic, and stir-fry for 2–3 minutes. Add the water chestnuts, bean sprouts, and peanut sauce. Bring to a boil and heat thoroughly. Season with salt to taste.

6 Drain the noodles and serve with the vegetable and nut stir-fry. Sprinkle with the reserved peanuts.

Quorn & Vegetable Stir-Fry

Quorn, like tofu, absorbs all of the flavors in a dish, making it ideal for this recipe, which is packed with classic Chinese flavorings.

NUTRITIONAL INFORMATION

Calories	167	Sugars	.........8g
Protein	........12g	Fat	...........9g
Carbohydrate	...10g	Saturates	.......1g

30 MINS   10 MINS

SERVES 4

INGREDIENTS

1 tbsp grated fresh gingerroot

1 tsp ground ginger

1 tbsp tomato paste

2 tbsp corn oil

1 garlic clove, crushed

2 tbsp soy sauce

12 oz/350 g Quorn or soya cubes

scant 1¾ cups sliced carrots

scant 1¾ cups green beans, sliced

4 celery stalks, sliced

1 red bell pepper, seeded and sliced

boiled rice, to serve

COOK'S TIP

Gingerroot will keep for several weeks in a cool, dry place. Gingerroot can also be kept frozen—break off lumps as needed.

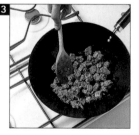

1 Place the grated fresh gingerroot, ground ginger, tomato paste, 1 tablespoon of the corn oil, garlic, soy sauce, and Quorn cubes in a large bowl. Mix well to combine, stirring carefully so that you don't break up the Quorn cubes. Cover and leave to marinate for 20 minutes.

2 Heat the remaining corn oil in a large preheated wok.

3 Add the marinated Quorn mixture to the wok and stir-fry for 2 minutes.

4 Add the carrots, green beans, celery, and red bell pepper to the wok and stir-fry for an additional 5 minutes.

5 Transfer the stir-fry to warm serving dishes and serve immediately with freshly cooked boiled rice.

Creamy Green Vegetables

This dish is very quick to make. A dash of cream is added to the sauce, but this may be omitted, if preferred.

NUTRITIONAL INFORMATION

Calories 111   Sugars 2g
Protein ....5g   Fat 8g
Carbohydrate ....7g   Saturates 2g

5 MINS   20 MINS

SERVES 4

INGREDIENTS

1 lb/450 g Napa cabbage, shredded

2 tbsp peanut oil

2 leeks, shredded

4 garlic cloves, crushed

1¼ cups vegetable stock

1 tbsp light soy sauce

2 tsp cornstarch

4 tsp water

2 tbsp light cream or plain yogurt

1 tbsp chopped cilantro

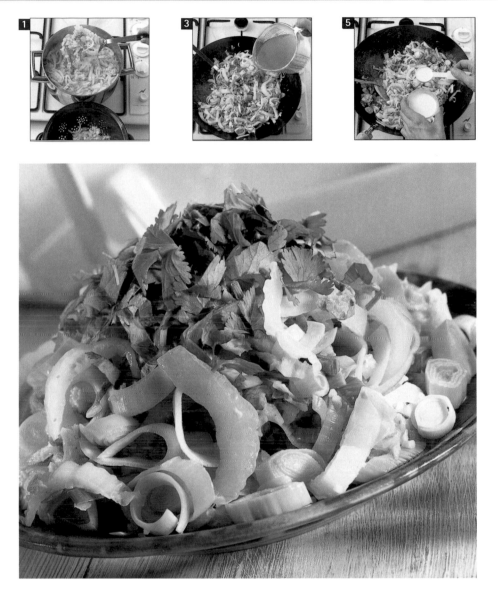

1 Blanch the Napa cabbage in boiling water for 30 seconds. Drain and rinse under cold running water, then drain thoroughly again.

2 Heat the oil in a preheated wok and add the Napa cabbage, leeks, and garlic. Stir-fry for 2–3 minutes.

3 Add the stock and soy sauce to the wok and reduce the heat to low, then cover and simmer for 10 minutes.

4 Remove the vegetables from the wok with a slotted spoon and set aside. Bring the stock to a boil and boil vigorously until reduced by about half.

5 Blend the cornstarch with the water and stir into the wok. Bring to a boil, and cook, stirring constantly, until thickened and clear.

6 Reduce the heat and stir in the vegetables and cream. Cook over a low heat for 1 minute.

7 Transfer to a serving dish. Sprinkle over the chopped cilantro and serve.

COOK'S TIP

Do not boil the sauce once the cream or yogurt has been added, as it will separate.

Crispy Cabbage & Almonds

This dish is better known as crispy seaweed. It does not actually contain seaweed, but consists of collard greens or bok choy.

NUTRITIONAL INFORMATION

Calories 431	Sugars 17g
Protein 9g	Fat 37g
Carbohydrate . . .17g	Saturates 4g

🥧 🥧

🍋 10 MINS   🕐 10 MINS

SERVES 4

I N G R E D I E N T S

2 lb 12 oz/1.25 kg bok choy or collard greens

3 cups vegetable oil

½ cup blanched almonds

1 tsp salt

1 tbsp light brown sugar

pinch of ground cinnamon

1 Separate the leaves from the bok choy or collard greens and rinse them well. Drain thoroughly and pat dry with absorbent paper towels.

2 Shred the collard greens into thin strips, using a sharp knife.

3 Heat the vegetable oil in a preheated wok or large, heavy-based skillet until the oil is almost smoking.

4 Reduce the heat and add the bok choy or collard greens. Cook for 2–3 minutes, until the greens begin to float in the oil and are crisp.

5 Remove the greens from the oil with a slotted spoon and leave to drain thoroughly on absorbent paper towels.

6 Add the blanched almonds to the oil in the wok and cook for 30 seconds. Remove the almonds from the oil with a slotted spoon and drain thoroughly on absorbent paper towels.

7 Mix together the salt, light brown sugar, and ground cinnamon and sprinkle onto the greens.

8 Toss the almonds into the greens.

9 Transfer the greens and almonds to a warm serving dish and serve immediately.

COOK'S TIP

Ensure that the greens are completely dry before adding them to the oil, otherwise it will spit. The greens will not become crisp if they are wet when placed in the oil.

Green & Black Bean Stir-Fry

A terrific side dish, the variety of greens in this recipe make it as attractive as it is tasty.

NUTRITIONAL INFORMATION

Calories 88   Sugars 2g
Protein . . . . .2g   Fat 7g
Carbohydrate . . . .4g   Saturates 4g

5 MINS   10 MINS

SERVES 4

INGREDIENTS

8 oz/225 g fine green beans, sliced

4 shallots, sliced

scant 2 cups thinly sliced shiitake mushrooms

1 garlic clove, crushed

1 iceberg lettuce, shredded

1 tsp chile oil

2 tbsp butter

4 tbsp black bean sauce

1 Using a sharp knife, slice the fine green beans, shallots, and shiitake mushrooms. Crush the garlic in a pestle and mortar and shred the iceberg lettuce.

2 Heat the chile oil and butter in a large preheated wok or skillet.

3 Add the green beans, shallots, garlic, and mushrooms to the wok and stir-fry for 2–3 minutes.

4 Add the shredded lettuce to the wok or skillet and stir-fry until the leaves have wilted.

5 Stir the black bean sauce into the mixture in the wok and heat through, tossing gently to mix, until the sauce is bubbling.

6 Transfer the green and black bean stir-fry to a warm serving dish and serve immediately.

COOK'S TIP

If possible, use Chinese green beans, which are tender and can be eaten whole. They are available from specialist Chinese stores.

Chestnut & Vegetable Stir-Fry

In this colorful stir-fry, vegetables are cooked in a wonderfully aromatic sauce that combines peanuts, chile, coconut, coriander, and turmeric.

NUTRITIONAL INFORMATION

Calories	446	Sugars	........17g
Protein	........14g	Fat	..........25g
Carbohydrate	...42g	Saturates	.......5g

🥧 🥧 🥧

🍲 10 MINS   🕐 15 MINS

SERVES 4

INGREDIENTS

scant 1 cup unsalted roasted peanuts

2 tsp hot chile sauce

¾ cup coconut milk

2 tbsp soy sauce

1 tbsp ground coriander

pinch of ground turmeric

1 tbsp dark muscovado sugar

3 tbsp sesame oil

3–4 shallots, finely sliced

1 garlic clove, finely sliced

1–2 red chiles, seeded and finely chopped

1 large carrot, cut into fine strips

1 yellow and 1 red bell pepper, sliced

1 zucchini, cut into fine strips

4½ oz/125 g sugar-snap peas, trimmed

3-inch/7.5-cm piece cucumber, cut into strips

9 oz/250 g oyster mushrooms,

9 oz/250 g canned chestnuts, drained

2 tsp grated fresh gingerroot

finely grated rind and juice of 1 lime

1 tbsp chopped fresh cilantro

salt and pepper

slices of lime, to garnish

1 To make the peanut sauce, grind the peanuts in a blender, or chop very finely. Put into a small pan with the hot chile sauce, coconut milk, soy sauce, ground coriander, ground turmeric, and dark muscovado sugar. Heat gently and simmer for 3–4 minutes. Keep warm and set aside until required.

2 Heat the sesame oil in a wok or large skillet. Add the shallots, garlic, and chiles and stir-fry for 2 minutes.

3 Add the carrot, bell peppers, zucchini, and sugar-snap peas to the wok or skillet and stir-fry for an additional 2 minutes.

4 Add the cucumber, mushrooms, chestnuts, ginger, lime rind and juice, and fresh cilantro to the wok or skillet and stir-fry briskly for 5 minutes, until the vegetables are crisp, yet crunchy.

5 Season to taste with salt and pepper.

6 Divide the stir-fry between four warmed serving plates, and garnish with slices of lime. Transfer the peanut sauce to a serving dish and serve with the vegetables.

Garlic Spinach

This has to be one of the simplest recipes, yet it is so tasty. Spinach is fried with garlic and lemon grass and tossed in soy sauce and sugar.

5 MINS   10 MINS

SERVES 4

I N G R E D I E N T S

2 garlic cloves

1 stem lemon grass

2 lb/900 g fresh spinach

2 tbsp peanut oil

salt

1 tbsp dark soy sauce

2 tsp brown sugar

1 Peel the garlic cloves and crush them in a pestle and mortar. Set aside until required.

2 Using a sharp knife, finely chop the lemon grass. Set aside until required.

3 Carefully remove the stems from the spinach. Rinse the spinach leaves and drain them thoroughly, patting them dry with absorbent paper towels.

4 Heat the peanut oil in a preheated wok or large, heavy-based skillet until it is almost smoking.

5 Reduce the heat slightly, then add the garlic and lemon grass and stir-fry for 30 seconds.

6 Add the spinach leaves and a pinch of salt to the wok or skillet and stir-fry for 2–3 minutes, until just wilted.

7 Stir the dark soy sauce and brown sugar into the mixture in the wok or skillet and cook for an additional 3–4 minutes.

8 Transfer the garlic spinach to a warm serving dish and serve as an accompaniment to a main dish.

COOK'S TIP

Lemon grass is available fresh, dried, and canned or bottled. Dried lemon grass must be soaked for 2 hours before using. The stems are hard and are usually used whole and removed from the dish before serving. The roots can be crushed or finely chopped.

Stir-Fried Eggplants

This dish would go well with rice and another vegetable dish such as stir-fried baby corn and green beans.

NUTRITIONAL INFORMATION

Calories	115	Sugars 2g
Protein	. . . . .3g	Fat 9g
Carbohydrate	. . . .6g	Saturates 1g

12¾ HOURS · 1¼ HOURS

SERVES 4

INGREDIENTS

generous ⅓ cup dried black beans

scant 1¾ cups vegetable stock

1 tbsp malt vinegar

1 tbsp dry sherry

1 tbsp soy sauce

1 tbsp sugar

1½ tsp cornstarch

1 red chile, seeded and chopped

½-inch/1-cm piece fresh gingerroot, chopped

2 eggplants

2 tsp salt

3 tbsp vegetable oil

2 garlic cloves, sliced

4 scallions, cut diagonally

shredded radishes, to garnish

1 Soak the beans overnight in plenty of cold water. Drain and place in a pan. Cover with cold water, bring to a boil and boil rapidly, uncovered, for 10 minutes. Drain. Return the beans to the pan with the vegetable stock and bring to a boil.

2 Blend together the vinegar, sherry, soy sauce, sugar, cornstarch, chile, and ginger in a small bowl. Add to the pan, cover and simmer for 40 minutes, until the beans are tender and the sauce has thickened. Stir occasionally.

3 Cut the eggplants into chunks and place in a colander. Sprinkle over the salt and leave to drain for 30 minutes. Rinse well to remove the salt and dry on paper towels. This process removes the bitter juices that would otherwise spoil the flavor of the dish.

4 Heat the vegetable oil in a wok or large skillet. Add the eggplant chunks and garlic. Stir-fry for 3–4 minutes, until the eggplant has started to brown.

5 Add the sauce to the eggplant with the scallions. Heat thoroughly, stirring to coat the eggplant, then garnish with radish shreds and serve.

Vegetable with Hoisin

This vegetable stir-fry has rice added to it and it can be served as a meal in itself.

NUTRITIONAL INFORMATION

Calories	120	Sugars	.........6g
Protein	.........4g	Fat	...........6g
Carbohydrate	...12g	Saturates	.......1g

20 MINS

10 MINS

SERVES 4

INGREDIENTS

1 red onion

3½ oz/100 g carrots

1 yellow bell pepper

2 tbsp corn oil

generous ⅔ cup cooked brown rice

2 cups snow peas

scant 1¼ cups bean sprouts

4 tbsp hoisin sauce

1 tbsp snipped fresh chives

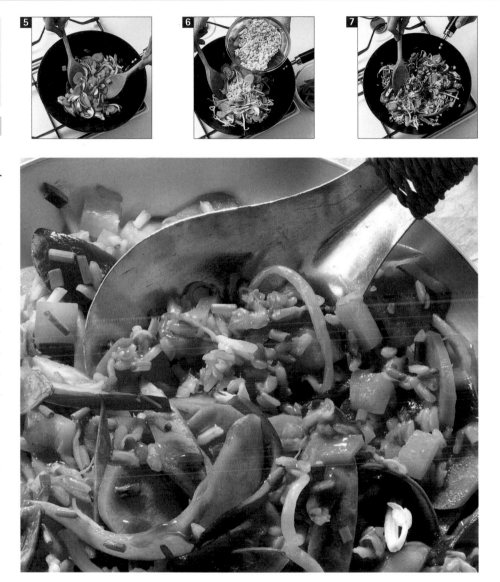

1 Using a sharp knife, thinly slice the red onion.

2 Thinly slice the carrots.

3 Seed and dice the yellow bell pepper.

4 Heat the corn oil in a large preheated wok or heavy-based skillet.

5 Add the red onion slices, carrots, and yellow bell pepper to the wok and stir-fry for 3 minutes.

6 Add the cooked brown rice, snow peas, and bean sprouts to the mixture in the wok and stir-fry for an additional 2 minutes. Stir briskly to ensure that the ingredients are well mixed and the rice grains are separated.

7 Stir the hoisin sauce into the vegetables and mix until well combined and completely heated through.

8 Transfer the vegetable stir-fry to warm serving dishes and scatter with the snipped fresh chives. Serve immediately.

COOK'S TIP

Hoisin sauce is a dark brown, reddish sauce made from soybeans, garlic, chile, and various other spices, and is commonly used in Chinese cookery. It may also be used as a dipping sauce.

Sweet & Sour Vegetables

Select vegetables from the suggested list, including scallions and garlic. For a hotter, spicier sauce add chile sauce.

NUTRITIONAL INFORMATION

Calories	160	Sugars	........16g
Protein	.........6g	Fat	...........7g
Carbohydrate	...18g	Saturates	.......1g

5 MINS   10 MINS

SERVES 4

INGREDIENTS

5–6 vegetables from the following:

1 bell pepper, red, green or yellow, cored, seeded and sliced

4½ oz/125 g green beans, cut into 2–3 pieces

4½ oz/125 g snow peas, cut into 2–3 pieces

9 oz/250 g broccoli or cauliflower, divided into tiny florets

9 oz/250 g zucchini, cut into thin 2-inch/ 5-cm lengths

6 oz/175 g carrots, cut into julienne strips

4½ oz/125 g baby corn cobs, sliced thinly

2 leeks, sliced thinly and cut into short thin sticks

4½ oz/125 g button or closed-cup mushrooms, thinly sliced

7 oz/200 g canned water chestnuts or bamboo shoots, drained and sliced

15 oz/425 g canned bean sprouts

4 scallions trimmed and thinly sliced

1 garlic clove, crushed

2 tbsp corn oil

SWEET & SOUR SAUCE

2 tbsp wine vinegar

2 tbsp clear honey

1 tbsp tomato paste

2 tbsp soy sauce

2 tbsp sherry

1–2 tsp sweet chile sauce (optional)

2 tsp cornstarch

1 Cut the selected vegetables into uniform lengths. Mix the sauce ingredients in a bowl. Heat the oil in the wok, then add the scallions and garlic and stir-fry for 1 minute.

2 Add the prepared vegetables—the harder and firmer ones first—and stir-fry for 2 minutes. Then add the softer ones such as mushrooms and snow peas and stir-fry for 2 minutes.

3 Add the sweet and sour mixture to the wok and bring to a boil quickly, tossing all the vegetables until they are thoroughly coated and the sauce has thickened. Serve hot.

Vegetable Stir-Fry

A range of delicious flavors are captured in this simple recipe that is ideal if you are in a hurry.

NUTRITIONAL INFORMATION

Calories 138	Sugars 5g
Protein 3g	Fat 12g
Carbohydrate 5g	Saturates 2g

🥘 5 MINS   🕑 25 MINS

SERVES 4

INGREDIENTS

3 tbsp vegetable oil

8 pearl onions, halved

1 eggplant, cubed

8 oz/225 g zucchini, sliced

2 cups open-cup mushrooms, halved

2 cloves garlic, crushed

14 oz/400 g canned chopped tomatoes

2 tbsp sun-dried tomato paste

2 tbsp soy sauce

1 tsp sesame oil

1 tbsp Chinese rice wine or dry sherry

freshly ground black pepper

fresh basil leaves, to garnish

1 Heat the vegetable oil in a large preheated wok or skillet.

2 Add the pearl onions and eggplant to the wok or skillet and stir-fry for 5 minutes, until the vegetables are golden and just beginning to soften.

3 Add the sliced zucchini, mushrooms, garlic, chopped tomatoes, and tomato paste to the wok and stir-fry for 5 minutes. Reduce the heat and leave to simmer for 10 minutes, until tender.

4 Add the soy sauce, sesame oil, and rice wine to the wok, then bring back to a boil and cook for 1 minute.

5 Season the vegetable stir-fry with freshly ground black pepper and scatter with fresh basil leaves. Serve immediately.

COOK'S TIP

Basil has a very strong flavor, which is perfect with vegetables and Chinese flavorings. Instead of using basil simply as a garnish in this dish, try adding a handful of fresh basil leaves to the stir-fry in step 4.

Green Stir-Fry

The basis of this recipe is bok choy, also known as pak choi or Chinese greens. If unavailable, use Swiss chard or savoy cabbage instead.

NUTRITIONAL INFORMATION

Calories	107	Sugars	6g
Protein	4g	Fat	8g
Carbohydrate	6g	Saturates	1g

5 MINS   10 MINS

SERVES 4

INGREDIENTS

2 tbsp peanut oil

2 garlic cloves, crushed

½ tsp ground star anise

1 tsp salt

12 oz/350 g bok choy, shredded

8 oz/225 g baby spinach

25 g/1 oz snow peas

1 celery stalk, sliced

1 green bell pepper, seeded and sliced

scant ¼ cup vegetable stock

1 tsp sesame oil

1 Heat the peanut oil in a preheated wok or large skillet, swirling the oil around the base of the wok until it is really hot.

2 Add the crushed garlic to the wok or skillet and stir-fry for about 30 seconds.

3 Stir in the ground star anise, salt, shredded bok choy, spinach, snow peas, celery, and green bell pepper and stir-fry for 3–4 minutes.

4 Add the vegetable stock, then cover the wok and cook for 3–4 minutes.

5 Remove the lid from the wok and stir in the sesame oil. Mix thoroughly to combine all the ingredients.

6 Transfer the green vegetable stir-fry to a warm serving dish and serve.

COOK'S TIP

Star anise is an important ingredient in Chinese cuisine. The attractive star-shaped pods are often used whole to add a decorative garnish to dishes. The flavor is similar to licorice, but with spicy undertones and is quite strong.

Spiced Eggplant

This is a spicy and sweet dish, flavored with mango chutney and heated up with chiles for a really wonderful combination of flavors.

NUTRITIONAL INFORMATION

Calories 208	Sugars 17g	
Protein 1g	Fat 15g	
Carbohydrate . . .17g	Saturates 2g	

5 MINS   25 MINS

SERVES 4

I N G R E D I E N T S

3 tbsp peanut oil

2 onions, sliced

2 garlic cloves, chopped

2 eggplant, diced

2 red chiles, seeded and very finely chopped

2 tbsp raw sugar

6 scallions, sliced

3 tbsp mango chutney

oil, for deep-frying

2 garlic cloves, sliced, to garnish

1 Heat the peanut oil in a large preheated wok or heavy-based skillet, swirling the oil around the base of the wok until it is really hot.

2 Add the onions and chopped garlic to the wok, stirring well.

3 Add the diced eggplant and chiles to the wok and stir-fry for 5 minutes.

4 Add the raw sugar, scallions, and mango chutney, stirring well.

5 Reduce the heat, then cover and leave to simmer, stirring from time to time, for 15 minutes, until the eggplant is cooked and tender.

6 Transfer the stir-fry to serving bowls and keep warm.

7 Heat the oil for deep-frying in the wok and quickly stir-fry the slices of garlic, until they brown slightly. Garnish the stir-fry with the deep-fried garlic and serve immediately.

COOK'S TIP

The "hotness" of chiles varies enormously so always use with caution, but as a general guide the smaller they are, the hotter they will be. The seeds are the hottest part and so are usually discarded.

Tofu

A popular ingredient in Chinese cooking, tofu is made from puréed and pressed yellow soybeans. Although it has a bland flavor it blends well with other ingredients and absorbs the flavors of spices and sauces. Tofu is extremely versatile—it can be stir-fried, deep-fried, or added to soups. It is also a healthy substitute for meat and fish,

being high in protein and low in fat. Tofu is sold in cakes and dried form, and it is also available marinated or smoked. The recipes in this chapter combine tofu with a variety of flavors and ingredients to create a selection of tasty snacks together with more filling main dishes—for example, Fried Tofu with Peanut Sauce, Braised Vegetables with Tofu, and Chinese Vegetable Casserole.

Fried Tofu with Peanut Sauce

This is a very sociable dish if put in the center of the table where people can help themselves with toothpicks.

NUTRITIONAL INFORMATION

Calories	338	Sugars 9g
Protein	........16g	Fat 22g
Carbohydrate	...21g	Saturates 4g

🍢 🍢 🍢 🍢

🍲 5 MINS   🕙 20 MINS

SERVES 4

I N G R E D I E N T S

1 lb 2 oz/500 g marinated or plain tofu

2 tbsp rice vinegar

2 tbsp sugar

1 tsp salt

3 tbsp smooth peanut butter

½ tsp chile flakes

3 tbsp barbecue sauce

4 cups corn oil

2 tbsp sesame oil

B A T T E R

4 tbsp all-purpose flour

2 eggs, beaten

4 tbsp milk

½ tsp baking powder

½ tsp chile powder

1 Cut the tofu into 1-inch/2.5-cm triangles. Set aside until required.

2 Combine the rice vinegar, sugar, and salt in a pan. Bring to a boil and then simmer for 2 minutes.

3 Remove the sauce from the heat and add the smooth peanut butter, chile flakes, and barbecue sauce, stirring well until thoroughly blended.

4 To make the batter, sift the all-purpose flour into a bowl, then make a well in the center and add the eggs. Draw in the flour, adding the milk slowly. Stir in the baking powder and chile powder.

5 Heat both the corn oil and sesame oil in a deep-fryer or large pan until a light haze appears on top.

6 Dip the tofu triangles into the batter and deep-fry until golden brown. You may need to do this in batches. Drain on absorbent paper towels.

7 Transfer the tofu triangles to a serving dish and serve with the peanut sauce.

COOK'S TIP

Tofu is made from puréed soybeans. It is white, with a soft cheese-like texture, and is sold in blocks, either fresh or vacuum-packed. Although it has a bland flavor, it blends well with other ingredients, and absorbs the flavors of spices and sauces.

Tofu Sandwiches

Slices of tofu are sandwiched together with a cucumber and cream cheese filling and coated in batter.

NUTRITIONAL INFORMATION

Calories ....398 Sugars 8g
Protein ....13g Fat 24g
Carbohydrate ...35g Saturates 7g

40 MINS   15 MINS

MAKES 28

INGREDIENTS

4 Chinese dried mushrooms (if
  unavailable, use thinly sliced
  open-cup mushrooms)

9½ oz/275 g tofu

½ cucumber, grated

½-inch/1-cm piece fresh gingerroot, grated

¼ cup cream cheese

salt and pepper

BATTER

scant 1 cup all-purpose flour

1 egg, beaten

½ cup water

½ tsp salt

2 tbsp sesame seeds

vegetable oil for deep-frying

SAUCE

⅔ cup plain yogurt

2 tsp honey

2 tbsp chopped fresh mint

1 Place the dried mushrooms in a small bowl and cover with warm water. Leave to soak for 20–25 minutes.

2 Drain the mushrooms, squeezing out the excess water. Remove the tough centers and chop the mushrooms.

3 Drain the tofu and slice thinly. Then cut each slice to make 1-inch/2.5-cm squares.

4 Squeeze the excess liquid from the cucumber and mix the cucumber with the mushrooms, grated ginger, and cream cheese. Season well with salt and pepper. Use as a filling to sandwich slices of tofu together to make about 28 sandwiches.

5 To make the batter, sift the flour into a bowl. Beat in the egg, water, and salt to make a thick batter. Stir in the sesame seeds. Heat the oil in a wok. Coat the sandwiches in the batter and deep-fry in batches until golden. Remove and drain on paper towels.

6 To make the dipping sauce, combine the yogurt, honey, and mint. Serve with the tofu sandwiches.

Braised Vegetables with Tofu

Also known as Buddha's Delight, the original recipe calls for 18 different vegetables to represent the 18 Buddhas—but 6-8 are quite acceptable!

NUTRITIONAL INFORMATION

Calories 300	Sugars 2g	
Protein 8g	Fat 28g	
Carbohydrate 6g	Saturates 3g	

3¾ HOURS   10 MINS

SERVES 4

INGREDIENTS

¼ oz/5 g dried wood ears

1 cake tofu

½ cup snow peas

4½oz/125 g Napa cabbage

1 small carrot

3 oz/85 g canned baby corn cobs, drained

3 oz/85 g canned straw mushrooms, drained

2 oz/55 g canned water chestnuts, drained

1¼ cups vegetable oil

1 tsp salt

½ tsp sugar

1 tbsp light soy sauce or oyster sauce

2–3 tbsp Chinese Stock (see page 30) or water

a few drops sesame oil

1 Soak the wood ears in warm water for 15-20 minutes, then rinse and drain, discarding any hard bits, and dry on paper towels.

2 Cut the cake of tofu into about 18 small pieces.

3 Top and tail the snow peas. Cut the Napa cabbage and the carrot into slices roughly the same size and shape as the snow peas. Cut the baby corn cobs, the straw mushrooms, and the water chestnuts in half.

4 Heat the oil in a preheated wok. Add the tofu and deep-fry for 2 minutes, until it turns slightly golden. Remove and drain on absorbent paper towels.

5 Pour off most of the oil, leaving about 2 tablespoons in the wok. Add the carrot, Napa cabbage, and snow peas and stir-fry for 1 minute. Add the corn, mushrooms, and water chestnuts.

6 Stir gently for 2 more minutes, then add the salt, sugar, soy sauce, and Chinese stock. Bring to a boil and stir-fry for 1 more minute. Sprinkle with sesame oil and serve hot or cold.

Ma-Po Tofu

Ma-Po was the wife of a Szechuan chef who created this popular dish in the middle of the 19th century.

NUTRITIONAL INFORMATION

Calories 235   Sugars 1g
Protein . . . . .16g   Fat 18g
Carbohydrate . . . .3g   Saturates 4g

3½ HOURS   15 MINS

SERVES 4

I N G R E D I E N T S

3 cakes tofu

3 tbsp vegetable oil

4½ oz/125 g coarsely ground beef

¼ tsp fincly chopped garlic

1 leek, cut into short sections

½ tsp salt

1 tbsp black bean sauce

1 tbsp light soy sauce

1 tsp chile bean sauce

3–4 tbsp Chinese Stock (see page 30) or water

2 tsp Cornstarch Paste (see page 31)

a few drops sesame oil

black pepper

finely chopped scallions, to garnish

1 Cut the tofu into ½-inch/1-cm cubes, handling it carefully.

2 Bring some water to a boil in a small pan or a wok, then add the tofu and blanch for 2-3 minutes to harden. Remove and drain well.

3 Heat the oil in a preheated wok. Add the ground beef and garlic and stir-fry for 1 minute, until the color of the beef changes. Add the leek, salt, and sauces and blend well.

4 Add the stock or water followed by the tofu. Bring to a boil and braise gently for 2-3 minutes.

5 Add the cornstarch paste, and stir until the sauce has thickened. Sprinkle with sesame oil and black pepper, then garnish and serve hot.

COOK'S TIP

Tofu has been an important element in Chinese cooking for more than 1000 years. It is made of yellow soybeans, which are soaked, ground, and mixed with water. Tofu is highly nutritious, being rich in protein and low in fat.

Tofu with Mushrooms

Chunks of cucumber and smoked tofu stir-fried with straw mushrooms, snow peas, and corn in a yellow bean sauce.

🕒 15 MINS   🕐 10 MINS

SERVES 4

INGREDIENTS

1 large cucumber

1 tsp salt

8 oz/225 g smoked tofu

2 tbsp vegetable oil

½ cup snow peas

8 baby corn cobs

1 celery stalk, sliced diagonally

15 oz/425 g canned straw mushrooms, drained

2 scallions, cut into strips

½-inch/1-cm piece fresh gingerroot, chopped

1 tbsp yellow bean sauce

1 tbsp light soy sauce

1 tbsp dry sherry

1 Halve the cucumber lengthwise and remove the seeds, using a teaspoon or melon baller.

2 Cut the cucumber into cubes, then place in a colander and sprinkle over the salt. Leave to drain for 10 minutes. Rinse thoroughly in cold water to remove the salt and drain thoroughly on absorbent paper towels.

3 Cut the tofu into cubes.

4 Heat the vegetable oil in a wok or large skillet until smoking.

5 Add the tofu, snow peas, baby corn cobs, and celery to the wok. Stir until the tofu is lightly browned.

6 Add the straw mushrooms, scallions, and ginger, and stir-fry for an additional minute.

7 Stir in the cucumber, yellow bean sauce, light soy sauce, dry sherry, and 2 tablespoons of water. Stir-fry for 1 minute and ensure that all the vegetables are coated in the sauces before serving.

COOK'S TIP

Straw mushrooms are available in cans from Asian suppliers and some supermarkets. If unavailable, substitute 9 oz/ 250 g baby white mushrooms.

Chinese Vegetable Casserole

This mixed vegetable casserole is very versatile and is delicious with any combination of vegetables of your choice.

NUTRITIONAL INFORMATION

Calories 218   Sugars 4g
Protein . . . . .7g   Fat 14g
Carbohydrate . . .12g   Saturates 2g

5 MINS   30 MINS

SERVES 4

I N G R E D I E N T S

4 tbsp vegetable oil

2 medium carrots, sliced

1 zucchini, sliced

4 baby corn cobs, halved lengthwise

4½ oz/125 g cauliflower florets

1 leek, sliced

4½ oz/125 g water chestnuts, halved

8 oz/225 g tofu, diced

1¼ cups vegetable stock

1 tsp salt

2 tsp dark brown sugar

2 tsp dark soy sauce

2 tbsp dry sherry

1 tbsp cornstarch

2 tbsp water

1 tbsp chopped cilantro, to garnish

1 Heat the oil in a preheated wok until it is almost smoking. Lower the heat slightly, then add the carrots, zucchini, corn cobs, cauliflower, and leek to the wok and stir-fry for 2–3 minutes.

2 Stir in the water chestnuts, tofu, stock, salt, sugar, soy sauce, and sherry and bring to a boil. Reduce the heat, then cover and simmer for 20 minutes.

3 Blend the cornstarch with the water to form a smooth paste.

4 Stir the cornstarch mixture into the wok. Bring the sauce to a boil and cook, stirring constantly until it thickens and clears.

5 Transfer the casserole to a warm serving dish. Sprinkle with chopped cilantro and serve immediately.

COOK'S TIP

If there is too much liquid remaining, boil vigorously for 1 minute before adding the cornstarch to reduce it slightly.

Oysters with Tofu

Oysters are often eaten raw, but are delicious when quickly cooked as in this recipe, and mixed with salt and citrus flavors.

NUTRITIONAL INFORMATION

Calories 175   Sugars 2g
Protein ....18g   Fat 10g
Carbohydrate ....3g   Saturates 1g

🦪 🦪

🍲 5 MINS   🕐 10 MINS

SERVES 4

INGREDIENTS

8 oz/225 g leeks

12 oz/350 g tofu

2 tbsp corn oil

12 oz/350 g shelled oysters

2 tbsp fresh lemon juice

1 tsp cornstarch

2 tbsp light soy sauce

scant ½ cup fish stock

2 tbsp chopped fresh cilantro

1 tsp finely grated lemon zest

1 Using a sharp knife, trim and slice the leeks.

2 Cut the tofu into bite-size pieces.

3 Heat the corn oil in a large preheated wok or skillet. Add the leeks to the wok and stir-fry for 2 minutes.

4 Add the tofu and oysters to the wok or skillet and stir-fry for 1–2 minutes.

5 Mix together the lemon juice, cornstarch, light soy sauce, and fish stock in a small bowl, stirring to blend.

6 Pour the cornstarch mixture into the wok and cook, stirring occasionally, until the juices start to thicken.

7 Transfer to serving bowls and scatter the cilantro and lemon zest on top. Serve immediately.

VARIATION

Shelled clams or mussels could be used instead of the oysters, if you prefer.

Tofu & Vegetable Stir-Fry

This is a quick dish to prepare, making it ideal as a mid-week supper dish, after a busy day at work.

NUTRITIONAL INFORMATION

Calories	124	Sugars	.........2g
Protein	.........6g	Fat	...........6g
Carbohydrate	....11g	Saturates	.......1g

5 MINS   25 MINS

SERVES 4

INGREDIENTS

6 oz/175 g potatoes, cubed

1 tbsp vegetable oil

1 red onion, sliced

8 oz/225 g firm tofu, diced

2 zucchini, diced

8 canned artichoke hearts, halved

⅔ cup strained tomatoes

1 tbsp sweet chile sauce

1 tbsp soy sauce

1 tsp superfine sugar

2 tbsp chopped basil

salt and pepper

1 Cook the potatoes in a pan of boiling water for 10 minutes. Drain well and set aside until required.

2 Heat the vegetable oil in a wok or large skillet and sauté the red onion for 2 minutes until the onion has softened, stirring.

3 Stir in the diced tofu and zucchini and cook for 3–4 minutes, until they begin to brown slightly.

4 Add the cooked potatoes to the wok or skillet, stirring to mix all the ingredients together.

5 Stir in the artichoke hearts, strained tomatoes, sweet chile sauce, soy sauce, sugar, and basil.

6 Season to taste with salt and pepper and cook for an additional 5 minutes, stirring well.

7 Transfer the tofu and vegetable stir-fry to serving dishes and serve immediately.

COOK'S TIP

Canned artichoke hearts should be drained thoroughly and rinsed before use because they often have salt added.

Black Bean Casserole

This colorful Chinese-style casserole is made with tofu, vegetables, and black bean sauce.

NUTRITIONAL INFORMATION

Calories 513   Sugars 5g
Protein . . . . .19g   Fat 25g
Carbohydrate . . .56g   Saturates 4g

30 MINS   30 MINS

SERVES 4

INGREDIENTS

6 Chinese dried mushrooms

9½ oz/275 g tofu

3 tbsp vegetable oil

1 carrot, cut into thin strips

1¼ cups snow peas

8 baby corn cobs, halved lengthwise

8 oz/225 g canned sliced bamboo shoots, drained

1 red bell pepper, cut into chunks

4½ oz/125 g Napa cabbage, shredded

1 tbsp soy sauce

1 tbsp black bean sauce

1 tsp sugar

1 tsp cornstarch

vegetable oil for deep-frying

9 oz/250 g Chinese rice noodles

salt

1 Soak the dried mushrooms in a bowl of warm water for 20–25 minutes. Drain and squeeze out the excess water, reserving 6 tablespoons of the liquid. Remove the tough centers and slice the mushrooms thinly with a sharp knife.

2 Cut the tofu into cubes. Boil in a large pan of lightly salted water for 2–3 minutes to firm up and then drain.

3 Heat half the oil in a pan. Add the tofu and fry until lightly browned. Remove and drain on paper towels.

4 Add the remaining oil and stir-fry the mushrooms, carrot, snow peas, baby corn, bamboo shoots, and bell pepper for 2–3 minutes. Add the Napa cabbage and tofu, and stir-fry for an additional 2 minutes.

5 Stir in the sauces and sugar, season with salt, and add the reserved liquid mixed with cornstarch. Bring to a boil, then reduce the heat and braise, covered, for 2–3 minutes, until thickened.

6 Heat the oil for deep-frying in a large pan. Deep-fry the noodles, in batches, until puffed up and lightly golden. Drain and serve with the casserole.

Spicy Fried Tofu Triangles

Marinated tofu is ideal in this recipe for added flavor, although the spicy coating is very tasty with plain tofu.

NUTRITIONAL INFORMATION

Calories	224	Sugars	........17g
Protein	........10g	Fat	..........13g
Carbohydrate	...18g	Saturates	.......2g

1¼ HOURS   10 MINS

SERVES 4

INGREDIENTS

1 tbsp sea salt

4½ tsp Chinese five-spice powder

3 tbsp light brown sugar

2 garlic cloves, crushed

1 tsp grated fresh gingerroot

2 x 8 oz/225 g cakes tofu

vegetable oil, for deep-frying

2 leeks, shredded and halved

shredded leek, to garnish

1 Mix together the salt, Chinese five-spice powder, sugar, garlic, and ginger in a bowl and transfer to a plate.

2 Cut the tofu cakes in half diagonally to form two triangles. Cut each triangle in half and then in half again to form 16 triangles.

3 Roll the tofu triangles in the spice mixture, turning to coat thoroughly. Set aside for 1 hour.

4 Heat the vegetable oil for deep-frying in a wok until it is almost smoking.

5 Reduce the heat slightly, then add the tofu triangles and deep-fry for 5 minutes, until golden brown. Remove the tofu from the wok with a slotted spoon, then set aside and keep warm until required.

6 Add the leeks to the wok and stir-fry for 1 minute. Remove from the wok and drain on paper towels.

7 Arrange the leeks on a warm serving plate and place the fried tofu on top. Garnish with the fresh shredded leek and serve immediately.

COOK'S TIP

Fry the tofu in batches and keep each batch warm until all of the tofu has been fried and is ready to serve.

Sweet & Sour Tofu

Sweet and sour sauce was one of the first Chinese sauces introduced to Western diets, and remains one of the most popular.

NUTRITIONAL INFORMATION

Calories	205	Sugars 12g
Protein	........11g	Fat 11g
Carbohydrate	...17g	Saturates 1g

5 MINS   10 MINS

SERVES 4

INGREDIENTS

2 celery stalks

1 carrot

1 green bell pepper, seeded

¾ cup snow peas

2 tbsp vegetable oil

2 garlic cloves, crushed

8 baby corn cobs

scant 1 cup bean sprouts

1 lb/450 g tofu, cubed

rice or noodles, to serve

SAUCE

2 tbsp light brown sugar

2 tbsp wine vinegar

scant 1 cup vegetable stock

1 tsp tomato paste

1 tbsp cornstarch

1 Using a sharp knife, thinly slice the celery, cut the carrot into thin strips, dice the bell pepper, and cut the snow peas in half diagonally.

2 Heat the vegetable oil in a preheated wok until it is almost smoking. Reduce the heat slightly, add the crushed garlic, celery, carrot, bell pepper, snow peas, and corn cobs and stir-fry for 3–4 minutes.

3 Add the bean sprouts and tofu to the wok and cook for 2 minutes, stirring constantly.

4 To make the sauce, combine the sugar, wine vinegar, stock, tomato paste, and cornstarch, stirring well to mix. Stir into the wok, bring to a boil and cook, stirring, until the sauce thickens and clears. Continue to cook for 1 minute. Serve with rice or noodles.

COOK'S TIP

Be careful not to break up the tofu when stirring.

Tofu with Bell Peppers

Tofu is perfect for marinating as it readily absorbs flavors for a great-tasting main dish.

NUTRITIONAL INFORMATION

Calories 267	Sugars 2g	
Protein 9g	Fat 23g	
Carbohydrate 5g	Saturates 3g	

25 MINS   15 MINS

SERVES 4

INGREDIENTS

12 oz/350 g tofu

2 garlic cloves, crushed

4 tbsp soy sauce

1 tbsp sweet chile sauce

6 tbsp corn oil

1 onion, sliced

1 green bell pepper, seeded and diced

1 tbsp sesame oil

1 Using a sharp knife, cut the tofu into bite-size pieces. Place the tofu in a shallow non-metallic dish.

2 Mix together the garlic, soy sauce, and sweet chile sauce and drizzle over the tofu. Toss well to coat and leave to marinate for about 20 minutes.

3 Meanwhile, heat the corn oil in a large preheated wok.

4 Add the onion to the wok and stir-fry over high heat until brown and crispy. Remove the onion slices with a slotted spoon and leave them to drain on absorbent paper towels.

5 Add the tofu to the hot oil and stir-fry for 5 minutes.

6 Remove all but 1 tablespoon of the corn oil from the wok. Add the bell pepper to the wok and stir-fry for 2–3 minutes, until softened.

7 Return the tofu and onions to the wok and heat through, stirring gently.

8 Drizzle with sesame oil. Transfer to serving plates and serve immediately.

COOK'S TIP

If you are in a real hurry, buy ready-marinated tofu from your supermarket.

Tofu Casserole

Tofu is ideal for absorbing all the other flavors in this dish. If marinated tofu is used, it will add a flavor of its own.

NUTRITIONAL INFORMATION

Calories 228   Sugars 3g
Protein . . . . .16g   Fat 15g
Carbohydrate . . . .7g   Saturates 2g

5 MINS   15 MINS

SERVES 4

I N G R E D I E N T S

1 lb/450 g tofu

2 tbsp peanut oil

8 scallions, cut into batons

2 celery stalks, sliced

4½ oz/125 g broccoli florets

4½ oz/125 g zucchini, sliced

2 garlic cloves, thinly sliced

1 lb/450 g baby spinach

rice, to serve

S A U C E

generous 1¾ cups vegetable stock

2 tbsp light soy sauce

3 tbsp hoisin sauce

½ tsp chile powder

1 tbsp sesame oil

1 Cut the tofu into 1-inch/2.5-cm cubes and set aside until required.

2 Heat the peanut oil in a preheated wok or large skillet.

3 Add the scallions, celery, broccoli, zucchini, garlic, spinach, and tofu to the wok or skillet and stir-fry for 3–4 minutes.

4 To make the sauce, mix together the vegetable stock, soy sauce, hoisin sauce, chile powder, and sesame oil in a flameproof casserole and bring to a boil.

5 Add the stir-fried vegetables and tofu to the pan, then reduce the heat, and simmer, covered, for 10 minutes.

6 Transfer the tofu and vegetables to a warm serving dish and serve with rice.

VARIATIONS

This recipe has a green vegetable theme, but alter the color and flavor by adding your favourite vegetables.

Add 2¾ oz/75 g fresh or canned and drained straw mushrooms with the vegetables in step 2.

Fried Tofu & Vegetables

Tofu is available in different forms from both Chinese and Western supermarkets. The cake form of tofu is used in this recipe.

NUTRITIONAL INFORMATION

Calories 367   Sugars 5g
Protein . . . . .13g   Fat 30g
Carbohydrate . . . .11g   Saturates 4g

5 MINS   15 MINS

SERVES 4

I N G R E D I E N T S

1 lb/450 g tofu

⅔ cup vegetable oil

1 leek, sliced

4 baby corn cobs, halved lengthwise

2 oz/55 g snow peas

1 red bell pepper, seeded and diced

½ cup canned bamboo shoots, drained and rinsed

rice or noodles, to serve

S A U C E

1 tbsp Chinese rice wine or dry sherry

4 tbsp oyster sauce

3 tsp light soy sauce

2 tsp superfine sugar

pinch of salt

scant ¼ cup vegetable stock

1 tsp cornstarch

2 tsp water

1 Rinse the tofu in cold water and pat dry with paper towels. Cut the tofu into 1-inch/2.5-cm cubes.

2 Heat the oil in a preheated wok until almost smoking. Reduce the heat, then add the tofu and stir-fry until golden brown. Remove with a slotted spoon and drain on absorbent paper towels.

3 Pour all but 2 tablespoons of the oil from the wok and return to the heat. Add the leek, corn cobs, snow peas, bell pepper, and bamboo shoots and stir-fry for 2–3 minutes.

4 Add the Chinese rice wine or sherry, oyster sauce, soy sauce, sugar, salt, and stock to the wok and bring to a boil. Blend the cornstarch with the water to form a smooth paste and stir it into the sauce. Bring to a boil and cook, stirring constantly, until thickened and clear.

5 Stir the tofu into the mixture in the wok and cook for 1 minute, until hot. Serve with rice or noodles.

Rice

Together with noodles, rice forms the central part of a Chinese meal, particularly in southern China. In the north, the staple foods tend to be more wheat-based. For an everyday meal, plain rice is served with one or two dishes and a soup. Rice can be boiled and then steamed or it can be fried with other ingredients such as eggs, shrimp, meat,

and vegetables and then flavored with soy sauce. The most common type of rice used in Chinese cooking is short-grain or glutinous rice, which become slightly sticky when cooked and is therefore ideal for eating with chopsticks. This chapter includes some delicious rice dishes, which can be eaten on their own or as an accompaniment. Fried rice is a particular favorite in Western restaurants, so several variations are included here.

Egg Fried Rice

In this classic Chinese dish, boiled rice is fried with peas, scallions, and egg and flavored with soy sauce.

NUTRITIONAL INFORMATION

Calories	203	Sugars	.........1g
Protein	.........9g	Fat	...........11g
Carbohydrate	...19g	Saturates	.......2g

20 MINS   10 MINS

SERVES 4

INGREDIENTS

¾ cup long-grain rice

3 eggs, beaten

2 tbsp vegetable oil

2 garlic cloves, crushed

4 scallions, chopped

generous 1 cup cooked peas

1 tbsp light soy sauce

pinch of salt

shredded scallion, to garnish

1 Cook the rice in a pan of boiling water for 10-12 minutes, until almost cooked, but not soft. Drain well, then rinse under cold water and drain again.

2 Place the beaten eggs in a pan and cook over gentle heat, stirring until softly scrambled.

3 Heat the vegetable oil in a preheated wok or large skillet, swirling the oil around the base of the wok until it is really hot.

4 Add the crushed garlic, scallions, and peas and sauté, stirring occasionally, for 1-2 minutes. Stir the rice into the wok, mixing to combine.

5 Add the eggs, light soy sauce and a pinch of salt to the wok or skillet and stir to mix the egg in thoroughly.

6 Transfer the egg fried rice to serving dishes and serve garnished with the shredded scallion.

COOK'S TIP

The rice is rinsed under cold water to wash out the starch and prevent it from sticking together.

Fried Rice with Pork

This dish is a meal in itself, containing pieces of pork, fried with rice, peas, tomatoes, and mushrooms.

NUTRITIONAL INFORMATION

Calories 285   Sugars 2g
Protein . . . . .18g   Fat 16g
Carbohydrate . . .19g   Saturates 4g

10 MINS   30 MINS

SERVES 4

INGREDIENTS

¾ cup long-grain rice

3 tbsp peanut oil

1 large onion, cut into 8

8 oz/225 g pork tenderloin, thinly sliced

2 open-cup mushrooms, sliced

2 garlic cloves, crushed

1 tbsp light soy sauce

1 tsp light brown sugar

2 tomatoes, skinned, seeded and chopped

½ cup cooked peas

2 eggs, beaten

1 Cook the rice in a pan of boiling water for 15 minutes, until tender, but not soft. Drain well, then rinse under cold running water and drain again thoroughly.

2 Heat the peanut oil in a preheated wok. Add the sliced onion and pork and stir-fry for 3-4 minutes, until just beginning to color.

3 Add the mushrooms and garlic to the wok and stir-fry for 1 minute.

4 Add the soy sauce and sugar to the mixture in the wok and stir-fry for an additional 2 minutes.

5 Stir in the rice, tomatoes, and peas, mixing well. Transfer the mixture to a warmed dish.

6 Stir the eggs into the wok and cook, stirring with a wooden spoon, for 2-3 minutes, until beginning to set.

7 Return the rice mixture to the wok and mix well. Transfer to serving dishes and serve immediately.

COOK'S TIP

You can cook the rice in advance and chill or freeze it until required.

Chinese Fried Rice

It is essential to use cold, dry rice with separate grains to make this recipe properly.

NUTRITIONAL INFORMATION

Calories	475	Sugars	.........3g
Protein	........16g	Fat	..........16g
Carbohydrate	...72g	Saturates	.......3g

5 MINS   30 MINS

SERVES 4

INGREDIENTS

3 cups water

½ tsp salt

1½ cups long-grain rice

2 eggs

4 tsp cold water

3 tbsp corn oil

4 scallions, sliced diagonally

1 red, green, or yellow bell pepper, cored, seeded and thinly sliced

3–4 lean bacon slices, rinded and cut into strips

7 oz/200 g fresh bean sprouts

generous 1 cup frozen peas, defrosted

2 tbsp soy sauce (optional)

salt and pepper

1   Pour the water into the wok with the salt and bring to a boil. Rinse the rice in a strainer under cold water until the water runs clear, then drain well and add to the boiling water. Stir well, then cover the wok tightly with the lid, and simmer gently for 12-13 minutes. (Don't remove the lid during cooking or the steam will escape and the rice will not be cooked.)

2   Remove the lid and give the rice a good stir, then spread out on a large plate or cookie sheet to cool and dry.

3   Beat each egg separately with salt and pepper and 2 teaspoons of cold water. Heat 1 tablespoon of oil in the wok, then pour in the first egg, swirl it around, and leave to cook undisturbed until set. Remove to a board and cook the second egg. Cut the omelets into thin slices.

4   Add the remaining oil to the wok and when really hot add the scallions and bell pepper and stir-fry for 1-2 minutes. Add the bacon and continue to stir-fry for an additional 1-2 minutes. Add the bean sprouts and peas and toss together thoroughly; stir in the soy sauce, if using.

5   Add the rice and seasoning and stir-fry for 1 minute or so, then add the strips of omelet and continue to stir for about 2 minutes, until the rice is piping hot. Serve at once.

Rice with Seven-Spice Beef

Beef fillet is used in this recipe as it is very suitable for quick cooking and has a wonderful flavor.

NUTRITIONAL INFORMATION

Calories 171   Sugars 8g
Protein . . . . .28g   Fat 15g
Carbohydrate . . .60g   Saturates 6g

5 MINS   30 MINS

SERVES 4

INGREDIENTS

generous 1 cup long-grain rice

2½ cups water

12 oz/350 g beef fillet

2 tbsp soy sauce

2 tbsp tomato ketchup

1 tbsp seven-spice seasoning

2 tbsp peanut oil

1 onion, diced

scant 1¾ cup diced carrots

1 cup frozen peas

2 eggs, beaten

2 tbsp cold water

1 Rinse the rice under cold running water, then drain thoroughly. Place the rice in a pan with 2½ cups of water, bring to a boil, then cover and leave to simmer for 12 minutes. Turn the cooked rice out on to a tray and leave to cool.

2 Using a sharp knife, thinly slice the beef fillet.

3 Mix together the soy sauce, tomato ketchup, and seven-spice seasoning. Spoon over the beef and toss well to coat.

4 Heat the oil in a preheated wok. Add the beef and stir-fry for 3–4 minutes.

5 Add the onion, carrots, and peas to the wok and stir-fry for an additional 2–3 minutes. Add the cooked rice to the wok and stir to combine.

6 Beat the eggs with 2 tablespoons of cold water. Drizzle the egg mixture over the rice and stir-fry for 3–4 minutes, until the rice is heated through and the egg has set. Transfer to a warm serving bowl and serve immediately.

VARIATION

You can use pork fillet or chicken instead of the beef, if you prefer.

Fragrant Coconut Rice

This fragrant, sweet rice is delicious served with meat, vegetable, or fish dishes as part of a Chinese menu.

NUTRITIONAL INFORMATION

Calories	306	Sugars	.........2g
Protein	.........5g	Fat	...........6g
Carbohydrate	...61g	Saturates	.......4g

5 MINS   15 MINS

SERVES 4

INGREDIENTS

scant 1½ cups long-grain rice

2½ cups water

½ tsp salt

⅓ cup coconut milk

¼ cup dry unsweetened coconut

1 Rinse the rice thoroughly under cold running water until the water runs completely clear.

2 Drain the rice thoroughly in a strainer set over a large bowl. This is to remove some of the starch and to prevent the grains from sticking together.

3 Place the rice in a wok with 2½ cups water.

4 Add the salt and coconut milk to the wok and bring to a boil.

5 Cover the wok with a lid or a lid made of foil, curved into a domed shape and resting on the sides of the wok. Reduce the heat and leave to simmer for 10 minutes.

6 Remove the lid from the wok and fluff up the rice with a fork—all of the liquid should be absorbed and the rice grains should be tender. If not, add more water and continue to simmer for a few more minutes until all the liquid has been absorbed.

7 Spoon the rice into a warm serving bowl and scatter with the dry unsweetened coconut. Serve immediately.

COOK'S TIP

Coconut milk is not the liquid found inside coconuts—that is called coconut water. Coconut milk is made from the white coconut flesh soaked in water and milk and then squeezed to extract all of the flavor. You can make your own or buy it in cans.

Stir-Fried Rice with Sausage

This is a very quick rice dish as it uses pre-cooked rice. It is therefore ideal when time is short or for a quick lunch-time dish.

5 MINS   20 MINS

SERVES 4

I N G R E D I E N T S

12 oz/350 g Chinese sausage

2 tbsp corn oil

2 tbsp soy sauce

1 onion, sliced

6 oz/175 g carrots, cut into thin sticks

generous 1½ cups peas

¾ cup canned pineapple cubes, drained

3⅔ cups cooked long-grain rice

1 egg, beaten

1 tbsp chopped fresh parsley

1 Using a sharp knife, thinly slice the Chinese sausage.

2 Heat the corn oil in a large preheated wok. Add the sausage to the wok and stir-fry for 5 minutes.

3 Stir in the soy sauce and let bubble for 2–3 minutes, until syrupy.

4 Add the onion, carrots, peas, and pineapple to the wok and stir-fry for an additional 3 minutes.

5 Add the cooked rice to the wok and stir-fry the mixture for 2–3 minutes, until the rice is heated through.

6 Drizzle the beaten egg over the top of the rice and cook, tossing the ingredients in the wok, until the egg sets.

7 Transfer the stir-fried rice to a large, warm serving bowl and scatter with plenty of chopped fresh parsley. Serve immediately.

COOK'S TIP

Cook extra rice and freeze it in preparation for some of the other rice dishes included in this book as it saves time and enables a meal to be prepared in minutes. Be sure to cool any leftover cooked rice quickly before freezing to avoid food poisoning.

Egg Foo Yong with Rice

In this dish, cooked rice is mixed with scrambled eggs and Chinese vegetables. It is a great way of using up leftover cooked rice.

NUTRITIONAL INFORMATION

Calories 258   Sugars 1g
Protein ....8g   Fat 16g
Carbohydrate ...21g   Saturates 3g

30 MINS   25 MINS

SERVES 4

INGREDIENTS

generous ¾ cup long-grain rice

2 Chinese dried mushrooms
   (if unavailable, use thinly sliced
   open-cup mushrooms)

3 eggs, beaten

3 tbsp vegetable oil

4 scallions, sliced

½ green bell pepper, chopped

½ cup canned bamboo shoots

⅓ cup canned water chestnuts, sliced

2 cups bean sprouts

2 tbsp light soy sauce

2 tbsp dry sherry

2 tsp sesame oil

salt and pepper

1 Cook the rice in lightly salted boiling water according to the packet instructions.

2 Place the Chinese dried mushrooms in a small bowl, then cover with warm water and leave to soak for 20–25 minutes.

3 Mix the beaten eggs with a little salt. Heat 1 tablespoon of the oil in a preheated wok or large skillet. Add the eggs and stir until just set. Remove the wok and set aside.

4 Drain the mushrooms and squeeze out the excess water. Remove the tough centers and chop the mushrooms.

5 Heat the remaining oil in a clean wok or skillet. Add the mushrooms, scallions, and green bell pepper, and stir-fry for 2 minutes. Add the bamboo shoots, water chestnuts, and bean sprouts. Stir-fry for 1 minute.

6 Drain the rice thoroughly and add to the pan with the remaining ingredients. Mix well, heating the rice thoroughly. Season to taste with salt and pepper. Stir in the reserved eggs and serve.

COOK'S TIP

To wash bean sprouts, place them in a bowl of cold water and swirl with your hand. Remove any long tail ends, then rinse and drain thoroughly.

Rice with Crab & Mussels

Shellfish makes an ideal partner for rice. Mussels and crab add flavor and texture to this spicy dish.

NUTRITIONAL INFORMATION

Calories	336	Sugars	.........4g
Protein	........32g	Fat	..........10g
Carbohydrate	...33g	Saturates	.......1g

20 MINS   10 MINS

SERVES 4

INGREDIENTS

1½ cups long-grain rice

6 oz/175 g white crabmeat, fresh, canned, or frozen (defrosted if frozen), or 8 crab sticks, defrosted if frozen

2 tbsp sesame or corn oil

1-inch/2.5-cm piece fresh gingerroot, grated

4 scallions, thinly sliced diagonally

generous 1 cup snow peas, cut into 2–3 pieces

½ tsp turmeric

1 tsp ground cumin

2 x 7 oz/200 g jars mussels, well drained, or 12 oz/350 g frozen mussels, defrosted

425 g/15 oz canned bean sprouts, well drained

salt and pepper

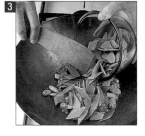

1 Cook the rice in boiling salted water, following the instructions given in Chinese Fried Rice (see page 310).

2 Extract the crabmeat, if using fresh crab (see right). Flake the crabmeat or cut the crab sticks into 3 or 4 pieces.

3 Heat the oil in a preheated wok and stir-fry the ginger and scallions for a minute or so. Add the snow peas and continue to cook for an additional minute.

Sprinkle the turmeric, cumin, and seasoning over the vegetables and mix together well.

4 Add the crabmeat and mussels and stir-fry for 1 minute. Stir in the cooked rice and bean sprouts and stir-fry for 2 minutes, until hot and well mixed.

5 Adjust the seasoning to taste and serve immediately.

COOK'S TIP

To prepare fresh crab, twist off the claws and legs, then crack with a heavy knife and pick out the meat with a skewer. Discard the gills and pull out the under shell; discard the stomach sac. Pull the soft meat from the shell. Cut open the body section and prize out the meat with a skewer.

Rice with Five-Spice Chicken

This dish has a wonderful color obtained from the turmeric, and a great spicy flavor, making it very appealing all round.

NUTRITIONAL INFORMATION

Calories	412	Sugars	.........1g
Protein	........23g	Fat	..........13g
Carbohydrate	...53g	Saturates	.......2g

5 MINS   20 MINS

SERVES 4

INGREDIENTS

1 tbsp Chinese five-spice powder

2 tbsp cornstarch

12 oz/350 g boneless, skinless chicken breasts, cubed

3 tbsp peanut oil

1 onion, diced

generous 1 cup long-grain rice

½ tsp turmeric

2½ cups chicken stock

2 tbsp snipped fresh chives

1 Place the Chinese five-spice powder and cornstarch in a large bowl and blend. Add the chicken pieces and toss to coat them all over.

2 Heat 2 tablespoons of the peanut oil in a large preheated wok. Add the chicken pieces to the wok and stir-fry for 5 minutes. Using a slotted spoon, remove the chicken and set aside.

3 Add the remaining peanut oil to the wok.

4 Add the onion to the wok and stir-fry for 1 minute.

5 Add the rice, turmeric, and chicken stock to the wok and gently bring to a boil.

6 Return the chicken pieces to the wok, reduce the heat and leave to simmer for 10 minutes, until the liquid has been absorbed and the rice is tender.

7 Add the snipped fresh chives, then stir to mix and serve hot.

COOK'S TIP

Be careful when using turmeric as it can stain the hands and clothes a distinctive shade of yellow.

Chinese Vegetable Rice

This rice can either be served as a meal in itself or as an accompaniment to other vegetable recipes.

NUTRITIONAL INFORMATION

Calories	228	Sugars	.........5g
Protein	.........5g	Fat	...........7g
Carbohydrate	...37g	Saturates	.......1g

5 MINS   25 MINS

SERVES 4

INGREDIENTS

1¾ cups long-grain rice

1 tsp turmeric

2 tbsp corn oil

8 oz/225 g zucchini, sliced

1 red bell pepper, seeded and sliced

1 green bell pepper, seeded and sliced

1 green chile, seeded and finely chopped

1 medium carrot, coarsely grated

1 cup bean sprouts

6 scallions, sliced, plus extra to garnish (optional)

2 tbsp soy sauce

salt

1 Place the rice and turmeric in a pan of lightly salted water and bring to a boil. Reduce the heat and leave to simmer until the rice is just tender. Drain the rice thoroughly and press out any excess water with absorbent paper towels. Set aside until required.

2 Heat the corn oil in a large preheated wok.

3 Add the zucchini to the wok and stir-fry for 2 minutes.

4 Add the bell peppers and chile to the wok and stir-fry for 2–3 minutes.

5 Add the cooked rice to the mixture in the wok, a little at a time, tossing well after each addition.

6 Add the carrots, bean sprouts, and scallions to the wok and stir-fry for an additional 2 minutes.

7 Drizzle with soy sauce and serve at once, garnished with extra scallions, if desired.

COOK'S TIP

For real luxury, add a few saffron strands infused in boiling water instead of the turmeric.

Green-Fried Rice

Spinach is used in this recipe to give the rice a wonderful green coloring. Tossed with the carrot strips, it is a really appealing dish.

NUTRITIONAL INFORMATION

Calories	139	Sugars	.........2g
Protein	.........3g	Fat	...........7g
Carbohydrate	...18g	Saturates	.......1g

🍲 5 MINS   🕒 20 MINS

SERVES 4

INGREDIENTS

¾ cup long-grain rice

2 tbsp vegetable oil

2 garlic cloves, crushed

1 tsp grated fresh gingerroot

1 carrot, cut into short, thin sticks

1 courgette zucchini, diced

8 oz/225 g baby spinach

2 tsp light soy sauce

2 tsp light brown sugar

1 Cook the rice in a pan of boiling water for about 15 minutes. Drain the rice well, rinse under cold running water and then rinse the rice thoroughly again. Set aside until required.

2 Heat the vegetable oil in a preheated wok or large, heavy-based skillet.

3 Add the crushed garlic and grated fresh gingerroot to the wok or skillet and stir-fry for 30 seconds.

4 Add the carrot sticks and diced zucchini to the mixture in the wok and stir-fry for 2 minutes, so the vegetables still retain their crunch.

5 Add the baby spinach and stir-fry for 1 minute, until wilted.

6 Add the rice, soy sauce, and sugar to the wok and mix together well.

7 Transfer the green-fried rice to serving dishes and serve immediately.

COOK'S TIP

Light soy sauce has more flavor than the sweeter, dark soy sauce, which gives the food a rich, reddish color.

Fruity Coconut Rice

A pale yellow rice flavored with coconut and spices to serve as an accompaniment—or as a main dish with added diced chicken or pork.

NUTRITIONAL INFORMATION

Calories	578	Sugars	........17g
Protein	.........8g	Fat	..........31g
Carbohydrate	....71g	Saturates	......15g

5 MINS   35 MINS

SERVES 4

INGREDIENTS

3 oz/85 g creamed coconut

3 cups boiling water

1 tbsp corn oil (or olive oil for a stronger flavor)

1 onion, thinly sliced or chopped

generous 1 cup long-grain rice

¼ tsp turmeric

6 whole cloves

1 cinnamon stick

½ tsp salt

½ cup raisins or golden raisins

⅓ cup walnut or pecan halves, coarsely chopped

2 tbsp pumpkin seeds (optional)

1 Blend the creamed coconut with half the boiling water until smooth, then stir in the remainder until well blended.

2 Heat the oil in a preheated wok, add the onion and stir-fry gently for 3-4 minutes, until the onion softens.

3 Rinse the rice thoroughly under cold running water, then drain well and add to the wok with the turmeric. Cook for 1-2 minutes, stirring all the time.

4 Add the coconut milk, cloves, cinnamon stick, and salt and bring to a boil. Cover and simmer very gently for 10 minutes.

5 Add the raisins, nuts, and pumpkin seeds, if using, and mix well. Cover the wok again and continue to cook for an additional 5-8 minutes, until all the liquid has been absorbed and the rice is tender. Remove from the heat and leave to stand, still tightly covered, for 5 minutes. Remove the cinnamon stick and serve.

COOK'S TIP

Add 9 oz/250 g cooked chicken or pork cut into dice or thin slivers with the raisins to turn this into a main dish. The addition of coconut milk makes the cooked rice slightly sticky.

Chinese Chicken Rice

This is a really colorful main meal or side dish that tastes just as good as it looks.

NUTRITIONAL INFORMATION

Calories	324	Sugars	.........4g
Protein	........24g	Fat	..........10g
Carbohydrate	...37g	Saturates	.......2g

5 MINS   25 MINS

SERVES 4

INGREDIENTS

1⅔ cups long-grain white rice

1 tsp turmeric

2 tbsp corn oil

12 oz/350 g skinless, boneless chicken breasts or thighs, sliced

1 red bell pepper, seeded and sliced

1 green bell pepper, seeded and sliced

1 green chile, seeded and finely chopped

1 medium carrot, coarsely grated

1 cup bean sprouts

6 scallions, sliced, plus extra to garnish

2 tbsp soy sauce

salt

1 Place the rice and turmeric in a large pan of lightly salted water and cook for about 10 minutes, until the grains of rice are just tender. Drain the rice thoroughly and press out any excess water with paper towels.

2 Heat the corn oil in a large preheated wok or skillet.

3 Add the strips of chicken to the wok or skillet and stir-fry over high heat until the chicken is just beginning to turn a golden color.

4 Add the sliced bell peppers and green chile to the wok and stir-fry for 2–3 minutes.

5 Add the cooked rice to the wok, a little at a time, tossing well after each addition until well combined and the grains of rice are separated.

6 Add the carrot, bean sprouts, and scallions to the wok and stir-fry for an additional 2 minutes.

7 Drizzle with the soy sauce and toss to combine.

8 Transfer the Chinese chicken rice to a warm serving dish. Garnish with extra scallions, if wished, and serve at once.

Curried Rice with Tofu

Cooked rice is combined with marinated tofu, vegetables, and peanuts to make this deliciously rich curry.

NUTRITIONAL INFORMATION

Calories 598	Sugars 2g	
Protein 16g	Fat 25	
Carbohydrate ...81g	Saturates 4g	

🥗 15 MINS   🕐 15 MINS

SERVES 4

I N G R E D I E N T S

1 tsp coriander seeds

1 tsp cumin seeds

1 tsp ground cinnamon

1 tsp cloves

1 whole star anise

1 tsp cardamom pods

1 tsp white peppercorns

1 tbsp oil

6 shallots, chopped very coarsely

6 garlic cloves, chopped very coarsely

2-inch/5-cm piece lemon grass, sliced

4 fresh red chiles, seeded and chopped

grated rind of 1 lime

1 tsp salt

3 tbsp corn oil

9 oz/250 g marinated tofu, cut into
   1-inch/2.5-cm cubes

1 cup green beans, cut into 1-inch/
   2.5cm lengths

5 cups cups cooked rice
   (2 cups raw weight)

3 shallots, diced finely and deep-fried

1 scallion, chopped finely

2 tbsp chopped roast peanuts

1 tbsp lime juice

1 To make the curry paste, grind together the seeds and spices in a pestle and mortar or spice grinder.

2 Heat the oil in a preheated wok until it is really hot. Add the shallots, garlic, and lemon grass and cook over low heat until soft, about 5 minutes. Add the chiles and grind together with the dry spices. Stir in the lime rind and salt.

3 To make the curry, heat the corn oil in a wok or large, heavy skillet. Cook the tofu over high heat for 2 minutes to seal. Stir in the curry paste and beans. Add the rice and stir over high heat for 3 minutes.

4 Transfer to a warmed serving dish. Sprinkle with the deep-fried shallots, scallion and peanuts. Squeeze over the lime juice.

Crab Congee

This is a typical Chinese breakfast dish, although it is probably best served as a lunch or supper dish at a Western table!

NUTRITIONAL INFORMATION

Calories . . . . . . .327 Sugars 0.1g
Protein . . . . .18g Fat 7g
Carbohydrate . . .50g Saturates 2g

5 MINS   1¼ HOURS

SERVES 4

INGREDIENTS

scant 1 cup short-grain rice

6¼ cups fish stock

½ tsp salt

3½ oz/100 g Chinese sausage,
    thinly sliced

8 oz/225 g white crabmeat

6 scallions, sliced

2 tbsp chopped fresh cilantro

freshly ground black pepper,
    to serve

1 Place the short-grain rice in a large preheated wok or heavy-based skillet.

2 Add the fish stock to the wok or skillet and bring to a boil.

3 Reduce the heat, then simmer gently for 1 hour, stirring the mixture from time to time.

4 Add the salt, sliced Chinese sausage, white crabmeat, sliced scallions, and chopped fresh cilantro to the wok and heat through for about 5 minutes.

5 Add a little more water to the wok if the congee "porridge" is too thick, stirring well.

6 Transfer the crab congee to warm serving bowls, then sprinkle with freshly ground black pepper and serve immediately.

COOK'S TIP

Always buy the freshest possible crabmeat; fresh is best, although frozen or canned will work for this recipe. In the West, crabs are almost always sold ready-cooked. The crab should feel heavy for its size, and when it is shaken there should be no sound of water inside.

Curried Rice with Pork

This rice dish is flavored with vegetables and pork, soy sauce, and curry spices with strips of omelet added as a topping.

NUTRITIONAL INFORMATION

Calories 436	Sugars 2g	
Protein 30g	Fat 20g	
Carbohydrate ...37g	Saturates 5g	

10 MINS   35 MINS

SERVES 4

INGREDIENTS

1½ cups long-grain rice

12 oz–1 lb 2 oz/350–500 g pork fillet or lean pork slices

3 tomatoes, peeled, cut into fourths, and seeded

2 eggs

4 tsp water

3 tbsp corn oil

1 onion, thinly sliced

1–2 garlic cloves, crushed

1 tsp medium or mild curry powder

½ tsp ground coriander

¼ tsp medium chile powder or 1 tsp bottled sweet chile sauce

2 tbsp soy sauce

generous 1 cup frozen peas, defrosted

salt and pepper

1 Cook the rice in boiling salted water, following the instructions given in Chinese Fried Rice (see page 310) and keep warm until required.

2 Meanwhile, cut the pork into narrow strips across the grain, discarding any fat. Slice the tomatoes.

3 Beat each egg separately with 2 teaspoons cold water and salt and pepper. Heat 2 teaspoons of oil in the wok

until really hot. Pour in the first egg, then swirl it around and cook undisturbed until set. Remove to a plate or board and repeat with the second egg. Cut the omelets into strips about ½ inch/1 cm wide.

4 Heat the remaining oil in the wok and when really hot add the onion and garlic and stir-fry for 1–2 minutes. Add the pork and continue to stir-fry for 3 minutes, until almost cooked.

5 Add the curry powder, coriander, chile powder, or chile sauce and soy sauce to the wok and cook for an additional minute, stirring constantly.

6 Stir in the rice, tomatoes, and peas and stir-fry for 2 minutes until piping hot. Adjust the seasoning to taste and turn into a heated serving dish. Arrange the strips of omelet on top and serve immediately.

Steamed Rice in Lotus Leaves

The fragrance of the leaves penetrates the rice, giving it a unique taste. Lotus leaves can be bought from specialist Chinese stores.

NUTRITIONAL INFORMATION

Calories 163	Sugars 0.1g
Protein 5g	Fat 6g
Carbohydrate ...2.1g	Saturates 1g

🍲 1 HOUR   🕐 40 MINS

SERVES 4

I N G R E D I E N T S

2 lotus leaves

4 Chinese dried mushrooms (if unavailable, use thinly sliced open-cup mushrooms)

generous ¾ cup long-grain rice

1 cinnamon stick

6 cardamom pods

4 cloves

1 tsp salt

2 eggs

1 tbsp vegetable oil

2 scallions, chopped

1 tbsp soy sauce

2 tbsp sherry

1 tsp sugar

1 tsp sesame oil

1 Unfold the lotus leaves carefully and cut along the fold to divide each leaf in half. Lay on a large baking sheet and pour over enough hot water to cover. Soak for 30 minutes, until softened.

2 Place the dried mushrooms in a small bowl and cover with warm water. Leave to soak for 20–25 minutes.

3 Cook the rice in a pan of boiling water with the cinnamon stick, cardamom pods, cloves, and salt for 10 minutes—the rice should be partially cooked. Drain thoroughly and remove the cinnamon stick. Place the rice in a bowl.

4 Beat the eggs lightly. Heat the oil in a wok and cook the eggs quickly, stirring until set. Remove and set aside.

5 Drain the mushrooms, squeezing out the excess water. Remove the tough centers and chop the mushrooms. Stir into the rice with the cooked egg, scallions, soy sauce, sherry, sugar, and sesame oil.

6 Drain the lotus leaves and divide the rice into four portions. Place a portion in the center of each leaf and fold up to form a packet. Place in a steamer, then cover and steam over simmering water for 20 minutes. To serve, cut the tops of the lotus leaves open to expose the rice inside.

Vegetable Fried Rice

This dish can be served as part of a substantial meal for a number of people or as a vegetarian meal in itself for four.

NUTRITIONAL INFORMATION

Calories	175	Sugars	.........3g
Protein	.........3g	Fat	..........10g
Carbohydrate	...20g	Saturates	.......2g

10 MINS 20 MINS

SERVES 4

INGREDIENTS

⅔ cup long-grain rice

3 tbsp peanut oil

2 garlic cloves, crushed

½ tsp Chinese five-spice powder

⅓ cup green beans

1 green bell pepper, seeded and chopped

4 baby corn cobs, sliced

1 oz/25 g canned bamboo shoots, chopped

3 tomatoes, skinned, seeded, and chopped

½ cup cooked peas

1 tsp sesame oil

1 Bring a large pan of water to a boil.

2 Add the long-grain rice to the pan and cook for 15 minutes. Drain the rice well, then rinse under cold running water and drain thoroughly again.

3 Heat the peanut oil in a preheated wok or large skillet. Add the garlic and Chinese five-spice and stir-fry for 30 seconds.

4 Add the green beans, chopped green bell pepper, and sliced corn cobs and stir-fry in the wok for 2 minutes.

5 Stir the bamboo shoots, tomatoes, peas, and rice into the mixture in the wok and stir-fry for 1 more minute.

6 Sprinkle with sesame oil and transfer to serving dishes. Serve immediately.

VARIATION

Use a selection of vegetables of your choice in this recipe, cutting them to a similar size in order to ensure that they cook in the same amount of time.

Chicken & Rice Casserole

This is a quick-cooking, spicy casserole of rice, chicken, vegetables, and chile in a soy and ginger flavored liquor.

NUTRITIONAL INFORMATION

Calories	502	Sugars	.........2g
Protein	........55g	Fat	..........9g
Carbohydrate	...52g	Saturates	.......3g

🍲 🍲 🍲

35 MINS   50 MINS

SERVES 4

INGREDIENTS

¾ cup long-grain rice

1 tbsp dry sherry

2 tbsp light soy sauce

2 tbsp dark soy sauce

2 tsp dark brown sugar

1 tsp salt

1 tsp sesame oil

2 lb/900 g skinless, boneless chicken meat, diced

3¾ cups chicken stock

2 open-cup mushrooms, sliced

⅓ cup water chestnuts, halved

2¾ oz/75 g broccoli florets

1 yellow bell pepper, sliced

4 tsp grated fresh gingerroot

whole chives, to garnish

VARIATIONS

This dish would work equally well with beef or pork.

Chinese dried mushrooms may be used instead of the open-cup mushrooms, if rehydrated before adding to the dish.

1 Cook the rice in a pan of boiling water for 15 minutes. Drain well, then rinse under cold water and drain again thoroughly.

2 Mix together the sherry, soy sauces, sugar, salt, and sesame oil.

3 Stir the chicken into the soy mixture, turning to coat the chicken well. Leave to marinate for about 30 minutes.

4 Bring the stock to a boil in a pan or preheated wok. Add the chicken with the marinade, mushrooms, water chestnuts, broccoli, bell pepper, and gingerroot.

5 Stir in the rice and reduce the heat, then cover and cook for 25-30 minutes, until the chicken and vegetables are cooked through. Transfer to serving plates, then garnish with chives and serve.

Special Fried Rice

This dish is a popular choice in Chinese restaurants. Ham and shrimp are mixed with vegetables in a soy-flavored rice.

NUTRITIONAL INFORMATION

Calories 301	Sugars 1g
Protein 26g	Fat 13g
Carbohydrate . . .21g	Saturates 3g

5 MINS   30 MINS

SERVES 4

INGREDIENTS

¾ cup long-grain rice

2 tbsp vegetable oil

2 eggs, beaten

2 garlic cloves, crushed

1 tsp grated fresh gingerroot

3 scallions, sliced

¾ cup cooked peas

1 cup bean sprouts

1 cup shredded ham

5½ oz/150 g shelled, cooked shrimp

2 tbsp light soy sauce

1 Cook the rice in a pan of boiling water for 15 minutes. Drain well, then rinse under cold water and drain thoroughly again.

2 Heat 1 tablespoon of the vegetable oil in a preheated wok.

3 Add the beaten eggs and an additional 1 teaspoon of oil. Tilt the wok so that the egg covers the base to make a thin omelet.

4 Cook until lightly browned on the underside, then flip the omelet over and cook on the other side for 1 minute. Remove from the wok and leave to cool.

5 Heat the remaining oil in the wok and stir-fry the garlic and ginger for 30 seconds. Add the scallions, peas, bean sprouts, ham, and shrimp. Stir-fry for 2 minutes.

6 Stir in the soy sauce and rice and cook for an additional 2 minutes. Transfer the rice to serving dishes. Roll up the omelet, then slice it very thinly and use to garnish the rice. Serve immediately.

COOK'S TIP

As this recipe contains meat and fish, it is ideal served with simpler vegetable dishes.

Sweet Chile Pork Fried Rice

This is a variation of egg fried rice and may be served as an accompaniment to a main meal dish.

NUTRITIONAL INFORMATION

Calories	366	Sugars	.........5g
Protein	........29g	Fat	..........16g
Carbohydrate	...28g	Saturates	.......4g

25 MINS   20 MINS

SERVES 4

I N G R E D I E N T S

1 lb/450 g pork tenderloin

2 tbsp corn oil

2 tbsp sweet chile sauce, plus extra
  to serve

1 onion, sliced

6 oz/175 g carrots, cut into thin sticks

6 oz/175 g zucchini, cut into sticks

⅔ cup canned bamboo shoots, drained

3⅔ cups cooked long-grain rice

1 egg, beaten

1 tbsp chopped fresh parsley

1 Using a sharp knife, cut the pork tenderloin into thin slices.

2 Heat the corn oil in a large preheated wok or skillet.

3 Add the pork to the wok and stir-fry for 5 minutes.

4 Add the chile sauce to the wok and let bubble, stirring, for 2–3 minutes, until syrupy.

5 Add the onion, carrots, zucchini, and bamboo shoots to the wok and stir-fry for an additional 3 minutes.

6 Add the cooked rice and stir-fry for 2–3 minutes, until the rice is heated through.

7 Drizzle the beaten egg over the top of the fried rice and cook, tossing the ingredients in the wok with two spoons, until the egg sets.

8 Scatter with chopped fresh parsley and serve immediately, with extra sweet chile sauce, if desired.

COOK'S TIP

For a really quick dish, add frozen mixed vegetables to the rice instead of the freshly prepared vegetables.

Crab Fried Rice

Canned crabmeat is used in this recipe for convenience, but fresh white crabmeat could be used—quite deliciously—in its place.

NUTRITIONAL INFORMATION

Calories 225	Sugars 1g	
Protein 12g	Fat 11g	
Carbohydrate ...20g	Saturates 2g	

5 MINS   25 MINS

SERVES 4

INGREDIENTS

⅔ cup long-grain rice

2 tbsp peanut oil

4½ oz/125 g canned white crabmeat, drained

1 leek, sliced

1 cup bean sprouts

2 eggs, beaten

1 tbsp light soy sauce

2 tsp lime juice

1 tsp sesame oil

salt

sliced lime, to garnish

1 Cook the rice in a pan of boiling salted water for 15 minutes. Drain well, then rinse under cold running water and drain again thoroughly.

2 Heat the peanut oil in a preheated wok until it is really hot.

3 Add the crabmeat, leek, and bean sprouts to the wok and stir-fry for 2-3 minutes. Remove the mixture from the wok with a slotted spoon and set aside until required.

4 Add the eggs to the wok and cook, stirring occasionally, for 2-3 minutes, until they begin to set.

5 Stir the rice and the crabmeat, leek, and bean sprout mixture into the eggs in the wok.

6 Add the soy sauce and lime juice to the mixture in the wok. Cook for 1 minute, stirring to combine, and sprinkle with the sesame oil.

7 Transfer the crab fried rice to a serving dish. Garnish with the sliced lime and serve immediately.

VARIATION

Cooked lobster may be used instead of the crab for a really special dish.

Noodles

Noodles are a symbol of longevity in China and are always served at birthday and New Year celebrations. It is considered bad luck to cut noodles into shorter lengths because the Chinese believe the longer they are the longer and happier your life will be. Noodles are available in several varieties, both fresh and dried, made from wheat,

buckwheat, or rice flours, or you can even make your own if you have time! They come in fine threads, strings, or flat ribbons and can be bought from large supermarkets or Asian food stores.

Like rice, noodles are very versatile and can be boiled, fried, added to soups, or served plain. Noodles are precooked as part of the manufacturing process so most only need soaking in hot water to rehydrate them.

Beef Chow Mein

Chow Mein must be the best-known and most popular noodle dish on any Chinese menu. You can use any meat or vegetables instead of beef.

NUTRITIONAL INFORMATION

Calories	341	Sugars	. . . . .3g
Protein	. . . . .27g	Fat	. . . . .17g
Carbohydrate	. . .20g	Saturates	. . . . . . .4g

10 MINS   20 MINS

SERVES 4

INGREDIENTS

1 lb/450 g egg noodles

4 tbsp peanut oil

1 lb/450 g lean beef steak, cut into thin strips

2 garlic cloves, crushed

1 tsp grated fresh gingerroot

1 green bell pepper, thinly sliced

1 carrot, thinly sliced

2 celery stalks, sliced

8 scallions

1 tsp dark brown sugar

1 tbsp dry sherry

2 tbsp dark soy sauce

few drops of chile sauce

VARIATION

A variety of different vegetables may be used in this recipe for color and flavor—try broccoli, red bell peppers, green beans, or baby corn cobs.

1 Cook the noodles in a pan of boiling salted water for 4–5 minutes. Drain well, then rinse under cold running water and drain again thoroughly.

2 Toss the noodles in 1 tablespoon of the peanut oil.

3 Heat the remaining oil in a preheated wok. Add the beef and stir-fry for 3–4 minutes, stirring constantly.

4 Add the crushed garlic and grated fresh gingerroot to the wok and stir-fry for 30 seconds.

5 Add the bell pepper, carrot, celery, and scallions and stir-fry for about 2 minutes.

6 Add the dark brown sugar, dry sherry, dark soy sauce, and chile sauce to the mixture in the wok and cook, stirring, for 1 minute.

7 Stir in the noodles, mixing well, and cook until completely warmed through.

8 Transfer the noodles to warm serving bowls and serve immediately.

Cellophane Noodles & Shrimp

Jumbo shrimp are cooked with orange juice, bell peppers, soy sauce, and vinegar and served on a bed of cellophane noodles.

NUTRITIONAL INFORMATION

Calories 118   Sugar 4g
Protein . . . . .7g   Fat 4g
Carbohydrate . . .15g   Saturates 1g

10 MINS   25 MINS

SERVES 4

INGREDIENTS

6 oz/175 g cellophane noodles

1 tbsp vegetable oil

1 garlic clove, crushed

2 tsp grated fresh gingerroot

24 raw jumbo shrimp, peeled and deveined

1 red bell pepper, seeded and thinly sliced

1 green bell pepper, seeded and thinly sliced

1 onion, chopped

2 tbsp light soy sauce

juice of 1 orange

2 tsp wine vinegar

pinch of brown sugar

⅔ cup fish stock

1 tbsp cornstarch

2 tsp water

orange slices, to garnish

1 Cook the noodles in a pan of boiling water for 1 minute. Drain well, then rinse under cold water and drain again.

2 Heat the oil in a wok and stir-fry the garlic and ginger for 30 seconds.

3 Add the shrimp and stir-fry for 2 minutes. Remove with a slotted spoon and keep warm.

4 Add the bell peppers and onion to the wok and stir-fry for 2 minutes. Stir in the soy sauce, orange juice, vinegar, sugar, and stock. Return the shrimp to the wok and cook for 8-10 minutes, until cooked through.

5 Blend the cornstarch with the water and stir into the wok. Bring to a boil, then add the noodles and cook for 1-2 minutes. Garnish and serve.

VARIATION

Lime or lemon juice slices may be used instead of the orange. Use 3–5½ teaspoons of these juices.

Cantonese Fried Noodles

This dish is usually served as a snack or light meal. It may also be served as an accompaniment to plain meat and fish dishes.

NUTRITIONAL INFORMATION

Calories 385	Sugars 6g
Protein 38g	Fat 17g
Carbohydrate ...21g	Saturates 4g

5 MINS   15 MINS

SERVES 4

INGREDIENTS

12 oz/350 g egg noodles

3 tbsp vegetable oil

1 lb 8 oz/675 g lean beef steak, cut into thin strips

4½ oz/125 g green cabbage, shredded

⅓ cup bamboo shoots

6 scallions, sliced

¼ cup green beans, halved

1 tbsp dark soy sauce

2 tbsp beef stock

1 tbsp dry sherry

1 tbsp light brown sugar

2 tbsp chopped parsley, to garnish

1 Cook the noodles in a pan of boiling water for 2-3 minutes. Drain well, then rinse under cold running water and drain thoroughly again.

2 Heat 1 tablespoon of the oil in a preheated wok or skillet, swirling it around until it is really hot.

3 Add the noodles and stir-fry for 1-2 minutes. Drain the noodles and set aside until required.

4 Heat the remaining oil in the wok. Add the beef and stir-fry for 2-3 minutes. Add the cabbage, bamboo shoots, scallions and beans to the wok and stir-fry for 1-2 minutes.

5 Add the soy sauce, beef stock, dry sherry and light brown sugar to the wok, stirring to mix well.

6 Stir the noodles into the mixture in the wok, tossing to mix well. Transfer to serving bowls, then garnish with chopped parsley and serve immediately.

VARIATION

You can vary the vegetables in this dish depending on seasonal availability or whatever you have at hand—try broccoli, green bell pepper, or spinach.

Sweet & Sour Noodles

This delicious dish combines sweet and sour flavors with the addition of egg, rice noodles, jumbo shrimp, and vegetables for a real treat.

NUTRITIONAL INFORMATION

Calories 352	Sugars 14g	
Protein 23g	Fat 17g	
Carbohydrate . . .29g	Saturates 3g	

🖐 🖐 🖐

🍲 10 MINS   🕙 10 MINS

SERVES 4

I N G R E D I E N T S

3 tbsp fish sauce

2 tbsp distilled white vinegar

2 tbsp superfine or palm sugar

2 tbsp tomato paste

2 tbsp corn oil

3 garlic cloves, crushed

12 oz/350 g rice noodles, soaked in boiling water for 5 minutes

8 scallions, sliced

6 oz/175 g carrot, grated

1 cup bean sprouts

2 eggs, beaten

8 oz/225 g peeled jumbo shrimp

⅓ cup chopped peanuts

1 tsp chile flakes, to garnish

1 Mix together the fish sauce, vinegar, sugar, and tomato paste.

2 Heat the corn oil in a large preheated wok.

3 Add the garlic to the wok and stir-fry for 30 seconds.

4 Drain the noodles thoroughly and add them to the wok together with the fish sauce and tomato paste mixture. Mix well to combine.

5 Add the scallions, carrot, and bean sprouts to the wok and stir-fry for 2–3 minutes.

6 Move the contents of the wok to one side, then add the beaten eggs to the empty part of the wok and cook until the egg sets. Add the shrimp and peanuts to the wok and mix well. Transfer to warm serving dishes and garnish with chile flakes. Serve hot.

COOK'S TIP

Chile flakes may be found in the spice section of large supermarkets.

Noodles with Chile & Shrimp

This is a simple dish to prepare and is packed with flavor, making it an ideal choice for special occasions.

NUTRITIONAL INFORMATION

Calories	259	Sugars	.........9g
Protein	........28g	Fat	...........8g
Carbohydrate	...20g	Saturates	.......1g

10 MINS 5 MINS

SERVES 4

INGREDIENTS

9 oz/250 g thin glass noodles

2 tbsp corn oil

1 onion, sliced

2 red chiles, seeded and very finely chopped

4 lime leaves, thinly shredded

1 tbsp fresh cilantro

2 tbsp palm or superfine sugar

2 tbsp fish sauce

1 lb/450 g raw jumbo shrimp, peeled

1 Place the noodles in a large bowl. Pour over enough boiling water to cover the noodles and leave to stand for 5 minutes. Drain thoroughly and set aside until required.

COOK'S TIP

If you cannot buy raw jumbo shrimp, use cooked shrimp instead and cook them with the noodles for 1 minute only, just to heat through.

2 Heat the corn oil in a large preheated wok or skillet until it is really hot.

3 Add the onion, red chiles, and lime leaves to the wok and stir-fry for 1 minute.

4 Add the cilantro, palm sugar, fish sauce, and shrimp to the wok or skillet and stir-fry for an additional 2 minutes, until the shrimp turn pink.

5 Add the drained noodles to the wok and toss to mix well, then stir-fry for 1–2 minutes or until heated through.

6 Transfer the noodles and shrimp to warm serving bowls and serve immediately.

Lamb with Noodles

Lamb is quick-fried and coated in a soy sauce, then served on a bed of transparent noodles for a richly flavored dish.

NUTRITIONAL INFORMATION

Calories	285	Sugars	.........1g
Protein	........27g	Fat	..........16g
Carbohydrate	...10g	Saturates	.......6g

5 MINS   15 MINS

SERVES 4

I N G R E D I E N T S

5½ oz/150 g cellophane noodles

2 tbsp peanut oil

1 lb/450 g lean lamb, thinly sliced

2 garlic cloves, crushed

2 leeks, sliced

3 tbsp dark soy sauce

1 cup lamb stock

dash of chile sauce

red chile strips, to garnish

1 Bring a large pan of water to a boil. Add the cellophane noodles and cook for 1 minute. Drain the noodles well and place in a strainer, then rinse under cold running water and drain thoroughly again. Set aside until required.

2 Heat the peanut oil in a preheated wok or skillet, swirling the oil around until it is really hot.

3 Add the lamb to the wok or skillet and stir-fry for 2 minutes.

4 Add the crushed garlic and sliced leeks to the wok and stir-fry for an additional 2 minutes.

5 Stir in the dark soy sauce, lamb stock, and chile sauce and cook for

3–4 minutes, stirring frequently, until the meat is cooked through.

6 Add the drained cellophane noodles to the wok or skillet and cook for 1 minute, stirring, until heated through.

7 Transfer the lamb and cellophane noodles to serving plates, then garnish with red chile strips and serve.

COOK'S TIP

Transparent noodles are available in Chinese supermarkets. Use egg noodles instead if transparent noodles are unavailable, and cook them according to the instructions on the package.

Quick Chicken Chow Mein

A quick stir-fry of chicken and vegetables, which are mixed with Chinese egg noodles and a dash of sesame oil.

NUTRITIONAL INFORMATION

Calories	300	Sugars	5g
Protein	23g	Fat	15g
Carbohydrate	18g	Saturates	2g

20 MINS   15 MINS

SERVES 4

INGREDIENTS

2 tbsp sesame seeds

9 oz/250 g thread egg noodles

6 oz/175 g broccoli florets

3 tbsp corn oil

1 garlic clove, sliced

1-inch/2.5-cm piece fresh gingerroot,
    peeled and chopped

9 oz/250 g chicken fillet, sliced thinly

1 onion, sliced

2 cups sliced shiitake mushrooms

1 red bell pepper, seeded and cut
    into thin strips

1 tsp cornstarch

2 tbsp water

15 oz/425 g canned baby corn cobs,
    drained and halved

2 tbsp dry sherry

2 tbsp soy sauce

1 tsp sesame oil

COOK'S TIP

As well as adding protein, vitamins, and useful fats to the diet, nuts and seeds add important flavor and texture.

1 Put the sesame seeds in a heavy-based skillet and cook for 2–3 minutes, until they turn brown and begin to pop. Cover the pan so the seeds do not jump out and shake them constantly to prevent them burning. Remove from the pan and set aside until required.

2 Put the noodles in a bowl. Cover with boiling water and leave to stand for 4 minutes. Drain thoroughly.

3 Meanwhile, blanch the broccoli in boiling salted water for 2 minutes, then drain.

4 Heat the corn oil in a wok or large skillet, then add the garlic, ginger, chicken and onion and stir-fry for 2 minutes, until the chicken is golden and the onion softened.

5 Add the broccoli, mushrooms, and red bell pepper and stir-fry for an additional 2 minutes.

6 Mix the cornstarch with the water, then stir into the pan with the baby corn, sherry, soy sauce, drained noodles, and sesame oil and cook, stirring, until the sauce is thickened and the noodles warmed through. Sprinkle with the sesame seeds and serve.

Pork Chow Mein

This is a classic basic recipe—nourishing and tasty, it is extremely quick and easy to make.

NUTRITIONAL INFORMATION

Calories	239	Sugars	.........1g
Protein	........17g	Fat	..........14g
Carbohydrate	...12g	Saturates	.......2g

15 MINS   15 MINS

SERVES 4

I N G R E D I E N T S

9 oz/250 g egg noodles

4–5 tbsp vegetable oil

9 oz/250 g pork fillet, cooked

generous ¾ cup green beans

2 tbsp light soy sauce

1 tsp salt

½ tsp sugar

1 tbsp Chinese rice wine or dry sherry

2 scallions, finely shredded

a few drops sesame oil

chile sauce, to serve (optional)

1 Cook the noodles in boiling water according to the instructions on the package, then drain and rinse under cold water. Drain again, then toss with 1 tablespoon of the oil.

2 Slice the pork into thin shreds and top and tail the beans.

3 Heat 3 tablespoons of oil in a preheated wok until hot. Add the noodles and stir-fry for 2-3 minutes with 1 tablespoon soy sauce, then remove to a serving dish. Keep warm.

4 Heat the remaining oil and stir-fry the beans and meat for 2 minutes. Add the salt, sugar, wine, the remaining soy sauce, and about half the scallions to the wok.

5 Stir the mixture in the wok, adding a little stock if necessary, then pour on top of the noodles, and sprinkle with sesame oil and the remaining scallions.

6 Serve the chow mein hot or cold with chile sauce, if desired.

COOK'S TIP

Chow Mein literally means "stir-fried noodles" and is highly popular in the West as well as in China. Almost any ingredient can be added, such as fish, meat, poultry, or vegetables. It is very popular for lunch and makes a tasty salad served cold.

Fried Noodles (Chow Mein)

This is a basic recipe for Chow Mein. Additional ingredients, such as chicken or pork, can be added if liked.

NUTRITIONAL INFORMATION

Calories	716	Sugars	2g
Protein	4g	Fat	12g
Carbohydrate	14g	Saturates	1g

5 MINS 15 MINS

SERVES 4

INGREDIENTS

9½ oz/275 g egg noodles

3–4 tbsp vegetable oil

1 small onion, finely shredded

4½ oz/125 g fresh bean sprouts

1 scallion, finely shredded

2 tbsp light soy sauce

a few drops of sesame oil

salt

1 Bring a wok or pan of salted water to a boil.

2 Add the egg noodles to the pan or wok and cook according to the instructions on the package (usually no more than 4-5 minutes).

COOK'S TIP

Noodles, a symbol of longevity, are made from wheat or rice flour, water, and egg. Handmade noodles are made by an elaborate process of kneading, pulling, and twisting the dough, and it takes years to learn the art.

3 Drain the noodles well and rinse in cold water; drain thoroughly again, then transfer to a large mixing bowl and toss with a little vegetable oil.

4 Heat the remaining vegetable oil in a preheated wok or large skillet until really hot.

5 Add the shredded onion to the wok and stir-fry for 30-40 seconds.

6 Add the bean sprouts and drained noodles to the wok, then stir and toss for 1 more minute.

7 Add the shredded scallion and light soy sauce and blend well.

8 Transfer the noodles to a warm serving dish, then sprinkle with the sesame oil and serve immediately.

Special Noodles

This dish combines meat, vegetables, shrimp, and noodles in a curried coconut sauce. Serve as a main meal or as an accompaniment.

NUTRITIONAL INFORMATION

Calories	409	Sugars	........12g
Protein	........24g	Fat	..........23g
Carbohydrate	...28g	Saturates	.......8g

5 MINS   25 MINS

SERVES 4

I N G R E D I E N T S

9 oz/250 g thin rice noodles

4 tbsp peanut oil

2 garlic cloves, crushed

2 red chiles, seeded and very finely chopped

1 tsp grated fresh ginger

2 tbsp Madras curry paste

2 tbsp rice wine vinegar

1 tbsp superfine sugar

scant 1 cup finely shredded cooked ham, finely shredded

½ cup canned water chestnuts, sliced

2 cups sliced mushrooms

¾ cup peas

1 red bell pepper, seeded and thinly sliced

3½ oz/100 g shelled shrimp

2 large eggs

4 tbsp coconut milk

¼ cup dry unsweetened coconut

2 tbsp chopped fresh cilantro

1 Place the rice noodles in a large bowl, then cover with boiling water and leave to soak for 10 minutes. Drain the noodles thoroughly, then toss with 2 tablespoons of peanut oil.

2 Heat the remaining peanut oil in a large preheated wok until the oil is really hot.

3 Add the garlic, chiles, ginger, curry paste, rice wine vinegar, and superfine sugar to the wok and stir-fry for 1 minute.

4 Add the ham, water chestnuts, mushrooms, peas, and red bell pepper to the wok and stir-fry for 5 minutes.

5 Add the noodles and shrimp to the wok and stir-fry for 2 minutes.

6 In a small bowl, beat together the eggs and coconut milk. Drizzle over the mixture in the wok and stir-fry until the egg sets.

7 Add the dry unsweetened coconut and chopped fresh cilantro to the wok and toss to combine. Transfer the noodles to warm serving dishes and serve immediately.

Seafood Chow Mein

Use whatever seafood is available for this delicious noodle dish—
mussels or crab would also be suitable.

NUTRITIONAL INFORMATION

Calories	.281	Sugars	.1g
Protein	.15g	Fat	.18g
Carbohydrate	.16g	Saturates	.2g

🍴 🍴 🍴

🍲 15 MINS   🕐 15 MINS

SERVES 4

INGREDIENTS

3 oz/85 g squid, cleaned

3–4 fresh scallops

3 oz/85 g raw shrimp,
  shelled

½ egg white, lightly beaten

1 tbsp cornstarch paste (see page 31)

9½ oz/275 g egg noodles

5–6 tbsp vegetable oil

2 tbsp light soy sauce

½ cup snow peas

½ tsp salt

½ tsp sugar

1 tsp Chinese rice wine

2 scallions, finely shredded

a few drops of sesame oil

1   Open up the squid and score the inside in a crisscross
pattern, then cut into pieces about the size of a
postage stamp. Soak the squid in a bowl of boiling water
until all the pieces curl up. Rinse in cold water and drain.

2   Cut each scallop into 3–4 slices. Cut the shrimp in half
lengthwise if large. Mix the scallops and shrimp with
the egg white and cornstarch paste.

3   Cook the noodles in boiling water according to the
package instructions, then drain and rinse under cold
water. Drain well, then toss with about 1 tablespoon of oil.

4   Heat 3 tablespoons of oil in a preheated wok. Add the
noodles and 1 tablespoon of the soy sauce and stir-fry
for 2-3 minutes. Remove to a large serving dish.

5   Heat the remaining oil in the wok and add the snow
peas and seafood. Stir-fry for 2 minutes, then add the
salt, sugar, wine, remaining soy sauce, and about half the
scallions. Blend well and add a little stock or water if
necessary. Pour the seafood mixture on top of the noodles
and sprinkle with sesame oil. Garnish with the remaining
scallions and serve.

COOK'S TIP

Chinese rice wine, made from
sticky rice, is also known as
"Yellow wine" because of its
golden amber color. If it is
unavailable, a good dry or medium
sherry is an acceptable substitute.

Sesame Hot Noodles

Plain egg noodles are tossed in a dressing made with sesame oil, soy sauce, peanut butter, cilantro, lime, chile, and sesame seeds.

NUTRITIONAL INFORMATION

Calories	...300	Sugars	...1g
Protein	...7g	Fat	...21g
Carbohydrate	...21g	Saturates	...3g

5 MINS 10 MINS

SERVES 4

INGREDIENTS

1 lb 2 oz/500 g medium egg noodles

3 tbsp corn oil

2 tbsp sesame oil

1 garlic clove, crushed

1 tbsp smooth peanut butter

1 small green chile, seeded and very finely chopped

3 tbsp toasted sesame seeds

4 tbsp light soy sauce

½ tbsp lime juice

salt and pepper

4 tbsp chopped fresh cilantro

1 Place the noodles in a large pan of boiling water, then immediately remove from the heat. Cover and leave to stand for 6 minutes, stirring once halfway through the time. At the end of 6 minutes the noodles will be perfectly cooked. Alternatively, cook the noodles following the package instructions.

2 Meanwhile, make the dressing. Mix together the corn oil, sesame oil, crushed garlic, and peanut butter in a mixing bowl until smooth.

3 Add the chopped green chile, sesame seeds, and light soy sauce to the

other dressing ingredients. Add the lime juice, according to taste, and mix well. Season with salt and pepper.

4 Drain the noodles thoroughly, then place in a heated serving bowl.

5 Add the dressing and chopped fresh cilantro to the noodles and toss well to mix. Serve hot as a main meal accompaniment.

COOK'S TIP

If you are cooking the noodles ahead of time, toss the cooked, drained noodles in 2 teaspoons of sesame oil, then turn into a bowl. Cover and keep warm until required.

Mushroom & Pork Noodles

This dish benefits from the use of colored oyster mushrooms. If these are unavailable, plain gray mushrooms will suffice.

NUTRITIONAL INFORMATION

Calories ....286 Sugars 3g
Protein ....23g Fat 13g
Carbohydrate ...21g Saturates 3g

10 MINS   20 MINS

SERVES 4

INGREDIENTS

1 lb/450 g thin egg noodles

2 tbsp peanut oil

12 oz/350 g pork tenderloin, sliced

2 garlic cloves, crushed

1 onion, cut into 8 pieces

8 oz/225 g oyster mushrooms

4 tomatoes, skinned, seeded, and thinly sliced

2 tbsp light soy sauce

scant ¼ cup pork stock

1 tbsp chopped fresh cilantro

1 Cook the noodles in a pan of boiling water for 2-3 minutes. Drain well, rinse under cold running water and drain thoroughly again.

2 Heat 1 tablespoon of the oil in a preheated wok or skillet.

3 Add the noodles to the wok or skillet and stir-fry for 2 minutes.

4 Using a slotted spoon, remove the noodles from the wok, then drain well and set aside until required.

5 Heat the remaining peanut oil in the wok. Add the pork slices and stir-fry for 4–5 minutes.

6 Stir in the crushed garlic and chopped onion and stir-fry for an additional 2-3 minutes.

7 Add the oyster mushrooms, tomatoes, light soy sauce, pork stock, and drained noodles. Stir well and cook for 1-2 minutes.

8 Sprinkle with chopped cilantro and serve immediately.

COOK'S TIP

For crisper noodles, add 2 tablespoons of oil to the wok and fry the noodles for 5-6 minutes, spreading them thinly in the wok and turning halfway through cooking.

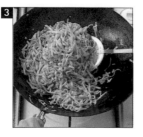

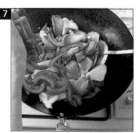

Beef with Crispy Noodles

Crispy noodles are terrific and may also be served on their own as a side dish, sprinkled with sugar and salt.

NUTRITIONAL INFORMATION

Calories	...244	Sugars	...9g
Protein	...20g	Fat	...10g
Carbohydrate	...19g	Saturates	...2g

5 MINS   30 MINS

SERVES 4

INGREDIENTS

8 oz/225 g medium egg noodles

12 oz/350 g beef fillet

2 tbsp corn oil

1 tsp ground ginger

1 garlic clove, crushed

1 red chile, seeded and very finely chopped

3¼ oz/100 g carrots, cut into thin sticks

6 scallions, sliced

2 tbsp lime marmalade

2 tbsp soy sauce

oil, for frying

1 Place the noodles in a large dish or bowl. Pour over enough boiling water to cover the noodles and leave to stand for 10 minutes while you stir-fry the rest of the ingredients.

2 Using a sharp knife, thinly slice the beef fillet.

3 Heat the corn oil in a large preheated wok or skillet.

4 Add the beef and ground ginger to the wok or skillet and stir-fry for 5 minutes.

5 Add the crushed garlic, chopped red chile, carrots, and scallions to the wok and stir-fry for an additional 2–3 minutes.

6 Add the lime marmalade and soy sauce to the wok and let bubble for 2 minutes. Remove the chile beef and ginger mixture, then set aside and keep warm until required.

7 Heat the oil for frying in the wok or skillet.

8 Drain the noodles thoroughly and pat dry with absorbent paper towels. Carefully lower the noodles into the hot oil and cook for 2–3 minutes, until crispy. Drain the noodles on absorbent paper towels.

9 Divide the noodles between 4 warm serving plates and top with the chile beef and ginger mixture. Serve immediately.

Egg Noodles with Beef

Quick and easy, this mouth-watering Chinese-style noodle dish can be cooked in minutes.

10 MINS   15 MINS

SERVES 4

INGREDIENTS

10 oz/280 g egg noodles

3 tbsp walnut oil

1-inch/2.5-cm piece fresh gingerroot,
   cut into thin strips

5 scallions, finely shredded

2 garlic cloves, finely chopped

1 red bell pepper, cored, seeded and thinly
   sliced

2 cups thinly sliced white mushrooms

12 oz/350 g fillet steak, cut into
   thin strips

1 tbsp cornstarch

5 tbsp dry sherry

3 tbsp soy sauce

1 tsp soft brown sugar

1½ cups bean sprouts

1 tbsp sesame oil

salt and pepper

scallion strips, to garnish

1 Bring a large pan of water to a boil. Add the egg noodles and cook according to the instructions on the package. Drain the noodles and rinse under cold running water, then drain thoroughly again and set aside.

2 Heat the walnut oil in a preheated wok until it is really hot.

3 Add the grated fresh gingerroot, shredded scallions and chopped garlic and stir-fry for 45 seconds.

4 Add the red bell pepper, white mushrooms, and steak and stir-fry for 4 minutes. Season to taste with salt and pepper.

5 Mix together the cornstarch, dry sherry, and soy sauce in a small jug to form a paste, and pour into the wok. Sprinkle over the brown sugar and stir-fry all of the ingredients for an additional 2 minutes.

6 Add the bean sprouts, drained noodles, and sesame oil to the wok, stir and toss together for 1 minute.

7 Transfer the stir-fry to warm serving dishes, garnish with strips of scallion and serve.

Chicken Noodles

Rice noodles are used in this recipe. They are available in large supermarkets or specialist Chinese supermarkets.

NUTRITIONAL INFORMATION

Calories . . . . .169 Sugars 2g
Protein . . . . .14g Fat 7g
Carbohydrate . . .12g Saturates 2g

🥟 5 MINS   🕐 15 MINS

SERVES 4

INGREDIENTS

8 oz/225 g rice noodles

2 tbsp peanut oil

8 oz/225 g skinless, boneless chicken breast, sliced

2 garlic cloves, crushed

1 tsp grated fresh gingerroot

1 tsp Chinese curry powder

1 red bell pepper, seeded and thinly sliced

¾ cup snow peas, shredded

1 tbsp light soy sauce

2 tsp Chinese rice wine

2 tbsp chicken stock

1 tsp sesame oil

1 tbsp chopped fresh cilantro

1 Soak the rice noodles for 4 minutes in warm water. Drain thoroughly and set aside until required.

2 Heat the peanut oil in a preheated wok or large heavy-based skillet and stir-fry the chicken slices for 2-3 minutes.

3 Add the garlic, ginger, and Chinese curry powder and stir-fry for an additional 30 seconds. Add the red bell pepper and snow peas to the mixture in the wok and stir-fry for 2-3 minutes.

4 Add the noodles, soy sauce, Chinese rice wine, and chicken stock to the wok and mix well, stirring occasionally, for 1 minute.

5 Sprinkle the sesame oil and chopped cilantro over the noodles. Transfer to serving plates and serve.

VARIATION

You can use pork or duck in this recipe instead of the chicken, if you prefer.

Oyster Sauce Noodles

Chicken and noodles are cooked and then tossed in an oyster sauce and egg mixture in this delicious recipe.

NUTRITIONAL INFORMATION

Calories	278	Sugars	.........2g
Protein	........30g	Fat	..........12g
Carbohydrate	...13g	Saturates	.......3g

5 MINS   25 MINS

SERVES 4

I N G R E D I E N T S

9 oz/250 g egg noodles

1 lb/450 g chicken thighs

2 tbsp peanut oil

⅔ cup sliced carrots

3 tbsp oyster sauce

2 eggs

3 tbsp cold water

1 Place the egg noodles in a large bowl or dish. Pour enough boiling water over the noodles to cover and leave to stand for 10 minutes.

2 Meanwhile, remove the skin from the chicken thighs. Cut the chicken flesh into small pieces, using a sharp knife.

3 Heat the peanut oil in a large preheated wok or skillet, swirling the oil around the base of the wok until it is really hot.

4 Add the pieces of chicken and the carrot slices to the wok and stir-fry for 5 minutes.

5 Drain the noodles thoroughly. Add the noodles to the wok and stir-fry for an additional 2–3 minutes, until the noodles are heated through.

6 Beat together the oyster sauce, eggs, and 3 tablespoons of cold water. Drizzle the mixture over the noodles and stir-fry for an additional 2–3 minutes, until the eggs set.

7 Transfer the mixture in the wok to warm serving bowls and serve hot.

VARIATION

Flavor the eggs with soy sauce or hoisin sauce as an alternative to the oyster sauce, if you prefer.

Garlic Pork & Noodles

This is a wonderful one-pot dish of stir-fried pork fillet with small shrimp and noodles that is made in minutes.

NUTRITIONAL INFORMATION

Calories 424	Sugars 1g	
Protein 33g	Fat 27g	
Carbohydrate ...13g	Saturates 5g	

5 MINS   15 MINS

SERVES 4

INGREDIENTS

9 oz/250 g medium egg noodles

3 tbsp vegetable oil

2 garlic cloves, crushed

12 oz/350 g pork fillet, cut into strips

4 tbsp dried small shrimp, or
    4½ oz/125 g shelled shrimp

1 bunch scallions, finely chopped

scant ⅔ cup chopped roasted and shelled
    unsalted peanuts

3 tbsp fish sauce

1½ tsp palm or raw sugar

1–2 small red chiles, seeded and finely
    chopped (to taste)

3 tbsp lime juice

3 tbsp chopped fresh cilantro

1 Place the noodles in a large pan of boiling water, then immediately remove from the heat. Cover and leave to stand for 6 minutes, stirring once halfway through the time. After 6 minutes, the noodles will be perfectly cooked. Alternatively, follow the instructions on the package. Drain and keep warm.

2 Heat the oil in a wok, then add the garlic and pork and stir-fry until the pork strips are browned—2-3 minutes.

3 Add the shrimp, scallions, peanuts, fish sauce, palm sugar, chiles to taste, and lime juice. Stir-fry for an additional 1 minute.

4 Add the cooked noodles and chopped fresh cilantro and stir-fry until heated through, about 1 minute. Serve the stir-fry immediately.

COOK'S TIP

Fish sauce is made from pressed, salted fish and is widely available in supermarkets and Asian stores. It is very salty, so no extra salt should be added.

Yellow Bean Noodles

Cellophane or thread noodles are excellent reheated, unlike other noodles that must be served as soon as they are ready.

NUTRITIONAL INFORMATION

Calories 212	Sugars 0.5g
Protein 28g	Fat 7g
Carbohydrate . . .10g	Saturates 2g

5 MINS   30 MINS

SERVES 4

INGREDIENTS

6 oz/175 g cellophane noodles

1 tbsp peanut oil

1 leek, sliced

2 garlic cloves, crushed

1 lb/450 g ground chicken

scant 1¾ cups chicken stock

1 tsp chile sauce

2 tbsp yellow bean sauce

4 tbsp light soy sauce

1 tsp sesame oil

chopped chives, to garnish

1 Place the cellophane noodles in a bowl, pour over boiling water and soak for 15 minutes.

COOK'S TIP

Cellophane noodles are available from many supermarkets and all Chinese supermarkets.

2 Drain the noodles thoroughly and cut into short lengths with a pair of kitchen scissors.

3 Heat the oil in a wok or skillet and stir-fry the leek and garlic for 30 seconds.

4 Add the chicken to the wok and stir-fry for 4-5 minutes, until the chicken is completely cooked through.

5 Add the chicken stock, chile sauce, yellow bean sauce, and soy sauce to the wok and cook for 3-4 minutes.

6 Add the drained noodles and sesame oil to the wok and cook, tossing to mix well, for 4-5 minutes.

7 Spoon the mixture into warm serving bowls, then sprinkle with chopped chives and serve immediately.

Crispy Noodles & Tofu

This dish requires a certain amount of care and attention to get the crispy noodles properly cooked, but it is well worth the effort.

NUTRITIONAL INFORMATION

Calories	242	Sugars	.........2g
Protein	........13g	Fat	..........17g
Carbohydrate	...10g	Saturates	.......3g

35 MINS   25 MINS

SERVES 4

INGREDIENTS

6 oz/175 g thread egg noodles

2½ cups corn oil, for deep-frying

2 tsp grated lemon peel

1 tbsp light soy sauce

1 tbsp rice vinegar

1 tbsp lemon juice

1½ tbsp sugar

9 oz/250 g marinated tofu, diced

2 garlic cloves, crushed

1 red chile, sliced finely

1 red bell pepper, diced

4 eggs, beaten

red chile flower, to garnish

1 Blanch the egg noodles briefly in hot water, to which a little of the oil has been added. Drain the noodles and spread out to dry for at least 30 minutes. Cut into threads about 3 inches/7 cm long.

2 Combine the lemon peel, light soy sauce, rice vinegar, lemon juice, and sugar in a small bowl. Set the mixture aside until required.

3 Heat the corn oil in a wok or large, heavy skillet, and test the temperature with a few strands of noodles. They should swell to many times their size, but if they do not, wait until the oil is hot enough; otherwise they will be tough and stringy, not puffy and light.

4 Cook the noodles in batches. As soon as they turn a pale gold color, scoop them out and drain on plenty of absorbent paper towels. Leave to cool.

5 Reserve 2 tablespoons of the oil and drain off the rest. Heat the reserved oil in the wok or skillet.

6 Add the marinated tofu to the wok or skillet and cook quickly over high heat to seal.

7 Add the crushed garlic cloves, sliced red chile, and diced red bell pepper to the wok. Stir-fry for 1–2 minutes.

8 Add the reserved vinegar mixture to the wok, then stir to mix well and add the beaten eggs, stirring until they are set.

9 Serve the tofu mixture with the crispy fried noodles, garnished with a red chile flower.

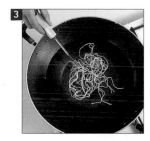

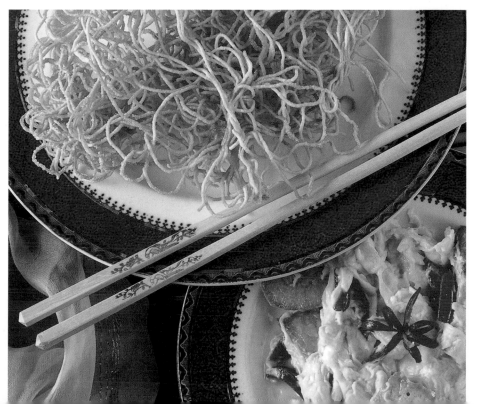

Twice-Cooked Lamb

Here lamb is first boiled and then fried with soy sauce, oyster sauce, and spinach and finally tossed with noodles for a richly flavored dish.

NUTRITIONAL INFORMATION

Calories	315	Sugars	.........5g
Protein	........27g	Fat	..........16g
Carbohydrate	...16g	Saturates	.......6g

5 MINS   30 MINS

SERVES 4

I N G R E D I E N T S

9 oz/250 g egg noodles

1 lb/450 g lamb loin fillet, thinly sliced

2 tbsp soy sauce

2 tbsp corn oil

2 garlic cloves, crushed

1 tbsp superfine sugar

2 tbsp oyster sauce

6 oz/175 g baby spinach

1 Place the egg noodles in a large bowl and cover with boiling water. Leave to soak for about 10 minutes.

2 Bring a large pan of water to a boil. Add the lamb and cook for 5 minutes. Drain thoroughly.

3 Place the slices of lamb in a bowl and mix with the soy sauce and 1 tablespoon of the corn oil.

4 Heat the remaining corn oil in a large preheated wok, swirling the oil around until it is really hot.

5 Add the marinated lamb and crushed garlic to the wok and stir-fry for 5 minutes, until the meat is just beginning to brown.

6 Add the superfine sugar and oyster sauce to the wok and stir well to combine.

7 Drain the noodles thoroughly. Add the noodles to the wok and stir-fry for an additional 5 minutes.

8 Add the spinach to the wok and cook for 1 minute, until the leaves just wilt. Transfer the lamb and noodles to serving bowls and serve hot.

COOK'S TIP

If using dried noodles, follow the instructions on the package as they require less soaking.

Speedy Peanut Pan-Fry

Thread egg noodles are the ideal accompaniment to this quick dish because they can be cooked quickly and easily while the stir-fry sizzles.

NUTRITIONAL INFORMATION

Calories	563	Sugars	.........7g
Protein	........45g	Fat	..........33g
Carbohydrate	...22g	Saturates	.......7g

5 MINS   15 MINS

SERVES 4

INGREDIENTS

10½ oz/300 g zucchini

9 oz/250 g baby corn cobs

9 oz/250 g thread egg noodles

2 tbsp corn oil

1 tbsp sesame oil

8 boneless chicken thighs or 4 breasts, sliced thinly

3⅔ cups white mushrooms

2⅓ cups bean sprouts

4 tbsp smooth peanut butter

2 tbsp soy sauce

2 tbsp lime or lemon juice

generous ⅓ cup roasted peanuts

salt and pepper

cilantro, to garnish

1 Using a sharp knife, trim and thinly slice the zucchini and baby corn. Set the vegetables aside until required.

2 Cook the noodles in lightly salted boiling water for 3–4 minutes.

3 Meanwhile, heat the corn oil and sesame oil in a large wok or skillet and fry the chicken over fairly high heat for 1 minute.

4 Add the zucchini, corn, and mushrooms and stir-fry for 5 minutes.

5 Add the bean sprouts, peanut butter, soy sauce, lime juice, and pepper, then cook for an additional 2 minutes.

6 Drain the noodles thoroughly. Scatter with the roasted peanuts and serve with the zucchini and mushroom mixture. Garnish and serve.

COOK'S TIP

Try serving this stir-fry with rice sticks. These are broad, pale, translucent ribbon noodles made from ground rice.

Curried Rice Noodles

Rice noodles or vermicelli are also known as rice sticks. The ideal meat to use in this dish is Barbecue Pork (see page 97).

NUTRITIONAL INFORMATION

Calories 223	Sugars 2g
Protein 15g	Fat 13g
Carbohydrate 11g	Saturates 2g

15 MINS   15 MINS

SERVES 4

INGREDIENTS

7 oz/200 g rice vermicelli

4½ oz/125 g cooked chicken or pork

2 oz/55 g shelled shrimp, defrosted if frozen

4 tbsp vegetable oil

1 medium onion, thinly shredded

scant 1 cup fresh bean sprouts

1 tsp salt

1 tbsp mild curry powder

2 tbsp light soy sauce

2 scallions, thinly shredded

1–2 small fresh green or red chiles, seeded and thinly shredded

1 Soak the rice vermicelli in boiling water for about 8-10 minutes, then rinse in cold water and drain well. Set aside until required.

2 Using a sharp knife or meat cleaver, thinly slice the cooked meat.

3 Dry the shrimp on absorbent paper towels.

4 Heat the vegetable oil in a preheated wok or large skillet.

5 Add the shredded onion to the wok or pan and stir-fry until opaque. Add the bean sprouts and stir-fry for 1 minute.

6 Add the drained noodles with the meat and shrimp, and continue stirring for another minute.

7 Mix together the salt, curry powder, and soy sauce in a little bowl.

8 Blend the sauce mixture into the wok, followed by the scallions and chiles. Stir-fry for one more minute, then serve immediately.

COOK'S TIP

Rice noodles are very delicate noodles made from rice flour. They become soft and pliable after being soaked for about 15 minutes. If you wish to store them after they have been soaked, toss them in a few drops of sesame oil, then place them in a sealed container in the refrigerator.

Hot & Crispy Noodles

These crispy noodles will add a delicious crunch to your Chinese meal. They can be served as a side dish or as an appetizer for people to share.

NUTRITIONAL INFORMATION

Calories	104	Sugars	.......0.3g
Protein	.........2g	Fat	...........6g
Carbohydrate	....11g	Saturates	.......1g

🥚 🥚 🥚

🍳 5 MINS   🕐 15 MINS

SERVES 4

INGREDIENTS

9 oz/250 g rice noodles

oil, for deep-frying

2 garlic cloves, chopped finely

8 scallions, trimmed and chopped finely

1 small red or green chile, seeded and chopped finely

2 tbsp fish sauce

2 tbsp light soy sauce

2 tbsp lime or lemon juice

2 tbsp molasses sugar

TO GARNISH

scallions, shredded

cucumber, sliced thinly

fresh chiles

 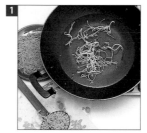 

1 Break the noodles into smaller pieces with your hands. Heat the oil for deep-frying in a wok or large skillet and fry small batches of the noodles until pale golden brown and puffed up. Lift the noodles out with a perforated spoon and leave to drain on paper towels.

2 When all of the noodles are cooked, pour off the oil, leaving 3 tablespoons in the wok. Add the garlic, scallions, and chile, and stir-fry for 2 minutes.

3 Mix together the fish sauce, soy sauce, lime juice, and sugar. Add to the wok or skillet and cook for 2 minutes, until the sugar has dissolved. Tip all the noodles back into the wok and toss lightly to coat with the sauce mixture.

4 Serve the noodles garnished with shredded scallions, thinly sliced cucumber, and chiles.

VARIATION

Stir-fry some uncooked shelled shrimp or chopped raw chicken with the scallions and garlic in step 2. Cook for an extra 3–4 minutes to make sure they are thoroughly cooked.

Chicken on Crispy Noodles

Blanched noodles are fried in the wok until crisp and brown, and then topped with a shredded chicken sauce for a delightfully tasty dish.

NUTRITIONAL INFORMATION

Calories	.376	Sugars	.2g
Protein	.15g	Fat	.27g
Carbohydrate	.17g	Saturates	.4g

🕒 35 MINS   ⏱ 25 MINS

SERVES 4

INGREDIENTS

8 oz/225 g skinless, boneless chicken breasts, shredded

1 egg white

5 tsp cornstarch

8 oz/225 g thin egg noodles

1¼ cups vegetable oil

2½ cups chicken stock

2 tbsp dry sherry

2 tbsp oyster sauce

1 tbsp light soy sauce

1 tbsp hoisin sauce

1 red bell pepper, seeded and very thinly sliced

2 tbsp water

3 scallions, chopped

1 Mix together the chicken, egg white, and 2 teaspoons of the cornstarch in a bowl. Leave to stand for at least 30 minutes.

2 Blanch the noodles in boiling water for 2 minutes, then drain thoroughly.

3 Heat the vegetable oil in a preheated wok. Add the noodles, spreading them to cover the base of the wok. Cook over a low heat for 5 minutes, until the noodles are browned on the underside. Flip the noodles over and brown on the other side. Remove from the wok when crisp and browned, place on a serving plate and keep warm. Drain the oil from the wok.

4 Add 1¼ cups of the chicken stock to the wok. Remove from the heat and add the chicken, stirring well so that it does not stick. Return to the heat and cook for 2 minutes. Drain, discarding the stock.

5 Wipe the wok with paper towels and return to the heat. Add the sherry, sauces, bell pepper, and the remaining stock and bring to a boil. Blend the remaining cornstarch with the water and stir it into the mixture.

6 Return the chicken to the wok and cook over low heat for 2 minutes. Place the chicken on top of the noodles and sprinkle with scallions.

Chile Pork Noodles

This is quite a spicy dish, with a delicious peanut flavor. Increase or reduce the amount of chile to your liking.

NUTRITIONAL INFORMATION

Calories	421	Sugars	.........3g
Protein	........27g	Fat	..........26g
Carbohydrate	...20g	Saturates	.......6g

35 MINS   10 MINS

SERVES 4

INGREDIENTS

12 oz/350 g ground pork

1 tbsp light soy sauce

1 tbsp dry sherry

12 oz/350 g egg noodles

2 tsp sesame oil

2 tbsp vegetable oil

2 garlic cloves, crushed

2 tsp grated fresh gingerroot

2 fresh red chiles, sliced

1 red bell pepper, seeded and finely sliced

scant ¼ cup unsalted peanuts

3 tbsp peanut butter

3 tbsp dark soy sauce

dash of chile oil

1¼ cups pork stock

1 Mix together the pork, light soy sauce, and dry sherry in a large bowl. Cover and marinate for 30 minutes.

2 Meanwhile, cook the noodles in a pan of boiling water for 4 minutes. Drain well, then rinse in cold water and drain again. Toss the noodles in the sesame oil.

3 Heat the vegetable oil in a preheated wok and stir-fry the garlic, ginger, chiles, and bell pepper for 30 seconds.

4 Add the pork to the mixture in the wok, together with the marinade. Continue cooking for 1 minute, until the pork is sealed.

5 Add the peanuts, peanut butter, soy sauce, chile oil, and stock and cook for 2-3 minutes.

6 Toss the noodles in the mixture and serve at once.

VARIATION

Ground chicken or lamb would also be excellent in this recipe instead of the pork.

Desserts

Desserts are rarely eaten in ordinary Chinese households except on special occasions. Sweet dishes are usually served as snacks between main meals, but fresh fruit is considered to be very refreshing at the end of a meal. The recipes in this chapter are adaptations of Imperial recipes or use Chinese cooking methods and ingredients to

produce mouthwatering desserts that round off any meal perfectly. There are delicious dinner party desserts that look as good as they taste, pastries that can be eaten as a tea-time snack, and a selection of refreshing fruit salads. Among the recipes to choose from are Mango Dumplings, in which a mango and litchi filling is sealed in dough and served with a sauce, or Battered Bananas, in which pieces of banana are deep-fried and then sprinkled with brown sugar.

Litchis With Orange Sherbet

This dish is truly delicious! The fresh flavor of the sherbet perfectly complements the spicy litchis.

NUTRITIONAL INFORMATION

Calories 313	Sugars 82g
Protein 1g	Fat 0g
Carbohydrate . . .82g	Saturates 0g

🔒 🔒 🔒

10½ HOURS   5 MINS

SERVES 4

INGREDIENTS

SHERBET

generous 1 cup superfine sugar

scant 1¾ cups cold water

12 oz/350 g canned mandarins
    in natural juice

2 tbsp lemon juice

STUFFED LITCHIS

15 oz/425 g canned litchis, drained

2 oz/55 g preserved ginger,
    drained and finely chopped

lime zest, cut into diamond shapes,
    to decorate

1 To make the sherbet, place the sugar and water in a pan and stir over low heat until the sugar has dissolved. Bring the mixture to a boil and boil vigorously for 2–3 minutes.

2 Blend the mandarins in a food processor or blender until smooth. Press the purée through a strainer, then stir into the syrup, together with the lemon juice. Set aside to cool. Once cooled, pour the mixture into a rigid, plastic container and freeze until set, stirring occasionally.

3 Meanwhile, drain the litchis on absorbent paper towels. Spoon the chopped preserved ginger into the center of the litchis.

4 Arrange the litchis on serving plates and serve with scoops of orange sherbet. Decorate with lime zest.

COOK'S TIP

It is best to leave the sherbet in the refrigerator for 10 minutes, so that it softens slightly, leaving you to scoop it to serve.

Mango Mousse

This is a light, softly set, and tangy mousse, which is perfect for clearing the palate after a Chinese meal of mixed flavors.

NUTRITIONAL INFORMATION

Calories 346	Sugars 27g	
Protein 7g	Fat 24g	
Carbohydrate ...27g	Saturates 15g	

🍤 🍤 🍤

40 MINS   0 MINS

SERVES 4

INGREDIENTS

14 oz/400 g canned mangoes in syrup

2 pieces preserved ginger, chopped

generous ¾ cup heavy cream

powdered gelatin

2 tbsp hot water

2 egg whites

1½ tbsp brown sugar

preserved ginger and lime zest,
    to decorate

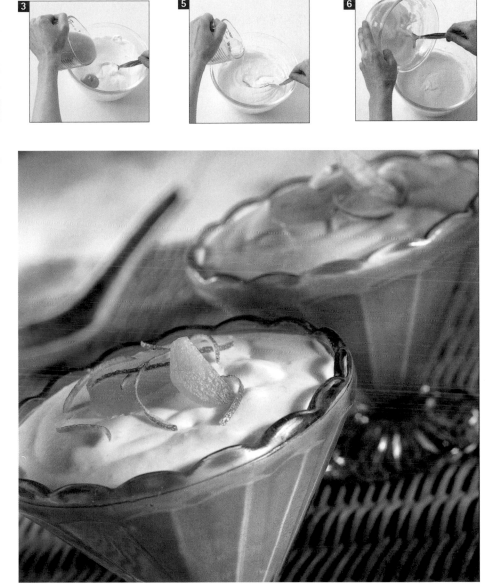

1 Drain the mangoes, reserving the syrup. Blend the mango pieces and ginger in a food processor or blender for 30 seconds, or until smooth.

2 Measure the purée and make up to 1¼ cups with the reserved mango syrup.

3 In a separate bowl, whip the cream until it forms soft peaks. Fold the mango mixture into the cream until well combined.

4 Dissolve the gelatin in the hot water and leave to cool slightly.

5 Pour the gelatin into the mango mixture in a steady stream, stirring.

Leave to cool in the refrigerator for 30 minutes, or until almost set.

6 Beat the egg whites in a clean bowl until they form soft peaks, then beat in the sugar. Gently fold the egg whites into the mango mixture with a metal spoon.

7 Spoon the mousse into individual serving dishes, decorate with preserved ginger and lime zest and serve.

COOK'S TIP

The gelatin must be stirred into the mango mixture in a gentle, steady stream to prevent it from setting in lumps when it comes into contact with the cold mixture.

Mango & Passion-Fruit Salad

The rich mascarpone cream that accompanies the exotic fruit salad gives this Chinese dessert an Italian twist.

NUTRITIONAL INFORMATION

Calories 211   Sugars 18g
Protein . . . . .6g   Fat 10g
Carbohydrate . . .18g   Saturates 6g

🍲 🍲

🍱 1¼ HOURS   🕐 0 MINS

SERVES 4

INGREDIENTS

1 large mango

2 oranges

4 passion-fruit

2 tbsp orange-flavored liqueur such as Grand Marnier

geranium leaves or mint, to decorate

MASCARPONE CREAM

½ cup mascarpone cheese

1 tbsp clear honey

4 tbsp thick, plain yogurt

few drops vanilla extract

1 Using a sharp knife, cut the mango in half lengthwise as close to the pit as possible. Remove the pit, using a sharp knife.

2 Peel off the mango skin, then cut the flesh into slices and place into a large bowl.

3 Peel the oranges, removing all the pith, and cut into segments. Add to the bowl with any juices.

4 Halve the passion-fruit, then scoop out the flesh and add to the bowl with the orange-flavored liqueur. Mix together all the ingredients in the bowl.

5 Cover the bowl with plastic wrap and chill in the refrigerator for 1 hour. Turn into glass serving dishes.

6 To make the mascarpone cream, blend the mascarpone cheese and honey together. Stir in the plain yogurt and vanilla extract until thoroughly blended.

7 Serve the fruit salad with the mascarpone cream, decorated with geranium leaves.

COOK'S TIP

Passion-fruit are ready to eat when their skins are well dimpled. They are most readily available in the summer. Substitute guava or pineapple for the passion-fruit, if you prefer.

Baked Coconut Rice Pudding

A wonderful baked rice pudding cooked with flavorsome coconut milk and a little lime rind. Serve hot or chilled with fresh or stewed fruit.

NUTRITIONAL INFORMATION

Calories	211	Sugars	.......27g
Protein	.........5g	Fat	..........2g
Carbohydrate	...46g	Saturates	.......1g

5 MINS   2½ HOURS

SERVES 4–6

INGREDIENTS

scant ½ cup pudding rice

2½ cups coconut milk

1¼ cups milk

1 large strip lime rind

¼ cup superfine sugar

knob of butter

pinch of ground star anise (optional)

fresh or stewed fruit, to serve

1 Lightly grease a 5-cup shallow ovenproof dish.

2 Mix the pudding rice with the coconut milk, milk, lime rind, and superfine sugar until all the ingredients are well blended.

3 Pour the rice mixture into the greased ovenproof dish and dot the surface with a little butter. Bake in the oven for 30 minutes.

4 Remove the dish from the oven. Remove and discard the strip of lime from the rice pudding.

5 Stir the pudding well, then add the pinch of ground star anise, if using. Return to the oven and cook for an

additional 1-2 hours, or until almost all the milk has been absorbed and a golden brown skin has baked on the top of the pudding.

6 Cover the top of the pudding with foil if it starts to brown too much towards the end of the cooking time.

7 Serve the baked coconut rice pudding warm, or chilled if you prefer, with fresh or stewed fruit.

COOK'S TIP

As the mixture cools it thickens. If you plan to serve the rice chilled, then fold in about 3 tablespoons cream or extra coconut milk before serving to give a thinner consistency.

Passion-Fruit Rice

This creamy rice pudding, adapted for the microwave, is spiced with cardamom, cinnamon, and bay leaf and served with passion-fruit.

NUTRITIONAL INFORMATION

Calories	534	Sugars	........42g
Protein	.........9g	Fat	..........22g
Carbohydrate	...80g	Saturates	......13g

1¼ HOURS   30 MINS

SERVES 4

INGREDIENTS

scant 1 cup jasmine fragrant rice

2½ cups milk

generous ½ cup superfine sugar

6 cardamom pods, split open

1 dried bay leaf

1 cinnamon stick

⅔ cup heavy cream, whipped

4 passion-fruit

soft berry fruits, to decorate

1 Place the jasmine fragrant rice in a large bowl with the milk, superfine sugar, cardamom pods, bay leaf, and cinnamon stick. Cover and cook on Medium power for 25–30 minutes, stirring occasionally. The rice should be just tender and have absorbed most of the milk. Add a little extra milk, if necessary.

2 Leave the rice to cool, still covered. Remove the bay leaf, cardamom husks, and cinnamon stick.

3 Gently fold the cream into the cooled rice mixture.

4 Halve the passion-fruits and scoop out the centers into a bowl.

5 Layer the rice with the passion-fruit in 4 tall glasses, finishing with a layer of passion-fruit. Leave to chill in the refrigerator for 30 minutes.

6 Decorate the passion-fruit rice with soft berry fruits and serve immediately.

COOK'S TIP

If you are unable to obtain passion-fruit, you can use a purée of another fruit of your choice, such as kiwifruit, raspberry or strawberry.

Chinese Fruit Salad

The syrup for this colorful dish is filled with Chinese flavors for a refreshing dessert.

NUTRITIONAL INFORMATION

Calories	405	Sugars	........81g
Protein	.........3g	Fat	...........6g
Carbohydrate	...83g	Saturates	.......1g

🅖 🅖 🅖

1¾ HOURS ⏱ 10 MINS

SERVES 4

I N G R E D I E N T S

⅓ cup Chinese rice wine or dry sherry

rind and juice of 1 lemon

3¾ cups water

generous 1 cup superfine sugar

2 cloves

1-inch/2.5-cm piece cinnamon stick, bruised

1 vanilla bean

pinch of allspice

1 star anise

1-inch/2.5-cm piece fresh gingerroot, sliced

⅓ cup unsalted cashew nuts

2 kiwifruits

1 carambola

4 oz/115 g strawberries

14 oz/400 g canned litchis in syrup, drained

1 piece preserved ginger, drained and sliced

chopped mint, to decorate

1 Put the Chinese rice wine, lemon rind and juice, and water in a pan.

2 Add the superfine sugar, cloves, cinnamon stick, vanilla bean, allspice, star anise, and gingerroot to the pan.

3 Heat the mixture in the pan gently, stirring constantly, until the sugar has dissolved and then bring to a boil. Reduce the heat and simmer for 5 minutes. Set aside to cool completely.

4 Strain the syrup, discarding the flavorings. Stir in the cashew nuts, then cover with plastic wrap and chill in the refrigerator.

5 Meanwhile, prepare the fruits: halve and slice the kiwifruit, slice the carambola, and hull and slice the strawberries.

6 Spoon the prepared fruit into a dish with the litchis and ginger. Stir through gently to mix.

7 Pour the syrup over the fruit, then decorate with chopped mint and serve.

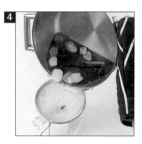

Melon & Kiwi Salad

A refreshing fruit salad, ideal to serve after a rich meal. Charentais or cantaloupe melons are also good.

NUTRITIONAL INFORMATION

Calories 88	Sugars 17g
Protein 1g	Fat 0.2g
Carbohydrate . . .17g	Saturates 0g

1¼ HOURS   0 MINS

SERVES 4

INGREDIENTS

½ galia melon

2 kiwifruit

1 cup green seedless grapes

1 papaya, halved

3 tbsp orange-flavored liqueur such as Cointreau

1 tbsp chopped lemon verbena, lemon balm, or mint

sprigs of lemon verbena or cape gooseberries, to decorate

1 Remove the seeds from the melon, then cut into 4 slices and cut away the skin. Cut the flesh into cubes and put into a bowl.

2 Peel the kiwifruit and cut across into slices. Add to the melon, together with the grapes.

3 Remove the seeds from the papaya and cut off the skin. Slice the flesh thickly and cut into diagonal pieces. Add to the fruit bowl and mix well.

4 Mix together the liqueur and lemon verbena, then pour over the fruit and leave for 1 hour, stirring occasionally.

5 Spoon the fruit salad into glasses, then pour over the juices and decorate with lemon verbena sprigs or cape gooseberries.

COOK'S TIP

Lemon balm or sweet balm is a fragrant lemon-scented plant with slightly hairy serrated leaves and a pronounced lemon flavor. Lemon verbena can also be used—this has an even stronger lemon flavor and smooth elongated leaves.

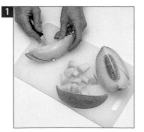

Fruit Salad with Ginger Syrup

This is a very special fruit salad made from the most exotic and colorful fruits that are soaked in a syrup made with fresh ginger and ginger wine.

NUTRITIONAL INFORMATION

Calories 225	Sugars 45g
Protein 2g	Fat 4g
Carbohydrate . . .45g	Saturates 3g

4½ HOURS   5 MINS

SERVES 4

I N G R E D I E N T S

1-inch/2.5-cm fresh gingerroot, peeled and chopped

¼ cup superfine sugar

⅔ cup water

grated rind and juice of 1 lime

¼ cup ginger wine

1 fresh pineapple, peeled, cored, and cut into bite-size pieces

2 ripe mangoes, peeled, pitted, and diced

4 kiwifruit, peeled and sliced

1 papaya, peeled, seeded and diced

2 passion-fruit, halved and flesh removed

12 oz/350 g litchis, peeled and stoned

¼ fresh coconut, grated

2 oz/55 g cape gooseberries, to decorate (optional)

coconut ice-cream, to serve (optional)

1 Place the ginger, sugar, water and lime juice in a pan and bring slowly to a boil. Simmer for 1 minute, them remove from the heat and let cool slightly.

2 Strain the syrup, then add the ginger wine and mix well. Cool completely.

3 Place the prepared fruit in a serving bowl. Add the cold syrup and mix well. Cover and chill in the refrigerator for 2–4 hours.

4 Just before serving, add half of the grated coconut to the salad and mix well. Sprinkle the remainder on top.

5 If using cape gooseberries to decorate the salad, then peel back each calyx to form a flower. Wipe the berries clean, then arrange them around the side of the fruit salad before serving.

COOK'S TIP

Despite their name, cape gooseberries are golden in color and more similar in appearance to ground cherries. They make a delightful decoration to many fruit-based desserts.

Honeyed Rice Puddings

These small rice puddings are quite sweet, but have a wonderful flavor because of the combination of ginger, honey, and cinnamon.

NUTRITIONAL INFORMATION

Calories 199   Sugars 15g
Protein ....3g   Fat 1g
Carbohydrate ...46g   Saturates 0g

10 MINS   50 MINS

SERVES 4

I N G R E D I E N T S

1½ cups pudding rice

2 tbsp clear honey, plus extra
    for drizzling

large pinch of ground cinnamon

15 no-need-to-soak dried apricots,
    chopped

3 pieces preserved ginger, drained and
    chopped

8 whole no-need-to-soak dried apricots,
    to decorate

1 Put the rice in a pan and just cover with cold water. Bring to a boil, then reduce the heat and cook, covered for 15 minutes, or until the water has been absorbed. Stir the honey and cinnamon into the rice.

2 Grease 4 x ⅔-cup ramekin dishes with a little butter.

3 Blend the chopped dried apricots and ginger in a food processor to make a smooth paste.

4 Divide the paste into 4 equal portions and shape each into a flat round to fit into the base of the ramekin dishes.

5 Divide half of the rice between the ramekin dishes and place the apricot paste on top.

6 Cover the apricot paste with the remaining rice. Cover the ramekins with waxed paper and foil and steam for 30 minutes, or until set.

7 Remove the ramekins from the steamer and let stand for 5 minutes.

8 Turn the puddings out on to warm serving plates and drizzle with honey. Decorate with dried apricots and serve.

COOK'S TIP

The puddings may be left to chill in their ramekin dishes in the refrigerator, then turned out and served with ice cream or cream.

Green Fruit Salad

This delightfully refreshing fruit salad is the perfect finale for a Chinese meal. It has a lovely light syrup made with fresh mint and honey.

NUTRITIONAL INFORMATION

Calories 157   Sugars 34g
Protein . . . . .1g   Fat 0.2g
Carbohydrate . . .34g   Saturates 0g

30 MINS   15 MINS

SERVES 4

INGREDIENTS

1 small Charentais or honeydew melon

2 green apples

2 kiwifruit

1 cup seedless white grapes

fresh mint sprigs, to decorate

SYRUP

1 lemon

⅔ cup white wine

⅔ cup water

4 tbsp clear honey

few sprigs of fresh mint

1 To make the syrup, pare the rind from the lemon using a potato peeler.

2 Put the lemon rind in a pan with the white wine, water, and clear honey. Bring to a boil, then simmer gently for 10 minutes.

3 Remove the syrup from the heat. Add the sprigs of mint and leave to cool.

4 To prepare the fruit, first slice the melon in half and scoop out the seeds. Use a melon baller or a teaspoon to make melon balls.

5 Core and chop the apples. Peel and slice the kiwifruit.

6 Strain the cooled syrup into a serving bowl, removing and reserving the lemon rind and discarding the mint sprigs.

7 Add the apple, grapes, kiwifruit, and melon to the serving bowl. Stir through gently to mix.

8 Serve the fruit salad, decorated with sprigs of fresh mint and some of the reserved lemon rind.

COOK'S TIP

Single-flower honey has a better, more individual flavor than blended honey. Acacia honey is typically Chinese, but you could also try clove, lemon blossom, lime flower, or orange blossom.

Chinese Custard Tarts

These small tarts are irresistible—a custard is baked in a rich, sweet pie dough. The tarts may be served warm or cold.

NUTRITIONAL INFORMATION

Calories	474	Sugars	........30g
Protein	.........9g	Fat	..........22g
Carbohydrate	...64g	Saturates	......12g

20 MINS

30 MINS

SERVES 4

INGREDIENTS

DOUGH

scant 1¼ cups all-purpose flour

3 tbsp superfine sugar

4 tbsp unsalted butter

2 tbsp shortening

2 tbsp water

CUSTARD

2 small eggs

¼ cup superfine sugar

¾ cup milk

½ tsp ground nutmeg, plus extra for sprinkling

cream, to serve

1 To make the dough, sift the all-purpose flour into a bowl. Add the superfine sugar and rub in the butter and shortening until the mixture resembles bread crumbs. Add the water and mix to form a firm dough.

2 Transfer the dough to a lightly floured surface and knead for 5 minutes, until smooth. Cover with plastic wrap and leave to chill in the refrigerator while you prepare the filling.

3 To make the custard, beat the eggs and sugar together. Gradually add the milk and ground nutmeg and beat until well combined.

4 Separate the dough into 15 even-size pieces. Flatten the dough pieces into rounds and press into shallow patty pans.

5 Spoon the custard into the pastry shells and cook in a preheated oven, at 300°F/150°C, for 25-30 minutes.

6 Transfer the Chinese custard tarts to a wire rack and leave to cool slightly, then sprinkle with nutmeg. Serve hot or cold with cream.

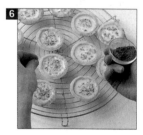

COOK'S TIP

For extra convenience, make the dough in advance, cover and leave to chill in the refrigerator until required.

Coconut Bananas

This elaborate dessert is the perfect finale for a Chinese banquet.
Bananas are fried in a citrus-flavored butter and served with coconut.

NUTRITIONAL INFORMATION

Calories	514	Sugars	........70g
Protein	.........4g	Fat	..........21g
Carbohydrate	...75g	Saturates	......14g

10 MINS   10 MINS

SERVES 4

INGREDIENTS

3 tbsp shredded fresh coconut

¼ cup unsalted butter

1 tbsp fresh grated gingerroot

grated zest of 1 orange

¼ cup superfine sugar

4 tbsp fresh lime juice

6 bananas

6 tbsp orange liqueur (Cointreau or Grand
Marnier, for example)

3 tsp toasted sesame seeds

lime slices, to decorate

ice-cream, to serve (optional)

1 Heat a small non-stick skillet until
hot. Add the coconut and cook,
stirring constantly, for 1 minute until
lightly coloured. Remove from the pan and
leave to cool.

2 Melt the butter in a large skillet and
add the ginger, orange zest, sugar,
and lime juice. Mix well.

3 Peel and slice the bananas lengthwise
(and halve if they are very large).
Place the bananas cut-side down in the
butter mixture and cook for 1-2 minutes,
or until the sauce mixture starts to
become sticky. Turn the bananas to coat in
the sauce.

4 Remove the bananas and place on
heated serving plates. Keep warm.

5 Return the pan to the heat and add
the orange liqueur, blending well.
Ignite with a taper, then let the flames die
down and pour over the bananas.

6 Sprinkle with the reserved coconut
and sesame seeds and serve at once,
decorated with slices of lime.

COOK'S TIP

For a very special treat
try serving this with a flavored
ice-cream such as coconut,
ginger, or praline.

Exotic Fruit Salad

This is a sophisticated fruit salad that makes use of some of the exotic fruits that can now be seen in the supermarket.

NUTRITIONAL INFORMATION

Calories ....149 Sugars 39g
Protein ....1g Fat 0.1g
Carbohydrate ...39g Saturates 0g

10 MINS   15 MINS

SERVES 6

INGREDIENTS

3 passion-fruit

generous ½ cup superfine sugar

⅔ cup water

1 mango

10 litchis, canned or fresh

1 star-fruit

1 Halve the passion-fruit and press the flesh through a strainer into a pan.

2 Add the sugar and water to the pan and bring to a gentle boil, stirring.

3 Put the mango on a cutting board and cut a thick slice from either side, cutting as near to the pit as possible. Cut away as much flesh as possible in large chunks from the pit.

COOK'S TIP

A delicious accompaniment to any exotic fruit dish is cardamom cream. Crush the seeds from 8 cardamom pods, add 1¼ cups whipping cream and whip until soft peaks form.

4 Take the 2 side slices and make 3 cuts through the flesh but not the skin, and 3 more at right angles to make a lattice pattern.

5 Push inside out so that the cubed flesh is exposed and you can easily cut it off.

6 Peel and pit the litchis and cut the star-fruit into 12 slices.

7 Add all the mango flesh, the litchis, and star-fruit to the passion-fruit syrup and poach gently for 5 minutes. Remove the fruit with a perforated spoon.

8 Bring the syrup to a boil and cook for 5 minutes, or until it thickens slightly.

9 To serve, transfer all the fruit to individual serving glasses, then pour over the sugar syrup and serve warm.

Sweet Rice

This dessert is served at banquets and celebratory meals in China, as it looks wonderful when sliced.

NUTRITIONAL INFORMATION

Calories 213   Sugars 15g
Protein . . . . .2g   Fat 7g
Carbohydrate . . .37g   Saturates 4g

🍰 20 MINS   🕐 1¼ HOURS

SERVES 4

INGREDIENTS

generous ¾ cup pudding rice

2 tbsp unsalted butter

1 tbsp superfine sugar

8 dried dates, pitted and chopped

1 tbsp raisins

5 candied cherries, halved

5 pieces angelica, chopped

5 walnut halves

½ cup canned chestnut purée

SYRUP

⅔ cup water

2 tbsp orange juice

4½ tsp light brown sugar

1½ tsp cornstarch

1 tbsp cold water

1 Put the rice in a pan, then cover with cold water and bring to a boil. Reduce the heat, then cover and simmer for 15 minutes, or until the water has been absorbed. Stir in the butter and superfine sugar.

2 Grease a 2½-cup heatproof pudding bowl. Cover the base and sides of the bowl with a thin layer of the rice, pressing with the back of a spoon.

3 Mix the fruit and walnuts together and press them into the rice.

4 Spread a thicker layer of rice on top and then fill the center with the chestnut purée. Cover with the remaining rice, pressing the top down to seal in the purée completely.

5 Cover the bowl with pleated waxed paper and foil and secure with string. Place in a steamer, or stand the bowl in a pan and fill with hot water until it reaches halfway up the sides of the bowl. Cover and steam for 45 minutes. Leave to stand for 10 minutes.

6 Before serving, gently heat the water and orange juice in a small pan. Add the light brown sugar and stir to dissolve. Bring the syrup to a boil.

7 Mix the cornstarch with the cold water to form a smooth paste, then stir into the boiling syrup. Cook for 1 minute, or until thickened and clear.

8 Turn the pudding out onto a serving plate. Pour the syrup over the top, then cut into slices and serve.

Mango Dumplings

Fresh mango and canned litchis fill these small steamed dumplings, making a really colorful and tasty treat.

1¾ HOURS   25 MINS

SERVES 4

INGREDIENTS

DOUGH

2 tsp baking powder

1 tbsp superfine sugar

⅔ cup water

⅔ cup milk

3½ cups all-purpose flour

FILLING AND SAUCE

1 small mango

3½ oz/100 g canned litchis, drained

1 tbsp ground almonds

4 tbsp orange juice

ground cinnamon, for dusting

1 To make the dough, place the baking powder and superfine sugar in a large mixing bowl.

2 Mix the water and milk together and then stir this mixture into the baking powder and sugar mixture until well combined. Gradually stir in the all-purpose flour to make a soft dough. Set the dough aside in a warm place for 1 hour.

3 To make the filling, peel the mango and cut the flesh from the pit. Coarsely chop the mango flesh; reserve half and set aside for the sauce.

4 Chop the litchis and add to half of the chopped mango, together with the ground almonds. Leave to stand for 20 minutes.

5 Meanwhile, make the sauce. Blend the reserved mango and the orange juice in a food processor until smooth. Using the back of a spoon, press the mixture through a strainer to make a smooth sauce.

6 Divide the dough into 16 equal pieces. Roll each piece out on a lightly floured counter into 3-inch/ 7.5-cm rounds.

7 Spoon a little of the mango and litchi filling on to the center of each round and fold the dough over the filling to make semi-circles. Pinch the edges together to seal firmly.

8 Place the dumplings on a heatproof plate in a steamer, then cover and steam for 20-25 minutes, or until cooked through.

9 Remove the mango dumplings from the steamer, then dust with a little ground cinnamon and serve with the mango sauce.

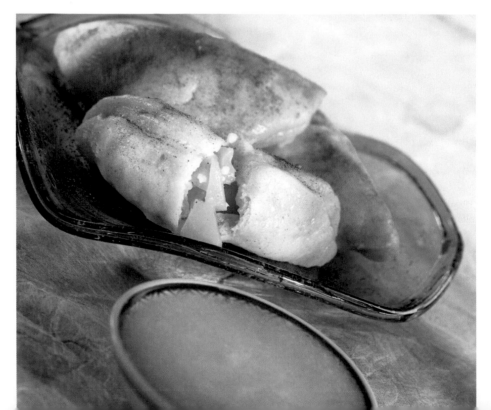

Battered Bananas

These bananas are quite irresistible, therefore it may be wise to make double quantities for weak-willed guests!

NUTRITIONAL INFORMATION

Calories 562	Sugars 79g
Protein 6g	Fat 10g
Carbohydrate ...118g	Saturates 1g

🍞 🍞

🥔 10 MINS   🕐 20 MINS

SERVES 4

INGREDIENTS

8 medium bananas

2 tsp lemon juice

½ cup self-rising flour

½ cup rice flour

1 tbsp cornstarch

½ tsp ground cinnamon

1 cup water

oil, for deep-frying

4 tbsp light brown sugar

cream or ice cream, to serve

1 Cut the bananas into even-size chunks and place them in a large mixing bowl.

2 Sprinkle the lemon juice over the bananas to prevent discoloration.

3 Sift the self-rising flour, rice flour, cornstarch, and cinnamon into a mixing bowl. Gradually stir in the water to make a thin batter.

4 Heat the oil in a preheated wok until smoking, then reduce the heat slightly.

5 Place a piece of banana on the end of a fork and carefully dip it into the batter, draining off any excess. Repeat with the remaining banana pieces.

6 Sprinkle the light brown sugar on to a large plate.

7 Carefully place the banana pieces in the oil and cook for 2-3 minutes, until golden. Remove the banana pieces from the oil with a slotted spoon and roll them in the sugar.

8 Transfer the battered bananas to serving bowls and serve immediately with cream or ice cream.

COOK'S TIP

Rice flour can be bought from health food stores or from Chinese supermarkets.

Mangoes with Sticky Rice

These delightful rice puddings make a lovely dessert or afternoon snack. You can have fun experimenting with different-shaped rice moulds.

NUTRITIONAL INFORMATION

Calories 202   Sugars 31g
Protein ....2g   Fat 2g
Carbohydrate ...47g   Saturates 0.3g

12¾ HOURS   50 MINS

SERVES 4

INGREDIENTS

generous ½ cup sticky rice

1 cup coconut milk

scant ⅓ cup light muscovado sugar

½ tsp salt

1 tsp sesame seeds, toasted

4 ripe mangoes, peeled, halved, pitted, and sliced

1 Put the rice into a colander and rinse well with plenty of cold water until the water runs clear. Transfer the rice to a large bowl, then cover with cold water and leave to soak overnight, or for at least 12 hours. Drain the rice thoroughly.

2 Line a bamboo basket or steamer with cheesecloth or finely woven cotton cloth. Add the rice and steam over a pan of gently simmering water until the rice is tender, about 40 minutes.

3 Remove the rice from the heat and transfer to a large mixing bowl.

4 Reserve 4 tablespoons of the coconut milk and put the remainder into a small pan with the light muscovado sugar and salt. Heat and simmer gently for 8 minutes, or until reduced by about one third.

5 Pour the coconut milk mixture over the rice, fluffing up the rice with a fork so that the mixture is absorbed. Set aside for 10–15 minutes.

6 Pack the rice into individual molds and then invert them onto serving plates.

7 Pour a little reserved coconut milk over each rice mound and sprinkle with the sesame seeds.

8 Arrange the sliced mango on the plates and serve, decorated with pieces of mango cut into different shapes with tiny cutters.

COOK'S TIP

Glutinous, or sticky, rice is available from stockists of Thai ingredients, although you can try making this recipe with pudding rice instead.

Lime Mousse with Mango

Lime-flavored cream molds, served with a fresh mango and lime sauce, make a stunning dessert.

NUTRITIONAL INFORMATION

Calories 254	Sugars 17g	
Protein 5g	Fat 19g	
Carbohydrate ...17g	Saturates 12g	

10 MINS   0 MINS

SERVES 4

INGREDIENTS

1 cup mascarpone cheese

grated rind of 1 lime

1 tbsp superfine sugar

½ cup heavy cream

MANGO SAUCE

1 mango

juice of 1 lime

4 tsp superfine sugar

TO DECORATE

4 cape gooseberries

strips of lime rind

1 Put the mascarpone, lime rind, and sugar in a bowl and mix together.

2 Whisk the heavy cream in a separate bowl and fold into the mascarpone.

3 Line 4 decorative molds or ramekin dishes with cheesecloth or plastic wrap and divide the mixture evenly between them. Fold the cheesecloth over the top and press down firmly.

4 To make the sauce, slice through the mango on each side of the large flat stone, then cut the flesh from the pit. Remove the skin.

5 Cut off 12 thin slices and set aside. Chop the remaining mango, then put into a food processor with the lime juice and sugar. Blend until smooth. Alternatively, push the mango through a strainer and mix with the lime juice and sugar.

6 Turn out the molds on to serving plates. Arrange 3 slices of mango on each plate and pour some sauce around, then decorate and serve.

COOK'S TIP

Cape gooseberries have a tart and mildly scented flavor and make an excellent decoration for many desserts. Peel back the papery husks to expose the bright orange fruits.

Index